MYRTLEFIELD

HOUSE

BRINGING
us to
GLORY

BRINGING
us to
GLORY

Daily Readings for the Christian Journey

DAVID GOODING

Cover design, interior design and composition: Matthew Craig
Cover image: Shutterstock

First published, 2020
Published by The Myrtlefield Trust
PO BOX 2216
Belfast
N Ireland
BT1 9YR

w: www.myrtlefieldhouse.com
e: info@myrtlefieldhouse.com

ISBN: 978-1-912721-36-8 (hbk.)
ISBN: 978-1-912721-37-5 (pbk.)
ISBN: 978-1-912721-38-2 (PDF)
ISBN: 978-1-912721-39-9 (Kindle)
ISBN: 978-1-912721-40-5 (EPUB without DRM)

25 24 23 22 21 20   10 9 8 7 6 5 4 3 2

Contents

THE CAPTAIN OF OUR SALVATION

THE DISCIPLE'S JOURNEY

THE FATHER'S PLAN OF REDEMPTION

Preface

Those of us who had the privilege of listening to Professor Gooding in person owe him a great debt for many reasons, not least that he taught us the value of God's word and how to study it. But one of his most enduring legacies, for which I will be eternally grateful, is that he was able to convey his own appreciation of the grandeur and glory of the character of our God. Sometimes the nature of God is presented in a way that engenders cringing fear and a sense of guilt. David Gooding exulted with a fierce joy in God's goodness. And it was by detailed analysis of the word of God that he discovered and conveyed the manifold glories of our Lord and Saviour.

So, it is the hope of the Myrtlefield Trust, to which I am grateful for the opportunity of editing this book, that these extracts will introduce others to the writings of Professor Gooding and, more importantly, inspire a greater love for and devotion to our risen Lord. Although it has been organized to follow a certain structure, it is not intended as a complete or systematic teaching of doctrine. Our prayer is that readers will come to appreciate something of the magnificence of God's plans and provision for bringing us to glory.

Helen Crookes
Belfast, 2020

Detailed Contents

THE CAPTAIN OF OUR SALVATION

Part 1—Christ's Devotion to the Father's Will

Part 2—The Lord Begins to Destroy the Works of the Devil

THE DISCIPLE'S JOURNEY

Part 1—Where We Begin: Our Justification and Salvation

Part 2—Holiness: The Goal of the Journey

Part 6—Prayer

Part 7—Hindrances, Challenges and Trials

Part 8—The World and Our Warfare

Part 9—Looking to the End

THE FATHER'S PLAN OF REDEMPTION

Part 1—God's Character and Government

Part 2—The Purpose of Our Redemption

Part 3—Implementing the Plan: Creation and the Fall

BRINGING
us to
GLORY

DAVID GOODING

THE CAPTAIN OF OUR SALVATION

Part 1—Christ's Devotion to the Father's Will

1st January

BRINGING MANY SONS TO GLORY

Reading: Hebrews 2:5–18

*For it was fitting that he, for whom and by whom all things
exist, in bringing many sons to glory, should make the
founder of their salvation perfect through suffering. (v. 10)*

Bringing many sons to glory is a task that God must do, if he does it at all, in a way that befits his holiness, dignity and love. Merely introducing a sinner into celestial glory by a sudden act of divine power would not change his rebellious and selfish heart and turn him into a saint, any more than suddenly introducing a tiger into your home will turn it into a civil, gracious and well-mannered guest. The sinner must first be brought to repentance and forgiven; the rebel be reconciled to God; the mere human creature be born again and become a child of God. And if the person concerned is going to have an *abundant* entrance into the eternal kingdom (see 2 Pet 1:11 KJV), and there carry an 'exceeding and eternal weight of glory' (2 Cor 4:17 KJV), some process, long or short, of preparation, training and refining is absolutely indispensable; and suffering will be an inevitable part of the process.

In order to bring his many sons to glory, then, God had first to provide them with a source and leader, a pioneer and pathfinder, of their salvation. And then God had to allow him to be qualified as their leader by first suffering himself. As the pre-incarnate Son of God he enjoyed equally infinite power as his Father. But how much did he know then about suffering from personal experience? And how, without that personal experience of suffering, could he ever understand and sympathize with his people in their suffering? In saying this, of course, the writer of Hebrews is not laying down conditions which he demands that God shall fulfil. Inspired by the Holy Spirit he is relaying to us how God himself felt about it all. And what a glorious insight into the character of God it gives us! Possessing infinite power he had the right, as Creator, to treat us in any way he pleased. But having decided to bring us to glory through a pathway of suffering, his infinite compassion insisted that it must be done not just anyhow, but in a way that would be fitting, even if it meant the suffering of his Son.

David Gooding, *An Unshakeable Kingdom: The Letter to the Hebrews for Today*, pp. 81–2

2nd January

THE INCARNATION ALLOWS US
TO COME CLOSE TO GOD

Reading: John 1:1–18

The Word became flesh and dwelt among us. (v. 14)

If, right from the beginning, Jesus had both announced and exhibited the divine majesty of his essential relationship with the Father, one of the major purposes of the incarnation would have been frustrated. His disciples might still have fallen flat on their faces and acknowledged him as the Creator in whom, by whom, and for whom, the universe was created. But God was seeking a relationship with men infinitely higher than that of a Creator with his creatures. He wanted to raise his creatures, by a spiritual 'birth from above' to a relationship of children, and then grown-up sons, with the Father. And that spiritual birth would depend on their forming a one-to-one personal relationship with his Son. That in turn would depend on their being attracted to him, and unafraid of him, with growing faith, and an ever-deepening understanding, with enough revealed of himself at any one time to draw out their faith and love still more, yet never so much that it overwhelmed their human personalities and made it impossible for them to act as friends toward him.

Many nations have in their folklore the story of a royal prince who unaccountably falls in love with a poor girl in the town. Determining to win her as his bride, he leaves the palace, puts on ordinary clothes, approaches her as an ordinary man, though somewhat above her level and handsome not only in looks but more importantly in his demeanour and behaviour. Yet generally he hides his glory so that she should not be afraid of him, nor, at the other extreme, love him simply for the sake of his wealth and position and not for his own sake. And then when he has won her heart and she has demonstrated her loyalty to him, gradually he reveals to her, so the story goes, ever more of his wealth and majesty until the stunning glory of the public wedding and the eventual coronation. Such—not in folklore, but in historical reality—is the story of the incarnation of God's Son, when he came to earth truly Man, yet God of very God, to seek us for himself. And what can we say but to exclaim, Oh blessed enigma! 'Great . . . is the mystery of godliness: He [God] was manifest in the flesh' (1 Tim 3:16).

David Gooding, In the School of Christ: Lessons on Holiness in John 13–17, pp. 208–9

3rd January

Reading: Matthew 11:20–30

All things have been handed over to me by my Father,
and no one knows the Son except the Father, and no
one knows the Father except the Son and anyone to
whom the Son chooses to reveal him. (v. 27)

Nothing has ever been known about the Father, the transcendent Lord, except what the second person in the Trinity, the Son of God, made known. 'No one has seen God at any time. The only begotten Son, who is in the bosom of the Father, he has made him known' (see John 1:18). And if you want to know what God's ideas are about colour, go to creation, but remember it was the Son of God who made the creation. If you want to know what God's ideas are on music, go to creation and the human ear, but remember it was the Son of God who made the human ear. 'No one knows the Father except the Son and anyone to whom the Son chooses to reveal him.' He has (forgive the term, this is not meant in the commercial sense) the exclusive monopoly on the knowledge of God.

In these days when Jesus Christ has been whittled down, even by Christendom, to being just 'a man for others' or 'a bright prophet' or 'a Jew in advance of his day', we should remember the exclusive claims of Jesus Christ our Lord. He has the exclusive monopoly on the revelation of the Father.

What are his terms? 'Come to me, all you who labour and are heavily burdened and I will give you rest' (see Matt 11:28). It doesn't even first say, 'Go and search your Bibles', good as that is. For the one who makes known God is a person, and he says, 'Come to me'. That is true, and we preach it to the unconverted. Let's preach it also to ourselves: not first my Bible, but first the Lord Jesus, using that office; but not the book without the person: first the person and then the book. So that even as I come to read these words as a believer, let me always remember I am not coming to a philosophical document or a theological system; I am coming to a person.

David Gooding, *The Gospel of Authority and the Path of Discipleship: Studies in Matthew*, pp. 60–1

4th January

THE SON OF GOD AND THE
CREATION OF THE UNIVERSE

Reading: Daniel 7:9–14

*He has spoken to us by his Son, whom he appointed the heir of all
things, through whom also he created the world. (Hebrews 1:2)*

The universe is not self-existent. It was made. And that inevitably raises the
question, 'What was it made for?' Instinctively we reject the idea that there
is no purpose or goal behind its existence. Our minds refuse to be satisfied
with the idea that while each part of the universe has a purpose and a function in regard to the whole, the whole itself has no purpose or function.

We ourselves are not self-existent either, and we certainly did not make
ourselves. Sooner or later we each start asking, 'Why am I here? What is
the purpose of life?' Most of us find that we ourselves are too small to be
a satisfying goal and purpose for our own lives. We must seek a bigger and
more satisfying purpose. But what? The family? Society? The nation? The
race? The behaviour of the nations and of the human race so far, as history
reveals it, seems to show the human race as a pretty unsatisfactory goal
to live for. 'Ah, but the human race', you say, 'has made, and will continue
to make, great progress; and I am satisfied if my individual life serves the
noble purpose of the progress of the human race.' Well said; but if the race
is making progress—and it certainly is in some directions—that raises once
again the same question: progress to what goal? And if there is no answer to
that question, 'serving the progress of the race' would ultimately be pointless.
What's the point of being a cog in the engine of a bus that serves the purpose
of making the bus go, if the bus itself doesn't know where it is going, and there
is in fact no place for it to go to and no reason for going anywhere anyway?

Where then shall we find a satisfactory and satisfying purpose and goal for
our existence? The answer is: in the Son of God. It was for him and for his
pleasure that the universe, and we within it, were made. He is the appointed
heir of all things; of the material universe, of all its creatures, of its history
and progress. Almighty and eternal Son of God, he alone is big enough and
worthy enough to be the final goal of the life of the individual and of the
human race and of the universe.

David Gooding, An Unshakeable Kingdom: The Letter to the Hebrews for Today, pp. 28–9

5th January

THE SON OF GOD AND THE
MAINTENANCE OF THE UNIVERSE

Reading: Romans 8:18–25; Job 38:1–18

. . . he upholds the universe by the word of his power. (Hebrews 1:3)

There is something else that Christ has ever done and ever will do. He upholds all things by the word of his power. He sustains the universe, which he himself made. He not only sustains it as though it were some dead weight that he has to hold up. He bears it in the sense that he is conveying it along, conveying it to its final goal and destiny. The scientists talk about the possibility of nuclear fission or fusion, about the possibility of man's blowing up the world on which we live. You need not be worried, for it is Christ whose powerful word maintains and guards its existence. We are told that the universe is expanding, that stars already millions of light years away are constantly travelling farther away from the earth at tremendous speeds. Where is it all going to? Where will it end? The fact is that the Son of God is upholding it all and leading it to its destiny.

There is more. He 'provided purification for sins', says Scripture. The King James Version reads: 'when he had by himself purged our sins . . .'; but the thought is bigger than that. It is not a question of our sins only—bad and big as they are—but of the whole defiled and disjointed universe. He made it all, he sustains it all; and when sin spoiled everything he himself came to put it right. He is not a mere creature, tinkering with a universe which he did not himself make. The universe's Creator, he has also become its Redeemer. He has done the work that makes possible the eventual reconciliation of all things to God 'whether things on earth or things in heaven, by making peace through his blood, shed on the cross' (Col 1:20 NIV).

David Gooding, *An Unshakeable Kingdom: The Letter to the Hebrews for Today*, pp. 30–1

6th January

THE PERSON OF THE SON OF GOD

Reading: Isaiah 6:1–4; John 12:41

The Son is the radiance of God's glory and the exact representation of his being. (Hebrews 1:3 NIV)

We have thought of the Son of God in relation to creation. But what is he in himself? He is the radiance of God's glory and the exact representation of his [essential] being. Notice the present tense. These are things that Christ has ever been, is and will always continue to be. He is the radiance of God's glory. None of us has ever seen God the Father at any time. Not even Moses. When Moses stood in the cleft of the rock and God made all his glory to pass by, Moses did not see the one whom we know as God the Father (Exod 33:17–23). He saw the one who subsequently became Jesus of Nazareth, but who ever was, and is through all eternity, the radiance of God's glory. He has displayed God's glory by creating the universe—showing that God is a God of colour and music and beauty and grandeur and might. Through Moses and his law he made God known as a God of moral order and purity, of righteousness and holiness. But in his own incarnation, death, resurrection and ascension, he has revealed the glory of the Father as only the Son could do. 'The Word became flesh and made his dwelling among us', says the Apostle John. 'We have seen his glory, the glory of the one and only, who came from the Father, full of grace and truth' (John 1:14 NIV).

Not only in his acts but in his own self he is the radiance of God's glory. Isaiah once looked up into heaven and saw the Lord high and lifted up and his train filled the temple. The seraphim were veiling their heads and feet as they cried, 'Holy, holy, holy is the Lord Almighty.' Isaiah saw, so he tells us, 'the King, the Lord Almighty' (Isa 6:1–5 NIV). John, the inspired Gospel writer, adds the information that the person whom Isaiah saw was the one whom we call Jesus (John 12:41). He is that person of the Trinity who reveals the glory of the Godhead. He does not merely reflect it as a mirror might reflect the rays of the sun but has no light of itself. Rather, just as the sun's rays reveal to us what the sun is like because they possess the same nature as the sun, so Christ reveals God because in his essential being he is God.

David Gooding, *An Unshakeable Kingdom: The Letter to the Hebrews for Today*, pp. 29–30

7th January

MAKING KNOWN THE FATHER'S NAME

Reading: John 17

I made known to them your name, and I will
continue to make it known. (v. 26)

God's name, that is, God's character, is infinite in its wealth and glory. God's people, therefore, must not remain spiritual infants. They must grow into the knowledge of God, becoming his mature sons, and always increasing in their understanding of the Father and the Son. To that end therefore Christ now pledges himself with a promise of never-ending revelation: 'I made known to them your name, and I will continue to make it known.'

True to that promise, Christ constantly makes known the Father's name to his people here on earth as they can bear it, using God's word and the education and discipline of life's experience. Few people have had a near-perfect human father; some have been emotionally dented or even scarred by the distorted interpretations of fatherhood given them (unintentionally) by their parents. It can take a lifetime for Christ to correct these false impressions and to inform the mind and, more importantly, to impress the heart with the perfect care, nurture, sympathy, patience and mercy of the Father's love, and to convince us that it is all more wonderful than we dare to dream of. Similarly, it can take Christ a long time to make us aware of the Father's insatiable ambition for his people's growth in holiness to the point where it matches his own, cost what it may (Heb 12:5–11).

But hear the climax to which Christ's prayer has been progressing. He plans to take his people at last to be with him where he is. There he will show them the inexhaustible riches that were his before creation was summoned into being. And the purpose of that never-ending display will be that they shall explore ever more profoundly the infinite extent of the glory given to him by the Father, and in doing so, perceive with ever increasing wonder the Father's love of the Son. And then, above the music of their adoration of the Father's love for the Son, shall be heard the voice of the Son revealing always more of the Father's name. Wave after wave of ecstatic wonder and joy shall then fill them in turn as they realize again and again, each time as though it were something completely new and fresh, that the Father loves them too, as fully and as richly and as infinitely as he loves the Son. And the love of God shall be in them, and the Son of God shall be in them, eternally.

David Gooding, *In the School of Christ: Lessons on Holiness in John 13–17*, pp. 255–6

8th January

SHOW US THE FATHER

Reading: John 14:5–12

Whoever has seen me has seen the Father. (v. 9)

Christ's reply to Philip must have left an expression of incredulity or incomprehension on Philip's face, for our Lord continued: 'Do you not believe that I am in the Father and the Father is in me? Take the words that I speak to you, and the marvellous works that I have performed. How do you suppose I do them, Philip? I am not the source of the words that I speak to you, nor of the works that I do. The source of both is the Father who dwells in me. Believe me, Philip, that I am in the Father, and the Father in me, or else if you cannot simply take my word for it, believe me on the evidence of the very works that I do' (see vv. 10–11).

That must have been a wonderful moment in that wonderful evening. Thomas and Philip had been thinking of God as being a long way off in heaven; but they now discovered that the Father was, so to speak, sitting at the other side of the table in the person of Jesus. All evening long they had been listening to Jesus' words, marvelling at their grace and their wonder. But all the while they were the Father's words they were listening to. As they had listened, they had watched Jesus' face and its expressions of love, encouragement and sorrow; and what in fact they had been watching was the light of the knowledge of the glory of God in the face of Jesus Christ. John had actually leaned on Jesus' bosom; and the love that throbbed in every heartbeat he heard was the love of God. And was that truly God who a few moments ago had knelt at their feet and washed them? Was God like that? Yes, precisely: 'The words that I say unto you I speak not on my own initiative; but the Father abiding in me does his works. He who has seen me has seen the Father.' This is what God is like. Certainly the apostles had not seen there in the Upper Room the external glories of God and Christ, as later John was privileged to see them in the revelation given to him on the island of Patmos (see the book of Revelation), and as all God's people shall one day see them. But they had seen the Father's heart and mind, character and attitude, words and works fully expressed. Christ had brought the Father to them.

David Gooding, *In the School of Christ: Lessons on Holiness in John 13–17*, pp. 87–8

9th January

IN HIS DEATH, RESURRECTION AND ASCENSION, CHRIST REVEALS THE FATHER

Reading: John 16:17–33

I have said these things to you in figures of speech. The hour is coming when I will no longer speak to you in figures of speech but will tell you plainly about the Father. (v. 25)

That hour came with his death, resurrection and ascension. His resurrection demonstrated, more eloquently than words could, that he was 'the Son of God in power' (Rom 1:4). His resurrection also demonstrated that the cross was neither an accident nor a disaster, and it was certainly not inconsistent with the being and character of God. It was, in fact, the clearest expression of the heart of God in all earth's history. The centre point of time and eternity, planned by God before the foundation of the world by his determinate counsel and foreknowledge (1 Pet 1:20; Acts 2:23), foretold in the prophecies of the Old Testament (Luke 24:25–27) and carried out at God's appointed hour, it was the mightiest and profoundest telling out of the Father's heart that man could ever hope for, or God himself devise. It was beyond all misinterpretation.

God possesses almighty power; but the Bible nowhere says that God is power—it says that God is love. If that, then, is what the Father is really like, where could we perceive it better than in the cross of Christ? 'In this the love of God was made manifest among us, that God sent his only Son into the world, so that we might live through him. In this is love, not that we loved God, but that he loved us and sent his Son to be the propitiation for our sins. . . . the Father has sent his Son to be the Saviour of the world' (1 John 4:9–10, 14). But Christ would not even so be content. What if he told out the Father's character to the full at Calvary, but we, for our part, were unable to take it in? And so to complete his plain and open revelation of the Father he would, after his ascension, send the Holy Spirit to every one of his people to pour out the love of God in their hearts to secure their subjective grasp and enjoyment of that love.

David Gooding, *In the School of Christ: Lessons on Holiness in John 13–17*, pp. 209–10

10th January

THE FIRST TEMPTATION

Reading: Luke 4:1–13

Jesus answered him, 'It is written, "Man
shall not live by bread alone."' (v. 4)

The flow of Luke's narrative—the son of Adam, son of God, being tempted by the devil in respect of eating—takes us back in thought to the story of Adam's disobedient eating of the tree; and that in turn throws further light on our two basic questions: who is Jesus and what has he come to do? He is the second man come to triumph where the first man failed, destined in resurrection to be the beginning and head of a new humanity as Adam was the beginning and head of the old. Yet the first temptation shows the difference between him and the first man. 'If you are the Son of God', said the devil, 'command this stone to become bread' (v. 3). Such a suggestion, needless to say, would never have been a temptation to Adam, any more than it would be to any of us. Adam did not have the power to turn stones into bread, nor has any mere man since. For Christ, by contrast, the whole force of the temptation lay in the fact that he, as Son of God, had the power to turn stones into bread if he pleased. He did not reply to the devil—let it be said reverently—'Don't be foolish: I have not the power to turn stones into bread', but 'Man shall not live by bread alone'. The Greek word for man which Luke uses is the one which means man in the sense of human being. Christ's reply, therefore, indicates that while he is indeed the Son of God, he is also human and proposes to live on the terms that are right and appropriate for a man, a son of Adam.

And so the first victory was won. It was not, however, a victory for mere asceticism. Human life, if it is going to be truly life, and not a form of living death, needs more than bread for its maintenance: it depends on God's word and on fellowship with him in loving obedience to that word. Israel in the desert was allowed to hunger (see Deut 8:3) and then fed with manna so as to be taught that man does not live by bread alone but by every word that proceeds out of the mouth of God. Now hungry after his forty days of fasting in the desert, Christ willingly submits to the written word—'It stands written'—and refuses to eat independently of God's word spoken to his heart.

David Gooding, *According to Luke: The Third Gospel's Ordered Historical Narrative*, pp. 77–8

11th January

THE MAN JESUS AND THE FULFILMENT
OF GOD'S PLAN FOR MANKIND

Reading: Hebrews 2:1–9

At present, we do not yet see everything in subjection to him. (v. 8)

At present we do not see everything subject to man. But that does not mean that God has abandoned his original purpose. Sin has spoiled everything, and man by his folly and disobedience has thrown away much of his dominion. But God has not admitted defeat. Far from it. In his original plan man was deliberately designed to be a little lower than the angels. Perhaps that was because the creation of man was God's tactical answer to rebellion that had broken out in the spirit realm to which angels naturally belong. Who knows? But when Satan very early on successfully corrupted God's viceroy, man, and set him on a course of disloyalty and rebellion against the very God in whose image he was made, the wisdom of God's strategy in making man a little lower than the angels eventually became apparent. Angels, in their proper state, do not marry or produce offspring. Man can do both. And that made possible God's long-planned strategic move by which he had himself born into our world as a man, so that as man he could defeat the enemy and bring to victorious fulfilment God's original purpose for mankind.

And already, says our writer, we see the first stage of that purpose fulfilled. 'We see Jesus'. Note his name: it is his human name, a Hebrew name, given him by human parents under the direction of an angel. 'We see Jesus, who was made a little lower than the angels. . .' (v. 9 KJV) just as the first man Adam was. He has taken on flesh and blood and has become what angels never were or will be: human. See him, then, lying as a baby in a crude manger in an obscure village called Bethlehem, apparently helpless. But don't suppose it is anything to be ashamed of! This is a tremendous leap forward for mankind. It is the first step on the way to mankind's redemption and triumphant glorification.

David Gooding, *An Unshakeable Kingdom: The Letter to the Hebrews for Today*, p. 79

12th January

HE IS NOT ASHAMED TO CALL THEM BROTHERS

Reading: Hebrews 2:10–18

*Both the Sanctifier and those who are being sanctified
are all of one; and for this reason he is not ashamed
to call them (his) brethren. (v. 11 own trans.)*

Why is it that the one who was the pre-existent, eternal Son of God, the second person of the Trinity, is not ashamed to call us his brothers? Because, when he does so, the term 'brothers' is not empty religious rhetoric or pious sentimental exaggeration: it is absolutely genuine and means exactly what it says. There is no pretence in it. He has become as truly human as we are (though not sinful: sin is no necessary part of humanity). He has experienced human joys and human sorrows. He knows from having suffered it, what it is to be hungry (Matt 4:2), tired (John 4:6), thirsty (John 19:28), sorrowful at the death of a loved friend (John 11:35), and broken-hearted in the face of blind, unreasoning rejection (Luke 13:32–35). He knows what temptation is, and he knows what death is more than we who trust him ever will.

When, therefore, he calls us his brothers, it is not empty talk. He is not afraid that anyone will ever compare his circumstances and experience with ours and accuse him of hypocrisy for daring to call us his brothers. The term represents reality. He is not ashamed to call us brothers because he and we are genuinely 'all of one'.

We must, of course, be careful to notice exactly who it is that the writer says are 'all of one'. He is not saying that because our Lord has become truly human, he calls every human being his brother. People nowadays constantly quote our Lord's words, 'Inasmuch as ye have done it unto one of the least of these my brethren, ye have done it unto me' (Matt 25:40 KJV), as if they meant to say that every man, woman, boy and girl on the face of the earth—all the unregenerate, all the deliberate atheists, religious hypocrites, criminals, child-molesters, cheats, liars and murderers—are one and all brothers of the Lord Jesus. It is not true of course. Our Lord himself was very careful to indicate precisely who his brothers are: 'My mother and brothers are those who hear God's word and put it into practice' (Luke 8:21 NIV).

David Gooding, An Unshakeable Kingdom: The Letter to the Hebrews for Today, p. 84

13th January

CHRIST'S FAITHFULNESS COMPARED WITH THAT OF MOSES

Reading: Hebrews 3

Christ is faithful over God's house as a son. (v. 6)

To give us some idea of our Lord's faithfulness to us, the Holy Spirit compares our Lord with Moses. We notice that the phrase he uses of Moses, 'who was faithful in all God's house' (v. 2), comes from a context where Miriam and Aaron had joined the ranks of those who were grumbling against him (Num 12:1–8). Israel was never slow, it seems, to grumble against Moses: their food and water supply and even his personal and private affairs, such as his getting married, all became reasons for grumbling against him, even though at that time he was the captain of their salvation. But in all this Moses' grace shone brightly. He was, says Scripture, more humble than anyone else on the face of the earth (v. 3). I wonder how he ever managed to keep his temper. He had given his life for this nation.

What was it that kept the man so faithful to Israel? It was his faithfulness to God who had appointed him to his house. Moses had been sent to Israel as God's apostle with the message of deliverance from Egypt. Moses thereafter acted as the mediator between Israel and God, and saved the people by his intercessions. In spite of all their grumblings and mistakes and personal insults, Moses remained faithful to the task that God had given him.

Moses broke down at last, in spite of his faithfulness. There came a day when the Israelites so angered him by their ungrateful complainings, that he erupted: 'Listen now, you rebels,' he shouted at them, 'must we bring you water out of this rock?' And with that he struck the rock with his staff instead of just speaking to it as God had told him to do (see Num 20:9–12).

That act of impatience cost Moses his entry into the promised land. It seems hard on Moses, doesn't it? But God had appointed Moses to look after Israel, and if Moses could not do it without losing his temper and so misrepresenting God to the people, then Moses must be set aside. God has appointed us a captain of our salvation, and made him responsible for seeing us through this world home to glory. Thank God we can count on his faithfulness and know that he will never fail, never once lose his patience or his temper with any of us, but will fulfil his God-appointed task to the very end. He will save to the uttermost all who come to God by him.

David Gooding, *An Unshakeable Kingdom: The Letter to the Hebrews for Today*, pp. 96–7

14th January

CHRIST LEARNED OBEDIENCE

Reading: Hebrews 5

*Son though he was, he learned obedience
from what he suffered. (v. 8 NIV)*

The wonder is that being the unique Son of God with right of command over every created being and force in the entire universe, nevertheless, Son though he was, he learned obedience, and learned it by suffering.

Moreover, as the eternal Son of the Father, he did not have to be taught to do the Father's will. He did not have to learn *to obey*. He had always obeyed flawlessly. But doing God's will in heaven is nothing but joy and gladness; and if as the pre-incarnate Son he had confined himself to heaven and left our world unvisited, he need never have learned, or paid the price of, obedience to God in this ungodly world. And who could have been surprised if he had done so? Who could have complained? But then how could he have learned what it costs to obey? And if he did not learn that by experience himself, how could he understand what it costs us to obey him?

And so he came and lived in our world and learned. Strong, sinless as he was, courageous to stand in the face of the bitterest opposition and the most painful physical and mental suffering, the experience nevertheless brought him to loud crying and tears. Let us recall Gethsemane. I know that when we stand in its dark shadows, we stand in a mysterious place, the juncture of the human and divine. We must take the shoes off our feet. The ground is holy. Worship rather than analysis becomes us. But when our Lord prayed, 'Abba, Father, everything is possible for you. Take this cup from me. Yet not what I will, but what you will' (Mark 14:36 NIV), he said what he meant and he meant what he said. There was no insincerity. He was not pretending that he did not want to drink the cup when all the while he did. And it certainly was not ostentatious stage show calculated to heighten the effect when later he would give in and say 'Your will be done'. In utter sincerity with bitter anguish and tears he cried to God to spare him having to drink that cup.

But the Father's will was that he drink it. So he willed God's will and drank the cup, unreservedly, unresentfully, to its last drop—and discovered by experience the cost of obedience. 'Son though he was,' says Scripture, 'he learned obedience from what he suffered.'

David Gooding, *An Unshakeable Kingdom: The Letter to the Hebrews for Today*, pp. 121–2

15th January

THE PRAYERS OF CHRIST AND THE VINDICATION OF GOD'S CHARACTER

Reading: John 12:27–33; 1 Timothy 6:13–16

In the days of his flesh, Jesus offered up prayers and supplications, with loud cries and tears, to him who was able to save him from death, and he was heard because of his reverence. (Hebrews 5:7)

Of all the prayers and intercessions that God has ever heard, those surely will prove the most effective that came from the lips and heart of the Son of God incarnate. For the amazing story is this: God has not only *looked* down from his sanctuary on high, but in the person of his Son he *came* down! The same Lord who will one day appear in his glory and rebuild Zion, once was manifested in the flesh, and walked the streets of Jerusalem. He not only viewed earth's pains, injustices and cruelties from on high, but personally came and experienced them. He not only heard the prayers of the distressed, but joined in them. He not only listened to the groanings of prisoners condemned to death, but became a prisoner himself; and though sinless, was numbered with the transgressors, was cut off out of the land of the living as a young man, bore the sin of many and made intercession for the transgressors (see Isa 53:8, 12). Son of God though the incarnate Messiah was, 'during the days of [his] life on earth, he offered up prayers and petitions with loud cries and tears to the one who could save him from death; and he was heard because of his reverent submission' (Heb 5:7). One day, not only in response to the prayers of the faithful of all ages, but supremely in answer to the prayers and intercessions of the Messiah, God will bring about the appearing of our Lord Jesus Christ (1 Tim 6:13–16).

What a vindication of the character of God that will be! What a declaration of his name, a demonstration of the glory of his faithfulness and compassion (Ps 102:13–16, 21)! What a vindication, before all the agnostics and atheists of the world, of the revelation of God in his word witnessed to by historic Israel and Jerusalem. Prayer too will be vindicated against all those unbelievers and critics who said so often that prayer was useless because either God did not hear, or, if he heard, did not care. The appearing of our great God and Saviour, Jesus Christ, will demonstrate overwhelmingly that God both heard and cared. God's name and character will be declared in Zion and his praise in Jerusalem. And the peoples and kingdoms of the world will assemble to worship the Lord (Ps 102:21; cf. Zech 14:16).

David Gooding, *An Unshakeable Kingdom: The Letter to the Hebrews for Today*, pp. 61–2

16th January

THE NEW AND LIVING WAY—THE VEIL

Reading: Exodus 26:31–37

Having therefore, brethren, boldness to enter into the holy place by the blood of Jesus, by the way which he dedicated for us, a new and living way, through the veil, that is to say, his flesh. (Hebrews 10:19–20 RV)

The veil was a merciful provision. It certainly barred access into the immediate presence of God; and yet it allowed the priests to come at least into the Holy Place, to the lampstand, the table, and the golden altar of incense and to all that they stood for. If there had been no veil, they could not have entered even the Holy Place; for without the veil, the Holy Place too would have been in the immediate presence of God. Whereas with the veil there, they could not only enter the Holy Place, but also come right up to the veil, inspect all its colours, figures and symbolism, and thereby learn something of the majesty of God. The veil, then, was a wonderful foreshadowing of Christ in his incarnation, his life and ministry on earth. The crowds could come right up to him, sinners could touch him, little children nestle in his arms. Yet all the fullness of deity dwelled in him bodily. Indeed, he so expressed the Father that he could say: 'he who has seen me has seen the Father' (see John 12:45; 14:9).

That was inexpressibly wonderful, but more wonderful still is the fact that he no longer acts as a veil. That same Jesus, still truly human and with a real human body, rent with the nails and the spear-thrust, has entered into heaven itself, into the immediate presence of God as our precursor, representative and high priest. In so doing he has inaugurated a new and living way for us ourselves to enter the immediate presence of God; and we may even now enter there in spirit as boldly as one day we shall do so in bodies refashioned and conformed to the body of his glory.

David Gooding, *The Riches of Divine Wisdom: The New Testament's Use of the Old Testament*, p. 302

17th January

WHY THE LORD WAS FORSAKEN AND MADE LIKE HIS BROTHERS

Reading: Psalm 22

My God, my God, why have you forsaken me? (v. 1)

Christ's life had been utterly perfect and sinless, whereas Israel's had been warped and sinful. In spite of that, when they cried to God they were heard and answered; but when he cried he was not heard—or at least, being heard, he was not answered. In his heart he knew why he was forsaken. It was because he insisted on taking his place alongside his brothers; because he refused to be separated from them in spite of their sin, weakness, frailty and rebellion against God. He bore their sins in his body on the tree, and for their sakes was forsaken by God. As the Apostle John puts it: 'having loved his own which were in the world, he loved them unto the end' (John 13:1 KJV).

World history has never seen a darker night for mankind than when the man, Jesus, mankind's representative, suffered the wrath of God against human sin, and was forsaken. 'He was delivered over to death for our sins' (Rom 4:25 NIV).

But that verse continues, he 'was raised to life for our justification'. The dark night of forsakenness gave way to the dawn of resurrection and to the noonday splendour of the ascension. Earth was now to be exchanged for heaven, suffering and shame for glory, the cross for the throne and the crown. The man Jesus was about to be invited to sit on the right hand of the Majesty on high. Would not that loosen somewhat the ties that bound him to his disciples? Would not the glorified Son of Man now feel a little ashamed before the majestic angels of God to acknowledge his humble followers on earth as his brothers? Never! On the very threshold of the ascension he said to Mary: 'Go . . . to my brothers and tell them, I am ascending to my Father and your Father, to my God and your God' (John 20:17 NIV); and in the bright morning of the second half of Psalm 22 we hear the glorified Messiah announce: 'I will tell of your name to my brothers; in the midst of the congregation I will praise you' (v. 22). And still wherever his people meet, there he is among them, revealing the Father's name to them (John 17:26) and leading the response of their praise. Here then rises the irrepressible and inexhaustible fountain of our hope for mankind.

David Gooding, *An Unshakeable Kingdom: The Letter to the Hebrews for Today*, p. 85–6

18th January

THE SECOND TEMPTATION

Reading: Isaiah 14:12–15; Deuteronomy 10:12–22

And Jesus answered him, 'It is written, "You shall worship the Lord your God, and him only shall you serve."' (Luke 4:8)

The second temptation did not rely for its force on the question of who Jesus was so much as on the authority which the devil himself claimed to have: 'all this authority . . . has been given to me and I give it to whomsoever I will'. We need not try to decide to what extent the claim was true. Some of it certainly was. Compare Revelation 13:2 where Scripture says of the beast 'the dragon gave him his power and his throne and great authority'. Admittedly, the very phrase 'all this authority . . . has been given to me' shows the devil's ineradicable sense that he is a creature and derives his power ultimately from the Creator. But in this very fact lies the force of the temptation: why does God allow the devil such long-lasting and apparently successful power? If the first temptation tested faith in God as the provider of life's necessities, the second is going to test faith in God as the moral governor of the universe, and in his promises that 'the Son of Man and the saints' (see Dan 7) should be given universal dominion.

The worship demanded by Satan did not presumably include that element of admiration and praise which worship of God normally includes. What Satan was demanding was that Christ should recognize him as an ultimate fact and authority which cannot be overcome but has to be reckoned with and compromised with. On those terms the devil was prepared to let Christ gain worldwide success. Many movements, before and since, both political and religious have bought success and power on those terms, justifying their attitude on grounds of expediency or realism or necessity. The result has been to leave mankind in spite of much apparent progress a prisoner to demonic forces of evil both in their personal lives and in their social and political institutions. Christ citing Scripture once more as the authoritative expression of God's absolute authority (see Luke 4:8), refused to bow down to any but God. In the mystery of God's purposes and government of the universe this refusal would cost Christ the cross; but it would win for mankind that possibility of freedom of which we shall soon hear him speak when he begins his public ministry.

David Gooding, *According to Luke: The Third Gospel's Ordered Historical Narrative*, p. 78–9

19th January

THE THIRD TEMPTATION

Reading: Matthew 4:1–11

If you are the Son of God, throw yourself
down from here. (Luke 4:9)

The third temptation relied for its power once more on the fact that Jesus was the Son of God, but also on his demonstrated determination to trust Holy Scripture and to obey God. The devil therefore quoted a Scripture which promised Messiah angelic protection, and challenged Christ not just to trust it, but to give evidence of his trust by acting upon it. The temptation was exceedingly subtle. We recall how John the Baptist had rightly urged it on the people that it was useless simply claiming to be children of Abraham: they must act, they must produce practical evidence of the validity of their claim. Moreover to the godly mind the challenge to trust God's word and 'step out in faith' has a powerful attraction, and refusal or even hesitancy to act can appear as lack of faith.

But Christ saw through the deception: it was in fact a challenge not to trust God but to tempt him, not to prove his Sonship, but to abuse it. No word had come from God bidding Christ to jump off the temple; no necessity of God's work or human need required it. The only motive for doing it would either be vainglory or the desire to test God to see whether he would keep his promise; and Scripture forbids man's testing of God in that way.

God is not on probation; there is no doubt about his faithfulness that has to be cleared up by putting him through an examination. To jump off the temple would have been to take the initiative and force God into a situation where he would have no choice but to back up the action in order to avert disaster, or else to be accused of unfaithfulness if he did not. That would have been to reverse the role of man and God, and of Son and Father. Satan's demand for action as evidence of Christ's Sonship was false, and Christ refused to act. All the devil had succeeded in doing was to demonstrate that Jesus was indeed the true Son of God.

David Gooding, *According to Luke: The Third Gospel's Ordered Historical Narrative*, p. 79–80

20th January

CHRIST CLEANSES THE TEMPLE

Reading: Luke 19:28–48

My house shall be a house of prayer. (v. 46)

On entering the city Christ went directly to the temple, as Malachi had said he would (Mal 3:1). It was not merely that as the Father's Son he would wish before all else to pay his respects to his Father's house. It was that as Zion's king who was about to be rejected by Zion he would go immediately to the source of the trouble and expose the cause that blinded Zion to the rightful claims of her owner-king: robbers had infested the very temple of God. The outward evidence of that robbery was the blatant commercialization of the temple services; bad in itself it was but the symptom of a deeper malaise.

Somebody, of course, had to sell the required sheep and birds to would-be worshippers; but these sales should have been left to secular trade, unassociated with the sacred precincts and activities of the temple. For the temple authorities not only to allow this trading to go on in the temple courts, but to profit unduly from the sales themselves was not only inappropriate, it was scandalous. Instead of being priestly intermediaries to help men find worship and be blessed by God, they had become middlemen, turning their priesthood into a commercial monopoly in order to make financial profit out of men's quest for God.

Thus they robbed men, for it is difficult to experience the grace of God and the free gift of his salvation through the services of men bent on making money out of one's spiritual need. They also robbed God, treating his word and sacraments as though they were the stock-in-trade of their business, and treating God's people not as God's possession, to be developed for God's enjoyment, but as a market to which they as the professionals had exclusive rights. In high indignation Christ drove out those who sold, and began to teach the people daily in the temple-courts. It was the beginning of a fight to the death. On the one side were the temple authorities, determined to maintain their status, power and income. On the other side was the Messiah, 'come in the name of the Lord' to secure the divine rights. At stake were the faith, love, obedience and devotion of the people; and from now on this struggle for the hearts of the people will be one of Luke's main concerns.

David Gooding, *According to Luke: The Third Gospel's Ordered Historical Narrative*, pp. 330–1

21st January

AN ASSURANCE OF VICTORY

Reading: John 14:15–31

*The ruler of this world is coming. He has no claim on me, but
I do as the Father has commanded me, so that the world may
know that I love the Father. Rise, let us go from here. (vv. 30–31)*

We notice at once that the secret of his victory was his undeviating and utterly unbreakable love of the Father. Now it is the fact that we ordinary men and women often talk, and sometimes quite easily, of our love for God, though often our behaviour contradicts our protestation of love. With the Saviour it was different. His love for his Father was always constant, full and true. Yet throughout the whole of the Gospels our Lord is on record only once as saying, 'I love the Father', and that once was on this occasion. Significantly so. For now had come the moment when he must demonstrate to the world and before heaven, earth and hell that his love for the Father was complete and unswerving.

Eve, in the garden of Eden, surrounded by all the delights that God in his creatorial ingenuity and love had given her, was deceived into thinking that God was against her. She chose the forbidden fruit instead of God and his word. She loved herself and the world more than she loved the Father. Now our Lord was to be met by Satan, the prince of this world, who would use all his venomous power to strip him of everything he possessed, down to his last shred of clothing; and would add to him all that he never deserved, the pain and the agony of Calvary which he might have avoided if only he had let go his love for the Father. But the prince of this world had nothing in Christ—no sin, no weakness that would yield either to his blandishments or to his hostilities. Christ would demonstrate to the whole universe what he thought of the Father. Given the choice between the kingdoms of the world and all its glories along with disloyalty to the Father, on the one hand, and on the other, loyalty to the Father along with all the agony that this world could inflict, he chose the latter. His love for the Father was unbreakable and unbroken.

David Gooding, *In the School of Christ: Lessons on Holiness in John 13–17*, pp. 110–1

22nd January

THE LORD'S FAITH IN HIS FATHER

Reading: Psalm 16:7–11

Therefore my heart was glad, and my tongue rejoiced; my flesh also will dwell in hope. For you will not abandon my soul to Hades, or let your Holy One see corruption. You have made known to me the paths of life; you will make me full of gladness with your presence. (Acts 2:26–28)

The immediately striking thing about this prophecy is that it does not simply talk about Messiah, but introduces Messiah himself talking. It does not simply announce that upon his death and burial God will intervene to raise him from the dead. It presents Messiah, in confrontation with death, telling out the secret of his relationship with God that abolished death's power over him. Utterly unswerving and undeviating in the concentration of his heart's love, his soul's energies, his mind's power and his body's strength on God, he never knew a moment when his inner vision was not fixed on God in uninterrupted obedience and devotion. He was God's 'Holy One', absolutely loyal and perfectly sinless. He 'saw the Lord always before him' and was conscious that God 'was at his right hand' so that he should 'not be moved'. It gave him a rock-like stability that opposition, persecution, and even death's approach could not demolish. His was a faith in God that not even the sufferings and dereliction of Calvary could obliterate and destroy; a perfect submission to the will of God that God himself could never do anything other than vindicate by raising him from the dead. As the writer to the Hebrews was eventually to phrase it, 'He offered up prayers . . . to the one who could save him from death, and he was heard because of his reverent submission' (Heb 5:7 NIV). God would cease to be moral if he finally disowned such faith, met such loyalty with ultimate disloyalty, or abandoned such flawless love and obedience to death, disintegration and decay. It was therefore in unshaken confidence in the character of God that Jesus bowed his head in death, with triumphant prayer on his tongue; and his flesh dwelt calmly in safety and certain hope that God would open to him the paths of life and fill him with eternal joy in his presence.

David Gooding, *True to the Faith: The Acts of the Apostles–Defining and Defending the Gospel*, pp. 74–5

THE CAPTAIN OF OUR SALVATION

Part 2—The Lord Begins to Destroy the Works of the Devil

23rd January

THE LORD'S WORK AND THE WORKS OF THE DEVIL

Reading: Luke 4:14–34

*He cried out with a loud voice, 'Ha! What have you to do
with us, Jesus of Nazareth? Have you come to destroy us?
I know who you are—the Holy One of God.' (vv. 33–34)*

At the temptation Satan's attempt to pervert the Son of God had failed;
now we see the Son of God turning to the offensive. Luke reports how the
demon-possessed man in the synagogue at Capernaum cried out at the
top of his voice, 'Ha! what do you want with us, Jesus of Nazareth? Have
you come to destroy us? I know who you are–the Holy One of God.' It was
a rhetorical question; but if we must answer it, we might well borrow the
words of John: 'For this purpose was the Son of God manifested, that he
might destroy the works of the devil' (1 John 3:8). It is at this level of spiritual
warfare that the battle for man's salvation must ultimately be fought out.

It would, of course, be untrue, foolish and dangerous to suggest that every
man is possessed by some demon or other. Demon possession, according
to the New Testament, is an extreme form of spiritual bondage. On the
other hand, the writers of the New Testament are serious in their assertion
that every unregenerate man is in a very real sense under the power of
Satan (see e.g. Acts 26:18; 2 Cor 4:3–4; Eph 2:2; Col 1:13; 1 Pet 2:9), and needs
to have his eyes opened to the fact, and allow Christ to bring him out of his
spiritual darkness and bondage into the freedom of God's light. And that
is, of course, what Christ was talking about when at Nazareth he asserted
that he had come to bring release to the captives and recovery of sight to
the blind. The congregation not only could not see he was the Messiah, but
actually became enraged, and in a frenzy tried to destroy him. It was all
too clear evidence that they were in captivity to Satan, blind to their own
condition and to where their salvation lay. If ever such people were going
to be liberated, Christ would have to break the power of Satan over them.

David Gooding, *According to Luke: The Third Gospel's Ordered Historical Narrative*, pp. 90–1

24th January

CHRIST PROVES THE EXISTENCE
OF THE UNSEEN WORLD

Reading: 2 Timothy 1:8–14

*I came from the Father and have come into the world, and now
I am leaving the world and going to the Father. (John 16:28)*

Satan, the prince of this world, has persuaded millions of people that this world is the only world there is. He has persuaded them that there was never any divine purpose behind the creation of the universe, since there was, and is, no God. And he has convinced them to believe that there is no heaven beyond this life. All talk of the paradise of God, according to him, is a fairy tale; and he has persuaded millions, who do not know enough about the philosophy of science to see through his lie, that belief in God and heaven is somehow unscientific. In this way Satan has, for them, turned this world into a prison house and life within it into literally hopeless existence.

To deliver mankind from this poverty-stricken bondage, God has sent his Son Jesus Christ into the world. But if ever we are going to be delivered, there is one thing above all others that we must come to see and believe. And that is not simply Christ's ethical teachings. It is this: 'I came out from the Father,' says Christ, 'and have come into the world.' So then, this world is not the only world there is! Nor is this world self-made. Behind and before it stands the Father. 'Again,' says Christ, 'I leave the world and go to the Father.' So then, this world is not the end: there is life beyond it. Since this is true, Satan's lie is exposed; and for those who believe Christ, Satan's power to turn this world into a prison house is broken.

David Gooding, *In the School of Christ: Lessons on Holiness in John 13–17*, pp. 213–4

25th January

CHRIST'S WEAPONS IN SPIRITUAL WARFARE

Reading: Luke 4:31–44

What is this word? For with authority and power he
commands the unclean spirits, and they come out! (v. 36)

We know of course that for mankind's deliverance and redemption Christ would later have to fight another battle of a different kind at Calvary. But that does nothing to diminish the importance of the point that Luke is making here: in the fight for man's deliverance from the power of Satan, the first and foremost tactic is the proclamation of the supremely and absolutely authoritative word of God. And it follows that to neglect the preaching of that word, or in any way to cast doubt in people's minds as to its authority and trustworthiness, is to play directly into Satan's hands and to help maintain his bondage over them. It was a sense of the supreme importance of preaching the word to as many as possible, says Luke (see vv. 4:42–44), that made Christ leave Capernaum, in spite of his popularity there, in order to preach elsewhere.

The second matter of supreme importance in the war against spiritual wickedness is the identity of Jesus. Twice over we are told (see vv. 4:34, 41) that demons as they left their victims cried out in recognition that Jesus was the Christ, the Son of God. On each occasion Christ silenced them. At first sight that is perhaps surprising. Throughout this stage of Luke's Gospel the question of the necessity of evidence to prove who Jesus is has been very much to the fore. We might have expected Jesus therefore to call the attention of the people to the testimony of these defeated demonic forces. But of course he did not. In the course of the great war, Satan and his demons may for tactical reasons sometimes say what is true—in the third temptation Satan even quoted Scripture—or they may be forced against their will to say what is true: they never say it out of loyalty to the truth or with any intention of leading people to believe the truth. Truth is ultimately a person; in the great warfare of the ages his identity is all-important. Only those are to be trusted, in the ultimate sense, who speak in loyalty to that person. Those of course who deny that Jesus is the Christ, the Son of God, thereby declare plainly that they fight on the other side.

David Gooding, *According to Luke: The Third Gospel's Ordered Historical Narrative*, pp. 91–2

26th January

THE HEALING OF THE DEMON-POSSESSED BOY

Reading: Luke 9:37–43; Deuteronomy 32:6–20

Jesus answered, 'O faithless and twisted generation,
how long am I to be with you and bear with
you? Bring your son here.' (Luke 9:41)

This is a very moving passage and its relevance to the situation in our story is at once evident. The boy's twisted limbs, convulsed features and disturbed personality, and the distress of the father at seeing his only son in that condition were an all too eloquent picture of the distress of the Father at seeing his sons and daughters in Israel gone from him, attracted by false religion and demonic powers, and become perverse, crooked and twisted at the deeper level of their spiritual relationships. And all this as a result of loss of faith in, and love of, and obedience to, the Father. For *the* Son of the Father it was an almost intolerable distress to have to remain among such faithless and perverted sons: 'how long shall I be with you, and bear with you?' he said. How then should the trouble be put right and Israel's sons and daughters be won back to the Father? If the trouble began with ingratitude and then unbelief, deepening into disobedience and alienation and faithlessness until any old religion, demonic power or superstition was more attractive and fascinating than the Father himself, it is obvious that mere moral sermons and exhortations would be inadequate to bring them back. They would need a new revelation of the Father, a vision of his majesty and glory, to break the fascination of sin and the attractiveness of idolatry, and to reawaken a sense of the incomparable wonder of God and evoke faith and worship and obedience.

And that is what Christ did for the people in our story. The disciples had been unable to do it. They were, of course, the ones who had been left behind when Christ and the three had gone up the mountain, and they had not even seen the glory and the cloud or heard the Father's voice. It took the Son of the Father to do it. From the splendour of the transfiguration where the voice from the 'Majestic Glory' had proclaimed him 'my beloved Son', he had come down the mountain to the spiritual squalor of the plain in order to make known what the Father was really like and to reveal his glory to some of his long-lost sons. And the effect on the people, says Luke, was this: they were all amazed at the majesty of God.

David Gooding, *According to Luke: The Third Gospel's Ordered Historical Narrative*, pp. 178–9

27th January

THE MAN WHO CALLED HIMSELF LEGION

Reading: Luke 8:26—39

What is your name? (v. 30)

The great Creator, who makes endless blades of grass and no two are the same, who scatters his snowflakes and no two are the same, made each one of us. Outwardly very similar in certain things, yet inwardly each of us is unique. Have you ever tried to think what you are—the you that God says is going to last somewhere for ever? You are almost a frightening thing! I don't mean your looks; I mean the fact that you, standing by yourself as a unique personality, are going to last for ever somewhere. How important you are, and what a tremendous lot that name of yours sums up.

Judge then how far this poor man had fallen. We read that when our Lord stood in front of him and said, 'What is your name?', he answered, 'Legion'. That wasn't his name; that wasn't the real him. That wasn't him as he had been born. 'Many demons had entered him' (v. 30). Demons from Satan himself had entered into that man and were in process of tearing his personality apart, making him a freak of a thing. What a tragedy. He was so far gone that he no longer recognized himself, and when he was asked, 'What is your name?' pathetically he replied, 'Legion'.

You say, 'He was an extreme case'.

He was indeed.

'The man surely had had a mental breakdown.'

Perhaps he had, but the Bible makes it clear that behind all his suffering was the fact that Satan himself had got hold of his life and was in process of tearing it apart.

You say, 'Why quote such a man, so far gone, to people like us? Surely you don't think that any of us are in that plight?'

Of course I don't, but can we not see here a vivid warning? Here on earth, this side of the grave, is a man whom Satan has taken almost to the limit. We begin to see what it will mean to be lost. What it means for a human soul, made in the image of God for happy fellowship with God, in all its mysterious, wonderful joy and gladness, to be now in the grip of Satan and almost lost on earth. He is a sad example of what it will mean to perish—to perish in body, to perish in mind—and land on the scrapheap of eternity.

David Gooding, *What is Your Name? The Healing of the Possessed Man in Luke 8*, p. 4

28th January

THE HEALING OF THE MAN WHO WAS MUTE

Reading: Luke 11:14–28

*But if it is by the finger of God that I cast out demons, then
the kingdom of God has come upon you. (v. 20)*

It was a glorious thing which the Saviour did when he cast out the demon responsible for the man's physical muteness. Luke tells us that when the silence of years was broken and for the first time in life the man spoke, the crowd was amazed (see v. 14). As well they might be: they had grown so used to this man being mute that they had never imagined he could be anything else. Even more glorious, however, is that great spiritual deliverance which Christ chose to illustrate by this miracle. To picture it we may perhaps be allowed to borrow some imagery from an analogy which he himself used in the argument that followed his miracle (see vv. 21–22). 'When a strong man fully armed guards his own court, his goods are in peace.' That is, they remain undisturbed and secure, they give him no trouble or anxiety. There for you is the true state of prayerless, spiritually mute mankind. Their peace, apparent contentment and spiritual silence is the peace of a prison. Chattels of the strong enemy, they ask God for nothing, not even for deliverance, because their prayerless tongues have been chained by a tyrant who has endless devices at his disposal for keeping them quiet and preventing any break-out or contact with the world above. Many of them have even been persuaded that there is no world above (cf. Eph 2:1–3).

In that grim situation we may thank God that he did not wait for the prisoners to invite him in before he intervened. He took the initiative. Strong and fully armed as the enemy was, by means of the incarnation a stronger than he began to invade the prison, overpower the tyrant, and talk to the prisoners. His miraculous release of one prisoner from a demon of physical muteness certainly astonished the rest of them; but the miracle was intended as more than an exhibition of supernatural power designed to demonstrate the existence of God and his kingdom. It was also meant as a sign to encourage men to break their silence, to set them free and get them talking to the Father. Since then, the stronger than the strong by his death has invaded the deepest of the enemy's dungeons and broken his last stronghold. Multitudes have been set free (see Col 2:13–15; Heb 2:14–15). The risen and triumphant Lord has 'distributed Satan's spoils' (Luke 11:22).

David Gooding, *According to Luke: The Third Gospel's Ordered Historical Narrative*, pp. 232–3

29th January

THE CLEANSING OF THE LEPER

Reading: Luke 5:12–16

*And Jesus stretched out his hand and touched him, saying,
'I will; be clean.' And immediately the leprosy left him. (v. 13)*

Christ's cleansing of the leper demonstrated two things simultaneously: his divine compassion and his miraculous power. He might have cured the man simply by speaking the command, 'Be clean'; but in his compassion he stretched out his hand and touched him. It requires little effort to imagine what the touch of that hand meant to a man who had been segregated from society as an untouchable. But we must not misinterpret Christ's compassion: it carried no criticism of the Jewish priests. He was not suggesting that if they had only been more compassionate they would not have segregated the man. Christ's touch had the miraculous ability to banish leprosy. The priests had no such power. For them to have touched the leper would have been to spread the uncleanness by contagion; and that would have been pseudo-compassion. Their God-given duty was to maintain standards of cleanliness, to diagnose leprosy, pronounce lepers unclean, and, painful and drastic though it was, to segregate them. In touching the leper Christ was doing nothing to undermine the priests' stand against uncleanness; on the contrary, he upheld their authority: for when he had cleansed the man he sent him to the priests for their inspection, and told him to offer the sacrifices required by the law of Moses (see v. 14).

The analogy will hold for moral and spiritual uncleanness too. Many people nowadays seem to imagine that Christ's compassion for unclean people justifies permissiveness. But that is mistaken and dangerous. The law of God condemns uncleanness, and warns that if persisted in it will lead to eternal segregation (see Rev 21:27). Christ certainly can do what the law cannot do: he can cleanse a man (see John 13:10; Eph 5:26). But that does not mean that he disagrees with the law. Cleansing a man is not the same thing as saying that on grounds of compassion dirt should no longer be so strictly regarded as dirty. Cleansing presumes that dirt is dirty, ugly, dangerous and unacceptable. Indeed Christ is on record (see Luke 16:14–18) as having explicitly denied that he had come to encourage a more permissive attitude towards the law's moral demands; and his apostles later on solemnly warn us that various forms of moral uncleanness are contagious (see 1 Cor 5:6; Heb 12:14–15).

David Gooding, *According to Luke: The Third Gospel's Ordered Historical Narrative*, p. 105–6

30th January

THE WOMAN WHO WAS BENT DOUBLE

Reading: Luke 13:1–17

And ought not this woman, a daughter of Abraham
whom Satan bound for eighteen years, be loosed
from this bond on the Sabbath day? (v. 16)

Whatever name is given to her physical condition, it had certainly robbed
her of a significant part of her human dignity: she was permanently bent
over and unable to straighten herself up. From one point of view it was
simply a physical condition. On the other hand, man's upright stance is
more than a mere anatomical fact. It is something distinctively human, an
appropriate physical expression of man's moral, spiritual and official dignity
as God's viceroy, created in the image of God to have dominion over all
other creatures (see Gen 1:26–27). By that same token the bent back is the
typical physical posture of the burden-bearer and the slave under the yoke,
and so becomes a natural and vivid metaphor for the effects of oppression
and slavery. Moreover the woman's physical condition was not due simply to
physical causes. Christ declared it to be a bondage induced by Satan, whose
malevolence has always sought from the very beginning to rob man of his
dominion and dignity and degrade him into a slave. Few men and women
have bent backs physically: but morally and spiritually all men and women
find themselves sooner or later bent and bowed by weaknesses of one kind
or another from which they have not the strength to free themselves.

One day, however, so the story tells us, the woman shuffled her way to
the synagogue to hear the word of God, for it was the Sabbath. What word
would the Bible have for her and her condition? Left to itself, uncomplicated
by Pharisaic traditions of interpretation, the Bible would have spoken clearly
enough. This perhaps: 'I am the Lord your God who brought you out of the
land of Egypt so that you should not be their slaves; and I have broken the bars
of your yoke and enabled you to walk upright and erect' (Lev 26:13). The ruler
of the synagogue, however, was a Pharisee, and he would have told her that
if ever God would be willing to set her free to stand up straight, it certainly
would not be today: this was the Sabbath, and it would not be glorifying to
God for her to be set free from bondage on the Sabbath. But before he had
the chance to say anything, mighty arms stretched out and laid their hands on
her, and another voice said, 'Woman, you are released from your weakness';
and immediately she stood erect and glorified God (Luke 13:12–13).

David Gooding, *According to Luke: The Third Gospel's Ordered Historical Narrative*, pp. 266–7

31st January

JESUS' MIRACLES—SIGNPOSTS TO GOD

Reading: Acts 10:34–44

Men of Israel, hear these words: Jesus of Nazareth, a man attested
to you by God with mighty works and wonders and signs that God
did through him in your midst, as you yourselves know. (2:22)

Peter rose to explain what it was, and what it meant; and very soon he was reminding them of other recent mighty acts. Throughout the last three years the regularities of nature had time and again been suspended or even reversed as up and down the length of Palestine Jesus of Nazareth had done mighty acts of power, wonders and signs. Many of the locals would have known about these miracles first hand; and those who were only visitors to the Passover festival at which he died would have heard about them from the endless conversations and discussions that had gone on in the temple and the city before the crucifixion (see, e.g. John 11:56; 12:9, 17–18). Everyone had heard about the nature and quality of those miracles. None of them had been a grotesque distortion of nature; none of them simply a display of power, a mere exhibition of supernatural fireworks. Every single miracle had been a work of mercy, producing life and peace, mental and physical wholeness, release from fear and bondage, joy, confidence and satisfaction. The only apparent exception was the cursing of the fig tree; but it harmed nobody, and conveyed a healthy spiritual lesson. The power that was invading nature through Jesus of Nazareth was no alien power. His miracles expressed, 'not simply a god, but God: that which is outside nature, not as a foreigner, but as her sovereign' (C S Lewis, *Miracles*). The attempt by the establishment to denounce Jesus' miracles as deceptions performed by satanic powers was patently absurd (Luke 11:14–20). They had been not only miracles of power: they had been signs of the greatness, love, mercy and compassion of God, miracles of physical provision, rescue and healing that at the same time were parables of the spiritual salvation which as Saviour of the world he offered to people who could not save themselves by their merely human powers. Jesus' whole life had been the epicentre of a constant invasion of our fallen, broken, sinful world by God's supernatural power and saving grace. With what more gracious gestures could God have accredited his Son to Israel when he sent him as their rightful Messiah and Sovereign?

David Gooding, *True to the Faith: The Acts of the Apostles–Defining and Defending the Gospel*, pp. 69-70

THE CAPTAIN OF OUR SALVATION

*Part 3—The Lord as Giver
and Sustainer of Life*

1st February

ETERNAL LIFE HERE AND NOW

Reading: 1 John 1:1–10

*That which we have seen and heard we proclaim also to you,
so that you too may have fellowship with us; and indeed our
fellowship is with the Father and with his Son Jesus Christ. (v. 3)*

This is not some mystical experience in which certain undefined and inde-finable shivers run through the intellect or the emotions. 'This is an eternal life that was manifested,' says John, and manifested in concrete forms here on this earth in the person of the Lord Jesus. He says, 'That which we have heard, that which we have seen with our eyes, and which we beheld, and our hands handled concerning the Word of life.' You notice how real this manifestation was: it could be handled, felt, seen and heard. This is the great historical reve-lation given us in the birth and life, death and resurrection of our blessed Lord.

Nowadays the Holy Spirit will make this revelation real in our hearts, but we need to hold that together with the actual historical facts that God has shown us in the historical Lord Jesus Christ. You can't escape John's feeling of excitement. What a thing that was! 'We write,' says John, 'so that you may have fellowship with us.' Fancy brushing against somebody as you got into a rowing boat and going across the lake, staying in the same inn, and then waking up to the fact that the person you had just touched was God incarnate. If that sounds like theological language to you, you must excuse the apostles for it's an excitement that they can scarcely contain—that they've actually seen and handled God incarnate! God forbid that in our generation we should ever lose the wonder of it.

Oh, my brother, my sister, that eternal life you have is not just the end of a theological proposition. God help us to wake up and see who it is that's in the midst of our thorn bush—twisted, gnarled and in danger of being consumed as we all may be. But what lights up your very inner man so that it glows brighter towards the eternal light, is already the person of the incarnate God in you. This is eternal life and the content of our fellowship; and the incarnation and life of our Lord is the basis of it.

Let's then notice what it is that we are to experience. John says, 'that we may have fellowship with him, that you believers also may have fellowship with us, the apostles. Yes, and our fellowship is with the Father and with his Son Jesus Christ.'

David Gooding, *Life in the Family of God: Twelve Seminars on the First Epistle of John*, pp. 14–15

2nd February

ETERNAL LIFE IS LIFE IN CHRIST

Reading: Colossians 3:1–15

*For the wages of sin is death, but the free gift of God is
eternal life in Christ Jesus our Lord. (Romans 6:23)*

Surely the eternal life is a gift; we get it at once. A baby has physical life.
Twenty years from now he or she could be an Olympic gold medallist. You'd
never have dreamed when you saw the baby that it had the potential for
that. The potential was developed, yes, but it had to be encouraged by rigorous, deliberate training; and the training increases the potential and has
its rewards.

But now we come to another important point. That is, that this eternal
life is a free gift of God *in Christ Jesus our Lord*. There is no eternal life
without Christ. We can't say, 'Now Lord, you've given me eternal life; that's
marvellously generous of you. Thank you, Lord, very, very much. Now, I'm
busy. Meet you in heaven, Lord, when I get there, because I don't need you
anymore for the time being. I've got eternal life, you see. You've just given me
eternal life, so goodbye for now, and I'll say a word for you now and again,
but we'll meet in heaven, Lord.'

That's a nonsense. 'Christ *is* your life,' says Paul (see Col 3:4). You don't have
any eternal life apart from him. And you won't be able to say when you get
to heaven, 'Lord, it's marvellous to be here, and it is your grace that brought
me here. That is stupendous, but, Lord, as you might expect, heaven is such
an interesting place, I shan't have much time to talk to you, because I've got
this infinite experience to explore. So I hope to see you sometime in the next
three hundred years. I've got eternal life!'

'No you haven't' says Christ, 'not apart from me, you haven't. Unless you
eat the flesh of the Son of Man and drink his blood, you have no life in
yourself' (see John 6:53).

That remains true of us. Christ is our life. We don't have any eternal life
apart from him; surely we don't. What did you symbolize by your baptism,
when you rose again from the water? It wasn't that, now that you are forgiven
you are going to try very hard. It was that you were buried with Christ, and
now you are risen with Christ. It is your being joined to Christ that brings
you eternal life.

David Gooding, *God's Power for Salvation: Paul's Letter to the Romans*, pp. 133–4

3rd February

CHRIST IS THE TRUE VINE

Reading: Isaiah 5:1–7

I am the true vine, and my Father is the vine dresser. (John 15:1)

In all Israel's—and the world's—history things were never so bad as when Jesus left the Upper Room with his disciples to go to Gethsemane and the cross. High heaven was about to witness the most outrageous act of oppression that Israel had ever committed, to hear the bitterest cry that Israel had ever forced from an innocent sufferer. The owner of the vineyard of Israel had sent his only Son to collect the fruit due to him, and the tenants of the vineyard were about to take that only Son, thrust him out of the vineyard and murder him (Luke 20:9–18).

What would the owner's response to that be? Abandon the whole project of growing grapes? No, far from it! Rather to set about growing even more grapes and still sweeter grapes, not just in Israel but throughout the whole world; but to do so—and here comes the secret—by using a different vine and a different method of cultivation and production. 'Yes,' says somebody, 'that's right. God would now set Israel aside as his vine and put the Christian church in Israel's place as the new and better vine.'

No, certainly not! If Israel, in spite of their long line of inspired prophets and godly saints, eventually failed, what realistic hope would the Christian church have of doing any better? Indeed, that unholy amalgam of religion and politics which men call Christendom has often been guilty of worse moral corruption, cruelty and oppression than Israel ever was. No, Christ did not say, 'Israel has failed, but you, my disciples, must try to do better.' To imagine he did would be to run the risk of missing the glory of the gospel of holiness which our Lord was now about to announce. God's answer to Israel's failure was not the Christian church, but Christ. The vine that was Israel had certainly failed; but, said Christ, '*I am* the true vine.'

David Gooding, *In the School of Christ: Lessons on Holiness in John 13–17*, pp. 128–9

4th February

Reading: Galatians 5:16–26

Therefore, as you received Christ Jesus the Lord, so walk in him, rooted and built up in him and established in the faith, just as you were taught, abounding in thanksgiving. (Colossians 2:6–7)

Let us pause to consider the magnificence of this great provision for our holiness. God gave Israel a law with clear directives as to what conduct and testimony he expected from them. There was nothing intrinsically wrong with the law: it was holy, righteous, and good. The reason for its failure as a scheme for growing grapes was, as Paul puts it, that it was 'weakened by the flesh' (Rom 8:3). Israel, fallen and failing human beings like the rest of us, had not the moral and spiritual strength necessary to carry out the law to God's standards and requirements. And Christians, in and of themselves, are no better or stronger than Israelites. Had God simply carried on with the same method, the result would have been as unsatisfactory as before.

No, God had a new method in mind, in fact since before the foundation of the world. It involved an altogether new and different kind of vine: the Son of God himself. Rooted—if we may use such a metaphor—in the Godhead since he is himself God, yet simultaneously truly human, he was and is and forever will be supremely able to express the character of God the Father in both deed and word, to God's unfailing delight and man's never fading blessing. He is, in his own words, the true vine. Not that Israel was a false vine. Christ is the true vine in the sense that he is the ideal, the ultimate, the perfect vine, of which Israel was at best an inadequate prototype. And Christ, the true vine, was altogether new in another respect as well. Redeemed men and women, regenerated by the Holy Spirit, could now be incorporated into him, like branches in a vine, so that his life, grace, goodness and power could circulate through them and produce the fruit of the Holy Spirit in them—love, joy, peace, long-suffering, kindness, goodness, faithfulness, meekness and self-control.

This was new, marvellously and exhilaratingly new. Toweringly great as were the famous saints of the Old Testament, nowhere in all the many records of their spiritual experiences does any one of them speak of being incorporated into the Messiah. Understandably not. But nothing less than this is God's provision for us who live this side of the incarnation, death, burial, resurrection and ascension of the Lord Jesus and the coming of the Holy Spirit at Pentecost.

David Gooding, In the School of Christ: Lessons on Holiness in John 13–17, pp. 129–30

5th February

I HAVE THE KEYS

Reading: Revelation 1:1–20

I have the keys of Death and Hades. (v. 18)

To add to the final part of the comfort, I think I hear him rattle the keys right at his side. Can you hear them rattling just now? Oh, I like the sound of those keys! 'I have the keys,' he says. 'Do you see them, John, my boy? I have the keys of death and of Hades' (see v. 18). Death is like the door. As we come to this door, we see it as death on our side. When you pass through it you are in the unseen world on the other side. 'I have the keys. I have the authority,' says Christ. 'I control them.' It is not the devil who controls those things. No, no. Hebrews 2 tells us that at one time Satan, that is the devil, had the power of death. Our Lord came and died 'to deliver them who through fear of death were all their lifetime subject to bondage' (see vv. 14–15). Christ has the keys.

You say, 'To let us in?'

No, to let us out! I think that's more likely. Yes, when we come to die physically, it is he who will control it. He will control our passage into the world beyond that's unseen. We have his blessed word as he gave it to the dying thief and to many since: 'Today you shall be with me in paradise' (Luke 23:43).

That is how the believers of the New Testament talk. They are not so much concerned with whether their 'soul' or their 'spirit' departs. You can talk like that if you care to. But it is: '*you* will be with me in paradise.'

'*I* want to depart,' says Paul, 'and be with Christ. If *we* are absent from the body *we* are present with the Lord' (see 2 Cor 5:6–8).

'I have the keys of death and of Hades,' Christ says. We need not fear then. Yes, we should fear, in the reverential sense. But we have no fear or dread as we stand before this glorious, blessed Lord Jesus Christ, Lord and head of the church, in all his official glory. He holds us with his right hand, and thus we shall find courage to listen to what he has to say, as he assesses us and encourages us, and exposes our faults and calls on us to repent and then to overcome.

David Gooding, *The Book of the Revelation: Major Themes of Revelation's Six Sections*, pp. 29–30

6th February

CHRIST THE SOURCE OF LIFE

Reading: John 5:1–30

*For as the Father has life in himself, so he has granted
the Son also to have life in himself. (v. 26)*

Sin takes many different forms: ungodliness, enmity with God and so forth,
but one of them is weakness: 'while we were still weak . . . Christ died for the
ungodly' (Rom 5:6). Similarly Romans 8 says, 'For what the law could not do,
in that it was weak through the flesh . . .' (v. 3 RV). That is precisely the word
that is used here of these people. They were weak: blind, lame, withered.

Galatians tells us that if the law (that is, the Old Testament law of Moses)
could have given life, then righteousness would have been by the law (3:21).
But the law can't give you life. It is true that God's law is healthy, good and
spiritual. If you follow its precepts it will guide you into healthy forms of
living. But the law could never give you life in the sense of spiritual life, eternal
life. Why not? Because we are too weak: 'what the law could not do, in that
it was weak through the flesh . . .'. It never could save us, therefore. We were
too weak to use the means!

People imagine Christ has come to do that, to give them a helping hand
to get into the 'pool', to give them a helping hand to keep the law, and by so
doing they will gradually improve. And though they will confess that at the
moment they have not improved enough, they hope life will last long enough
so that Christ will eventually be able to help them enough to get through
the final judgment.

That is a fundamental misconception of what Christ has come to do! To put
it in the terms of this incident, he hasn't come to give sinners a helping hand
to get into the pool—to keep the law—and thus be saved. He is the source
of life! And when the man said, 'I have no one to put me into the pool', our
Lord didn't reply, 'Well, I will, because I'm the strong Son of God, and I will
give you immense help!' He said, in effect, 'Pool? I don't need any pool! Get
up!' And the man got up and walked. It was instantaneous salvation, because
Christ is the source of life.

David Gooding, Four Journeys to Jerusalem: A Series of Seminars on the Gospel of John, pp. 50–1

7th February

CHRIST THE MEANS OF LIFE

Reading: John 6:1–15

This was to fulfil the word that he had spoken: 'Of those whom you gave me I have lost not one.' (John 18:9)

Consider what the bread is. It is not only 'the bread of life' it is 'the *living* bread'. The manna came down from heaven, but it wasn't alive itself! Our Lord is the living bread. This bread is alive. When the miracle of the feeding of the five thousand took place, we are told that, after the crowds had eaten and were filled, our Lord instructed the apostles to go around and gather up the broken pieces of the bread that remained so 'that nothing may be lost' (6:12). That is an interesting remark. We might say, 'But if our Lord had the power to multiply loaves and fishes to feed five thousand, what does it matter if a few broken pieces were left lying around and left to rot? He could easily make some more, couldn't he?' But he gave them instructions, and they had to gather up the broken pieces that remained so that nothing of that bread would be lost.

How much more the people he has saved. You claim that Christ saved you and is your bread of life, and he is in you? Well, I can tell you now that that bread shall *never* be lost. 'Christ in you'—the living bread. It is a magnificent concept, but an even more magnificent reality: Christ has come to live *in* us!

We have to be prepared for life in a spirit world. Our Lord's resurrection body is said to be a 'spiritual body'. That doesn't mean, as some people say, that our resurrection body is made of spirit and is not genuinely material, any more than if I told you that this man's car has a petrol engine you would imagine that the engine is made of petrol. Petrol is the stuff that makes it go as distinct from a diesel engine or an electric motor.

So too with the resurrection body of Christ. He said, 'Touch me, and see. For a spirit does not have flesh and bones as you see that I have' (Luke 24:39). It was a real and, in our sense, a physical body, but of a different order. It is a *spiritual body*. If you are Christ's, you have within you that very power that shall raise you at the resurrection when the Lord comes (if you have to be raised), or shall transform you when you meet the Lord in the air.

David Gooding, *Four Journeys to Jerusalem: A Series of Seminars on the Gospel of John*, pp. 82–3

THE CAPTAIN OF OUR SALVATION

Part 4—The Servant King

8th February

THE LORD'S EXAMPLE OF SERVICE

Reading: Luke 18:31–43

I am among you as the one who serves. (Luke 22:27)

How true that was! Luke tells us (18:35–43) that once when Christ was approaching the town of Jericho, a blind beggar sitting by the roadside heard the commotion of the approaching crowd, and discovering that it was Jesus coming, surrounded by a vast throng of people, decided to appeal to Christ to do something about his blindness. Being very tactful—or was it that for all his blindness he had a good deal more insight than most?—he hailed Christ as the Son of David, that is, as the great and glorious king of Israel, and pleaded with him to have mercy on him.

The crowd told him to shut up. 'Look,' they doubtless said, 'there's no use your shouting like that. Jesus is a very important person. In fact, it's quite possible that, like you say, he is the great king himself; and if not that, he is certainly a tremendous preacher and prophet. Kings and prophets can't keep stopping at every corner to see to the needs of fleabitten beggars. Jesus has more important things to see to.' But at that moment Christ came up level with the blind beggar. He stopped. 'Help that man up and bring him to me,' he said to some of the bystanders. And then as the man came near, he asked him, 'Did you call me? Did you want something?' 'Yes,' faltered the man, 'my eyes . . . I'm blind, you know. Could you, I mean, would you give me sight?' 'Why, of course,' said Christ, 'that's why I've come, to serve people.' And immediately he gave the man sight.

That was dramatic; and doubtless was meant to be, not in order to make a good showing and get a good write-up in the press, but that all might know that this is Christ's idea of what it means to be great, to be king: it means serving even the lowest. And we may be sure that now Christ has left our lowly world and sits enthroned in glory, his ideas on being great are the same as they were then. Any one of us in need may kneel and pray; and Christ will still come toward us and say, 'Did you call? Did you want something?' Happy the subjects who have a king like that!

David Gooding, *Windows on Paradise: Scenes of Hope and Salvation in the Gospel of Luke*, pp. 99–100

9th February

Reading: 1 Peter 3:8–22

Therefore I will divide him a portion with the many,
and he shall divide the spoil with the strong,
because he poured out his soul to death. (Isaiah 53:12)

If we are going to preach the gospel effectively, the gospel of the suffering servant of God, we must be prepared to follow the pattern of the suffering servant.

'Christ has left us an example,' says Peter, 'that we should follow his steps; he who "committed no sin, neither was deceit found in his mouth. When he was reviled, he did not revile in return; when he suffered, he did not threaten"' (1 Pet 2:22–23). He was 'like a lamb that is led to the slaughter' (Isa 53:7); and he 'bore our sins in his body on the tree, that we might die to sin and live to righteousness' (1 Pet 2:24).

The suffering servant not only made atonement for sin; he left us an example that we might follow his steps. Says Peter to the slaves, 'You know, when your masters are unreasonable and they flog you even when you don't deserve it, and you could curse them, try and remember the pattern of the suffering servant. Where would you have been if Christ had cursed you when he suffered?' (see 1 Pet 2:18–20).

'And you women,' says Peter, talking to the married women who were converted and their husbands weren't converted, 'when your husbands are very difficult and they won't listen to you, try in your heart to remember the pattern of the suffering servant. Living like him, you could win your husbands by your behaviour, even if you can't win them by your words' (see 3:1–2).

Let's seek the rewards that are going. Don't let's be like James and John, who could think only of sitting on thrones in the day to come, and had to be taught that the Son of Man came, not to be served, but to serve, and to give his life as a ransom for many (Matt 20:28). If we are going to be effective to preach to the world about a Saviour who poured out his soul unto death, the most effective way of preaching it is for us to be willing, likewise, to pour out our souls and our bodies and all we have for our fellow men.

David Gooding, *The Restoration of Israel: A Study in Isaiah 43, 53 and 59*, pp. 5–6

10th February

THE POWER OF CHRIST'S EXAMPLE

Reading: John 13:1–17

For I have given you an example, that you also
should do just as I have done to you. (v. 15)

A capable teacher knows that the most effective way of teaching is when theory is accompanied by practical demonstration. And so the perfect teacher gave his disciples an example of humble, loving, practical service, so vivid that they would immediately grasp its general significance and never forget it for the rest of their lives. But there was infinitely more to it than that. He was not simply a teacher. Indeed he was not first and foremost the perfect teacher. He was first and foremost their Lord; in fact, the Lord of the universe. They had no claim on him that he should serve them, nor any right to expect him to do it. On the contrary, it was already a grievous fault in them that they had not hastened to do their duty towards him, their Lord, and wash his feet. That he, their Lord and Creator incarnate should, in spite of it, divest himself of his clothes, gird himself with a towel like a humble servant, kneel at their feet, wash them and dry them with the towel which his own body had warmed, was astounding. When he had done this for them, how could they resent his command that they should similarly serve others? 'Truly, truly, I say to you,' said Christ, 'a servant is not greater than his master, nor is a messenger greater than the one who sent him' (v. 16).

The time would come when he would send them into the wide world as his apostles with apostolic authority. But there was a danger that their high office in the church might cause them to forget that their duty was humbly to serve their fellow-believers, and instead to think that their fellow-Christians ought to bow down before them and serve them. So they were always to remember that the Christ they represented had, like a humble servant, done the menial task of washing their feet. After that how could they become arrogant and proud and behave as if they were greater and more important than their Lord? The feel of the touch of his hands on their feet would never fade from their memory, a silent rebuke to their pride, an irrepressible and undeniable call to act as the servants of even the lowliest of men.

David Gooding, *In the School of Christ: Lessons on Holiness in John 13–17*, pp. 40–1

11th February

THE KING EATS IN JERUSALEM

Reading: Mark 14:12–26

*This is my blood of the covenant, which
is poured out for many. (v. 24)*

Let's bring our thoughts to the situation as it was in Jerusalem just before the Passover at the end of Holy Week. The religious authorities naturally had their preparations to make for the celebration of the national feast. Pressing even more urgently on their minds, however, was the necessity of isolating Jesus from the crowds so that they could destroy him. Presently Judas gave them the opportunity they were looking for, and they went ahead with their preparations for the kill.

And now we are to behold the most spectacular demonstration of the way God governs a rebellious universe. Human rebellion, initially induced in Eden's garden by Satan, is at this stage in history by Satan's continued inspiration (see Luke 22:3) determined that Jesus shall die. And Jesus for his part in order to counter that rebellion and to establish God's kingdom here on earth in the very teeth of that rebellion is determined—to die! To that end he once more makes preparations to enter Jerusalem, and sends two disciples, not this time to borrow an ass on which to ride in ceremonial procession as Zion's king, but to borrow a room in which to eat the Passover. The Passover, of course, had to be eaten at night; but, humanly speaking, it was dangerous for Christ to be in the city at night without the protection of the crowds around him, which is why all through the past week as soon as evening came and the crowds dispersed our Lord had left the city and disappeared into the dark shadows of the Mount of Olives to avoid premature arrest (see 19:47–48; 21:37–38). His entry into the city at night and the place where he would eat the Passover had to be kept secret. The two disciples were therefore given certain prearranged signals that would eventually bring them to an unnamed man who was prepared to lend Christ a room in his house in which to celebrate the Passover in Jerusalem. It was the king's own capital city; but the authorities had a price on his head and Jerusalem was now the earthly headquarters of rebellion against the king.

David Gooding, *According to Luke: The Third Gospel's Ordered Historical Narrative*, p. 349

12th February

CHRIST'S OFFER OF FRIENDSHIP TO JUDAS

Reading: Psalm 41

It is he to whom I will give this morsel of bread
when I have dipped it. (John 13:26)

In the Upper Room it was not other people who were about to be damaged. Judas's sin was hurting Christ personally, thrusting a poisoned arrow at Christ's own heart. How, then, and in what terms, and in what tone of voice, and by what action would he expose this viper's treachery against his own person? In answer to John's question as to who the traitor was, he said, 'It is the one to whom I will give this piece of bread, when I have dipped it in the dish.' Then, dipping the piece of bread, he gave it to Judas Iscariot, the son of Simon.

This eloquent action was more than a convenient way of indicating who the traitor was. Judas, we remember had for the last three years been taking Christ's bread, pretending to be his friend. Now by betraying Christ, he was about to fling the bread of Christ's friendship back into his face. How would Christ react to that? By offering him once more that self-same bread! There was no burning indignation, no vitriolic vituperation. Only the offer of the sop which said with unspoken eloquence: 'Judas, you have taken the bread of my friendship, and, in spite of it, you have treacherously lifted up your heel to kick me. Now you are about to betray me. I know all about it. But in spite of it, before you do it, Judas, I offer you once more the bread of my friendship! Will you not accept it?'

The gesture was neither cynical nor sarcastic. Nor was it a bribe to curry favour with Judas. It was a genuine, last minute attempt to save him from his self-chosen hell. According to the unwritten laws of ancient Middle Eastern hospitality, if a host took a piece of bread, dipped it in the dish and personally handed it to one of his guests, it did not only mean that he was honouring the guest by offering him a specially tasteful morsel of food from the banquet: it meant in addition that he was pledging himself to that guest, to be his loyal friend. And we may be sure that, even at this dark and dramatic moment in Judas's pathway to hell, our Lord's offering to him of the sop was a genuine gesture, late as the time was, to urge upon Judas his friendship and love and with them the forgiveness, the pardon and the eventual glory that they implied.

David Gooding, *In the School of Christ: Lessons on Holiness in John 13–17*, pp. 57–8

13th February

THE AMBITION OF THE SERVANT

Reading: Isaiah 49:1–21

It is too light a thing that you should be my
servant to raise up the tribes of Jacob. (v. 6)

That magnificent task of bringing Israel back was far too big for any but him, God's infinite Son. But just to bring Israel back couldn't be enough to satisfy him; what did it need to be? 'I couldn't give him so small a thing,' said God, 'I'm going to set you as a light to the Gentiles'—the whole earth shall hear of his fame.

Oh, how lovely a task has been given to the Son of God, God's holy servant—*big enough for his divine capabilities.* As I listen to him summon us Gentiles to hear what he's got to say about his service for the Lord, I find gratitude rising in my heart because I have a personal interest in it. Very selfish, I know, but I am so glad he wasn't content just to save Israel; aren't you? To come from heaven to be called from the womb to bring back Israel and Jacob, that's what he was formed for. Had he gone back to heaven having done nothing more, what right had we to complain? But I thank God he couldn't be content with such a small thing. To be honest with you, we don't add a lot compared with the multimillions he has saved, but he couldn't be content without us. Oh, thank God for the horizons of the blessed Lord Jesus.

And one day, the man whom men despised and the nation abhorred, who seemed to be but a servant of rulers, 'Kings shall see and arise; princes, and they shall prostrate themselves; because of the Lord, who is faithful, the Holy One of Israel, who has chosen you' (v. 7). He shall come to be admired amidst the ten thousand times ten thousand (Rev 9:16); and then you will see the aim of the task that he so gladly accepted.

This then is our Lord; and would it be altogether wrong for us to lean upon his breast and hear his emotions and his feelings, and in our tiny little level echo them? You will find profound satisfaction in serving the Lord, so make sure the Lord opens your eyes to *a task big enough for your abilities.* Don't be content with too small a thing.

David Gooding, *Satisfaction in Serving the Lord: Three Principles from the Prophecy of Isaiah*, p. 6

14th February

THE GRACE OF GOD TO PAUL AND TO US

Reading: Acts 9:1–19

But I received mercy for this reason, that in me, as the foremost, Jesus Christ might display his perfect patience as an example to those who were to believe in him for eternal life. (1 Timothy 1:16)

What a king, who had had mercy on Saul of Tarsus. Would you have had mercy on him? If an impertinent mosquito were to alight on my forehead and start to bite me, I wouldn't hesitate to smash it into oblivion, and neither would you. Tell me, how did the King of all ages, the King of kings and Lord of lords, find it in his heart to put up with Saul of Tarsus, as he agreed with those who had taken a crown of thorns and rammed it on the head of God incarnate?

How did God break him? Well, he broke his enmity. What a marvellous story it is. Christ did the job of representing God to Saul of Tarsus, and that was amazing because Christ was the very one whom Paul was attacking and blaspheming and trying to eliminate. God gave to his dear Son the task of subduing that rebel and putting him into his service.

Excuse the term, but what *courage* our blessed Lord Jesus had. If I'd pardoned Saul, I might have said, 'All right Saul, but you'll just get inside heaven and sit on one of the draughtiest seats.' In that moment Christ counted him faithful and trusted him, and put him into his service.

'I opposed him ignorantly in unbelief,' said Paul (v. 13). 'Now that he's changed my heart and judged me faithful, he has appointed me to serve his people in his church. He didn't just give me forgiveness, he overflowed me with grace and love that have their source in Christ. He did it so that I should be a beacon light, an example of the way God treats all who dare to repent and trust his dear Son' (see vv. 14–16).

So may we too discover something more of the grace of God ministered by Jesus Christ, and may it turn us around. O may God continue to reveal himself to us, that his revelation may leave its mark upon us that shall last from now to eternity.

David Gooding, *Take Hold of Eternal Life: Major Themes in Paul's First Letter to Timothy*, pp. 11–12

THE CAPTAIN OF OUR SALVATION

Part 5—The Shepherd King

15th February

OUR SECURITY

Reading: Hebrews 6:1–20

By myself I have sworn, declares the LORD, because you have done this and have not withheld your son, your only son, I will surely bless you, and I will surely multiply your offspring as the stars of heaven. (Genesis 22:16–17)

If it is security that we are interested in, these next few verses (Heb 6:13–20), are one of the strongest statements in the whole of the Bible of the utterly unbreakable security that every believer may constantly enjoy. It starts by citing the experience of Abraham. God made him a tremendous promise: 'Surely blessing I will bless thee, and multiplying I will multiply thee' (6:14 KJV), or as the NIV puts it, rather less vigorously, 'I will surely bless you and give you many descendants.' Now God cannot lie. So when God makes a promise, his bare word ought to be enough for anyone to rest on with unshakeable confidence. But on this occasion God was not content simply to make the promise; he swore an oath as well: 'By myself have I sworn . . . that in blessing I will bless thee, and in multiplying I will multiply thy seed' (Gen 22:16–17 KJV). He did it, the writer explains, not simply for Abraham's sake. He did it for the sake of all those who down the centuries would inherit the benefits of this promise, that is, all those who would truly believe in God and in his Son, Abraham's seed, Jesus Christ our Lord. And he did it because he wanted us to have as strong encouragement as he could possibly give us in the knowledge that his purpose to bless us is utterly unchangeable. 'God did this so that, by two unchangeable things [that is, his promise and his oath] in which it is impossible for God to lie, we who have fled to take hold of the hope set before us may be greatly encouraged' (Heb 6:18 NIV) or 'may have a strong encouragement' (RV).

What a hope Christians have! They have cast their anchor not in their fluctuating moods or feelings, or in their varying circumstances, or in anything else in this changing world. Christ himself as their precursor has taken their anchor right through into heaven itself and embedded it in the immovable ground of the presence and throne and character of God (6:19–20).

David Gooding, *An Unshakeable Kingdom: The Letter to the Hebrews for Today*, pp. 140–1

16th February

THE MAN ABOVE THE RIVER

Reading: Daniel 12:1–13; Mark 5:45–52

*I heard the man clothed in linen, who was above the
waters of the stream; he raised his right hand and
his left hand towards heaven. (Daniel 12:7)*

As Daniel watched the waters flow by and remembered the past, he thought
of what must lie over the horizon where the waters were going. As he looked,
there stood a man above the water—not in the water being carried with the
tide, nor on the bank watching the river, but over the water (vv. 6–7). His
appearance was glorious and his knowledge wonderful, for as he starts to
talk to Daniel you perceive that he could see beyond the horizon; not only
the geographical horizon but beyond the horizons of time.

As he talks to Daniel, he begins to talk about the great time of trouble that
shall come. As we now know, it was distant to Daniel by thousands of years.
He even pierced the great eternity and told Daniel that when it was all over
his 'lot' forever stood secure (v. 13 KJV).

It must have been of immense comfort to Daniel's heart in the first place,
to see this figure standing above the river. Like in another sense it was to the
twelve apostles as they toiled one dark stormy night, and amidst the wind
and the waves they saw a man walking above the waters. He stepped into
their boat, demonstrating his control of those waters.

So it was for Daniel; and shall I not add, so it is for us? We don't have the
burdens that a great prophet like Daniel had to bear, but we have them too,
don't we? Sometimes things happen; shocking things. My heart went out to
the mother reported on the news the other day. She was out for a walk by
a canal with three children and two fell in and were drowned. As she tried to
save them, the baby fell in as well and drowned. What things could happen
tomorrow? This is no fairy story, but what happened to Daniel and what
happened to the twelve in the boat, surely happens to us at times? Through
the mist of tears, the flurry of the storm and the rage of the torrent, we see no
flash of lightening, no wonderful vision, but we sense the approach of the
Saviour. When we bid him into our boat there ensues the calm of knowing
that even sorrow and the ways of men and the politics of earth and the
seeming accidents of life stand under his gracious control.

David Gooding, *Days Yet to Come: Israel's Future and Ours in Daniel 10–12*, pp. 8–9

17th February

CHRIST HAS POWER OVER THE SPIRIT WORLD

Reading: Matthew 8:28–34

*And the men marvelled, saying, 'What sort of man is
this, that even winds and sea obey him?' (v. 27)*

We come now to the other side of the sea. We have learnt the lessons at the beginning, when the boat was by the quay, and now we've had the lessons that you learn in midstream. On the other side of the sea when they came out, they next had to learn our Lord's relationship, not to the physical powers of the universe, but to the spiritual powers of the universe. For though the physical powers of the universe can be terrifying sometimes, they are as nothing compared with the spiritual opposition that is raised against us.

When they got out of the boat, they met two people possessed of demons, and Matthew is the one who tells us what the other Gospel writers don't quite: They were 'so fierce that no one could pass that way' (v. 28). Anybody trying to journey through there, when they met those demons, found the demons so fierce that they turned around and went back.

That's a common experience with people who set forth on the path of discipleship. They begin to make some marvellous progress, and then his satanic majesty sees to it that there is some spiritual opposition in the way. It is so fierce! And Satan tries to defy the new convert, or the serious disciple, and stop him going home. He will try to get it into his head: 'It's no good; you'd better give this up. You were silly to try to start, you know. So pack up. Ignore the call of Jesus; turn tail and go back!' For ranged against us to try and stop us ever getting home to glory is all the power of hell itself. What hope have I of getting through?

What hope? Well, if it were left to my strength, I'd have no hope whatsoever. But thank God that he who is Lord of wind and wave, Lord of the physical powers, is sovereign over the spiritual powers. He cast out the opposition, and he opened the way for progress to be made. This is the pathway of discipleship, but we have one with us who is all-powerful to see us through.

David Gooding, *The Gospel of Authority and the Path of Discipleship: Studies in Matthew*, p. 19

18th February

THE FIRST AND THE LAST

Reading: Revelation 1:16–20; 2:8–11

*I am the first and I am the last; besides me
there is no god. (Isaiah 44:6)*

'And he laid his right hand upon me, saying, "Fear not; I am the first and the last . . ."' (Rev 1:17). Oh, I like that: 'I am the first and the last.' Well, he's the first and the last of a lot of things. He existed before the universe. He'll exist long after it goes to pieces, however it goes to pieces, by heat death or cold death or whatever. When it's long since gone, our Lord will still be there.

This is an indication of his deity. In the Old Testament, Jehovah says, 'I am the first and I am the last' (Isa 44:6). So does Christ say it here. But I take comfort in this: when it comes to me, he is the first and the last. He is the alpha and omega as far as I am concerned: the first letter of the alphabet and the last letter of the alphabet that makes up the story of me.

I don't think you'd ever think of writing the story of me; you haven't got the time to waste, but, if you were to do it, you'd have to use an alphabet of some kind. Do you know what the first letter will be in my story? Well, it won't be me, but Christ. I'm his idea; he thought me up. You mustn't believe I created myself. Well, whose idea are you then, if you're not Christ's idea? 'In him were all things created . . . and through him' (Col 1:16). And what is the last letter in all the story of my life going to be? Where is its goal? It is Christ, isn't it? In him, through him and to him were all things created. When your life is finished, and the whole story is told of what it's all been about here on earth, if you are one of his redeemed, it will be shown how you and your life have been turned by the redeeming grace of Christ to glorify Christ for all eternity! It will have been part of the eternal programme of the Word of God and part of his glorification. He is the first and the last.

19th February

CHRIST COMES TO US

Reading: John 6:16–24

When they had rowed about three or four miles, they
saw Jesus walking on the sea and coming near the
boat, and they were frightened. (v. 19)

He taught them to walk on the water that night, not merely empowering them by interceding for them, but we are told that at the fourth watch when the going was tough, he came to them. It was not something that the world at large saw or ever knew of. How would you explain such a thing to your ordinary, cynical man of the world? The Christians didn't try anyway: neither did Christ. Here is a secret for those in the family of God, and what a blessed secret it is. It reminds me of what our Lord Jesus said to his disciples just before he left, 'I will not leave you as orphans; I will come to you.' Note carefully what he meant. Not merely that one day he would come again, with the voice of the archangel and the trump of God at the second coming and take his people home. That he will do, but in the course of life and from time to time he has promised, 'I will not leave you as orphans; I will come to you. Yet a little while and the world will see me no more, but you will see me' (John 14:18–19).

Judas (not Iscariot) didn't quite understand and enquired further, 'Lord, how is it you'll manifest yourself to us and not to the world?' (v. 22).

Said Christ, 'If anyone loves me, he will keep my word, and my Father will love him, and we will come to him and make our home with him' (v. 23).

Christ comes to his people. I am not promising that he'll give you visions or spectacular sights, though I can't say he never will. But at that deeper level which is far more important than sight, the level of our spirit, it is still blessedly true that from time to time, Christ comes to his people.

Without excitement, without voices from the blue but in the profoundest level of reality, believers will tell you again and again of how, in their times of need, the Saviour has come to them. They have, so to speak, heard the rustling of the shepherd's robes and they said, 'It is the Lord.' Friend, do you know what it is to walk with the Saviour like that? If the Saviour comes, it has an effect. Although the storm may rage still, somehow all seems well.

David Gooding, *The Church's Witness to Christ: Faith Strengthening Evidence from Matthew*, pp. 15-17

20th February

THE SECURITY OF THE NEW COVENANT

Reading: Jeremiah 31:31–40

*For I will forgive their iniquity, and I will
remember their sin no more. (v. 34)*

Why is there no need for Christ to continue offering himself as a sacrifice? Why does he not still have to suffer the legal sanctions against sin whenever a believer sins? To this question the Holy Spirit himself gives the answer (Heb 10:17–18). He points to the third clause in the new covenant, 'I will remember their sins and their lawless deeds no more.' He then asks us to make the simple and obvious deduction: if all sins are completely forgiven, there is no need for the process of sacrifice to continue, 'where there is forgiveness of these, there is no longer any offering for sin.'

One final point about the third clause of the new covenant. It begins with the little word 'for': 'For I will be merciful towards their iniquities, and I will remember their sins no more' (8:12). This shows that the third clause is meant to explain how the promises of the previous clause can be put into effect. That clause promised that every believer would enjoy an intimate knowledge of God based on a direct and personal relationship with him. But how could anyone enjoy a personal and direct relationship with God, if he had to live in constant uncertainty whether God would eventually accept or reject him?

We all know the lasting psychological damage that a child can suffer if in his formative years he is uncertain of acceptance by his parents and lives in fear, conscious or subconscious, that one day they might reject him. And yet there are multitudes even of religious folk whose relationship with God is haunted by that basic fear and uncertainty, so much so that the very idea of claiming to be sure of salvation strikes them as alarming presumption. And yet it is God's wish to cast out that fear. As John puts it: 'There is no fear in love, but perfect love casts out fear. For fear has to do with punishment, and whoever fears has not been perfected in love' (1 John 4:18). Therefore, in order that the promise of clause two (Heb 8:10–11) of the covenant should be realized and the believer enjoy a secure relationship with God, clause three (v. 12) provides the guarantee of complete and utter forgiveness. And it does so not merely in order that the believer should feel secure and be free from the servility of fear, but because perfect security of relationship with God is the only adequate basis from which could be developed the holiness of character that clause one (v. 10) guarantees to develop in him.

David Gooding, *Windows on Paradise: Scenes of Hope and Salvation in the Gospel of Luke*, pp. 94–5

21st February

CHRIST'S AUTHORITY TO FORGIVE

Reading: Luke 5:17–26

The Son of Man has authority on earth to forgive sins. (v. 24)

Now the lesson which Christ taught them was not that God being a forgiving God delights to forgive the repentant sinner. That the Jewish theologians (one suspects, even the Jewish schoolchildren) knew already from the Old Testament. What Christ taught them was something startlingly new: he personally released a man from the guilt of his sins (v. 20). The theologians immediately picked up the implications of this claim. The Old Testament gave no one, not priest, nor prophet, nor theologian any such authority. They could pronounce in God's name that God had forgiven, or would forgive, such and such a sin; but none had authority to pronounce forgiveness in his own name, as Christ had just done. They accused him of blasphemously arrogating to himself a divine prerogative (see v. 21). And Christ's reply was not to explain that they had misunderstood him. Far from it. He proceeded to demonstrate by a miracle that he personally as Son of Man had authority here on earth, without waiting for some final judgment, to pronounce absolute and final forgiveness in his own name (see vv. 22–25).

Astonishing as this was to the theologians, an even fuller statement of the wonderfully new element which Christ has introduced into the concept and enjoyment of forgiveness, came with Christ's death, resurrection and ascension. Judaism, it goes without saying, had all the way along, known and enjoyed divine forgiveness. But it was forgiveness of a kind that left even the saintliest of them with a conscience 'not yet made perfect' (Heb 10:1–23), with no sense at all that sin had been finally and fully put away, and therefore with the need constantly to bring further sacrifices to put away further sin. With them, therefore, the question of forgiveness was always at any given time incomplete. They had no freedom to enter the most holy place of God's presence, and the question of ultimate acceptance with God was left uncertain. By contrast the forgiveness which Christ gives makes the conscience 'perfect', in the sense that the one forgiven is assured that God will never again 'remember his sins against him', will never raise again in the court of divine judgment the question of his guilt and its legal penalty. It therefore frees the one forgiven from the need to offer any more sacrifices for his sins and gives him complete freedom of access into, and welcome in, the presence of God both here and now, and in the hereafter.

David Gooding, *According to Luke: The Third Gospel's Ordered Historical Narrative*, pp. 107–8

22nd February

CHRIST IS WITH US IN THE STORM

Reading: Matthew 8:23–27

No, in all these things we are more than conquerors through him who loved us. (Romans 8:37)

It's easy to think, when the tempests come and the physical elements begin to assail us and threaten to destroy us, that something's gone wrong with the path of discipleship. But that isn't so. Our Lord was so confident that he was asleep in the middle of the storm. It wasn't anything unusual to him, for as he now demonstrated, he was in perfect control of those winds and waves, and had it been God's will that they should have drowned him to the bottom of the sea, well that's okay then. He was in control of them. And it wasn't by accident that the journey led through this storm; that was the way he'd planned it. It obviously took a lot of courage and nerve, even for those hardened fishermen, to stand in that rocking boat with the boat shipping water and the wind tearing at the old sails and making them think it could go down any moment. It took a lot of nerve to trust that Jesus Christ was in control, but he was.

If we are to go on our path of discipleship home to glory, then this is a lesson that all of us presently must learn. What is my relation to the big, physical powers of the universe? First of all I have the assurance that neither life nor death, things present nor things to come, nor height nor depth nor any other creature, shall be able to separate me from the love of God, which is in Christ Jesus our Lord (see Rom 8:38–39). In that sense I'm safe. I'm not told that there shall never come any storm. I'm not told that there is no depth. I'm not told there is no disease, no germ, no virus, no threat. What I am told is that none of these things can separate me from the love of God that is in Christ Jesus. Secondly, I am told that, in all these things, I am more than a *conqueror*.

Consider this for a moment. What is your relationship as a believer to the big, physical powers of this universe? My brother, my sister, the whole universe was made for you! It was made for you as the pathway by which you will arrive home to God. It will sometimes scare the very life out of you, but Christ stands in your boat and tells you, 'Don't be afraid', for he's master of it. And before you get to be aged ninety-six, you'll need courage to believe it.

David Gooding, *The Gospel of Authority and the Path of Discipleship: Studies in Matthew*, pp. 17–18

23rd February

THE CERTAINTY OF PETER'S RESTORATION

Reading: John 13:31–14:1

I tell you the truth, before the cock crows, you
will disown me three times. (v. 38)

But Christ was certain, of course, that Peter would eventually be restored, and triumph. 'Where I am going you cannot follow me now,' he said to Peter, 'but you shall follow afterwards' (13:36). And so Peter did. Though his courage left him, and he denied and deserted Christ in order to escape suffering in the high priest's court and at the cross, he was afterwards restored, then served and followed Christ magnificently for many years, and finally, like the Lord, went home to glory via a martyr's death.

And we should not fail to notice this: when the breakdown came, as our Lord predicted, and Peter failed to follow the Lord in his suffering as he should have done, it must have been a tremendous source of encouragement and new hope for Peter to remember what the Lord said before it all happened: 'You cannot follow me now, *but you will follow afterwards*'. All through the ups and downs of the rest of Peter's life, he would constantly have repeated the Lord's words to himself over and over again, giving them their fullest meaning. He had not yet been allowed to follow the ascending Lord bodily into the glory of the Father's presence in heaven. But there was no doubt he would one day. Christ had said he would; and his promise would not fail. And what is more, entry into the glory of the Father's presence in heaven, and the direct sight of the blessed Lord Jesus, would instantaneously complete Peter's sanctification and complete it forever beyond danger of any further collapse. This too, then, our Lord let Peter know by implication, before he fell. The certainty of this promise and the courage it gave him enabled him to face his failure, to come back, and follow the Lord devotedly for the rest of his life. And since Christ has no favourites, all who trust him may take this same promise to themselves.

David Gooding, *In the School of Christ: Lessons on Holiness in John 13–17*, pp. 74–5

24th February

THE EFFECTIVENESS OF THE LORD'S PRAYER

Reading: John 17:1–19

*While I was with them, I kept them in your name, which
you have given me. I have guarded them, and not one
of them has been lost except the son of destruction,
that the Scripture might be fulfilled. (v. 12)*

Not one lost! That was a magnificent claim; but it was not an exaggeration, nor a rare and exceptional statement that could not be taken too literally because of its unusualness. Our Lord had said the same thing earlier just as emphatically:

> And this is the will of him who sent me, that I should lose nothing of all that he has given me, but raise it up on the last day. For this is the will of my Father, that everyone who looks on the Son and believes in him should have eternal life, and I will raise him up on the last day. (John 6:39–40)

So then, the disciples were safe while Christ was with them; safe, not because of their own strength to maintain their own faith, but safe because he kept them and preserved their faith. But what about the future, now that he was leaving them and was no more in the world? Who, or what, would keep them now? The answer is that Christ now asks the Father to take on the task of keeping them: 'While I was with them, I kept them: now, Father, you keep them.' The only question each true believer nowadays needs to ask, therefore, is this: 'Will the Father be less diligent, less effective in keeping me and preserving my faith, than the Lord Jesus was in keeping the faith of his eleven apostles?' The answer is self-evident: 'Of course, not!' But for the sake of double certainty, let us listen again to what our Lord said about it on a previous occasion: 'My Father, who has given them to me, is greater than all, and no one is able to snatch them out of the Father's hand. I and the Father are one' (10:29–30). At this, every true believer will experience a surge of profound joy, which is exactly what our Lord intended. He had gathered his disciples round him as he prayed that they might hear exactly what he prayed for them, and be certain that it would be answered: 'These things I speak in the world,' said he, 'that they might have my joy fulfilled in themselves' (17:13).

David Gooding, *In the School of Christ: Lessons on Holiness in John 13–17*, pp. 231–2

25th February

ETERNAL SECURITY

Reading: John 6:21–51

All that the Father gives me will come to me, and
whoever comes to me I will never cast out. (v. 37)

How can we be sure of eternal life? The tremendous truth is given in our Lord's statement here: 'I have come down from heaven.'

What for?

'To save the lost,' you say.

Well, that is perfectly true. He came 'to seek and to save the lost' (Luke 19:10). But in this context he says:

> For I have come down from heaven, not to do my own will but the will of him who sent me. And this is the will of him who sent me, that I should lose nothing of all that he has given me, but raise it up on the last day. For this is the will of my Father, that everyone who looks on the Son and believes in him should have eternal life, and I will raise him up on the last day' (John 6:38–40).

Hallelujah for that! For my eternal security rests on Christ doing the will of the Father. It is the Father's will that he should 'lose nothing'. He will lose nothing and none of those that the Father has given him. I like to think of it with a childlike mind (not 'childish' I hope). Imagine the whole assembly of heaven being presented to the Father and counted in by name, so to speak. And when it gets to the end the Father says, 'Is that all?'

'Yes.'

'Well, what about that Gooding chap? Is he here?'

The Son says, 'Oh, he was a bit of an oddity, and he lost his way, and he's not here.'

And the Father says, 'But I thought you went to do my will; and my will was that you should lose nothing!'

So if Christ loses a genuine believer, he then has failed to do the will of God. That is unthinkable! He will bring home to the Father all who have trusted him.

David Gooding, *Four Journeys to Jerusalem: A Series of Seminars on the Gospel of John*, pp. 77–8

26th February

HE GIVES HIS LIFE FOR HIS SHEEP

Reading: John 10:1–21

*For this reason the Father loves me, because I lay
down my life that I may take it up again. (v. 17)*

A man need not be a robber or a thief. He could simply be shepherding
the sheep for what he got out of it as an employee: so much money a week
for looking after sheep. 'I am not one of those,' says Christ. 'I am not an
employee. In fact, the sheep belong to me. They are my sheep.'

Now, the employee will look after them as well as he can, but if he sees the
wolf or the lion coming, then he has to make up his mind: 'Is it worth trying
to save the sheep from this wolf?' It wouldn't be worth it, if he lost his life,
would it? What is your weekly wage worth if you lose your life on the job? So
he runs off, for the sheep don't belong to him. He is merely an employee, and
if they get destroyed, well, what does he care? He's not going to lay down his
life for them! He's only doing it for the money he gets out of it, and that's all!

But Christ is not an employee; the sheep belong to him, and he lays down
his life for the sheep. He does it voluntarily, not because he was overcome.

> I know my own and my own know me, just as the Father knows me
> and I know the Father; and I lay down my life for the sheep . . . For
> this reason the Father loves me, because I lay down my life that I may
> take it up again. (vv. 14–15, 17)

And in so saying, he points out that there comes an intimate reciprocal
knowledge: the sheep know him, and he knows his own sheep. It sets up
the kind of relationship of knowledge between his sheep and him that he
enjoyed already, the one between him and the Father. That is astounding! It
is a relationship between him and us on the model of his relationship with
the Father: he knows the Father, and the Father knows him.

David Gooding, *Four Journeys to Jerusalem: A Series of Seminars on the Gospel of John*, pp. 132–3

27th February

QUALIFICATIONS OF THE TRUE SHEPHERD

Reading: John 10:22–42

My Father, who has given them to me, is greater than all, and
no one is able to snatch them out of the Father's hand. (v. 29)

We are told at this time that it was the Feast of Dedication. Dedication recalled the time when the great, sinister Gentile ruler, Antiochus Epiphanes, came and desecrated the temple at Jerusalem. He set up a pagan image, sacrificed a pig upon the altar, forbade circumcision and destroyed the Scriptures as best he could. The chief priests in Israel at the time agreed with him and went over to syncretism.

But that reminds us what is meant in the Old Testament by a 'shepherd'. When our Lord says, 'I am the good shepherd,' we think simply of a shepherd with his sheep, but in Israel in the Old Testament, shepherd is also the description of the king. The true king is a shepherd. What about the false king, the false leaders and the high priests? And what about that sinister figure, Antiochus Epiphanes, who put the abomination of desolation in the Holy Place in Jerusalem? And what about this Jesus, claiming to be shepherd and king? Dare you trust him? What claim will he make? So the final part of John 10 is extraordinarily delightful.

I don't know if you have ever applied for a job with a lot of management responsibility. But if you have, you might be brought before an interview committee, and they might ask you how you would solve a particularly difficult problem. You would have to advertise your abilities in order to prove that you were a good applicant.

And here come the crowds around Jesus, and they say, 'Look here, why won't you tell us plainly and straightforwardly, are you the Christ, or aren't you?'

And Christ says, 'Well, I told you before, and you didn't believe, but if you now want to know whether I'm the Christ or not, let me . . .' (may I use the term?) '. . . advertise myself as the true shepherd. Here are my qualities as a shepherd: I give to my sheep eternal life and they shall never perish, and no one will snatch them out of my hand. My Father, who has given them to me, is greater than all, and no one is able to snatch them out of the Father's hand. I and my Father are one' (see vv. 24–30). Here are the marvellous qualifications of the shepherd, and the eternal security that he gives to all his sheep.

David Gooding, *Four Journeys to Jerusalem: A Series of Seminars on the Gospel of John*, p. 133

28th February

CHRIST SAVES HIS DISCIPLE FROM SINKING

Reading: Matthew 14:22–36

Jesus immediately reached out his hand
and took hold of him. (v. 31)

You wouldn't be the last person to commit yourself to Christ for salvation and have begun the Christian life and then find it too much and begin to sink. Because it was Peter's fault, our Lord eventually had to chide him saying, 'Oh, you of little faith, why did you doubt?' But notice the order of events. Peter had responded to the word of Christ. Now in his weakness and with his faith all jittery, he was beginning to sink. Would the Saviour let him sink and be lost? The music of heaven would stop and heaven itself grow black if the Saviour would encourage anybody to put their faith in him and then let them down and let them perish. Christ has given his word, 'whoever comes to me I will never cast out'; 'this is the will of him who sent me, that I should lose nothing of all that he has given me' (John 6:37, 39).

That night, as the storm raged and the water began to come up round Peter's waist and up across his shoulders and neck, what heaven was interested in was what the Saviour would do. Would he be faithful to the man? What do you think he said? Did he stand there and lecture him? 'Peter, you foolish man, you've lost your faith, haven't you? Yes, I will save you, but obviously I can't save you until your faith is perfected. Now try to believe a little bit better, and when you've learnt to believe perfectly, then I can save you.' By that time the water would have dragged him down.

As Peter went down, he simply cried, 'Lord, save me.' And Scripture says 'Everyone who calls on the name of the Lord will be saved' (Rom 10:13). You won't be able to keep it up, but the Saviour who invites you to come, promises you now that in the day when you fall, when you call upon him, he will save you. Fellow Christian, if you feel as if you can't stick it, that you don't know whether you can keep it up, whether you can maintain your faith, if you feel you're going down, then cry, 'Lord, save me'; knowing that everyone who calls on the name of the Lord will be saved, and saved to the uttermost (Heb 7:25).

David Gooding, *The Church's Witness to Christ: Faith Strengthening Evidence from Matthew*, pp. 17-18

THE CAPTAIN OF OUR SALVATION

Part 6—The Joys of Fellowship with the King

1st March

AN ABIDING PLACE FOR THE FATHER
AND THE SON IN OUR HEARTS

Reading: Revelation 3:20; 2 John

*Jesus answered him, 'If anyone loves me, he will keep my
word, and my Father will love him, and we will come
to him and make our home with him.' (John 14:23)*

Because he is the life, and shares that divine life with us, he is for us the way
to the Father. But he also shows us how, and on what conditions, the Father
and the Son are prepared to come and make their abiding place in our hearts.
It stands to reason, of course, that anyone who professes to have the hope of
being taken to the Father's house at the second coming of Christ will be keen
to make the Father and the Son a dwelling place in his heart here and now.

What, then, are the conditions? 'If anyone loves me,' says Christ, 'he will
keep my word, and my Father will love him, and we will come to him and
make our home with him. Whoever does not love me does not keep my
words. And the word that you hear is not mine but the Father's who sent
me' (John 14:23–24). If we were expecting to welcome a merely human guest
into our literal homes, mere courtesy would lead us to consult our guest's
wishes, and to carry them out as best we can.

So then, if we are going to make the Father and the Son a dwelling place
in our hearts, the conditions are that we first love them, and loving them,
study their word to discover their likes and dislikes; and then show our love
by gladly and humbly seeking to please them by doing what they like, and
abstaining from what they dislike. So shall we experience ever more deeply
their love and fellowship. Of course, there is a side to God's love that is utterly
unconditional. He loved us even while we were still sinners and still his
enemies, and he will go on loving his people with that kind of unconditional
love. But here we are thinking of our mutual enjoyment of one another's love,
in intimate fellowship with the Father and his Son; and devoted attention and
obedience to their commandments are the only way towards that practical
enjoyment of their love.

David Gooding, In the School of Christ: Lessons on Holiness in John 13–17, pp. 102–3

2nd March

THE VINE'S GENIUS FOR JOY

Reading: John 15:9–17; Judges 9:12–13

This is my commandment, that you love one another as I have loved you. (John 15:12)

Christ who knew his apostles' hearts, and ours too, added an explanation at this point: 'These things I have spoken to you, that my joy may be in you, and that your joy may be full' (v. 11). In other words, he assured them that his commandments were not aimed at diminishing their joy but increasing it. It is after all the pride and joy of a vine to produce grapes that by their fruit and wine bring joy to others. If dumb nature could speak, a vine stock would never complain that it was always having to pass on its rich nutriments to the branches to produce grapes for other people's consumption. Vines, if they could feel, would hugely enjoy their God-given function of producing joy for others, as Jotham's parable long since observed (Judg 9:12–13).

Christ, the true vine, certainly did, and does still. After a long, dusty, and tiring journey to bring spiritual satisfaction to one lonely woman, he explained to his disciples that doing God's will in this way and bringing his work to completion was food and drink to him (John 4:31–34). He rejoiced in the Holy Spirit, says Luke (10:21), and thanked his Father, the Lord of heaven and earth, that God had used him to reveal his treasures to babes. And he sang a hymn even as he left the Upper Room for the sacrifice of himself at Calvary (Matt 26:30).

His instructions to us, therefore, that the only way of remaining in the practical enjoyment of his love is to keep his commandments, are designed so that his joy as the self-giving vine should flow unimpeded to and through us to others, and that we in turn should find our own joy brought to its peak as we thus fulfil our God-given function as branches in the vine. The commandment therefore above all others that he gives us, as he brings this small section of his teaching to a close, is that we love one another after the same pattern of love that he has shown to us (John 15:12).

David Gooding, *In the School of Christ: Lessons on Holiness in John 13–17*, pp. 155–6

3rd March

THE TRANSFORMING EFFECT OF GRACE

Reading: Luke 19:1–10

And Zacchaeus stood and said to the Lord, 'Behold,
Lord, half of my goods I give to the poor.' (v. 8)

Zacchaeus was a little man himself; that was why he was up the tree, so that he could see over the heads of the crowd. But he was a little man in more senses than one, or else he would never have taken such delight in exacting extortionate taxes out of poor people who had difficulty in making ends meet. Perhaps, indeed, being very short, he may early in life have developed a deep-seated inferiority complex and a feeling of rejection, which was forever driving him on to try and prove his 'superiority'. He turned to making money, perhaps with the subconscious idea that by becoming exceedingly wealthy he would make people respect him. In actual fact it only made them despise him and avoid his company. That in turn only increased his sense of rejection, and made him determine all the more to get his own back, demonstrating his superiority by hurting people and exacting ever more taxes from them, while filling his own house with extravagantly rich furniture, designed to impress everybody with his wealth and provoke their envy.

It was an endless and vicious spiral. How could it be broken? Not by more ethical teaching—Zacchaeus already knew his conduct was wrong; but in a very real sense he could not help himself. He was driven to it by urges that he did not understand and could not control. And social ostracism only made those urges stronger. Reading in his desire to see Jesus the faint beginnings of repentance— the bleating of a sheep that has got itself caught in a thicket and doesn't know how to get out—Christ cut through all the entanglements by accepting the man as he was. And he publicly demonstrated that acceptance by calling him down from the tree and announcing that he was coming to stay in his home.

At last Zacchaeus had found, by the unmerited grace of God, what years of his own misguided toil had never been able to achieve—the sense of acceptance not only with men but at the highest level with the Creator himself. What was the effect on Zacchaeus? More extortion and endless taking advantage of the grace of God? No. He quit his extortion immediately and announced a magnificent programme of philanthropy—not in order to try and persuade Christ to accept him but simply because Christ *had* accepted him. 'Today salvation has come to this house', commented Christ, 'since he also is a son of Abraham' (19:9).

David Gooding, *Windows on Paradise: Scenes of Hope and Salvation in the Gospel of Luke*, pp. 22–3

4th March

THE ENCOURAGEMENT OF THE LORD

Reading: 2 Thessalonians 2:5–17

Now may our Lord Jesus Christ himself, and God our
Father, who loved us and gave us eternal comfort and good
hope through grace, comfort your hearts. (vv. 16–17)

Paul pleads that the Lord *himself* will pay personal attention to his appeal. I don't know what your need is this very day, but 'may our Lord Jesus Christ himself'—not some archangel, not even Michael or Gabriel, nor even some great learned apostle like Paul—'comfort and establish your hearts'. May he draw near and give you the inner strength and determination that you need to be effectual and persistent in the work to which God has called you. When he was on earth he not only preached to crowds but drew near and comforted his disciples personally by name, and he does it still. As he sees our need he comforts and establishes our hearts.

So, once more, God the Father has set his love on us and given us eternal encouragement and good hope. He knew that we should very often need encouragement, just as the angel of the Lord stood by Paul in his particular distress as the ship was being tossed about by the waves (Acts 27:23).

But not only does God do that from time-to-time; his encouragement is eternal. When you come in weary from your work, discouraged, and your heart is low, his encouragement is there for you. All believers shall be like Christ one day (1 John 3:2). That's built-in encouragement, isn't it? 'My word shall not return to me empty' (Isa 55:11). That's his promise, and the encouragement is built-in. The mansions are nearly ready now (John 14:2)! Our Lord has gone to make a place for us; he's coming back, and when we see him we shall be like him. The encouragement is built in to the very scheme of salvation that he has given us. Let us not get so overwhelmed with the work that we lose the very joy of salvation and the hope of the gospel. He has given us, as Thomas Chisholm's hymn says, 'Strength for today and bright hope for tomorrow | blessings all mine, with ten thousand beside.'

David Gooding, *Eternal Encouragement and Good Hope: 2 Thessalonians 2:13-17*, p. 6

5th March

CHRIST BRINGS US NEAR

Reading: Ephesians 2:11–22

*But now in Christ Jesus you who once were far off have
been brought near by the blood of Christ. (v. 13)*

We found that God's dealing with the nations in the time of Israel wasn't his final answer to mankind's need, and because it wasn't the final answer, but only one of the preliminary stages, it caused in its way (if you don't mind me saying so) some unfortunate results. It did it this way round: the very fact that God chose Abraham and started the new race from him, distinct from the other Gentile nations, emphasized the distance between the Gentiles and God. It wasn't God's fault: they had already gone away. It wasn't God who created the distance. Men had once known God, but not wanting to retain him in their knowledge they had gone into all their philosophical notions. Lost in their idolatry, they were already at a distance. But when God chose out Abraham and revealed himself to Abraham and the nation of the Jews, it emphasized the vast distance that had opened up between God and the Gentiles.

The first thing these verses tell us is that he abolished the distance. What volumes that tells us about the heart of God, a God who desired to dwell with men and in men. The sight of Gentiles going off into their perversions broke his heart, but the first thing that broke his heart was the distance. He had it in his heart from all eternity not only to make man but to come and dwell in man. The thing that broke the very heart of God was the distance that opened up. Therefore, when the inspired apostle comes to tell of what Christ came to do, the very first thing he notices is that he abolished the distance: 'But now in Christ Jesus you who once were far off have been brought near by the blood of Christ' (v. 13).

Notice it is not now so much a question of forgiveness, though that is true. It is a case of redemption—notice the reference to the blood of Christ. But now it is not so much the redemption that has been bought for us; it is this great and marvellous fact that we have been brought near. All that terrible distance that his law had to emphasize has been done away through the redemption that is in Christ Jesus.

David Gooding, *Ephesians: A Bird's Eye View of the Major Movements of Thought*, pp. 70–1

6th March

THE AUTHORITY OF THE KING

Reading: Hebrews 8:6–13

*Behold, the days are coming, declares the LORD, when
I will make a new covenant with the house of Israel
and the house of Judah. (Jeremiah 31:31)*

Some people react quite strongly against the whole idea that Christ's relationship with his people should be expressed in terms of a covenant; they say it makes it sound far too severe and legal, when legality is the last thing that should enter into truly personal relationships. And further, when Christ is described as a king and his people as subjects, their resentment boils over into opposition.

Their reaction springs from one of two sources, or perhaps a mixture of both. One source is the modern fashion of thought according to which all assertion of authority is by definition a bad thing, and all submission to authority a mark of servility. People of this persuasion would have everyone equal, with no one possessing or exercising any authority over anyone else. They do not normally campaign, it is true, for the abolition of the force of gravity on the ground that the sun exercises a greater gravitational pull over the earth than the earth does over the sun. But the physical chaos they would cause if they could switch off gravity, would be no greater than the moral chaos that would result if they could abolish all authority in human relationships, let alone between humanity and God. A mother who declined to exercise any authority over her two-year-old child would cease to be a mother; she would probably find herself prosecuted on grounds of gross neglect. Should her baby grab a bottle of poison and go to drink it, she must exercise her authority fast and firm. Love and instinct both demand it.

David Gooding, *Windows on Paradise: Scenes of Hope and Salvation in the Gospel of Luke*, pp. 96–7

7th March

THE LORD JUDGES US NOW

Reading: 1 Peter 4:12–19

The Lord will judge his people. (Hebrews 10:30)

There is a present judgment of the individual and there is a present judgment of the church. Peter says, 'For it is time for judgment to begin at the household of God; and if it begins with us, what will be the outcome for those who do not obey the gospel of God?' (1 Pet 4:17). That isn't an emphasis which evangelicals often sound. We have a very big example of judgment beginning at the house of God in the book of Revelation. Chapters 4–20 of that book tell of the solemn judgments that shall fall on the world at the end of this world and chapters 1–3 depict our blessed Lord in the solemn robes of a judge walking among the lampstands that are his churches, judging them.

It is not a thing that we should shun, surely. As we thank the blessed Lord for being our Saviour, should we not praise him for being our judge? He who died for us comes alongside us in life and gently but firmly and solemnly points out our mistakes and waywardness and tells us how we may be delivered from them.

There was a solemn moment when the apostle John saw the risen Lord in all his glory, his face shining as the sun shines in its strength, and in that instant he fell at his feet as dead. He was the man who leaned on the bosom of the Lord Jesus at the last supper; seeing him now in his risen glory as judge he was overcome, almost to the point of death. Thank God for the blessed things that he heard and felt in that moment.

> He laid his right hand on me, saying, 'Fear not, I am the first and the last, and the living one. I died, and behold I am alive for evermore, and I have the keys of Death and Hades. (Rev 1:17–18)

In those moments John learned the secret of being able to stand as a believer and face his judge. This glorious Son of God, now in resurrection, has the keys of death and hell; not to unlock the gates of it and let us in, but to let us out! In virtue of his death, his resurrection and the guarantee of his eternal resurrection, he gives us the strength to stand and face his judgment and listen to his criticism. In our listening and in our obeying is abundant treasure of reward.

David Gooding, *James's Vision of the Perfect Man and Woman: The Epistle of James*, p. 35

8th March

THE HEALING OF THE WOMAN
WITH THE HAEMORRHAGE

Reading: Luke 8:40–56

And he said to her, 'Daughter, your faith has
made you well; go in peace.' (v. 48)

In the case of the second woman the crucial question was Christ's ability to perceive not merely something about the woman but also something about himself. He knew, so he said, that someone had touched him in a more than casual or superficial way, because he perceived that power had gone out from him (see v. 46). This tells us the supremely important fact that the power that saves us is not an impersonal power. True, the power of Christ was transmitted to the woman when she touched not him but merely the border of his garment. She was healed because hers was genuine faith and not mere superstition; but she found out what genuine faith must mean: we cannot be saved by the power of Christ without having to do with Christ as a person. It is impossible, for the simple reason that we cannot exercise faith in Christ and draw on his power without his knowing; but the impossibility saves us from at least two dangers. It saves faith from degenerating into superstition and regarding Christ (or his garments) like a relic possessed of some magical impersonal power. It also saves faith from being merely a form of selfishness and salvation from being regarded as merely self-improvement. Many a man has first come to Christ simply to get power to overcome some weakness or other like, say, obsessive gambling or alcoholism that is ruining his body and wasting his resources. Christ stands ready to answer every such call for help. But in his mercy he will not have such a person treat his salvation as a cure; he will insist that such a man comes to know him as a person, and, like the woman, to confess him publicly as Saviour.

David Gooding, *According to Luke: The Third Gospel's Ordered Historical Narrative*, pp. 153–4

9th March

WASHING OUR FEET

Reading: Luke 9:51–56

Jesus answered him, 'If I do not wash you, you have no share with me.' (John 13:8)

On one occasion, when Jesus was travelling through Israel preaching the gospel, he sent messengers ahead into a nearby village to book lodgings for himself and his disciples for the night. But the people of the village were all Samaritans who for ethnic and religious reasons hated Jews; and they all refused to let Jesus and his disciples stay the night in the village. Two of Jesus' disciples, James and John, were so angry at this that they wanted to call down fire from heaven on these Samaritans. But in giving way to such desires for revenge, John and James showed themselves altogether out of fellowship with Christ who had come not to destroy men's lives but to save them. Had they continued in such an attitude toward people of other cultures and religions, they could have had no part with Christ in his evangelism and in his love even for his enemies. And so our Lord rebuked them (Luke 9:55); or to put it in other words, he 'washed their feet'.

Similarly, if as believers we do not allow Christ constantly to wash away our ethnic and nationalistic animosities, our outbursts of bad temper, our selfishness, dishonesty, jealousy, pride, and all other moral and spiritual uncleannesses, we shall enjoy little practical communion with Christ and little practical fellowship with him in his mission of love to the world.

Thus, as believers who have been born again, we are assured that we shall not be condemned along with unbelievers at the final judgment. But that does not mean we are free to live careless and sinful lives. We are constantly to examine ourselves; and where we find in ourselves wrong attitudes and deeds, we are to judge ourselves, confess it to the Lord, and seek his pardon. And if we do so, all will be well. But if we grow careless and do not judge ourselves and 'wash our feet', then the Lord in his love and faithfulness will take us in hand and discipline us so as to bring us to repentance and back to close and practical daily fellowship with himself (see 1 Cor 11:31–32).

David Gooding, *In the School of Christ: Lessons on Holiness in John 13–17*, pp. 36–7

10th March

THE FEEDING OF THE FIVE THOUSAND

Reading: John 6:25–59

For the bread of God is he who comes down from
heaven and gives life to the world. (v. 33)

But first Christ did an interesting thing: he told his apostles to feed the crowds themselves. Now the apostles had never seen a miracle on this scale before. They had witnessed the healing of individuals; indeed, they had themselves been allowed in their recent mission to use supernatural power to expel demons and to heal. But to feed this tremendous mass of people, numbering some five thousand males let alone women and children, was altogether a different proposition. Even so their response was not all that intelligent. Christ was not in the habit of talking practical nonsense, nor was he mocking their feeble powers. If he told them to feed the crowd, it ought at least to have startled them into thinking that there might be more to the kingdom of God and the powers of Jesus than they had yet realized. Instead of that, the highest their thoughts could rise to was the possibility of going to the nearest merchants (wholesalers, of course) and of buying the necessary quantity of food; otherwise, they remarked, they had only five loaves and two fish.

But the pitiful inadequacy of their resources and the utter impossibility of the situation, as long as their ideas were limited to the ordinary natural processes of life in this world, provided the contrasting background against which Christ could vividly demonstrate what will be involved in the coming of the kingdom. Looking up into heaven (see Luke 9:16) he brought the powers of heaven irrupting once more into this world and transformed its meagre resources into more than enough to feed the multitudes. The lesson is still needed. We rightly stress the moral laws of the kingdom of God, and strive to see them applied even now to the world's social and economic problems. But we should beware of allowing that present concern to limit our ideas of what the kingdom of God will one day involve. The kingdom of God, fully come, will not mean simply the carrying on of present activities in a more caring, more just, more efficient way. It will be nothing less than the invasion of our world by the powers of the world beyond, releasing nature from her groanings and frustrations, and transforming creation from a system of inevitable decay into a world of freedom, satisfaction and perfect fulfilment, with death destroyed and sorrow gone.

David Gooding, *According to Luke: The Third Gospel's Ordered Historical Narrative*, pp. 166–7

11th March

Reading: Luke 17:1–10

*Truly, I say to you, [the master] will dress himself
for service and have them recline at table, and
he will come and serve them. (Luke 12:37)*

The apostles asked Christ to increase their faith. They received the stimulating reply that even faith as small as a mustard seed would uproot a tree and plant it in the sea. To faith so strong few duties would prove difficult. But powerful faith such as that might possibly create in us wrong attitudes: the very success it achieved might make us spiritually overbearing and arrogant. And so Christ proceeds to teach us what our attitude toward God must ever be as his servants.

'Which one of you', asks Christ, 'having a servant ploughing or keeping sheep, will say to him when he comes in from the field, "Come at once and sit down to eat", and will not rather say to him, "Get my dinner ready, and dress yourself and wait on me until I have eaten and drunken, and after that you shall eat and drink"?' (see 17:7–10).

If God will always put man's salvation before the ceremonies and celebrations of his own praise, we who have been saved must always put God's service before our own interests. We certainly must never get it into our heads that we have served God so superbly well that now we have a right to put our own needs and satisfactions before his requirements. And never can we put God in our debt by serving him. If after we have served him well, as we think, he appears not to thank us or to be grateful (see v. 9), why should we expect him to? When we have done everything he asks of us, it is what we were only duty-bound to do anyway. At the great banquet the master himself will serve us (see 12:37). Does not that inspire us to grasp every opportunity of serving him first?

David Gooding, *According to Luke: The Third Gospel's Ordered Historical Narrative*, pp. 294–5

12th March

CHRIST'S INHERITANCE IS OUR INHERITANCE

Reading: Galatians 3:26–4:7

*For the promise to Abraham and his offspring that he
would be heir of the world did not come through the law
but through the righteousness of faith. (Romans 4:13)*

He is going to rule from shore to shore! He is going to claim dominion over
this planet, and any others that exist, anyway. So, Christ is going to inherit it
because he is Abraham's seed. But now look at the end of Galatians 3:

> For as many of you as were baptized into Christ did put on Christ.
> There can be neither Jew nor Greek, there can be neither bond nor
> free, there can be no male and female: for you all are one man in
> Christ Jesus. And if you are Christ's, then are you Abraham's seed,
> heirs according to promise. (vv. 27–29 RV)

If you've not seen that before, you might feel yourself richer than you ever
imagined you were. You are an heir to the promises covenanted to Abraham
about this great inheritance, because it was promised to Abraham and his
seed, and now by God's grace you have been incorporated into Christ, you
have put on Christ! You are Abraham's seed therefore, and if you are Abraham's seed you are heirs, in the terms of that covenant: 'to you and your
seed'. Now, do it internally and don't disturb the peace, but shout a quiet
'Hallelujah!' You are richer than you might have imagined!

That being so, if you have got any common sense in your head and any
practicality, you will want to know: is that inheritance secure for me? On what
ground is this given? Was it given after the law was given or before the law was
given? Well, historically there's no doubt about it. Abraham was justified before
the law was given. Abraham was given this covenant of inheritance before the
law was given, and the law that came over four hundred years afterwards (v. 17)
cannot change that covenant to make it of no effect. It did not depend on the
law but on God's gracious promise that Abraham believed. And the reason
why it is through faith and grace is this, as we come back to Romans 4: 'For
this cause it is of faith, that it may be according to grace; to the end that the
promise may be *sure* to all the seed' (v. 16 RV). Do shout 'Hallelujah!' What
magnificent things these are.

David Gooding, *God's Power for Salvation: Paul's Letter to the Romans*, p. 79

13th March

LOOKING TO THE REWARD

Reading: Matthew 10:29–42

The one who receives a prophet because he is
a prophet will receive a prophet's reward. (v. 41)

There are some people who tell us that we should serve the Lord without looking for reward. What marvellously spiritual people they are, and I'm delighted to hear that they can keep going with undiminished puff and zeal without any prospect of reward. They have a little unrealistic idea, however, because there's one standing in front of you who, if it weren't for the reward, might have given up a long while ago. And in his mercy, the Lord encourages us with reward, and if he holds out the reward I'm not quite sure that it is too spiritual to say to him, 'No, I don't want it,' for he holds it out.

What a lovely antidote there is here to that feeling that comes to us all from time to time: 'Well I'm not much good, and what can I do anyway? I shall never get a very big reward.' Don't you be so sure of that. You could have a prophet's reward if you wanted it, couldn't you? I should think that might be sizeable. I think I should be happy to get a prophet's reward. I think it's unlikely, but I should be happy to.

'How do you get that?'

You get it in one of two ways: either by being a prophet or, from time to time, looking after a prophet. Whoever receives a prophet (that is, into his home) in the name of a prophet so as to be a partaker of his work, receives the reward that the prophet gets (see v. 41). 'And if it were only a cup of cold water,' says our Lord, using a very vivid example, 'you'll not lose your reward' (v. 42). Tap water is pretty abundant, most times in the year at any rate. If you can get a reward for tap water, I think I've got a bit more than tap water I could bring to bear upon the need, if it wasn't for myself, then for somebody else. I've noticed preachers get thirsty, and if supplying the water for them, like some good soul has done for me as I preach (he's going to get a reward) then I could do that at least. But then how much do I believe it?

David Gooding, *The Gospel of Authority and the Path of Discipleship: Studies in Matthew*, p. 38–9

14th March

INVESTMENT INTEREST

Reading: Malachi 3:6–16

Your words have been hard against me, says the Lord. But
you say, 'How have we spoken against you?' (v. 13)

God finally tells them that their words have been stout, arrogant against him. How was that? They had asked what they were getting out of their service for the Lord. They called the wicked happy, and asked what they themselves were getting out of it (vv. 14–15).

We have not yet seen nor imagined what God will do when he repays our sacrifices. We shall be ashamed of what we said about him, if we are not careful. Not one person will stand before Christ to get his reward and say that he deserves it. We shall all be eternally ashamed (if that will be possible) that we did so little and he gave us so much. Are we aware of what the going rate is for any sacrifice that we make for Christ? It is certainly not merely the current building society interest. The ordinary flat rate is ten thousand per cent!

> Jesus said, 'Truly, I say to you, there is no one who has left house or brothers or sisters or mother or father or children or lands, for my sake and for the gospel, who will not receive a hundredfold now in this time, houses and brothers and sisters and mothers and children and lands, with persecutions, and in the age to come eternal life. But many who are first will be last, and the last first' (Mark 10:29–31).

That, in the terms of present day business, is ten thousand per cent! And on top of that there will be the eternal enjoyment of eternal life. It will take some faith to believe this. We are not having heaven here; we shall be having it above. Now is the time for service, for sacrifice and suffering for Christ until the Lord comes. The Old Testament ends with the promise that he will come. They had to wait four hundred years, but he did come. We have had to wait nearly two thousand years for his return, and he will come. 'Yet a little while, and the coming one will come and will not delay' (Heb 10:37). 'If it seems slow, wait for it; it will surely come; it will not delay' (Hab 2:3).

May God grant that in the meanwhile we do not lose heart, and however long the period of restoration may be we shall carry on, lest we shall be ashamed before him when he comes (1 John 2:28).

David Gooding, *Spiritual Dullness: A Study in the Prophet Malachi*, pp. 7–8

15th March

GREATNESS IN THE KINGDOM

Reading: Luke 22:24–30

*But not so with you. Rather, let the greatest among you become
as the youngest, and the leader as one who serves. (v. 26)*

All three synoptic Gospels make it clear that nothing angered our Lord so
much as the sight of people being oppressed by religious leaders abusing
their authority. And he took no pains to conceal his anger. Listen to him
preaching in Jerusalem (see 20:45–47).

And so it was that when an argument broke out among the apostles at
the Last Supper, our Lord took the occasion to teach them what is the true
nature of rule and office and service in his kingdom. The argument on that
solemn and most sacred occasion had been about which of them was to be
regarded as greatest. That one apostle should desire to be regarded as greater
than another apostle would surely strike us as incredible, did we not know
our own hearts and recognize that the apostles, for all the importance of their
office, were human like ourselves. But so it was, and our Lord had to point
out to them how thoroughly unregenerate an idea of power and ruling they
had, without thinking, imbibed: 'The kings of the Gentiles exercise lordship
over them, and those in authority over them are called benefactors' (22:25).

And still today all too often greatness is felt to lie not in actually serving
other people but in the personal aggrandisement that accompanies high office
and in the sense of power and the ability to control other people's lives that
high position brings. And by some curious twist in logic the title of Benefactor
goes, not to the people who actually do the work and serve, but to the people
who sit aloft and are served by others. 'But not so among you', said our Lord
to his apostles. They might be destined to hold high office in the church, so
high that none could be higher save Christ himself; but they were not to get
it into their heads that office in the church was like office in the great pagan
empires. 'But not so with you', said Christ, 'Rather, let the greatest among
you become as the youngest, and the leader as one who serves' (22:26).

David Gooding, *Windows on Paradise: Scenes of Hope and Salvation in the Gospel of Luke*, pp. 98–9

THE CAPTAIN OF OUR SALVATION

Part 7—The Road to the Cross

16th March

SUFFERING—THE WAY TO GLORY

Reading: John 12:20–26

*But we see him who for a little while was made lower than
the angels, namely Jesus, crowned with glory and honour
because of the suffering of death, so that by the grace of
God he might taste death for everyone. (Hebrews 2:9)*

And so the first stage in the programme has already been completed: the man, Christ Jesus, has been born. But so has the second stage. For see him now: he is already crowned with glory and honour.

I think I hear the Hebrew Christians sigh. 'Yes, that is true. He suffered on the cross and was rejected and shamefully treated. But in spite of it all, yes, it's true—he is now crowned with glory and honour.'

'Oh, but cheer up,' says the writer, 'it is not that way. He is crowned with glory and honour *because of*, not in spite of, the fact that he suffered death. Do you not see that because man threw away his dominion, and lost his glory by sin, the only possible way that man could reach that glory again was by suffering? Instead of the cross being a mistake, instead of those sufferings being a tragic accident, they have been in God's hand the way of bringing Messiah himself to his crowning with glory and honour: *On account of the suffering of death he is crowned with glory and honour.* Cheer up! His sufferings are something to be gloried in. There is in them the evidence of divine strategy.'

Not only is he himself crowned with glory and honour because of the suffering of death; by God's wonderful grace this has been the means of securing reconciliation for everything. When he went into death and tasted its bitterness, he tasted death for everything. And because of that a day will eventually come (of which the Apostle Paul speaks in his letter to Colossians, 1:20–21), when all things, both that are upon earth and that are in heaven, shall be reconciled to God. God will be presented with a heaven and earth freed from sin, cleansed and reconciled in every part, an honour to God and a pleasure to man for ever. It shall all be done by this very means of Christ's suffering, because the man, Jesus, tasted death for everyone.

David Gooding, An Unshakeable Kingdom: The Letter to the Hebrews for Today, p. 80

17th March

THE REWARD OF THE SERVANT

Reading: Isaiah 53

Out of the anguish of his soul he shall see and be satisfied. (v. 11)

Crucified by his nation, crushed by God, despised and rejected of men, considered to be dying under God's disapproval (so his nation thought), yet it is written, 'He shall see his offspring . . . Out of the anguish of his soul he shall see and be satisfied' (Isa 53:10–11). To my mind, these are astonishing words, bordering on the incredible. 'Satisfied'—the infinite Son of God satisfied?

The same prophet in chapter 40 asks what could possibly satisfy God. Even to sacrifice the whole beef stock throughout the world as a burnt offering couldn't begin to satisfy him. The nations are like the dust left after potatoes have been weighed and you're left with the dust in the pan that weighed them (Isa 40:15). That's all the nations are to God, and his hand is big enough to measure all the distance of space. How then could you satisfy him? And here it speaks of the Son of God himself, 'He shall see of the travail of his soul, and shall be satisfied' (53:11 KJV). It borders on the incredible that I'm to be part of that satisfaction, but there it is.

You say, 'It's not just you, Gooding, it's going to be the multimillions of the redeemed.' But even if you take me and multiply me by 3 trillion you don't get much, do you? But you see, I'm looking at it from my point of view and I shouldn't do that, should I? It's a question of what he's going to make of me and that's a different story. The glorious thing is this, that when he gets us home at last, perfected—not only redeemed, but perfected and matured and made like himself—he shall be satisfied not only with the work of his hands, but compensated for the sacrifice and the suffering that he's entailed. For it is written, 'Who for the joy that was set before him [he] endured the cross, despising the shame' (Heb 12:2)—the shame he counted as but nothing.

It was different with the cross—it wasn't despised and it had to be endured. Who of us can say that, during those dark hours of enduring the cross, the thought wasn't in his mind of the joy of having his redeemed perfected and with him forever?

David Gooding, *Satisfaction in Serving the Lord: Three Principles from the Prophecy of Isaiah*, p. 7

18th March

THE WISDOM OF THE CROSS

Reading: Luke 9:44–50

The Son of Man is about to be delivered
into the hands of men. (v. 44)

While, then, everyone was still amazed at the tremendous acts of power which Christ was performing (see v. 43), Christ impressed on his apostles that he who was doing these powerful deeds would eventually be 'delivered up into the hands of men'. The apostles did not understand what he said. In the first place they did not apparently understand to what 'being delivered up into the hands of men' referred, and they were afraid to ask (was it because they were subconsciously afraid of what the answer would be?). And then the phrase itself seemed to imply weakness and helplessness; and it probably did not make sense to them that someone who could wield the supernatural power that Christ was wielding, would be delivered into the hands of men as though completely unable to save himself. Luke explains that it was not altogether their fault that they could not understand the lesson: 'it was concealed from them so that they should not perceive it' (v. 45). When Christ was arrested, condemned and crucified they saw all too clearly what it meant, and saw it with shock and consternation. In a world that worshipped power, to be crucified was the extreme of disgrace and shameful weakness, and a crucified Messiah seemed an absurd contradiction in terms. Later they came to see and admire the divine wisdom of the strategy of the cross. They saw that mere power is inadequate to change a man's heart, to reconcile a man to God, to change his rebellion into faith and love and obedience; and inadequate therefore to solve the human problem and bring in the kingdom of God. And then they saw that the cross with all its apparent weakness and shame was able to do what power by itself could not do: 'the weakness of God is stronger than men' (1 Cor 1:25). They saw too that Christ's suffering of the cross was not an unfortunate obstacle on Christ's path to glory: he had come down from glory deliberately in order to suffer the cross. The cross was an expression of the wisdom of the 'Majestic Glory'. And then they woke up to the fact that the message of the cross is the only message of any use in the evangelization of the world, and the principle of the cross the only safe principle to follow in the organization and running of the churches (see 1 Cor 1:18–4:13).

David Gooding, *According to Luke: The Third Gospel's Ordered Historical Narrative*, pp. 179–80

19th March

AN ACCEPTED SACRIFICE

Reading: Leviticus 9:9–24

*How much more will the blood of Christ, who through the
eternal Spirit offered himself without blemish to God, purify our
conscience from dead works to serve the living God. (Hebrews 9:14)*

Did you notice that descriptive passage we read where, on the first occasion,
the offerings having been ordained and the priesthood prepared, there came
that public occasion when now the priest and the people gathered and they
brought their sacrifices? The priest brought his sacrifices for he too was a sinful man, and Israel the nation brought theirs, and they did with them appropriately as they had been told. Then, as each sacrifice had been offered, finally
they came to the burnt offering and the fat upon the altar. The priests lifted up
their hands to bless the people and then Aaron and Moses went in to meet God
and came out again to bless the people. And in that moment, says Leviticus,
the glory of the Lord appeared, and the very fire of God came out and burnt
that burnt offering and consumed it to ashes upon the altar (Lev 9:23–24).

When the people saw it they shouted in automatic reaction of wonder.
Wonder beyond explanation—to see the very glory of God come and the fire
of God come and, before their very eyes, accept their sacrifice, so to speak.
What a thing to have brought a sacrifice, but now to be made conscious that
the living God was there, and the living God had actually accepted your
sacrifice, what a thing it was! The people shouted as the reality of it gripped
their hearts, and in that split second they fell upon their faces.

Those days have long since gone by. We do not now think in terms of
literal fire, not even miraculous fire, coming down from heaven. But it is
given to God's people to know a far more wonderful thing. To stand in spirit,
in memory, in heart, by the great sacrifice of Christ until God's Holy Spirit
makes it as vivid to you as he could possibly make it. God, the living God,
has accepted that sacrifice on your behalf. What a wonder it is when our
blessed Lord, in his redeeming office and by his sacrifice, brings us in touch
with the living God and you know his reality and you know that Christ's
sacrifice has been accepted for you. What shouts of triumph, even if nobody
else hears them, come up from our hearts and how, without any ostentation
or pretence, we fall upon our faces in adoring worship.

David Gooding, *The Beauty of Holiness: Israel's Sacrificial System and the Christian Faith*, p. 7

20th March

THE CROSS EXPOSES THE FOLLY
OF HUMAN WISDOM

Reading: 1 Corinthians 1:18–28

Where is the one who is wise? Where is the scribe?
Where is the debater of this age? Has not God made
foolish the wisdom of the world? (v. 20)

You'll see that the first step God had to take in restoring us human beings to being truly human must be to smash that false confidence of trusting in man—in ourselves, in other people—as the ultimate ground of our salvation. How will God smash it? He did it by the cross of Christ. Now Paul is using his terms very carefully and exactly. He could have devoted his first four chapters to the death of Christ. If Christ died for our sins, is that not the gospel (see 1 Cor 15:3)? Of course it is. Why won't it do then? What does it matter whether you refer to 'the *cross* of Christ' or you refer to 'the *death* of Christ'? Well, it matters everything.

The death of the great Greek philosopher Socrates was a very noble death, as in quiet confidence he took the poisoned cup from the jailer, drank it, and with all dignity lay down and died. That would not offend anybody's sense of nobility, but the cross would. The cross as a means of death was thought to be the most disgraceful, shameful death that anybody could die. God chose the cross as the way Jesus should die, and he did it on purpose.

What for? To deliberately expose man's folly. Jesus was crucified by the so-called wisdom of this world, wasn't he? High political and religious wisdom: Caiaphas the high priest, negotiating with Pilate the Roman governor, and consulting with Herod. 'You know nothing at all,' said Caiaphas to his fellow members of the council. 'When it comes to high powered religion and politics, you can't afford to be innocent little children. It is expedient for the cause of God and for the good health of the body politic that this Jesus must die, and the faith that the common people have in him be smashed' (see John 11:49–50). And they devised a cross.

What fools they were, for three days later God raised him from the dead. What sheer ignoramuses were these men that crucified Christ: 'None of the rulers of this age understood this, for if they had, they would not have crucified the Lord of glory' (1 Cor 2:8). None of them knew this hidden wisdom of God. God was making a fool of mere human wisdom—he did it on purpose.

David Gooding, *The Christian Philosophy of Man: Eight Studies in 1 Corinthians*, p. 17

21st March

RECONCILING ALL THINGS BY
THE BLOOD OF HIS CROSS

Reading: Colossians 1:15–23

And you, who once were alienated and hostile in mind,
doing evil deeds, he has now reconciled in his body
of flesh by his death, in order to present you holy and
blameless and above reproach before him. (vv. 21–22)

Revelation chapter 5 helps us to understand what shall yet happen when the blessed Lamb of God takes the book from him that sits upon the throne and proceeds with judgment to bring back the world and the universe to God's obedience. The cry shall go out, not merely, 'Who is able?' or 'Who has the power?' but 'Who has the moral worth to do it?' How shall God deluge the universe with his judgments of destruction and retrieve his name? With his dying gasp Satan would say that he had been proved right—the Creator was a tyrant, and God himself would be left with an empty world.

The question is, 'Who is morally right?' When the Lamb takes the book, then not only those in heaven and on the earth, but those under the earth shall confess that Jesus Christ is worthy to take it. How is he worthy? 'Worthy is the Lamb who was slain' (Rev 5:12). And from the caverns of the lost nobody shall be able to say otherwise. 'At the name of Jesus every knee [shall] bow, in heaven and on earth and under the earth, and every tongue confess that Jesus Christ is Lord, to the glory of God the Father' (Phil 2:10–11). The whole universe shall be pacified and glorified, and God's honour proved to the remotest boundary.

'And you . . .' (v. 21). It matters to God what you think of him. It mattered so much to him that the divine decree was that all the fullness should dwell in the Lord Jesus, and he would reconcile you to God. To win you, to remove your fear and to show you what the infinite God is really like, he became an innocent baby in the womb and arms of a virgin. The guilt of our sins that had made us fear God has been removed: 'He has now reconciled [us] in his body of flesh by his death' (v. 22). Even though life may be difficult, you find yourself saying, 'If that's God on Calvary and he's there for me what a great God he is.' And not only so, but eventually he shall 'present you holy and blameless and above reproach before him.' So we marvel at the method and, as the hymn puts it, 'stand all amazed at the love Jesus offers me.'

David Gooding, *Christ Is All: Twelve Seminars on the Letter to the Colossians*, p. 32

22nd March

VICTORY THROUGH DEFEAT

Reading: Joshua 8:1–19

For the foolishness of God is wiser than men, and the
weakness of God is stronger than men. (1 Corinthians 1:25)

When the armies came to execute the wrath of God upon Jericho, the great captain with his sword outstretched led the way, but as Israel came to be delivered from that terrible sin at Ai, how did he do it? The first time Israel came up to Ai they were defeated and they ran away. Says Joshua, 'The way to victory at Ai will be to re-enact, to rehearse, the defeat.' So he took the troops up to Ai and he said, 'When the enemy come out, you run away as though you were defeated.' I think I would have preferred to be in the ambush, the all-victorious ambush, around the other side of the city, wouldn't you? I'd like that role. You'd get a medal for that. You wouldn't get a medal for running away; and admitting yourself defeated and remembering all those past mistakes.

'No, please Joshua, put me in the other lot.'

Says Joshua, 'Wouldn't you prefer to be where I am?'

'Oh, what brigade will you be with? Will you be with the people who give the victory?'

'No,' says Joshua, 'I shall lead the defeated.'

Oh, what grace is it that Joshua, this delightful prototype of Christ, with his javelin in his hand led that band of defeated, sinful Israelites, now repentant, and got them to re-enact the defeat.

Oh yes, my long defeat; and Christ took my side, and in his apparent weakness joined my defeat even so far as the curse of Calvary's cross. Satan thought he'd won forever, but it was another story, for just as Joshua didn't withdraw the javelin until the enemy found to their surprise that what looked like defeat was the divine strategy of final victory, so as the hymn says of our Lord, 'By weakness and defeat | He won a glorious crown, | Trod all our foes beneath his feet | By being trodden down.'

Oh, let's praise him in our hearts. Let's praise the divine grace that had mercy on us Gentiles, and has brought us the promise of Abraham, that in Abraham and his seed shall all the nations of the world be blessed.

David Gooding, *Entering the Inheritance: Studies in Joshua 1–12*, p. 37

23rd March

DISARMING THE PRINCIPALITIES

Reading: Colossians 2:6–23

He disarmed the rulers and authorities and put them to
open shame, by triumphing over them in him. (v. 15)

It wasn't merely that the law and our trespasses stood against us; God had to find a way of forgiving us that upheld his law and maintained God's justice. He has found it in Christ. The rulers and authorities were arraigned against him. The greatest of those is Satan and we are told that he is 'the accuser of our brothers' (Rev 12:10). How should God shut his mouth? You say, 'Squash him out, he's only a creature anyway. Don't listen to him.'

But the charge had an element of truth in it. Said Satan, 'God, are you going to forgive this fallen human race? What's this I hear about you raising them and putting them above angels? Look at their sins! You're going to throw me out of heaven because of my sin and then let them in—what about their sins? Cross me out if you like, God, but what about your character? I'm afraid that your whole experiment with the human race has come unstuck. I've destroyed it beyond your ability to repair, because I tempted them to sin. They've trespassed against your law and your own righteousness forbids your forgiving them.'

They gathered around the cross of Jesus Christ our Lord, thinking it was the last step in their victory. That fair flower of humanity was dying as a reputed sinner on the tree. None of the princes of this world knew it, did they? Not Caiaphas, Herod or Pilate, nor his satanic majesty. 'None of the rulers of this age understood this, for if they had, they would not have crucified the Lord of glory' (1 Cor 2:8). In their ignorance and folly they went and crucified him. God raised him from the dead and you with him. Every spirit opposition was silenced eternally, not by destroying them but by the great answer of the cross of Christ.

What a magnificent salvation it is. No angel could have done it for you. He hung there solitary, your only Saviour, and he triumphed because he is God's incarnate Son. Then let us take heed to the message: 'Therefore, as you received Christ Jesus the Lord, so walk in him' (Col 2:6). He is your only hope, your only Saviour—find everything for your sanctification in him.

David Gooding, *Christ Is All: Twelve Seminars on the Letter to the Colossians*, p. 54

24th March

TO DESTROY HIM WHO HAD THE POWER OF DEATH

Reading: Joshua 3:9–17

Since therefore the children share in flesh and blood,
he himself likewise partook of the same things, that
through death he might destroy the one who has the
power of death, that is, the devil. (Hebrews 2:14)

The prince of this world has had one mighty great defence line all down history. It's called in Hebrews 'the power of death'. And, says Hebrews, using that power of death he has subjected people to bondage—'them who through fear of death were all their lifetime subject to bondage' (v. 15 KJV). Where he has been allowed his way, anybody that professes loyalty to the God of heaven, he will threaten them with death. And multitudes of men and women, because they fear death, give in. Oh, I pray God, if ever conditions come in which I find myself faced with the stake, or the psychiatric hospital, or the torture camp for loyalty to Christ, may God give me the grace to look death in the face, that I shall not let myself be scared by him who has the power of death.

When the Son of God came down to earth, Satan made a great effort to keep him away and to stop his gospel. Satan knew no better than to put him to death, and they thought they'd seen the last of him. But see the wonder, brothers and sisters, as the blessed transcendent Lord, creator of heaven and earth, became incarnate. He was scarce thirty years old when he went to Jordan and literally stood with sinners in the mud of its river bed. A few years later, stand back if you can, and see the wonder as those holy feet entered the river of death.

I wish I could tell you that when he stood there the waters kept back, but the record is that they went over his head, for he bore our sins, all sinless himself, in his body. He tasted death's waters, dark, bitter, offensive, and for his lost sheep he went down to the grave. Oh, but hail his victory: death couldn't keep its prey. Jesus my Saviour, Lord of heaven and earth, tore the bars away, and the third day he rose again and went triumphantly to the right hand of God. He destroyed him that had the power of death and took his defence away, and has opened up the way to our great inheritance.

David Gooding, *Entering the Inheritance: Studies in Joshua 1–12*, pp. 21–2

25th March

A JUST FORGIVENESS

Reading: Romans 3:21–31

It was to show his righteousness at the present
time, so that he might be just and the justifier of
the one who has faith in Jesus. (v. 26)

As our Lord instituted the Lord's Supper, he took wine as a symbol of his blood. He said, 'This is my blood of the covenant, which is poured out for many for the forgiveness of sins' (Matt 26:28). Notice that term. You will perceive at once that it is not merely an airy and breezy matter of coming back to God and saying, 'All right, now let's start from square one.' There are accounts to be settled. God's morality will not be at peace until those accounts are honoured and fully settled. What did Christ mean when he said that he was going to shed his blood for forgiveness? Let me quote you another saying of his that he made around about this time: 'The Son of Man came not to be served but to serve, and to give his life as a ransom for many' (Mark 10:45).

He was alluding to the great prophecy of Isaiah (ch. 53) in which, before Messiah came, his redemptive role was sketched out—how that Messiah was to be pierced for our transgressions and crushed for our iniquities. How the chastisement that brought us peace was to be on him; how we were to be healed through his wounds. That famous prophecy contains the profound phrase, 'Yet it was the will of the LORD to crush him; he has put him to grief' (v. 10). I would not pretend to try and explain the atonement. Who can pierce through that veil of thick darkness which God caused to surround our Lord's cross? Or adequately describe what our Lord meant when he cried that God had forsaken him? But it is evident that when our Lord hung upon the cross, God bruised him. God put him to grief. That somehow on that occasion, God took up with him the controversy of human sin. And in the coin of suffering, Christ paid the ransom that would deliver mankind from an impasse that would otherwise be eternal.

Oh yes, God certainly wanted to forgive, but the love of God that seeks to forgive people is not an easy-going carefree love that will take the view that sin doesn't matter. If God took that view, who knows but that heaven wouldn't turn out to be the hell that this earth has turned out to be? God cares. And because sin matters, our Lord informed us that he would have to be lifted up (John 3:14–15).

David Gooding, *The Unexpected Person and Character of Jesus Christ*, p. 28

26th March

THE KING SETS UP HIS KINGDOM

Reading: Luke 22:1–23

*I have earnestly desired to eat this Passover
with you before I suffer. (v. 15)*

On the night of the Last Supper, Christ determined to eat the supper with his disciples in the middle of the city in spite of all the hostility that surrounded them. And so it had to be done secretly, and elaborate precautions were taken.

To get the supper ready, two disciples were sent into the city with instructions to look out for a man carrying a pitcher of water. This evidently was some prearranged sign. Without saying anything to him, they were to follow him, notice the house he went into, and presently enter the house themselves and ask for the owner. When he appeared, they were simply to say, 'The Teacher says to you, Where is the guest room, where I may eat the Passover with my disciples?' (v. 11). At this, the man would show them a large upper room and they were to prepare the meal there.

When all was ready and night had fallen, Christ unobtrusively entered the city and gathered his disciples round him in this borrowed upper room. For a few brief hours the upper room, cosy and comfortable in the mellow light of its oil lamps, gave them shelter from the hostility that breathed in the darkness outside. But not from all hostility, nor even from the worst; for Satan, who had dogged the path of Christ throughout his earthly ministry, now began to take up position for the final assault. For months past he had worked on the love of money that enslaved the heart of Judas Iscariot until Judas no longer had any power or desire to resist evil; and now at this opportune moment he began to press home his advantage. He first put it into his heart to betray the Saviour, and before the supper was ended he demanded personal entry into Judas to commandeer and rule him completely.

Consider, then, the situation. A few days earlier, Christ had ridden into the city formally claiming to be her king, and he had been acclaimed by the multitudes. But the city of the great king was now in the hands of rebel forces; and even one of the disciples had sold himself to the archenemy. Yet that night in the face of implacable hatred and in the teeth of satanic opposition, the king set up his kingdom, and instituted the covenant that should define the relations between himself as sovereign and his subjects.

David Gooding, *Windows on Paradise: Scenes of Hope and Salvation in the Gospel of Luke*, pp. 79–80

27th March

THE DISPLAY OF GOD'S GLORY

Reading: John 13:18–30

Then after he had taken the morsel, Satan entered into him. (v. 27)

Let's get this straight to start with: neither Jesus' choice of Judas to be an apostle, nor his prediction that Judas would betray him, made Judas betray him. Suppose, looking down from a helicopter, you saw two cars approaching each other at high speed round a blind corner, you could predict that they were bound to crash into each other. But your prediction, though true, would not make them crash. The crash would be the drivers' fault. And so it was with Judas. Jesus knew in advance and predicted that he would betray him; but that did not make Judas betray him or excuse him for doing it. Judas did what he did of his own free will, out of the sinfulness of his own heart. Nor did Satan have any intention of fulfilling the Old Testament prophecies that the Messiah must die, when he infiltrated into Judas's mind the idea of betraying Jesus. He too acted out of the scheming of his own mind. To his fallen and devilish way of thinking, the betrayal of Jesus and his death on a cross could only be a disastrous defeat for Jesus. Death by crucifixion was the most opprobrious punishment known to the ancient world. The shame of it would drown the cause of Jesus in an ocean of disgrace. And so he thought it a masterful stroke of strategy when he suborned one of Jesus' chosen apostles to betray him to that public humiliation.

But how mistaken Satan was! The Son of God had come to our world on purpose to die the death of the cross! Knowing in advance that Judas would betray him to that death, he had deliberately chosen him as an apostle. And when Judas finally left the Upper Room to go out to do his dastardly deed, Christ commanded him: 'What you are going to do, do quickly' (v. 27). So far from the shame of the cross destroying the reputation of Christ, the suffering of the cross would become the greatest exhibition of the glory of God and of the Son of God that the world has ever seen or that the universe will ever see. Which is why, when Judas had gone out and Christ's crucifixion was now imminent, Christ declared: 'Now is the Son of Man glorified, and God is glorified in him' (v. 31).

David Gooding, *In the School of Christ: Lessons on Holiness in John 13–17*, pp. 61–2

28th March

GOD'S GLORY IN RECONCILIATION

Reading: Luke 20:9–19

In Christ God was reconciling the world
to himself. (2 Corinthians 5:19)

Ever since Satan had polluted mankind's heart with slanderous misrepresentations of God's character, God had been planning and working towards this moment. In due course God's own Son set foot on our rebel planet. Then came the climax when the Creator incarnate came face to face in the Upper Room with the creature that was about to betray him to a cross. Now the world would see what God was like! Now God's reaction to this traitor would reveal exactly what was in God's heart. Deliberately, and in full knowledge of what Judas was about to do, he offered Judas the sop of his friendship.

Magnificent though this gesture was, it formed but the prelude to the even more majestic display of God's glory at Calvary. For just as Christ's giving of the sop to Judas exposed the traitor and his evil treachery, so God's giving of his Son into the hands of mankind exposed man's rebel hatred against God. 'This is the heir,' they said; 'Let us kill him, so that the inheritance may be ours' (Luke 20:14). But even as they nailed his hands and feet to the cross, God was offering Christ to the world as the sop of his friendship, as the pledge of his forgiveness and eternal love to all who would repent and receive him in sincerity and truth. 'In Christ God was reconciling the world to himself, not counting their trespasses against them' (2 Cor 5:19). For 'God shows his love for us in that while we were still sinners, Christ died for us. . . . For if while we were enemies we were reconciled to God by the death of his Son, much more, now that we are reconciled, shall we be saved by his life' (Rom 5:8, 10). And right down to us in our century comes God's call through Christ's apostles: 'We are ambassadors for Christ, God making his appeal through us. We implore you on behalf of Christ, be reconciled to God. For our sake he made him to be sin who knew no sin, so that in him we might become the righteousness of God' (2 Cor 5:20–21).

If after that, people take all the Creator's natural gifts, but reject the sop of his friendship, they will, like Judas, go out into a night of eternal darkness where the light of God's friendship never comes and the awareness of his holiness burns like an unquenchable fire. But they will have only themselves to blame.

David Gooding, In the School of Christ: Lessons on Holiness in John 13–17, pp. 62–3

29th March

THE LORD PRAYS IN GETHSEMANE

Reading: Luke 22:39–45

And he said, 'Abba, Father, all things are possible
for you. Remove this cup from me. Yet not what
I will, but what you will.' (Mark 14:36)

When the king came out from the upper room, he went to 'the place' (Luke 22:40) on the Mount of Olives where every day throughout the past week he had gone when he left the temple at nightfall, the place which Judas knew well and to which he would soon come with the arresting party. There was no thought of running away. If the kingdom of God was going to be set up, then the battle with the powers of darkness must be fought and the sooner it was joined the better. 'Pray', said Christ to his disciples, 'that you enter not into temptation'. Hell itself would now unite all its forces and combine with human evil to prevent, if possible, the will of God from being done. And this would be their temptation: to avoid facing the battle, to give in, to run away, to fail to do the will of God.

So then, as if to make clear where at this crucial, fateful hour in the history of the universe the battle-centre lay, he withdrew from his disciples about a stone's throw (see v. 41). The battle and its outcome would depend on him alone. If he failed, all would for ever be lost: if he triumphed, he secured irreversible victory.

And he kneeled down. What a sight! What a victory! The king kneeling on the Mount of Olives! Only a few days ago he had come riding down this same Mount of Olives in royal procession rightly acclaimed as the king (19:35–38). But he had found Jerusalem his capital city in the hands of rebels, the temple infested with robbers. How could such opposition be overcome? How could such rebels be saved from the condemnation of God and the penalty of their rebellion, and restored to obedience and the worship of God? Riding on the royal mount through the streets of the city would hardly do it. Pomp and ceremony never yet turned a rebel into a saint. If ever Jerusalem, Israel and the world were to be brought back to God's obedience, it must all start here: Messiah must himself establish the will of God on earth by obeying it himself.

So the king kneeled down. He would obey on his own behalf as always, but on behalf of Israel and all the human race. 'For as through the one man's disobedience the many were made sinners, even so through the obedience of the one should the many be made righteous' (see Rom 5:19).

David Gooding, *According to Luke: The Third Gospel's Ordered Historical Narrative*, pp. 353–4

30th March

THE ARREST OF THE LORD

Reading: Luke 22:47–71

Have you come out as against a robber, with
swords and clubs? (v. 52)

The sudden shock of seeing through Judas's sickening pretence and of realizing what was going to happen provoked an instantaneous reaction from the other disciples: 'Lord, shall we use our swords on them?' One of them indeed did not wait for permission, but drew his sword and with poor aim but stout intention cut off the right ear of one of the high-priest's servants. This reaction was natural, the all too natural reaction of mere human nature, unprepared by prayer, ungoverned by the will and wisdom of God, and utterly inappropriate and inadequate to the nature of the conflict that was now upon them. What they were up against was not mere flesh and blood but principalities and powers, the world-rulers of this darkness (v. 53) whose power lies in twisting all that is genuinely human and true into a diabolical but specious lie. That is not a power from which a man can be delivered by physical weapons. Christ restrained his followers and healed the man's ear. One man at least should hear loud and clear, in spite of all the confusion in the garden that night, exactly what Christ really stood for, as Christ now exposed the deceit of the chief priests, captains of the temple and elders who were conducting the operation. There they stood professed ministers of God, guardians of his temple, upholders of his sanctity and truth, making out they were on an expedition against some political activist. The whole thing was a deliberate pretence; and we can now see how beautifully Peter would have unthinkingly played into their hands, if he had been allowed to continue with his armed resistance. Then they could have told the public that they had caught Jesus at dead of night at the head of an armed band, engaged on some subversive guerrilla action, and that when challenged, he and his followers had attacked the authorities with weapons. How Satan would have laughed to see the Saviour of the world represented as a guerrilla fighter who thought that the problem of evil could be solved by political subversion and armed conflict.

The fact is that publicly in broad daylight they had been unable to find any basis for a political charge against him and they were obliged therefore to concoct one and try to pin it on him under cover of darkness. Their very tactics and the timing of their arrest proclaimed the source of their power: 'This is your hour,' said Christ, 'and the authority of darkness' (v. 53).

David Gooding, *According to Luke: The Third Gospel's Ordered Historical Narrative*, pp. 355–6

31st March

CHRIST BEFORE PILATE

Reading: John 18:28–40

You say that I am a king. For this purpose I was born and for this purpose I have come into the world—to bear witness to the truth. Everyone who is of the truth listens to my voice. (v. 37)

Pilate was beginning to lose his temper: 'You'd better start speaking, young man. Don't you realize I have power to crucify you? And power to release you? You'd better start speaking! I'm asking you where you're from.' And our Lord replied,

> You would have no authority over me at all unless it had been given you from above. Therefore he who delivered me over to you has the greater sin. (19:11)

What did our Lord mean? He meant, of course, that this very occasion was God's arrangement. God had given Pilate the authority to take this decision; it was given him 'from above'. We know it from what the Gospel of John has said, that Jesus Christ was God incarnate. What is the truth about Calvary?

'I came to bear witness to the truth,' says Christ.

'What is truth?' says Pilate (see 18:37–38).

Well, what is truth, then? Truth, ultimately, is a person. 'I am . . . the truth,' says Christ (14:6). The truth of this situation, as Jesus stood before Pilate, is that God had given Pilate the authority; and the one who stood in front of him was God incarnate!

Do you believe it? Can it be true that the God of the universe—God incarnate—would come and stand before a human being, and let a human being decide what to do with him, to crucify him or release him? You do believe some extraordinary things, you know, if I may point it out!

It is no good saying, 'Christ, prove it! Show Pilate that you are God incarnate!' Well, our Lord could have done it, but the very sight of it would have shrivelled Pilate to a cinder. It is the fact that, as you preach, as you witness, this is God incarnate putting himself before men. And they can decide what they are going to do with Jesus who is called the Christ. That is the truth about God, you know. That is the kind of god that God is! That is the amazing truth.

David Gooding, *Four Journeys to Jerusalem: A Series of Seminars on the Gospel of John*, p. 160

THE CAPTAIN OF OUR SALVATION

Part 8—The Lord's Death and Resurrection

1st April

THE LORD COMMITS HIS MOTHER TO JOHN

Reading: John 19:19–27

*When Jesus saw his mother and the disciple whom he loved
standing nearby, he said to his mother, 'Woman, behold, your
son!' Then he said to the disciple, 'Behold, your mother!' And from
that hour the disciple took her to his own home. (vv. 26–27)*

There is Mary at the death of her son. This is what the *cross* does to relationships. It is not just physical death, but the world's enmity, taking this
son from his mother. But then it shows the compensation of being fellow
believers in a new family. He said to Mary: 'Behold your son'; and to John,
'Behold your mother.' It is a new family relationship.

It could have been that John was more well off than some of the others.
You will notice that John, when Christ caught him, left his father and 'the
hired servants' in the boat (Mark 1:19–20). He and his father were employers
and had employees working for them. They were in a bigger way of fishing
than was Peter who manned his own boat. And it may be that John was
more in a position to look after her. And finally, John was a young man, and
he looked after her for years. She lived with him, according to tradition, in
Ephesus, when he was there.

Also it seems to me it was no accident that our Lord said it at the cross
because, first, Mary had come to the cross, and he was about to give up his
spirit, and he wanted somebody to look after her when he was gone, so to speak.
And it was the John who leaned on his bosom, who was so near the Lord—in
the Lord's affections—who had the mother committed to him to look after.

Secondly, there is the meaning of 'the cross'. I don't know whether it is
still said around here, but you know the way it is sometimes said, 'I've got
very bad rheumatism, but that's the cross that God has given me.' Well, that's
talking nonsense, actually. It has nothing to do with the cross. The cross is
what the world gives you. Jesus bore his own cross. You'll notice it is never
said 'he took it up'. The cross was what the world gave him. It is not a burden
such as we all bear, and some of us have different burdens to bear; but the
cross is the world's enmity to Christ.

This was said next to the cross. It was the world's hostility and crucifixion
of Christ that was robbing Mary of her son. It was fellowship in the cross of
Christ that made John so suitable to take Mary.

David Gooding, *Four Journeys to Jerusalem: A Series of Seminars on the Gospel of John*, pp. 37–8, 186

2nd April

THE 'THORN BUSH' OF CALVARY

Reading: Exodus 3:1–10

*[Moses] looked, and behold, the bush was
burning, yet it was not consumed. (v. 2)*

Have you discovered the thorn bushes of life? You had your ideas of what life could be. Is it now the unreasonableness of your children, the spitefulness of some you have loved dearly, the cruelty and perversity of men in industry? Be it what it will, it has disillusioned you. Well, perhaps that's the place where God will meet with you in your disillusionment, to begin for you a pilgrimage to a fairer world and a glorious inheritance that shall never fade.

Have you not seen his glory? In your mind's eye once more and in a spirit of worship, with the shoes off your feet, come with me to the most barren place this world has ever known, or shall know—Calvary. See a human figure spiked on a cross, torn with thorns and mutilated by men. Their envy, ambition, power-lust, greed, spite and sadism have worked until they have wrecked that human form and made it scarcely recognizable as human. O the poverty, the disillusionment of Calvary! Is there any hope?

Ah, see it again! See the crown of thorns and the emblem of a curse. But why wasn't he consumed? And the answer comes back, 'God was in Christ reconciling the world unto himself, not imputing unto them their trespasses' (see 2 Cor 5:19). As the hymn says, 'Here we find the dawn of heaven, while upon the cross we gaze.' Here we find hope that 'creation itself will be set free from its bondage to corruption and obtain the freedom of the glory of the children of God' (Rom 8:21). Here I find hope, not for the tangle that is this world and my contemporaries merely; here I find hope for that thorn bush of my own life. My tangled, gnarled, broken personality, for which there would be no hope were it not for a God who is faithful to what he has created. Here I find hope that through Christ, who bore my curse, one day I too shall be fully and finally delivered and fashioned to the image of God's Son. That thorn bush is not the end of the journey, but it is the beginning that guarantees the end.

David Gooding, *No Longer Bondmen: Thirteen Studies in the Book of Exodus*, pp. 22–3

3rd April

THE DYING THIEF AND THE NATURE
OF CHRIST'S KINGSHIP

Reading: Luke 23:26–43

*And he said, 'Jesus, remember me when you
come into your kingdom.' (v. 42)*

The story of the so-called dying thief is very well known. And it deserves to be. It illustrates as few other stories do the almost incredible extent of the forgiveness of God. After a life of lurid crime, a professional criminal in the eleventh hour, indeed in the fifty-ninth minute of the eleventh hour, repents and trusts Christ; and Christ forgives him immediately and absolutely.

How was he to get right with God? His past held no merit. To promise reform in the future was useless: he had but a few hours left, spiked hand and foot to a cross. Soon the pain that was tearing through every fibre and searing his brain would make even prayer impossible. And anyway, he didn't know any prayers to say; praying had never been much in his line. There was no doubt that this Jesus was God's king as he said he was, and that he would one day come again in all his kingly power. That was as certain as God himself, as certain as the fact of coming judgment. Personally he had never thought much of kings, had never felt like obeying any of them. But a king who would pray forgiveness for the very men who were spiking his hands and feet to a cross . . . you could respect a king like that. He wouldn't mind being in his kingdom and obeying him. But what chance had he, a self-confessed anarchist, of being allowed so much as to enter his kingdom? And yet, what if he had not prayed, 'Father, forgive them for they know not what they do'? If those soldiers could be forgiven because they had not realized exactly what they were doing, then certainly he hadn't realized before how wonderful God's king was. He hadn't meant to rebel against a king like that.

'Jesus,' he said, 'would you ever let me into your kingdom? Would you let me obey you? Lord, remember me when you come in your kingdom.' And at once, to that poor broken rebel against man and God in the last few hours of his tortured life, there came clearly and without reserve that most kingly word from the King of kings himself: 'Assuredly, I say to you, today you will be with me in paradise.'

David Gooding, *Windows on Paradise: Scenes of Hope and Salvation in the Gospel of Luke*, pp. 37–43

4th April

CHRIST'S RESURRECTION DESTROYED DEATH

Reading: John 20:1–31

*God raised him up, loosing the pangs of death, because it
was not possible for him to be held by it. (Acts 2:24)*

If Jesus was in fact God's Son, why did not God intervene with some further
spectacular miracle to save him, and so put his accreditation beyond doubt?
The answer appears from the sequel. God had purposed in Jesus to teach not
only Israel but all mankind a fundamental fact about the universe: death
is not a permanent, unbreakable, irreversible regularity of nature. Death,
therefore, is not a final disaster for the good, nor an impregnable barricade
of protection for the evil. The Sadducees did not believe in resurrection.
They held that death ends everything. God, therefore, deliberately allowed
the Sadducees to use their final weapon; but it broke in their hands. They put
Jesus to death, but God raised him from the dead. Here then, for people who
had refused the message of the previous mighty acts, was the mightiest act
of all; and its message was gospel indeed. 'Christ Jesus', as Paul was later to
say (2 Tim 1:10), had 'destroyed death and . . . brought life and immortality
to light through the gospel'; not life and then survival after death, but life and
deathlessness. God had made known to him the paths of life and filled him
with joy in his presence (Acts 2:28). The resurrection of Christ has altered
the face of the universe. Not only is death not an irreversible process; it is not
even a permanent institution. Moreover, if it has been reversed, destroyed
and abolished in the case of one man, Jesus Christ, so it can be, on certain
conditions, for all others. 'For since death came through a man, the resurrection of the dead comes also through a man. For as in Adam all die, so in
Christ all will be made alive' (1 Cor 15:21–22).

David Gooding, *True to the Faith: The Acts of the Apostles–Defining and Defending the Gospel*, pp. 71-2

5th April

CHRIST VINDICATED AS THE SON OF GOD

Reading: Acts 13:32–41

Therefore he says also in another psalm, 'You will not let your Holy One see corruption.' (v. 35)

There is another piece of highly significant evidence bearing on the question of the fulfilment of the promise, 'I will be his father, and he shall be my son' (Heb 1:5). With the birth of Jesus Christ in the royal line of David there entered our world someone who had an unparalleled sense of God as his Father and of himself as God's Son. As a boy of twelve he astounded his hearers by referring to the temple as 'my Father's house' (Luke 2:49). In the twenty-one chapters of the Gospel of John's record of his life and teaching he refers to God as his Father over one hundred times.

We are so used to thinking of God as Father that if we are not careful we shall fail to see how doubly unique Jesus was in this respect. First, no prophet, priest, poet or king in the Old Testament ever spoke of God as his personal Father in the way and to the extent that Jesus did. Verify this claim for yourself. Secondly, though Jesus taught his disciples that God was their Father, he consistently maintained that God was his Father and that he was God's Son in a unique sense. He taught his disciples, 'This, then, is how you should pray: "Our Father . . ."' (Matt 6:9 NIV); but he never joined them in saying 'Our Father'. Rather he expressed himself, as to Mary in the Garden: 'I am returning to my Father and your Father' (see John 20:17). Or as in Matthew: 'All things have been committed to me by my Father. No one knows the Son except the Father, and no one knows the Father except the Son and those to whom the Son chooses to reveal him' (11:27 NIV). It was language like this that astonished, and then infuriated, many of his contemporaries: 'he was even calling God his own Father, making himself equal with God' (John 5:18 NIV).

The resurrection has vindicated his teaching about himself, and it becomes apparent that God's promise to David has been fulfilled magnificently. David's line will never peter out. God's promise to provide the world with a Saviour-King is secure. The Messiah is not a mere man or even an angel, both of whom might fall out of divine favour. He is the eternal Son of the eternal Father. The relationship is indestructible; and the future is in his hands.

David Gooding, *An Unshakeable Kingdom: The Letter to the Hebrews for Today*, pp. 46–7

6th April

THE RESURRECTION WAS INEVITABLE

Reading: Luke 20:27–47

He is not God of the dead, but of the living. (v. 38)

According to Christ (vv. 34–40) the Sadducees' objection was based on two false presuppositions. The first was that conditions in the world to which resurrection admits a man are simply a continuation of this life, and that therefore the marriage relationships which people have contracted here will continue there. That, of course, is not so. In the resurrection the redeemed will be like the angels in two respects: they will never die, and they will not marry.

The second mistaken presupposition lay at the other extreme. It implied that the relationship formed between God and men in this life was only temporary. But that is not so. God being eternal, the relationships he forms are eternal. Centuries after Abraham, Isaac and Jacob lived, God was announcing himself to Moses, so Christ pointed out, as the God of Abraham and the God of Isaac and the God of Jacob (v. 37). The eternal cannot be characterized by something that no longer exists. Resurrection then is not a fantasy dreamed up by the wishful thinking of less than rigorous theologians; resurrection is a necessary outcome of the character and nature of God.

Christ, however, was not content to leave the matter there, but went over to the offensive and in his turn cited a passage from the Old Testament. In Psalm 110:1, Christ observed, David called Messiah his Lord. What sense could that possibly make if (1) Messiah was not already existent in David's day, and (2) if by the time Messiah was born, David had completely ceased to exist? How could David call a non-existent Messiah his Lord? How could Messiah be Lord of a non-existent David? Moreover no oriental father, let alone an oriental monarch, would ever call one of his own sons Lord. Joseph's brothers might eventually call him Lord; Jacob never did! But David called Messiah his Lord: how could he therefore be simply his son?

The rest of the New Testament supplies the answer to these questions: Messiah was not simply the son of David. He was and is both the Root and Offspring of David (see Rev 22:16). He could have said with reference to David what he said with reference to Abraham: 'Before Abraham was, I am' (John 8:58). It was, therefore, impossible for him to be executed and then to cease to exist. He was the owner's beloved Son in the fullest possible sense of the term. His death would inevitably be followed by his resurrection.

David Gooding, *According to Luke: The Third Gospel's Ordered Historical Narrative*, pp. 340–1

7th April

THE IMPLICATIONS OF THE RESURRECTION
FOR THE MESSIANIC KINGDOM

Reading: Acts 17:1–15

Explaining and proving that it was necessary for the
Christ to suffer and to rise from the dead. (v. 3)

We may briefly remind ourselves of some of the implications of that bodily resurrection. First, it shows that our Lord has not abandoned earth, and gone off as a disembodied spirit into some purely spiritual heaven. He has a body still, which, though glorified, is as literal and physical a body as it was when he was here on earth. The resurrection of his body carries implications for the whole of the physical universe. In him the restoration of all things has already commenced. Christians may, and do, differ over how many phases there will be in that restoration; but we can certainly affirm that God's programme for the establishment of our Lord's messianic reign involves earth. Creation herself, groaning though she is now, shall be delivered from her bondage to corruption. Her groanings will cease, her frustration and futility be ended (Rom 8:20–22). Even in the eternal state, we are told, there will be a new earth as well as a new heaven. God will always have a material expression of his purposes: that is guaranteed by our Lord's eternal retention of his complete human nature including his human body. We do well to remember that the last view that John was given to see of the eternal city was of that city not speeding away from earth into some immaterial heaven, but descending out of heaven towards earth (Rev 21:2).

Secondly, as Acts early reminded us, the bodily resurrection and ascension of Christ are to be followed by his bodily return. Indeed the emphasis of the New Testament is everywhere laid on the fact that the Lord Jesus will *come* again: not merely that men and women will be summoned one day to meet him in some distant heaven, but that he himself will come back again. We empty the New Testament's language of its plain significance if we reduce all its talk of his coming back to mean nothing more than his staying where he now is and our going to him. The earth where he was crucified has not seen the last of him (Rev 1:7). And thirdly, our Lord's death and bodily resurrection, so Paul subsequently told the Thessalonians in a letter he wrote them after he left, carried the guarantee that those believers who died before he returned would not miss the enjoyment of participating in his future messianic reign.

David Gooding, *True to the Faith: The Acts of the Apostles–Defining and Defending the Gospel*, pp. 339-40

8th April

JERICHO AND JUDGMENT ON THE PRINCE OF THIS WORLD

Reading: Joshua 5:13–6:21

Now is the judgment of this world; now will the ruler of this world be cast out. (John 12:31)

When Israel came into that land hitherto filled by worldliness and sinfulness of a shocking degree, how did God save them from that present evil world, with all its iniquity? There were two battles: the conquest of Jericho and the conquest of Ai. At this historical and physical level, they are twins: two sides of one coin as far as military strategy goes. In Jericho it was a question of getting in through the walls and there destroying the enemy. In Ai it was a question of drawing the enemy out of the walls, and there grasping them in a pincer movement and so destroying them.

There were two sides to the story, and if ever the law was to be established on Mount Ebal and Gerizim, both Jericho and Ai must be destroyed. When Jericho came to be destroyed, how was it done? The ark of the Lord of the whole earth led by the captain of the host—not Joshua but his greater captain (5:13–15)—marched round the city. Israel did nothing for the moment but watch as the ark and the presence of God came to judge that wicked city. But the ark had been down under the waters of Jordan, and now arisen. What must its resurrection mean to Jericho, and what must it mean that the Lord of glory, who went down to Calvary and to death, is risen and ascended? Says the Holy Spirit, 'It means this, it is evidence of the judgment of this world, for now has the prince of this world been judged' (John 12:31).

The trumpets blared, and the ark now risen went around the city. On the last day, on the seventh occasion, Joshua said, 'Shout,' and the very walls fell down and Jericho's inhabitants were destroyed. How would we be delivered from the world and all its evil? Ask the Epistle to the Galatians. By circumcision, by legalism? Certainly not. Well, then how? We'll borrow a word from Joshua's address to Achan: 'Give God the glory' (Josh 7:19). Had you found the secret of overcoming the world and being delivered from all its iniquity, you'd give God the glory too, wouldn't you? 'God forbid that I should glory, save in the cross of our Lord Jesus Christ, by whom the world is crucified unto me, and I unto the world' (Gal 6:14 KJV).

David Gooding, Entering the Inheritance: Studies in Joshua 1–12, p. 36

9th April

THE RESURRECTION CALLS FOR REPENTANCE

Reading: Acts 17:16–34

He has fixed a day on which he will judge the world in
righteousness by a man whom he has appointed. (v. 31)

Why has the resurrection of Christ made it necessary *now* to call people of all nations everywhere to repent, in a way that was not done during the preceding centuries? We shall find the answer if we recall the meaning of the phrase 'judge the world in righteousness'. Paul is not thinking simply of the judgment to be faced after death. There will, of course, be such a judgment, and it will be Christ who does the judging. 'I saw the dead', says John in the Revelation, 'great and small, standing before the throne, and . . . the dead were judged according to what they had done as recorded in the books. The sea . . . and death and Hades gave up the dead that were in them, and each person was judged according to what he had done' (Rev 20:12–13).

But Christ is going to do more than judge the dead: he is going to judge the living as well, as the New Testament repeatedly affirms, 'he is the one whom God appointed as judge of the living and the dead' (Acts 10:42); [he] is ready to judge the living and the dead' (1 Pet 4:5); 'Christ Jesus . . . will judge the living and the dead' (2 Tim 4:1). Then when will he judge the living? At his second coming, of course. The New Testament speaks of 'the coming wrath' in the sense not merely that it is future, but that it will come when the Lord Jesus comes. Recall again what Paul later wrote to the believers at Thessalonica not all that long after he left Athens:

> This will happen when the Lord Jesus is revealed from heaven in blazing fire with his powerful angels. He will punish those who do not know God and do not obey the gospel of our Lord Jesus. They will be punished with everlasting destruction and shut out from the presence of the Lord and from the majesty of his power on the day he comes . . . . (2 Thess 1:7–10)

It was indeed Paul's preaching of this coming of the Lord Jesus and the wrath that would accompany it that led many Thessalonians to turn 'to God from idols to serve the living and true God, and to wait for his Son from heaven, whom he raised from the dead—Jesus, who rescues us from the coming wrath' (1 Thess 1:9–10).

David Gooding, *True to the Faith: The Acts of the Apostles–Defining and Defending the Gospel*, pp. 356-7

10th April

THE RESURRECTION OF THE BODY

Reading: 1 Corinthians 15:35–58

It is sown a natural body; it is raised a spiritual body. (v. 44)

You sow a bare grain and what you get out is remarkably different from what went in. A brownish, wrinkled, bare grain goes in and out comes something beautifully green and luscious, with forty grains on it. It is different from what went in; yet you cannot get something out without putting something in. There is a vital connection somewhere between the two.

This applies also to our bodies. We are not altogether the same as we were some years ago. Except for those in our brain, the cells are constantly changing. We are not what we used to be; yet somehow we retain our identity. There is a connection between what is now and what there was. God is able to do it so let us be content to leave those mysteries there.

But if we would understand what the Bible means by *resurrection*, we must look a bit further. Plato, the Greek philosopher, talked about the survival of the 'never-dying soul.' He also taught that the body is a very poor thing and a wise man would keep as far away from the body as he possibly could. From those wrong and foolish notions have sprung centuries of misery for generations of people. They got it into their heads that the human body was evil, and that true spirituality was in keeping away from it. From this there arose ideas of forbidding to marry and being harsh to the body. But God made the body and he is determined that we shall have bodies eternally. He has given to the human body the supreme compliment; God himself has been manifest in flesh.

It is a wonderful thing to contemplate this mystery. In the process of redemption the Godhead has been changed, and our blessed Lord shall retain his holy and glorified body eternally. The human body is a glorious thing and what shall it be when we reach our inheritance and have a 'body to be like his glorious body' (Phil 3:21). Poets and artists have raved about the glory of even our present human bodies. But even at its best, it is a natural body 'from the earth'—descending from Adam, a living soul like Adam. The new body will be a different kind of thing; the second man, the Lord from heaven, is a 'life-giving spirit' (1 Cor 15:45). If we have borne the image of the earthy, so we shall bear the image of the heavenly, but still human.

David Gooding, *The Feasts of the Lord: Studies on the Feasts Appointed by the Lord for Israel*, p. 26

THE CAPTAIN OF OUR SALVATION

Part 9—Christ's Ascension and Exaltation

11th April

THE ASCENSION

Reading: Acts 1:1–11

*This Jesus, who was taken up from you into heaven, will come
in the same way as you saw him go into heaven. (v. 11)*

According to Luke's own record, the goings and the comings again of the
Lord during the forty days had often been instantaneous. On this occasion,
however, it was different. He chose first to ascend visibly a certain distance
up into the sky before the cloud of the shekinah glory of God enveloped
him, and there took place (by mechanisms that are as inconceivable by us
as they were invisible to the apostles) his transition into the world beyond.

That preliminary physical ascent served at least three purposes. It marked
the end of the earlier appearances: there would be no more of them. It
formed also a simple yet awe-inspiring and eloquent ceremony, expressing
in symbolic action the infinitely higher reality that, by the invitation of
the Father, Jesus of Nazareth, the Son of God, was being exalted above all
heavens, to the glory which he had had with the Father before the world
began. It served finally as a model for the second coming. The angels fixed
no dates for that coming, for angels know no more about that than anyone
else, except the Father. But they called attention to the manner of his going,
and they assured the apostles that the manner of his return would be the
same: 'This same Jesus . . . will come back in the same way you have seen
him go into heaven' (1:11). The Jesus who was the Word of God incarnate,
in and through whom God entered our space and time, was no docetic
Christ who appeared to be man when in fact he was not. He was as truly
man as he was truly God. Nor was his humanity a temporary phase in God's
self-revelation, to be superseded by some 'higher' form of revelation. The
manner of the ascension tells us that he remains this same Jesus now, when
he has returned to God's space and time, as he was in his earthly life, and as
he was when in resurrection he bade his disciples handle him and see that it
was he himself. And if in him God could and did enter our space and time
once, we are to believe the angels that he will do so again; and that he will
do so just as physically and as visibly as he was seen to leave it. In becoming
genuinely human in the cause of our redemption, the second person of the
Trinity has become what he never was before. And he will remain so eternally.

David Gooding, *True to the Faith: The Acts of the Apostles–Defining and Defending the Gospel*, p. 51

12th April

THE EXALTATION OF CHRIST DEMONSTRATED IN THE GIVING OF THE HOLY SPIRIT

Reading: Acts 2:1–21

And in the last days it shall be, God declares, that
I will pour out my Spirit on all flesh. (v. 17)

The Christian witness is not simply that Jesus of Nazareth has been raised from the dead, but that in addition to being raised he has been exalted. In the first place physically and bodily exalted, by and to the right hand of God, into the immediate presence of God. And secondly, exalted in the sense that God has made him both Lord and Messiah; that is, by exalting him God has demonstrated that he is both Lord and Messiah by giving him the position in the universe that is suited to his being both Lord and Christ, the position and status that declare him to be so. This, and no less than this, is the astounding fact that the Holy Spirit has come to earth to attest!

'This Jesus, whom you crucified', is not only Messiah; he is Lord, and Lord in the fullest sense of the term: he is Yahweh incarnate (v. 36). And the evidence of this exaltation was not that he should appear before the crowd—how would that demonstrate that he had been exalted?—but that he should be the one responsible for the pouring out of the Holy Spirit, which they could see and hear around them. At this point Peter comes back to the topic with which he began. He first identified the miraculous phenomenon taking place before their very eyes: it was the promised outpouring of the Holy Spirit. But that necessarily raised the question: 'Why now? Why after so many centuries of delay was the promised Holy Spirit being poured out at this particular festival of Pentecost?' And the answer is: 'Because of Jesus'. And it is not merely that the outpouring followed the death, resurrection and exaltation of Jesus in order to call attention to him; it is that he, upon his exaltation, did the outpouring. As the one sinless man in all of human history, he has won for mankind this supreme gift, and has received it from the Father with authority to dispense it to whomever he will. It vindicates his sinless life, but it does more. The Holy Spirit is not some created force, which any other (superior) creature could rightly control. The Holy Spirit is an uncreated, divine person. No mere human, even if sinless, could impart him to others. If Jesus Christ has poured out the Holy Spirit—and he has—the whole house of Israel might know beyond all doubt that Jesus of Nazareth is not only Messiah: he must be God.

David Gooding, *True to the Faith: The Acts of the Apostles–Defining and Defending the Gospel*, pp. 77–8

13th April

THE IMPLICATIONS OF THE LORD'S ASCENSION FOR THE BELIEVER'S JOY

Reading: John 16:17–33

In that day you will ask nothing of me. Truly, truly,
I say to you, whatever you ask of the Father in
my name, he will give it to you. (v. 23)

This promise must of course be read in its context. They would ask him for information about various things. But when it came to his resurrection and ascension, they would not need to ask him for any explanation. The direct experience of these things would be enough. And in an extended sense, this is true of all believers even though they have not physically seen the risen Lord. They do not have to ask agonizing questions about the ascension, or demand explanations as to how the Lord Jesus can still have a human body and be in the presence of God, and yet be with and in every one of his people here on earth. A believer, because he knows God as a child knows its father, knows without question that these things are true. We, as scientists, ask questions about birds: how do they manage to fly; how do they know to migrate at the right time, to the right places, even when they have never done it before? But birds don't need to ask such questions. Their 'knowledge' of these things is part of their very life as birds. And so it is with believers: since they share the life of the risen Saviour, they instinctively know the witness of the apostles to be true, the resurrection and ascension of Christ to be facts.

But experience of the risen Christ and of his 'going to the Father' would make a profound difference to their praying. They had been used to praying to God; but never before had they asked for anything from God in the name of Jesus, any more than they would have asked God for anything in the name of some now dead saint like Moses, or Jeremiah. But when they saw the risen Christ ascend, and under the Holy Spirit's instruction came to understand what it meant for him, who had come forth from the Father, to return to the Father, they would find that if they asked the Father for things which Jesus had taught them to ask for and which they could thus ask for in his name, the Father would grant their requests. And their joy in consequence would be filled full. Experience would thus show that the Jesus who had lived and walked and talked with them on earth was now not only at the pinnacle and throne of the universe, but at the heart of the Godhead.

David Gooding, *In the School of Christ: Lessons on Holiness in John 13–17*, pp. 203–4

14th April

CHRIST OUR FORERUNNER

Reading: Leviticus 23:9–14; Psalm 24

But when Christ had offered for all time a single sacrifice for sins, he sat down at the right hand of God. (Hebrews 10:12)

There is another side of our Lord's resurrection to be considered. As to his body, he is the firstfruits—he shall come for us and take us to glory. But he is firstfruits in another sense too. He is our forerunner (see Heb 6:18–20). *Firstfruits* says that there is a harvest coming. *Forerunner* says that a whole cavalcade is coming, so he has entered within the veil, informing heaven that there is a vast cavalcade coming.

You can know by the way the forerunner is treated how the cavalcade will be treated when it arrives. When the president of the United States proposes to go to China, he does not just turn up some afternoon hoping that the Chinese will welcome him. For him not to be welcomed would be a shocking blow. So he takes the precaution of sending a forerunner who goes and sees the Chinese; and if they like the look of him, then it is safe for the president to come.

Christ is risen from the dead and has gone in as the forerunner for all those who are coming behind him. He made it known from the very moment he entered glory that he was not entering for himself alone but on behalf of all the great harvest coming behind him. How was he received? He was received with open arms: 'We have such a high priest, one who is seated at the right hand of the throne of the Majesty in heaven . . . But when Christ had offered for all time a single sacrifice for sins, he sat down at the right hand of God' (Heb 8:1; 10:12). In two thousand years he has not been asked to move one centimetre. It is comforting to know that when he received our Lord Jesus Christ, God knew that he came representing us. What a Firstfruits! What a Forerunner!

In the ancient world the Jews waved the sheaf of firstfruits before the Lord. The idea is like that of a child; if he wants you to look at something and you do not look at once he will wave it in front of you. God already knew that the harvest was coming, but the priests still waved the sheaf before him. We stand here in the wilderness and 'wave' Jesus Christ our Lord before God, saying 'Look at him, I am coming behind him. You accepted him and in him you have accepted me.'

David Gooding, *The Feasts of the Lord: Studies on the Feasts Appointed by the Lord for Israel*, pp. 28–9

15th April

CHRIST'S FUTURE GLORY

Reading: Luke 9:26–36

He received honour and glory from God the Father, and the
voice was borne to him by the Majestic Glory, 'This is my
beloved Son, with whom I am well pleased'. (2 Peter 1:17)

The conversation between Christ, Moses and Elijah was about Christ's exodus at Jerusalem, about the fact that he must leave the glory of the transfiguration mount, go down into the squalid sinful world below, on to Jerusalem and death: the Son of Man had to go even as it had been ordained. Moses and Elijah therefore were now already beginning to depart when Peter suggested that it would be good if they did not go, but all stayed where they were on the mountain. He proposed in fact to make three tents, one each for Christ, Moses and Elijah, to facilitate their stay. He, like the other two apostles, had been asleep, Luke says, and he did not realize what he was saying. It was nonetheless a most unfortunate suggestion. Not only did it imply putting Moses and Elijah on a level with Christ, but it would have impeded and delayed the very going which had been planned from eternity and for which the time had now come. It was at that point in the proceedings, when having discussed his exodus Moses and Elijah were departing and Christ was turning to go down the mountain and on to his exodus, that the cloud came and Jesus received from the 'Majestic Glory' himself the tremendous accolade of honour and glory: 'This is my Son, my Chosen One; hear him'. Not only had the exodus been planned by the Father: Christ's willingness to fulfil it filled the Father's heart with delight and moved him thus to honour the Son.

As Peter reflected on this glorious event in later life, it convinced him of two things. First, the death of Christ was no tragic accident: it was foreknown, that is foreordained, before the foundation of the world (see 1 Pet 1:20). Secondly, the shame and death of the cross were no obstacle in the way of Christ's setting up of the kingdom. His willingness to suffer was the reason for the Father's delight, the grounds for his bestowing on Jesus the supreme glory. Not only had he already raised him from the dead and given him glory: one day he would do before the whole universe what he had done on the mount of transfiguration. He would glorify and vindicate his Son: Christ would come again not only in his personal glory but in the glory of the Father himself and of the holy angels. No glory would be too great for the Father to bestow upon the one crucified.

David Gooding, *According to Luke: The Third Gospel's Ordered Historical Narrative*, pp. 174–5

16th April

AUTHORITY OVER THE POWERS OF SATAN

Reading: Luke 10:1–18

The seventy-two returned with joy, saying, 'Lord, even the demons are subject to us in your name!' (v. 17)

The Seventy returned from their mission exultantly joyful in a discovery they had made: 'Even the demons, Lord,' they said, 'are subject to us in your name'. Without their knowing it, theirs was the first expression of a theme which after Pentecost and the ascension was to rise to a mighty crescendo of joy and praise as the early Christians realized the significance of Christ's being 'received up' into heaven. 'He has gone into heaven,' says Peter, 'angels and authorities and powers being made subject to him' (1 Pet 3:22). '[God] has made him to sit at his right hand in heavenly places, far above all rule, and authority, and power, and dominion, and every name that is named, not only in this [age], but also in that which is to come: and [God] put all things in subjection under his feet,' says Paul (Eph 1:20-22). Indeed Christ saw what was happening in this mission to Israel as the early successes in a war which would end in Satan being cast out of heaven completely. 'I beheld Satan fall as lightning from heaven,' he said (Luke 10:18). His vision was prophetic. The Christians after Pentecost were aware that they still had to fight against 'spiritual hosts of wickedness in the heavenly realms' (Eph 6:12). But they had no doubt about the outcome (see Rom 16:20); and what excited them as it did the Seventy was that here on earth they might exercise the triumphant authority of Christ's name. 'I have given you' said Christ, 'authority. . . over all the power of the enemy, and nothing will by any means hurt you' (Luke 10:19).

Again, the Seventy were yet to learn that possessing this authority would not exempt them from suffering or even martyrdom. It would mean, however, that nothing could hurt them by separating them from God's love; in all things they would be 'more than conquerors', and they certainly would never be hurt by the second death (see Rom 8:37; Rev 2:11).

David Gooding, *According to Luke: The Third Gospel's Ordered Historical Narrative*, p. 207

17th April

THE EXALTATION OF JESUS AND
THE PROBLEM OF EVIL

Reading: Psalm 110

*For David did not ascend into the heavens, but he himself
says, 'The LORD said to my Lord, Sit at my right hand, until
I make your enemies your footstool.' (Acts 2:34–35)*

Perhaps even so there were some in the crowd who still had a major objection: If Jesus really was King Messiah, where was there any evidence of his kingdom? When was he going to start putting an end to the problem of evil? And if he didn't do that, how could he be the Messiah? The question strikes us today with even greater force than it may have struck the Jerusalem crowd. Almost two thousand years have passed since Jesus' exaltation. But where has there ever been any serious evidence that he has even attempted to solve the problem of evil? The twentieth century in fact witnessed in the Holocaust, in Stalin's purges, in the killing fields of Cambodia, and in a thousand atrocities besides, an out-flowering of evil greater perhaps than any previous century. Jesus has obviously not attempted to stamp out evil. How then is it credible that he is both Lord and Messiah?

Once more the psalm has the answer. It was never part of God's programme that the Messiah should proceed immediately upon his exaltation to stamp out evil. The invitation was: 'Sit at my right hand *until* I make your enemies your footstool.' There was to be an interval between his exaltation and the subjugation of his enemies, during which he would be seated at God's right hand, awaiting the time of his second coming. Only then would his enemies be made the footstool of his feet. And what a mercy it was that this interval was written into the programme, for the sake of us all, of course, but particularly for the crowd who stood listening to Peter. They had crucified God incarnate, and he was now elevated to the position of supreme power in the universe. What if there had been no interval and he had proceeded at once to stamp out evil? We are, Peter pointed out, already in the last days of this present age. The cosmic convulsions will occur soon enough, to be followed by the great and resplendent Day of the Lord and the dawning of the messianic age to come. But thank God for the present interval.

David Gooding, True to the Faith: The Acts of the Apostles–Defining and Defending the Gospel, pp. 78–9

18th April

OUR FUTURE IS SECURE

Reading: Psalm 102:18–28

*The children of your servants shall dwell secure; their
offspring shall be established before you. (v. 28)*

The Creator is eternal, but the created heavens and earth are only temporary
and one day must perish and be discarded. We human beings are creatures.
What assurance can we have that the Creator will never discard any human
being who by faith has entered into a personal relationship with God? See
here the explicit and absolute assurance! The Creator himself has become
human, has entered our temporary world of space and time with authority
to give us eternal life; he has prayed to be saved from death, to be glorified in
the Father's presence with the glory he had with the Father before the world
began (John 17:1–5). And his prayer has been answered! God has raised
him from the dead and he has carried his humanity to the very bosom
of the Godhead. The eternal Creator who is eternally the same (Ps 102:27)
has for ever become Jesus the man, 'the same yesterday and today and
for ever' (Heb 13:8). And God the Father has assured him in the words of
Psalm 102:28: 'The children of your servants will live in your presence; their
descendants will be established before you.' Or in the words of the New
Testament: 'God raised us up with Christ and seated us with him in the
heavenly realms in Christ Jesus, in order that in the coming ages he might
show the incomparable riches of his grace, expressed in his kindness to us in
Christ Jesus' (Eph 2:6–7). For this is what God had in mind when he chose
us in Christ before the creation of this temporary world (Eph 1:4).

And what is more: none of those who have believed in him, and have lived
and worked for his coming kingdom, will miss it, no matter in what distant
century they lived and died. For those who are Christ's shall be made alive
at his coming (1 Cor 15:22–23); and when the Lord appears in his glory, and
sets up his kingdom, them also will God bring with him (1 Thess 4:13–18).

David Gooding, *An Unshakeable Kingdom: The Letter to the Hebrews for Today*, pp. 67–8

THE CAPTAIN OF OUR SALVATION

Part 10—Our Great High Priest

19th April

GOD'S GIFT OF A HIGH PRIEST

Reading: Hebrews 7:23–8:6

*For it was indeed fitting that we should have such
a high priest, holy, innocent, unstained, separated from
sinners, and exalted above the heavens. (7:26)*

In view of Israel's waywardness, uncleanness and the weakness and inherent imperfection of their worship, it was merciful of God to provide them with a high priest and representative who could intervene between them and God and offer incense on their behalf before God. A thin plate of gold which Aaron had to wear on his forehead carried the words: 'Holy to the Lord'. Their significance was this:

> Aaron shall bear any guilt from the holy things that the people of Israel consecrate as their holy gifts. It shall regularly be on his forehead, that they may be accepted before the Lord. (Exod 28:38 ESV)

These were not idle words. Early on in Aaron's ministry, two of his sons each took his censer and put fire in it and laid incense on it and offered unauthorized fire before the Lord which he had not commanded them. And fire came out from before the Lord and consumed them, and they died before the Lord.

> Then Moses said to Aaron, 'This is what the Lord has said, "Among those who are near me I will be sanctified, and before all the people I will be glorified."' (Lev 10:3 ESV)

To modern sensibilities this may sound barbarous; but that is because our modern western world has lost awareness of the infinite glory and holiness of God. If an otherwise sane person were to imagine he could improve a painting by Rembrandt by dabbing paint on it, the art-loving world would be outraged. The living God is 'a consuming fire'; and we must learn to offer service to him with reverence and awe (Heb 12:28–29). We lose that sense of awe at our peril. Aaron himself eventually failed. At Sinai he was too lenient with the people (Exod 32:1–5, 21). Later he misrepresented God and paid the penalty (Num 20:12–13, 23–29). It did but emphasize the need for another priest to arise, not after the Aaronic order, but after the order of Melchizedek.

David Gooding, *The Riches of Divine Wisdom: The New Testament's Use of the Old Testament*, p. 295

2Oth April

THE NECESSITY OF OUR HIGH PRIEST

Reading: Hebrews 9:11–28

He entered once for all into the holy places, not by means of the blood of goats and calves but by means of his own blood, thus securing an eternal redemption. (v. 12)

Many of us have too small an idea of our Lord's high priesthood. We speak of him in that capacity as though he held a sinecure, as though we should be saved anyway, even if he did not minister as a high priest. But that is not true. We would all be lost if we did not have a high priest who constantly and incessantly intercedes for us. We began our spiritual path when we realized that his sacrifice put away all the guilt of our sin. We look back to that with joy. But there is more to his saving ministry than that. It is not enough to begin the path of spiritual pilgrimage. Beginning would all be in vain if we did not continue all the way through our spiritual journey and enter our heavenly inheritance at last. How then shall we continue? How can we be sure of entering in at last?

The answer is: we have a high priest! In spite of our failures in the past, through him there is mercy for us at God's throne: we need not abandon our confession of faith. In spite of the temptations ahead, he understands what temptation means, and through him there will be grace to help us in our time of need. He is able to save us completely (7:25). What is more, our high priest has himself gone through the heavens, says 4:14. He has sat down at the right hand of the Majesty in heaven, says 8:1. That is, he has already entered and arrived in the heaven towards which we are making our way. He has gone before us not merely because he started out before we did and therefore has arrived first. He has entered heaven on our behalf as our official forerunner, or precursor, announcing to all concerned that we are coming on behind, and by his ministry as our high priest guaranteeing our eventual safe arrival (6:20).

David Gooding, An Unshakeable Kingdom: The Letter to the Hebrews for Today, pp. 115–6

21st April

CHRIST'S DIVINE APPOINTMENT AS HIGH PRIEST

Reading: Hebrews 7:1–22

You are a priest for ever, after the order of Melchizedek. (v. 17)

Only remember what we are talking about. We are discussing an office invented for the purpose of looking after ignorant and straying people and designed to bring them, in spite of their weaknesses and wanderings, safely through their spiritual pilgrimage home to God's heaven. How important is this office of looking after such ignorant, wayward weaklings? To our astonishment we discover that it is an office of immeasurable majesty. It is doubly so. First, because of the transcendent glory of the one who confers the office: he is the almighty God. And secondly, because of the unique relationship with God of the one on whom the office is conferred. The proclamation of conferment brings both together. It is the very one, observes our writer, who said to Messiah, 'You are my Son; today I have begotten you,' who also says, 'You are a priest for ever, in the order of Melchizedek.'

Contemplate too the indescribable majesty of the appointment ceremony. Psalm 2 graphically depicts the triumph of our Lord's resurrection and ascension: Jesus, as God's King installed by God on God's holy hill of Zion, declaring before the entire universe the divine decree: '[The LORD] said to me, "You are my Son, today I have begotten you."' Now we listen as the composer of Psalm 110 takes over as commentator on this same awesome occasion. We hear first the Lord God Almighty address the words of the invitation to the ascended Lord Messiah: 'Sit at my right hand until I make your enemies a footstool for your feet' (Ps 110:1). And then as the ceremony proceeds we hear the Almighty utter the great oath of appointment: 'The LORD has sworn and will not change his mind: You are a priest for ever in the order of Melchizedek' (Ps 110:4). 'Priest for whom?' we ask; for instinct tells us that if induction into this office is attended with such exalted ceremony, the office itself must be of cosmic significance, its objectives infinitely important, and its beneficiaries blessed beyond all possible calculation.

'For whom is he priest?' we repeat. And the answer comes back 'For those who have trusted the Saviour.' 'What for?' we ask. 'To save them from their ignorance and wandering, to save them completely, and to present them faultless at last before the presence of his glory with exceeding joy' (see Jude 24 KJV).

David Gooding, An Unshakeable Kingdom: The Letter to the Hebrews for Today, pp. 117–8

22nd April

A HIGH PRIEST OVER THE HOUSE OF GOD

Reading: Exodus 28:6–43

It shall be on Aaron's forehead, and Aaron shall
bear any guilt from the holy things that the people
of Israel consecrate as their holy gifts. (v. 38)

We have a great priest, that is a high priest, over the house of God. When the young Israelite priests began their complicated duties in the solemn courts of the temple, it must have been a comfort to them to have a high priest who was an expert and could show them just what to do and how to behave in the divine presence.

Thank God, as we come into the awesome dwelling place of God, we have a high priest to take us by the hand, to present us at court, to prompt and lead our praise and prayer, and to tell us how to behave before the Majesty in the heavens. Israel's high priest wore on his mitre a plate of pure gold engraved with the words 'Holy to the LORD'. He did this, Scripture explains, so that he might 'bear the guilt involved in the sacred gifts the Israelites consecrate. . . It will be on Aaron's forehead continually so that they will be acceptable to the LORD' (v. 36–38). So Christ—only in a far fuller sense—has made himself responsible for the imperfections of our worship and prayers. He has borne the guilt not only of the sins we did as sinners, but also of our sins and imperfections as saints and worshippers. We may therefore enter boldly into the very presence of God through the veil, not because we have merit, or have attained to an advanced stage of sanctification; but in spite of all our imperfections, thanks solely to Jesus Christ, our Lord, Saviour and high priest.

David Gooding, *An Unshakeable Kingdom: The Letter to the Hebrews for Today*, pp. 193–4

23rd April

THE SCOPE OF THE ETERNAL PRIESTHOOD

Reading: John 13:33–14:7

*In my Father's house are many rooms. If it were not so, would
I have told you that I go to prepare a place for you? (14:2)*

In the ancient earthly temple of God in Jerusalem the service of God was
not performed by all the people of God. It was restricted to members of one
special tribe, the tribe of Levi, who were set apart and consecrated to act as
priests on behalf of the laity. Because of their ordination, they were regarded
as specially holy and privileged to enter into parts of the temple where the
laity were not allowed to come. But in Christ all such limitations, distinctions,
and special privileges are abolished. Now all the people of God are priests.
They are so here and now: 'You yourselves . . . are being built up as a spiritual
house, to be a holy priesthood, to offer spiritual sacrifices acceptable to God
through Jesus Christ' (1 Pet 2:5). All the redeemed sing their praise to Christ,
along with the Apostle John, 'To him who loves us and has freed us from our
sins by his blood and made us a kingdom, priests to his God and Father, to
him be glory and dominion for ever and ever' (Rev 1:5–6). And for all the
redeemed in heaven the promise is given:

> Therefore they are before the throne of God, and serve him day and
> night in his temple . . . and his servants will worship him. They will
> see his face, and his name will be on their foreheads. (Rev 7:15; 22:3–4)

Words are inadequate to express the grandeur and the magnificence of this
provision of a place in the Father's house on high. Its effect will be perfect
and eternal. It is something, moreover, that we do not have to provide or
work out for ourselves. It is altogether the unaided work and provision of
Christ. And our Lord tells us about it already while we are still on earth, not
to make us careless, but for the very opposite purpose: to foster our determination to be holy. While we are still surrounded by trials and temptations,
and while from time to time we still stumble and fall, we are to know that the
ultimate goal is secure. We need never give up, we need never lose heart. We
shall one day be conformed to the Lord Jesus. We shall one day be perfectly
holy. We shall be with him forever. There will come a day when our devotion
to the divine persons will never again be less than complete.

David Gooding, *In the School of Christ: Lessons on Holiness in John 13–17*, pp. 81–2

24th April

THE INTERCESSION OF CHRIST

Reading: Zechariah 1:1–17

*Consequently, he is able to save to the uttermost those
who draw near to God through him, since he always
lives to make intercession for them. (Hebrews 7:25)*

Where now shall come the initiative for revival and restoration? We hear the answer as that terrible silence is broken by the intercessions; not of Israel to be sure, many of whom were snoring in their beds. The silence is broken by the intercessions of the one the prophet here describes as the angel of the LORD— none other than the one we would call the second person of the Trinity.

Now indeed we are introduced to something most wonderful and most sacred. Not only to hear the intercessions of him whom we in subsequent ages have learnt to love so well, but to hear the actual contents of his intercession as he interceded with God on the behalf of his people. Our hearts take a leap and our spiritual pulses begin to race. How many a night, my brother and sister, when you've gone to bed exhausted, worried, tired and depressed, and you were sunk in sleep, sleeping maybe for very sorrow, there was heard in the heavenly courts above the voice of your great intercessor calling upon the divine Father, discussing with him his discipline of your case and pleading for you. A time of new initiative, new beginnings, new surges of power and new accomplishments.

We owe more than we can imagine, not to our zeal but to his; to the one who daily intercedes for us and ever shall. And if, thinking in human terms, we observe how successful his intercessions were then, what shall we feel in our age? We live in days when the blessed second person of the Trinity has long since become human and known from practical experience what temptation and opposition means; he has learnt obedience by the things which he suffered. He has run the race and knows the energy required for running it to the end. He has endured the cross and now has sat down. God has given him to us, appointed by divine oath as our priest forever, after the order of Melchizedek. Surely you will be restored if it depends upon his intercession. Hear him now as he discusses with God the matter of God's discipline and hear an infinitely touching thing. He cries to God the Father, 'How long will you have no mercy on Jerusalem and the cities of Judah, against which you have been angry these seventy years?' (Zech 1:12).

David Gooding, The God of Restoration: Four Studies in the Prophecy of Zechariah, pp. 8–9

25th April

TO HIM WHO IS ABLE TO KEEP YOU

Reading: John 17:6–19

Now unto him that is able to keep you from falling, and to present
you faultless before the presence of his glory with exceeding joy, to
the only wise God our Saviour, be glory and majesty, dominion
and power, both now and ever. Amen. (Jude 24–25 KJV)

Ponder it again in these quiet moments as you sit before the Lord. And
if you're a believer in the Lord Jesus, know this: that you only became
a believer because the transcendent Lord of heaven and earth bowed down
to you and personally caused you to hear his voice, like little Samuel in the
temple, and called you by name. You are known to God himself, personally
and individually called by God himself. And he shall keep you: 'Now unto
him that is able to keep you from falling and to present you faultless before
the presence of his glory with exceeding joy' (v. 24 KJV).

I love those words that our Lord uttered in his prayer before the shades
of Gethsemane closed in upon them. Reviewing his life's ministry and the
handful of men that were around him, he said to his Father, 'Of all you have
given me, I have lost not one, save the son of perdition; that the Scripture
might be fulfilled. But of all those who were genuine believers, I have lost
not one.' And then with very deep poignancy he turns to his Father and
says, 'But now I'm no longer in the world, and I must hand to you the task
of keeping them. Now I come to thee, Holy Father, keep them—you keep
them' (see John 17:11–12).

And I say to myself, 'I say, my good man, ponder a moment; if the Lord
Jesus in his ministry could say, "I have kept them and not one of them is
lost", shall the Father do less than the Son, and shall the Father not keep
them with all that same devotion and with all that same effectiveness and
success as the blessed Lord Jesus kept them in the days of his flesh?' Ah, he
shall indeed, and he shall present you before the presence of his glory with
exceeding joy! And the time draws near.

David Gooding, *How Religion Goes Wrong: Four Studies in the Epistle of Jude*, pp. 10–11

THE CAPTAIN OF OUR SALVATION

Part 11—The Lord's Return

26th April

THE COMING OF THE LORD MEANS
JOY FOR THE OPPRESSED

Reading: Luke 18:1–8

*And will not God give justice to his elect, who cry to him
day and night? Will he delay long over them? (v. 7)*

For the ungodly the coming of the Son of Man will be an event of unrelieved disaster; but for God's elect the assurance of that coming is a veritable gospel, for then all the wrongs which they have suffered will be put right. All down the ages God's elect have from time to time suffered injustices and persecutions, and the sufferings which they will be called upon to endure at the end of the age before the appearance of Christ will be of unparalleled severity (see Matt 24:21–22). It is only natural that they should cry to God, not for revenge on their enemies, but for God to intervene and put a stop to all the evils perpetrated on them by unprincipled individuals and governments. After all, is God not interested in justice and in seeing justice done?

The problem then is not that Christians should cry to God to be avenged but that when they cry he remains silent and appears to do nothing, until in the end God's elect are tempted to think that it is no use appealing to God. Either he does not hear them, or else he does not really care. Yet, Christ insists, it is imperative that God's elect should persist in praying and not give up (see Luke 18:1); for to cease praying would be to call in question the very character of God. The judge in the parable was wicked and unprincipled enough, caring for neither God nor man. But even he eventually gave in to the widow's persistent pleading. And shall we give up appealing to God and so make him out to be more unfeeling, more unjust than the unjust judge himself? To give up praying would be calamitous: it would imply that God, if there is one, is so indifferent to justice that we can have no reasonable hope for a coming reign of justice on earth nor of any heaven above worth going to.

One day God will avenge his elect. Christ stakes his truthfulness on it. God will intervene: the Son of Man will come. Justice will be done. But will he find us still believing in God's justice (v. 8)? If meanwhile we have stopped praying, how shall we then satisfactorily explain to him why we doubted his character?

David Gooding, *According to Luke: The Third Gospel's Ordered Historical Narrative*, pp. 307–8

27th April

THE RESURRECTION OF LAZARUS
AND THE COMING OF THE LORD

Reading: John 11:1–44

*Then Jesus told them plainly, 'Lazarus has died, and
for your sake I am glad that I was not there, so that
you may believe. But let us go to him.' (vv. 14–15)*

The resurrection of the believer will not take place in our Lord's absence. He will not sit on the throne of heaven and suddenly speak the word, and then all the dead will rise. So the raising of Lazarus is a sign of the great reality of the resurrection and the reuniting of the living and the dead when the Lord comes. Therefore we have the demonstration that Martha and Mary sent the letter to him: 'He whom you love is sick'. It was a prayer for Lazarus's recovery, for healing from his sickness. But our Lord stayed away and let Lazarus die. And then raised him when he came!

What a simple parable that is. It is a miracle, but it is also a parable, of course. It is put here to prepare the Lord's people for our Lord's going away. He was crucified, is risen, has ascended back to heaven. What happens now when our loved ones get sick? Well, of course, we send a message to the Lord, don't we? 'Lord, dear brother so-and-so has been taken into hospital with a heart attack.' If it pleases the Lord, he will give him recovery, and often he does. But ultimately he doesn't, does he? Am I not right in saying that, since the Lord ascended to heaven, most believers have died? I'm not denying that sometimes the Lord answers our prayer and heals our loved ones when they are sick; he does that. But, ultimately, until the Lord comes, we shall all die. There's no need to get upset about it. Look at the pattern. The dead will be raised and reunited with the living when the Lord comes.

This sign for Martha and Mary and Lazarus is also a parable for us, so that we should not be disturbed when our Lord in his absence allows our loved ones to die. It holds out the promise of his second coming. He will come again!

David Gooding, *Four Journeys to Jerusalem: A Series of Seminars on the Gospel of John*, pp. 144–5

28th April

THE SECOND COMING OF THE LORD

Reading: Luke 17:20–37

But first he must suffer many things and be
rejected by this generation. (v. 25)

In regard to this coming our Lord proceeded to issue two warnings. First, his disciples would naturally come to long for his appearing; but that very longing could lead them into wishfully thinking he had come when he had not. He therefore pointed out once more the folly of those who would say 'See, there,' or 'See, here' (v. 23); only this time the folly lay differently from before. In verse 21 it was foolish to say 'See, here,' when what was supposedly being pointed at was by definition invisible. Here in verse 23 the folly lies in suggesting that something needs to be pointed out when in fact it is impossible for anyone not to see it. The disciples, therefore, were to be wary of all claims that the Messiah had been actually sighted somewhere or other, or that the kingdom had already come. When the Son of Man appeared, no one would need to tell anybody.

The second warning was that before his glorious appearing he must first be rejected by this generation (see vv. 25-30). When his disciples eventually saw him suffer, this prediction would steady their faith (24:6–8). But in its context in the discourse it serves another purpose as well. It explains why, in spite of generations of Christian preaching, the second coming will take the world by surprise. The term 'rejected by this generation' points specifically to the fact that his generation would examine his claims to be Messiah and repudiate them. As long, therefore, as Israel, or the nations for that matter, held that view, they would deny the very possibility of his return. Hence their surprise and unpreparedness when it takes place.

Two analogies are used to drive the lesson home. During 'the days of Noah' men disbelieved his preaching (see 2 Pet 2:5); the day of the flood surprised and destroyed them. During 'the days of Lot' the people of Sodom mocked at his testimony; the day Lot left, to their consternation the judgment of God actually fell and destroyed them. In the same way, after a long period of warning largely disregarded by the world, there shall come a day when the Son of Man shall suddenly and unexpectedly be revealed (Luke 17:30; 1 Thess 5:3). It will be a day of apocalyptic judgment (see 2 Thess 1:7–9; 2:8–12).

David Gooding, *According to Luke: The Third Gospel's Ordered Historical Narrative*, pp. 305–6

29th April

FINAL SALVATION AT THE LORD'S RETURN

Reading: Genesis 5:18–24; Hebrews 11:5–6; Matthew 24:36–51

Enoch walked with God, and he was not, for
God took him. (Genesis 5:24)

Enoch's removal to heaven without dying naturally reminds us of the final stage of our salvation, when the Lord comes. Millions of believers from all over the world will similarly be removed to heaven without dying. 'We will not all sleep, but we will all be changed—in a flash, in the twinkling of an eye, at the last trumpet. For the trumpet will sound, the dead will be raised imperishable, and we will be changed' (1 Cor 15:51–52).

So we may take a lesson from Enoch. 'By faith Enoch was taken from this life, so that he did not experience death.' How 'by faith'? And how does our author know it was by faith? Because, he points out, before Enoch was removed, it was said of him that he pleased God. And since (so the author argues) it is impossible to please God without faith—indeed, you cannot truly come to God at all without believing—Enoch must have been a true believer. And it was because he was a true believer that he was taken to heaven without dying.

The lesson is clear. The Lord's coming draws ever nearer. If we are alive when he comes, and we wish to be caught up to meet him in the air (1 Thess 4:17), we too must be true believers. How, then, shall we show we are? By daily walking with God, by living constantly to please him. The Apostle John makes the same point. When the Lord appears, he says, 'we shall be like him, for we shall see him as he is' (1 John 3:2). The hope is glorious. But then he adds, 'Everyone who has this hope in him purifies himself, just as he is pure' (v. 3). Notice that this is a statement of fact, not an exhortation. It is the fact that every one that has the hope purifies himself. Anyone who consistently neglects to purify himself shows that he does not possess the hope. He is not a true believer.

David Gooding, *An Unshakeable Kingdom: The Letter to the Hebrews for Today*, p. 206

30th April

WAITING FOR THE MESSIAH

Reading: Daniel 1:17–21; 6:1–10; Matthew 25:14–30

*For it will be like a man going on a journey, who called his
servants and entrusted to them his property. (Matthew 25:14)*

While Daniel did hold that the only hope for the world was the coming of
the Messiah, he didn't run away from life. It stares you in the face, if you
read the historical chapters of his memoirs. Given the chance of a university
education in Babylon, he didn't say, 'No, why would you bother about education? Messiah is coming!' Given the chance, though in a Gentile society, he
thought it was worth taking. For God's sake, for his own sake, for his people's sake, it was worth taking. He sweated away at learning Akkadian (not
an easy language), and all the business of cuneiform and administration.
Though a lot of that education was based on funny mythologies, he thought
it worthwhile learning what these people believed. Offered a place in the
civil service later on, he took it. He must have applied himself diligently
because he rose to great eminence. He was adviser to sundry of the kings of
Babylon, and when the Persians took over he became for a little while head
of the Persian administration. He did not run away from life.

I might add at once that the belief that the only hope for the world is
the coming of Christ, is not a recipe for running away from life. Not even
now! Why didn't he run away from life? Because, as he himself will make
clear, even suppose the Messiah were not due to come for centuries, life
is still worth living. It is in the daily affairs of life, in the here and now (in
business, in school, in the factory, in the lawyer's office, and in the home
predominantly), as we face life and live it under God, that we are facing
life's chief purpose. This temporary life is given to us as the time in which
we prepare for the eternal beyond.

Daniel was told that the Messiah would not come for centuries. He did
not say, 'Then it's no good living.' He gave himself to life, in the fear of God,
because he knew and believed that this life was given to prepare him for
meeting God. Though the Messiah would not come for centuries, when
Daniel's short life was over he knew he would have to meet God.

David Gooding, Daniel: Civil Servant and Saint, pp. 14–15

THE DISCIPLE'S JOURNEY

Part 1—Where We Begin: Our Justification and Salvation

1st May

SALVATION AS A GIFT

Reading: Psalm 50:1–9

*Nor is he served by human hands, as though he
needed anything, since he himself gives to all mankind
life and breath and everything. (Acts 17:25)*

From the earliest days, so the Old Testament indicates, God taught people
to offer sacrifices for sin. They were never intended as payments to God that
purchased forgiveness from him, and certainly not as bribes to encourage
him to forgive. They were divinely appointed symbols that taught mankind
that sin cannot be forgiven without the payment of the penalty of sin. The
animal sacrifices never paid that penalty themselves: they were but symbols
and foreshadowings of the great 'payment for sin' that God himself in the
person of Christ would one day pay at the cross. Similarly, God ordained
that people could bring animals and other things as offerings to express
their gratitude to him for his many gifts. But again those offerings were only
symbolic; none of them were payments to God for the gifts given.

Much later in Israel the more subtle idea came to be prevalent that somehow the sin offerings paid God for his forgiveness and that sacrifices could
purchase God's blessings. It led to God's protest: 'I have no need of a bull
from your stall or of goats from your pens, for every animal of the forest is
mine . . . If I were hungry I would not tell you, for the world is mine, and all
that is in it' (Ps 50:9–12). You cannot pay God with coins that are his anyway.
The idea that you can is self-evidently false.

More sophisticated versions of this basic fallacy have troubled Christendom.
One of them is that if we are good, we can accumulate merit that we can then use
in order to gain God's forgiveness, or a place in his heaven. And another is that the
work of our hands and the offering of ourselves in service to God can somehow
become part of Christ's sacrifice for sin, and so help to procure forgiveness for us.

All this is but a refined expression of the pagan idea which Paul exposed at
Athens. Its sadness lies in the way it misreads and misinterprets the heart and
character of the true God. He is not in business. He does not sell his love or his
forgiveness to us spiritually bankrupt sinners, nor can we buy his salvation. His
love gives it to us freely. If he uses the metaphor of buying, he does so in order
to emphasize that we have no price to pay: 'Come, all you who are thirsty . . .
Come, buy wine and milk without money and without cost' (Isa 55:1).

David Gooding, *True to the Faith: The Acts of the Apostles–Defining and Defending the Gospel*, pp. 363–4

2nd May

THE WASHING OF REGENERATION

Reading: Titus 3

He saved us, not because of works done by us in righteousness,
but according to his own mercy, by the washing of
regeneration and renewal of the Holy Spirit. (v. 5)

The very description of this initial experience of salvation introduces two
ideas. In the first place it is a washing, a cleansing away of evil and polluted
things. In the second place it is regeneration, the positive implanting of
a new life, and a new order of living. The Holy Spirit washes us by bringing
us to see the wrong and evil in our sinful attitudes and desires. He makes us
feel their uncleanness, and leads us to repent of them and repudiate them.
More deeply than that, he brings us to see that, in spite of all our efforts
to improve ourselves, we cannot eradicate these evil powers within us: we
need a Saviour. We cry out in the secret of our hearts: 'O wretched man that
I am! Who shall deliver me? For all too often the good things I want to do,
I don't do; and the bad things I don't want to do, I do' (see Rom 7:15–25).
And he brings us to the point where we are prepared for all the changes of
lifestyle that we must be willing to accept, if we receive Christ from now
on as Saviour and Lord of our lives.

But then Christ does not leave it there. Nor does he simply exhort us from
now on to try to do good works and to lead a Christian life. His provision
for making us holy is much more radical than that. He implants within us
the very life of the Holy Spirit of God, an utterly new and spotlessly clean
life that we never possessed before, a new life with new powers and new
desires and new abilities to lead a life pleasing to God, since it is the life
of the Spirit of God himself. That does not mean that when a person first
trusts the Saviour and receives the new life of the Spirit of God, that person
immediately becomes sinlessly perfect, but it does mean that there is now
within that person a life that has the power to rise up and overcome the wrong
desires and attitudes of his sinful heart. It is as though one planted an acorn
inside a sepulchre. It would not improve the corpse that lay rotting inside; but
from that acorn and amidst all that corruption there would grow up a new
life, vigorous, strong, perfectly clean and beautiful, that was not there before.

David Gooding, *In the School of Christ: Lessons on Holiness in John 13–17*, pp. 24–5

3rd May

AGREEING WITH GOD'S VERDICT ON SIN

Reading: Joshua 5:13–6:21

*And when the LORD your God gives them over to you, and
you defeat them, then you must devote them to complete
destruction. You shall make no covenant with them
and show no mercy to them. (Deuteronomy 7:2)*

When God took Israel into the land of Canaan he insisted that they join him
in the execution of his judgment upon those evil cities. Why do you think
he did that? God needn't have done it that way. He could have said to the
Israelites, 'You stay in one of the oases like Kadesh-Barnea. There's plenty of
palm trees and beautiful water. You can stay there for a few months while
I execute my long threatened wrath upon the evil cities of Canaan.'

He could have used the same method that he used with Sodom and
Gomorrah and burned them up. Having cleaned the whole place up, then
he could have brought his people into their promised land. But he didn't do
that. When God executed his wrath upon the cities of Canaan with all their
evil, he said to Israel, 'You'll come with me and do it. What is more, you will
agree with me that it's right to do it.'

I find there are many people who profess to be Christians but have no
assurance of salvation in their hearts. I have long since come to the conclusion
that one of the reasons for this is that they have bypassed this initial step in
their conversion. This stands at the very entry—this is our Jericho. It is to
agree with God's judgment that we all have sinned. Not only have we sinned
in the past, but no matter how long we live it will still be true of us that we
come short of the glory of God. God will not bend his law, the penalty of
his law must be carried out. When God says therefore that nobody can be
saved through keeping the law he's not disparaging his law, he's maintaining
it. None of this, 'Do the best you can and in the end, even if you come short,
God will be merciful.' That's nonsense. No heaven can be built on the principle
of anything being near-enough right.

David Gooding, What Moses Could Not Do: Nine Studies in the Book of Joshua, pp. 35–6

4th May

RAHAB AND TRUE REPENTANCE

Reading: Joshua 2

*You turned to God from idols to serve the living and true God, and
to wait for his Son from heaven, whom he raised from the dead,
Jesus who delivers us from the wrath to come. (1 Thess 1:9–10)*

God's judgment on Jericho was severe, but Rahab and all her family were
saved, and any of her friends that gathered in her house. On what grounds
were they saved, when all the rest of Jericho perished? Was Rahab better than
the others? Well hardly—she'd been the town prostitute. On what principle
was she saved and how did she escape the judgment of God? Indeed, on what
principle did she become incorporated with the people of God and enjoy the
inheritance with them for the rest of her lifetime? The Bible has the answer,
'By faith Rahab the prostitute did not perish with those who were disobedient, because she had given a friendly welcome to the spies' (Heb 11:31).

It was simply by faith. She had no good works to recommend her, nothing
but a tarnished past. But she turned to God from idols, to serve the living and
the true God, and to wait. As the armies of God massed outside the wall she
knew that any day now they'd be coming and Joshua would destroy the city.
Rahab knew in her heart she would be saved because she believed the word of
God. But the apostle James says that Rahab was justified by her works, 'And
in the same way was not also Rahab the prostitute justified by works when
she received the messengers and sent them out by another way?' (Jas 2:25).

I believe what James says as well—was Rahab not justified by her works? Of
course she was, but what works? She received the spies with peace, showing
that her repentance was real. She left the side of Jericho, her citizens and the
king, and came over to the side of the people of God. She received the spies,
believed the word of God and declared her loyalty with the people of God.
It was a genuine conversion, and to make it clear she bound the cord in the
window of her little house up on the wall.

This is salvation. Accepting the fact that judgment is coming and owning
we are worthy of it; upholding therefore the law of God. It is repenting,
acknowledging we cannot save ourselves and putting our faith in the Saviour,
receiving the oath that has guaranteed we shall be saved from the coming
wrath. By taking our stand with the people of God and binding his word in
our hearts we show that our repentance is genuine.

David Gooding, What Moses Could Not Do: Nine Studies in the Book of Joshua, pp. 37–8

5th May

RECEIVING THEN WORKING

Reading: Genesis 17

When Abram was ninety-nine years old the LORD appeared to Abram and said to him, 'I am God Almighty; walk before me, and be blameless'. (v. 1)

I was sitting recently with a colleague of mine at dinner, and he was talking about the sundry religions that had come knocking on his front door offering their goods. And when opportunity arose I said, 'Have you noticed that there is one difference between true Christianity and all other religions?' He hadn't, so I had to tell him. It comes in many different ways and forms, but it amounts to the same thing. Religion says, 'Work out your salvation, discipline yourself, do this, do that, do this other; and by doing it perhaps at length you will arrive at your goal.' Religion is a matter of *doing*.

'But you will notice,' I said, 'that when you come to Christ he offers you salvation as a free gift.' That is the great difference. 'For the wages of sin is death, but the free gift of God is eternal life in Christ Jesus our Lord' (Rom 6:23).

It is a simple matter, then, to tell the difference between true Christianity and religion. Religion says do, earn, merit, achieve. Christ says, *'Come and receive a gift!'*

My colleague immediately said, 'That cannot be! If salvation is a gift you can go out and do as you please!' It is understandable that unsaved people should talk like that, but it is not true. When we do believe God and enter into a personal relationship with him, something new begins. The believer is required to walk before God now, with no time off! There are no holidays from this holy occupation; we are constantly walking before God living in fellowship with him. God holds this goal out before us, 'Walk before me, and be blameless.'

Please notice which way round it is! God did not say to Abraham, 'I want you to try and walk perfect before me, and if you succeed I will receive you in the end.' It was the other way round. 'I have received you. Therefore, walk before me and be perfect.' There are those two parts, but they come in that order. It is important at the outset that we see this. Receiving salvation as a gift does not mean that we are then free to go and live as we please. Receiving salvation is entering a relationship with God that is meant to be active every moment from then on.

David Gooding, The God of New Beginnings: Eighteen Seminars on the Book of Genesis, p. 114

6th May

THE LEGAL BASIS OF OUR SANCTIFICATION

Reading: Romans 6

*Knowing this, that our old man was crucified with
him, that the body of sin might be done away, that
so we should no longer be in bondage to sin; For he
that has died is justified from sin. (vv. 6–7 RV)*

It does not say 'sanctified' but 'justified'. Do notice the term and resist any temptation to make it mean something different here from what it means in chapter 3. What does it mean, 'he that has died is *justified* from sin'?

Well, suppose you had committed murder, and you were convicted in the old days when murder was a capital offence. The law wouldn't be satisfied until you were hanged. If somehow you got out of prison, the law would follow you around the whole earth until it caught up with you and insisted the penalty be paid. When it was paid, and you were executed, the law wouldn't chase you anymore. You would have been *justified*. Why? Well, the penalty had been paid. This is justification by the penalty having been paid.

'He that has died has been justified from sin.' If it is true that Christ died for our sins according to the Scriptures—that he paid the penalty of the law, then the law has no more against us. We are justified. Now, I'll tell you something. There is said to be a book up in heaven that records all the deeds and sins of every single person that has ever lived (see Rev 20:12). So, my name is there on the list. Wouldn't you like to get to heaven and (if you could) bribe the archangel and the recording angel just to have a look inside that book? 'Please turn under the letter G. We'd like to see what the truth is about this chap who sits there pontificating to us. I daresay there are some hidden things and red ink all over the place.' Well, you would see that. And a sorry list it would be! But if you then asked the law what it was going to do about it, it would look and say, 'The whole lot's crossed out. Don't you see that? He is dead.'

You'd say, 'That's funny, I saw him the other Saturday morning (talking rather too much). What do you mean, he has died?'

'Well,' the law says, 'as far as I know he has died, because he has accepted Christ and, as far as I am concerned, when Christ died, he died too.' What a tremendous relief to the likes of me to know it: 'He that has died has been justified from sin.' This is the basis of our practical sanctification.

David Gooding, God's Power for Salvation: Paul's Letter to the Romans, pp. 120–1

7th May

Reading: Exodus 27:1–8, 30:17–21; Hebrews 10:19–25

*Let us draw near with a true heart in full
assurance of faith. (Hebrews 10:22)*

With complete and utter confidence, then, and with a sincere heart in full assurance of faith, we are now to draw near and enter the Most Holy Place. How the Holy Spirit does delight to emphasize the confidence which every true believer has to enter the Holiest of All! It goes without saying that such confidence is not presumption. It is based on God's own provision. For ancient Israel's priests God provided a double ceremonial cleansing. There was cleansing by literal blood at the altar, and cleansing by literal water at the laver. We have the double reality of which Israel's cleansings were only symbolic.

First, our hearts have been sprinkled with the blood of Jesus (not literally, of course, but metaphorically), and so cleansed from a guilty conscience. That is justification. We do not have to suppress our guilty consciences, or force them in any way. When our consciences see that the wrath of God against us has been righteously appeased, and the penalty of our sins fully paid, they rightly lose all fear and can approach God with total confidence and in peace.

Secondly, our bodies have been bathed with pure water (not literally, again, but metaphorically). Not *sprinkled* with water (as our consciences have been with blood), or even rinsed with water, but bathed all over with water. The Greek word for 'bathed' is the same as that used in John 13:10 where our Lord says, 'A person who has been bathed all over needs only to rinse his feet; his whole body is clean' (my translation). The language, of course, is metaphorical once more. Our Lord is talking of that initial, complete and once-for-all sanctification which takes place when in true repentance and faith someone trusts the Saviour. He is not talking of baptism (one big baptism to start with and many minor baptisms thereafter!?), nor of literal water whether common or holy. In virtue of this once-and-for-all bathing all over in water, when our Lord added, 'You are clean, though not every one of you,' he knew who was going to betray him, and that was why he said that not everyone was clean. But he obviously did not mean, 'You have all been baptized except Judas.' Judas had doubtless been baptized along with the rest; but he had not been 'bathed all over', he had not been sanctified. But every true believer has. 'You were washed,' Paul says, 'you were sanctified, you were justified in the name of the Lord Jesus Christ and by the Spirit of our God' (1 Cor 6:11).

David Gooding, *An Unshakeable Kingdom: The Letter to the Hebrews for Today*, pp. 192–3

8th May

THE SALVATION OF INDIVIDUALS

Reading: Acts 16

One who heard us was a woman named Lydia, from the city of Thyatira, a seller of purple goods, who was a worshipper of God. The Lord opened her heart to pay attention to what was said by Paul. (v. 14)

We can see that by the time Paul left Philippi, the nucleus, at least, of a church had been formed; though Luke nowhere mentions what he surely knew when he later compiled Acts, that this nucleus eventually grew into a vigorous church that contributed significantly to Paul's evangelization of both Europe and Asia. Instead, ninety-five per cent of his narrative in this movement concentrates on two individuals, Lydia and the jailer. The whole sweep of the first half of the movement climaxed in Lydia's conversion and the instalment of Paul and his team in her capacious house (16:6–15); and all the exciting details of the second half climax, not in the magistrates' being obliged to come and personally conduct Paul and Silas out of prison and then, if you please, asking them to leave the city!—a poor climax that would be—but in the conversion of the jailer and the intensely joyous midnight scene as he 'brought them into his house and set a meal before them', and rejoiced with all his household (16:34). Not since the story of Cornelius (ch. 10) has the narrative concentrated in such detail on the conversion of individuals.

Here, then, is our first lesson: From the proportions of Luke's narrative we learn God's sense of proportion too. God loves the whole world. He is not uninterested in the conquest of whole continents and countries by the gospel. This very section will eventually tell us that, as a result of Paul's teaching in Ephesus, all the Jews and Greeks who lived in the province of Asia heard the word of the Lord (19:10). But when it comes to salvation, God does not think in terms of continents and masses of people: he is interested in people as individuals. He knows each one of them, their hearts, their aspirations, their longings; he knows their work, their businesses, families and travels; he knows exactly where they are. Indeed, he has 'determined . . . the exact places where they should live . . . so that men would seek him and perhaps reach out for him and find him' (17:26–27). He knows those who do actually seek him, and he rewards their seeking.

David Gooding, *True to the Faith: The Acts of the Apostles–Defining and Defending the Gospel*, pp. 309–10

9th May

Reading: Romans 8:18–30

How shall we escape if we neglect such
a great salvation? (Hebrews 2:3)

'Salvation' and 'being saved' are ideas which often embarrass even the most sincerely religious people. They are associated in their minds with the mystery religions of the ancient world or with the multifarious cults in modern times.

The writer of Hebrews will show them that there is nothing to be ashamed of either in salvation or in the Saviour who has made it possible. Salvation, as he describes it, certainly concerns individuals at the personal level. But it is far from being a little individual private matter. When he talks of 'such a great salvation', he is thinking of God's programme for 'the world to come' (2:5), a programme that will one day liberate creation itself from its bondage to decay, and put it under the perfect control of redeemed men and women, who themselves have been reconciled to their Creator, have become children of God through faith in Christ Jesus, and have been trained and matured into moral and spiritual conformity with the Son of God (see Rom 8:18–30). He is talking of releasing men and women from the sense of nonsignificance and non-worth that haunts so many of them; from the feelings of fear and futility that afflict them and make life a kind of bondage; from the violence, desecration and disease that degrade and humiliate their bodies. He is talking of restoring to people the vision and the hope and, one day, the reality of attaining that noble purpose for which God originally created mankind.

It is not the worst thing you can say about people, but it is perhaps the saddest, that many of them have no real hope. And without hope life becomes a dead end. They do not believe in God; they know of no satisfying goal and purpose for their lives or for the world to aim at, nor of any credible Messiah figure who could bring either them or the world to that goal. They are, as the New Testament puts it, 'separate from Christ . . . without hope . . . and without God in the world' (Eph 2:12). But if many people have lost their hope, God has not given up hope for mankind! In the world to come, God's original purpose will be fully achieved. Indeed, in the man, Jesus, that purpose is already far advanced towards its fulfilment.

David Gooding, *An Unshakeable Kingdom: The Letter to the Hebrews for Today*, pp. 76–7

10th May

SALVATION FROM PHYSICAL ELEMENTS

Reading: Luke 8:22–25

He said to them, 'Where is your faith?' (v. 25)

Granted then that the disciples' fear was natural and instinctive; but where was their logic? If Jesus was what even at this early stage in their experience they believed him to be, logic should have told them that the divine plan for the redemption of mankind was not about to founder because a sudden storm had caught the long-promised Messiah asleep and he had inadvertently perished. But fear is a powerful demolisher of logic, and in any case they were still learners: they believed John and they believed Jesus and accepted his miraculous demonstrations of his messiahship; yet it still surprised them to find he was Lord of the physical elements.

There is less excuse for our lapses of faith and logic, if at one extreme we confess Jesus as God incarnate and then dismiss this present story contemptuously as a mere 'nature-miracle', or if at the other extreme, we confess Jesus as Lord of the universe and then fear that he has forgotten about us and our circumstances.

We live in a universe that is lethally hostile to human life: only the miracle of creation and divine maintenance preserves our planet and its wonderful adaptations and provisions for the propagation of human life. Within our earth itself, wind, wave, lightning, storm, flood, drought, avalanche, earthquake, fire, heat, cold, germ, virus, epidemic, all from time to time threaten and destroy life. Sooner or later one of them may destroy us. The story of the stilling of the storm is not, of course, meant to tell us that Christ will never allow any believer to perish by drowning, or by any other natural disaster. Many believers have so perished. It does demonstrate that he is Lord of the physical forces in the universe, that for him nothing happens by accident, and that no force in all creation can destroy his plan for our eternal salvation or separate us from the love of God, which is in Christ Jesus our Lord (see Rom 8:38–39).

David Gooding, According to Luke: The Third Gospel's Ordered Historical Narrative, pp. 144–5

11th May

SALVATION FROM A BROKEN CREATION

Reading: Revelation 7:13–17

They shall hunger no more, neither thirst any more; the sun shall not strike them, nor any scorching heat. (v. 16)

Coming victoriously through the great tribulation, this great multitude cry with a loud voice: 'Salvation belongs to our God who sits on the throne, and to the Lamb!' (v. 10). What is the ground of their salvation, and what will their salvation involve? Verses 14–15 tell us, 'These are the ones coming out of the great tribulation. They have washed their robes and made them white in the blood of the Lamb. Therefore they are *before the throne of God . . .*' That is the basis of their *standing*. You say, 'But they're not in heaven, are they? This is an earthly people.' Whether they're on earth or in heaven, notice their theological standing. They are 'before the throne.' It's not just a question of local position, being before him and standing in his presence. As distinct from those who call upon the rocks to cover them, these stand before the throne, *accepted*.

Now some lovely things are said relevant to creation, 'they . . . serve him day and night in his temple [so they're in his temple]; and he who sits on the throne will shelter them with his presence. They shall hunger no more, neither thirst any more; the sun shall not strike them, nor any scorching heat' (vv. 15–16). What a marvellous promise.

You'll notice that the description is in terms of the created powers of the universe—no hunger, no thirst, neither shall the sun strike them, nor any scorching heat. It's no good hiding our eyes from the fact that creation has hurt a lot of people, and not merely by physical sunstroke. This is a broken creation, and it's not just physical thirst that has tormented people, but a deeper thirst. Nature cries out to have its proper desire satisfied, but when life doesn't satisfy, it creates an almost intolerable thirst; wind and wave and sun causing death and disablement and disease. Creation has hurt people, for it's a broken world. Salvation will not only protect us from the wrath of God, but one day he who sits on the throne will shelter his redeemed people with his presence. The sun won't hurt them any more; neither shall they thirst any more. The one who made the universe will gear it towards their blessing and none of the powers of the universe will hurt them.

David Gooding, Daniel and Revelation: A Comparative Study, pp. 97–8

12th May

SALVATION INVOLVES A JOURNEY

Reading: Exodus 12

In this manner you shall eat it: with your belt fastened, your sandals on your feet, and your staff in your hand. And you shall eat it in haste. It is the LORD's Passover. (v. 11)

All who would be saved from the wrath of God must eat that Passover Lamb. All who eat it must go out and depart. They couldn't eat of it just anyhow; they had to put their shoes on, fasten their belts, take their staffs in their hands and be ready to move, for this very day they would begin the journey towards the inheritance.

Shall we get it clear in our minds that those two parts of the scheme were inextricably linked together? There was no gospel that said the main thing was to escape the wrath of God. Imagine the unlikelihood, if you can (the impossibility, if you will), of Moses coming to preach such a gospel.

'My fellow Israelites, you know the main thing is to get yourselves saved from the wrath of God. Then, in addition, if you would care—if you would be interested—there is a further course for advanced people! Once out of Egypt you could perhaps consider taking it. The second course is that you leave Egypt behind and you begin the journey to the promised land. Of course if you're not interested in that, well all right; but the main thing of course is to escape from the wrath of God in Egypt.'

No, indeed not! Moses didn't preach that, for the good reason there is no such gospel. There never was and there never will be. The gospel is that God has come down to deliver them and bring them into that land flowing with milk and honey, and between it lies a journey. If you take the one bit you take the other; there is no having the one without the other. The very moment I take Christ as the sacrifice for my sin I declare that I am leaving my Egypt and beginning my journey.

And thus Peter spoke to the believers of his day, exhorting them to see the implications of being redeemed 'with the precious blood of Christ' (1 Pet 1:19) He says, 'I beseech you my dear brethren, prepare your minds for action' (see v. 13). Take your jacket off, do some thoroughgoing thinking and work out logically what the implications are of trusting Christ as your great Passover lamb, for you have a journey before you and all who are redeemed must start their journey.

David Gooding, No Longer Bondmen: Thirteen Studies in the Book of Exodus, pp. 57–8

THE DISCIPLE'S JOURNEY

Part 2—Holiness: The Goal of the Journey

13th May

ASSURED OF ATTAINING THE GLORY OF HOLINESS

Reading: Romans 5:1–11

Through him we have also obtained access by faith into this grace in which we stand, and we rejoice in hope of the glory of God. (v. 2)

As we study Romans 5–6, we find that before God proceeds to tell us how he proposes to make us holy, and what practical steps he intends to take to make us like himself, God delays a moment to assure our hearts of one fundamental thing. He delays to assure us that every believer in the Lord Jesus Christ is utterly secure in the love of God and that his security does not depend on his spiritual progress, but that God has, for Christ's sake, received him and will never cast him out and never abandon him.

He does so through this lovely argument that the Holy Spirit engages in with all who belong to Christ (5:1–11). The Holy Spirit is pouring out God's love for them in their hearts through this argument. He is arguing that if God loved you *while* you were yet a sinner, so much that he gave his Son for you while you were yet a sinner, it is all the more certain that God will never abandon you now that you have become his child. And therefore we may confidently exult: we 'shall be saved from the wrath of God through him' (v. 9); we 'shall be saved by his life' (v. 10). What is even more glorious, we shall attain 'the glory of God' (v. 2).

Personally, I like that phrase: 'the glory of God'. God is talking here about what we shall be one day when he has made us perfectly holy. But sometimes we think of holiness as a kind of negative thing: not doing that and not doing the other and not going here or there. Holiness seems to us to be a kind of a refrigerator—a state next to death—in which there are so many things that we don't do that we scarce do anything at all. That is not the biblical idea of holiness! Here God describes perfect holiness as the very glory of God! It is all the wonder and beauty of his life—the majesty and glory of that positive pulsating eternal life of God! *That* is the state to which God is determined to bring us. Before we start the long and lengthy course in holiness in the school of Christ, God gives us courage to know we shall attain it one day. We shall attain the glory of God. And in the meantime we are to know that if we are truly Christ's, then our acceptance with God does not depend on our progress, even in holiness.

David Gooding, *Wreckage and Recovery: God's Way of Making Believers Holy: Romans 5–8*, p. 17

14th May

THE SECRET OF HOLINESS

Reading: Romans 7

Likewise, my brothers, you also have died to the law through the body of Christ, so that you may belong to another, to him who has been raised from the dead, in order that we may bear fruit for God. (v. 4)

Though there is a true legal basis for Christian holiness, the heart of the matter lies here. The secret of living a holy life is to let it be an affair of the heart. I mean that: an affair of the heart between you and the lover of your soul.

Have you ever come across a couple when they've just started courting, or are newlyweds? She's got his trousers pressed, and she's been studying what he likes for birthdays. He's been studying the particular flowers that she likes. He never would have done it before—he was a crusty old bachelor. But now, it's all this affair of the heart business, and he's wanting to please her, and she's wanting to please him. They'll do the crankiest things (well, I mustn't say that!), they'll do the *loveliest* things just to please one another!

Thus does God design a holy life to be, not my trying to keep some hard rule, but an affair of the heart between me and Christ. Oh, you can count it sentimental if you like. But it means saying, 'Christ, now is there something you'd like changed in me? And, overall that was pretty disgraceful today, wasn't it? I'm sorry about that. I can't change it myself. Would you, in your mighty arms, embrace me and put your life in me, that I might bring forth your fruit to God?'

There is a part of our personality that should never be ceded, not to anybody! For the human personality in its most intimate is a marvellous thing, and God gave it to you. Be yourself. Don't you let anybody ever trespass on that inner personality of yours! Save for one. Your blessed Lord and the lover of your soul invites you to let him penetrate that very shrine of your personality. So, as Paul puts it: 'It is I, yet it is no longer I; it is Christ in me. It is an affair of the heart by which I have become strong and full of his life, thus to bring forth fruit to God' (see Gal 2:20).

David Gooding, *Wreckage and Recovery: God's Way of Making Believers Holy: Romans 5–8*, p. 41

15th May

HOLINESS IS BOTH POSITIVE AND NEGATIVE

Reading: Leviticus 10

You are to distinguish between the holy and the common,
and between the unclean and the clean. (v. 10)

If we ask the book of Leviticus to tell us what holiness is, it will reply by giving us several different component parts. One of them is concerned with all the rules and regulations that forbid physical, spiritual and moral uncleanness. There are the prohibitions, 'You shall not . . . and if you do, then you must be cleansed from the uncleanness that is involved.' That is the negative side of holiness.

Nowadays the negative side of Christianity does not get people jumping for sheer joy; they are found half-apologizing for it and trying to emphasize the positive side of Christianity. In some ways that is good, but the negative side of holiness is important. We are glad that God sets his face against all impurity, just like we are glad that doctors take a very negative attitude towards germs. We pray that they always will and that the permissive age will never enter hospitals. Imagine a doctor, about to operate on an appendix, saying that he is not as strict on this matter of germs as his forefathers were. I think we would prefer that doctors were more progressive on the negative attitude to germs and unclean things. We must never let the attitude of the present age creep into us individually or into our churches. The call from God is 'Be holy, as I am holy' (see 1 Pet 1:16). He is exceedingly negative when it comes to physical or spiritual germs.

But holiness is not only negative. 'You shall love your neighbour as yourself' (Lev 19:18). This second of the two great Old Testament commandments tells us that one of the major evidences of holiness is to be warm-hearted and to have a positive attitude towards our neighbours.

'[Jesus] said to him, "You shall love the Lord your God with all your heart and with all your soul and with all your mind. This is the great and first commandment. And the second is like it: You shall love your neighbour as yourself"' (Matt 22:37–39).

To love your neighbour as yourself means a lot of different things. For example, 'You shall not go around as a slanderer among your people' (Lev 19:16). That would mean an end to all gossip. In all we do we should think, 'Would I like someone to do that to me, tell that story about me, drive that kind of bargain with me?' If we would not like it, we are not to do it to our neighbours; we are to love our neighbours as ourselves.

David Gooding, *The Feasts of the Lord: Studies on the Feasts Appointed by the Lord for Israel*, pp. 5–6

16th May

HOLINESS MEANS FREEDOM TO SERVE THE LORD

Reading: Exodus 6

*I am the LORD your God, who brought you out of the land of
Egypt, that you should not be their slaves. And I have broken
the bars of your yoke and made you walk erect. (Lev 26:13)*

This is another side to holiness, and what a lovely and vivid metaphor it
is. God found these people in Egypt, their backs broken with slavery; he
redeemed them, desiring that they should be holy. What will holiness mean
to them? It will mean that they can now go through life as free men with
their shoulders back and their heads up. No longer were they bondmen; by
God's grace they were free!

God wants to make us free from bondage to guilt, but he also wants to
make us free in all the affairs of daily life. Free from those attitudes that would
make us slaves to our homes, our duties or our businesses. He wants to make
us walk upright so that we may feel confident in his grace and power; not
as slaves to the guilt of our past or to the responsibilities of our present, but
as free men and women. That does not mean we should be lazy. God is not
lazy. Let us remember, in all reverence, that he does not have to work for
a living. What he does, he does for the sheer joy of doing it and he will fill
the whole of eternity with his glorious activity. But he never makes himself
a slave to it and he wants us to learn that the secret of true, holy living is not
to make ourselves into slaves.

For that reason, God ordained that Israel should have their year inter-
spersed with seven major holidays. They were seven occasions when the
Israelites left their daily routine of work and rested—not by going to the
beach with their children, but by taking the time to rest and think about God
and to be with God. There is a recurrent phrase through the details of these
feasts, 'You shall not do any ordinary work' (e.g., Lev 23:7–8). And there is
a little paragraph interjected before the details of the seven feasts where God
reminds them about the weekly day of rest, the Sabbath. He was trying to get
something across to them when he told them to observe a weekly Sabbath
and also when he told them to observe seven holidays each year during which
they were not to do any ordinary work.

David Gooding, *The Feasts of the Lord: Studies on the Feasts Appointed by the Lord for Israel*, p. 6

17th May

TRUE HOLINESS

Reading: Acts 9:20–35

Therefore lift your drooping hands and strengthen your weak knees, and make straight paths for your feet, so that what is lame may not be put out of joint but rather be healed. (Heb 12:12–13)

The paralysis was literal and the healing a physical miracle. But we shall not be far wrong if we suppose that, as with our Lord's miracles of physical healing, this miracle too conveyed a deeper lesson.

Aeneas's healing was in the first instance an exhibition of supernatural physical power that advertised the reality of the risen Christ. But surely it was more. It did not of course carry an implicit promise that every paralytic or quadriplegic will be instantaneously healed upon becoming a Christian. History has shown otherwise. But it did point to Christ's ability to empower all his people; in the metaphorical language of Hebrews 12:12–13, to reinvigorate their drooping hands and paralysed knees. Then, as the NEB puts it, 'the disabled limb will not be put out of joint, but regain its former powers'.

It is all too easy for Christians to give people an impression of holiness that repels them. It is true, of course, that all believers are 'saints' by calling. They have been sanctified by the offering of the body of Jesus Christ once for all (Heb 10:10). In this sense one believer is no more a saint than another. The members of the church at Corinth, troubled by faults and failings and impurities and divisions though they were, are addressed as 'saints' (1 Cor 1:2), just as the believers at Rome (Rom 1:7) or at Philippi (Phil 1:1) or anywhere else are. But that is only one side of the story. True saintliness will sooner or later begin to make its presence felt; for it is not a form of weakness, encouraging people to remain in spiritually immature dependence on others, all the while obsessed with 'difficulties' and 'problems'. True saintliness is positive, vigorous, active, maturely self-supporting, and able spiritually to stand on its own feet. Jesus Christ our Lord has the power to make us holy in this practical sense; to release us from unhealthy inhibitions and weaknesses; to make us strong and active in the work he gives us to do and so to make us an advertisement to the world of what true Christian saintliness is.

David Gooding, *True to the Faith: The Acts of the Apostles–Defining and Defending the Gospel*, p. 199

18th May

THE GOAL OF LIFE'S JOURNEY

Reading: Philippians 3:1–14

Master, it is good that we are here. Let us make three tents, one
for you and one for Moses and one for Elijah. (Luke 9:33)

Luke adds that Peter did not realize what he was saying. Obviously not, since the whole conversation had been about Christ's going away, and Peter suggested staying put.

We may smile at Peter, but we often appear to be saying the same thing by the way we live. We know that the Bible declares that life is a journey to an eternal heaven—or hell; we have heard it many times. But we live as though we are going to stay here forever, as though this life is everything and there is no eternal goal. Of course, Peter's remark was very understandable. The life of a Galilean fisherman was hard and humdrum; so when a rare occasion of splendour and enchantment came his way, it was only natural that he should want to make it last as long as possible. Nor is there anything necessarily wrong with his or our desire to enjoy life to the full and to pack as much interest and adventure into it as possible. If life has an eternal goal, then every step of the journey has eternal significance. And if the goal is to be enjoyed, that is no reason why the journey should not be enjoyed as well. Most of us enjoy travelling as well as arriving.

On the other hand, if while sailing from America to Ireland the captain of the vessel presently forgot he was on a journey, and simply steered the ship in never-ending circles round the middle of the Atlantic instead of making for his destination, most of the passengers in the ship would eventually become disenchanted with the voyage. And the danger is that in our effort to enjoy this life to the full, we lose sight of the goal, and thereby defeat the very object that we set out to achieve. We rob this life of its eternal, and therefore of its most important and enjoyable, dimension. We cease travelling and begin meandering through life, and all this at the peril of arriving in eternity utterly unprepared.

Perhaps this is why the Bible, unlike a good deal of popular preaching, very seldom uses the phrase 'go to heaven', but constantly urges us to receive eternal life now. For eternal life is not a something that we must wait until we get to heaven before we receive it; it is an added, eternal dimension to this life, which is enjoyed by those who enter now into a personal relationship with the eternal God through Jesus Christ.

David Gooding, *Windows on Paradise: Scenes of Hope and Salvation in the Gospel of Luke*, pp. 60–1

19th May

THE JOURNEY TO HEAVEN

Reading: Luke 10:1–21

Nevertheless, do not rejoice in this, that the spirits are subject to you, but rejoice that your names are written in heaven. (v. 20)

Suppose then we take Christ seriously and determine to set out on the journey that leads to God's heaven. Two questions naturally arise. The first is: Where does the journey start? The answer is simple and may be given in Peter's own words. He describes the goal as 'an inheritance that is imperishable, undefiled, and unfading, kept in heaven for you' (1 Pet 1:4). Then he describes the start of the spiritual pilgrimage that leads to the goal: 'since you have been born again, not of perishable seed but of imperishable, through the living and abiding word of God . . .' (v. 23). In other words, the journey begins when we first receive the word of God and personally trust the Saviour and are born again as newborn babies into the family of God.

The second question is: Can we be sure that, having started out on the journey, we shall arrive in God's heaven, and not miss our way and end up disastrously elsewhere? The straight and certain answer to this question is: Yes! We can be sure! Let Luke answer this time. Very early in his narrative of the journey, Luke tells us about an occasion when the disciples came to Christ elated and overjoyed at the success they had had at casting out demons in his name. He replied, 'Nevertheless, do not rejoice in this, that the spirits are subject to you, but rejoice that your names are written in heaven' (Luke 10:20). So here was assurance that, as they journeyed through life, they were already registered as citizens of heaven—as men whose fatherland is heaven, and who by the grace of God have citizens' right to be in the heavenly city.

David Gooding, *Windows on Paradise: Scenes of Hope and Salvation in the Gospel of Luke*, pp. 62–3

20th May

THE AARONIC BLESSING

Reading: Exodus 33:12–23

The Lord bless you and keep you; the Lord make his face to shine upon you and be gracious to you. (Numbers 6:24–25)

'The Lord bless you' (v. 24). You see, if it should ever happen that the enemy of souls should insinuate into their hearts that God was not a God of love and cared little for them, then it might invalidate the whole journey. The thing that would be vital in the testings that would come upon them was the preservation of the blessing of God, God's attitude toward them. 'The Lord bless you and keep you'—this is the number one requirement, in all that hazardous, howling wilderness, to be kept by the power of God. For however prosperous life may be, should it be that we lose the sense of the grace and the keeping of God, then we should be lost indeed.

'The Lord bless you, and keep you. The Lord make his face to shine upon you, and be gracious to you' (vv. 24–25). Being of a simple mind myself, I do admire the way that the ancient Hebrew dares to speak of God in ordinary, everyday language as though he had a face. 'The Lord bless you and . . . make his face to shine upon you.' What a delightful notion. When I think of that, I think of a little child I knew. It was her father's birthday, and Mum had given the child the necessary cash to make her think she was buying Daddy a present, shaving cream or something of little actual value. And here's the little one coming to Daddy, and she's going to give the present. Look at her face. It is all shining, isn't it? And it challenged me to ask, when did I last look up into the face of God and sense the face of God shining towards me, because of the grace, the ten thousand and one graces that he has provided for me? 'The Lord make his face to shine upon you, and be gracious unto you,' so that we may revel in the inexhaustible wealth of the grace of God.

David Gooding, Understanding the Old Testament: An Overview of Genesis to Joshua, pp. 36–7

21st May

SANCTIFICATION AND FREE WILL

Reading: Romans 6:11–23

*Do not present your members to sin as instruments for
unrighteousness, but present yourselves to God as those who
have been brought from death to life, and your members
to God as instruments for righteousness. (v. 13)*

If you're going to make a human being holy, you will find you are in for
a very, very delicate task. God could of course, if he chose, come in like
a tank and override our free will, override our choice and our consent, and
stop us sinning. But what good would that be? He might get a something
that didn't sin, but it wouldn't be a human being, would it? God would have
reduced us to machines, and God will never do that.

It is a solemn though majestic thing that God, having given us a free will,
a human personality, will never destroy that free will or personality. So much
so that if we choose to say, 'No' to God and continue in saying, 'No' and go
out into eternity saying 'No', even then God will not destroy our free will in
order to save us. God respects human personalities so much that if we take
our human personality and free will and say, 'No' to God, in the end God will
put up with that eternally. Not even to save us would he destroy our free will.

That means that though God proceeds to make us holy, he has got to carry
us with him all the time, hasn't he? You'll never become holy automatically.
I shall become holy as I am made to face my sins, my wrong attitudes, and
recognize and confess them, saying, 'Yes, I have been wrong; these things
are wrong', and repent of them.

Let us get that settled from the start. Sometimes we think that repenting
is a thing that the unconverted have to do before they get saved, and that is
very true, but it is something that the child of God has to do every day of
the week almost, and all the way home to glory. We are to allow God's Holy
Spirit to point out what is wrong and then to agree with God that it is wrong,
and to seek God's grace for it to be put away and overcome.

David Gooding, Wreckage and Recovery: God's Way of Making Believers Holy: Romans 5–8, p. 18

22nd May

HOLINESS DOESN'T COME EASILY

Reading: 1 Peter 1:3–9; Revelation 3:19–22

For the Lord disciplines the one he loves, and chastises
every son whom he receives. (Hebrews 12:6)

The discipline process can at times be painful; let's not deceive ourselves. When it's over, then we shall find how pleasant it is—after the chastening is over, after the bitter lessons are learned, 'it yields the peaceful fruit of righteousness' (Heb 12:11).

But we're like a lot of kids, aren't we? Here's Tommy. He's having such a lovely time scribbling on the wallpaper. He's scribbled and scribbled and it's marvellous! And he doesn't at all enjoy the process when it is pointed out to him that people shouldn't scribble on the wallpaper. Of course one day he'll grow up and say how stupid it was anyway. But for the moment, Tommy is kicking wildly at being restrained and being told it's wrong.

Alas, we are often like that aren't we? God's Holy Spirit begins, by this means or the other, to point out to us that we are wrong. Then, instead of welcoming it, out go the old defences with every reason under the sun why people want to criticize us like this, or why we should do it, and thus, and thus! (You know the old story.) Then God insists, and we begin to feel sore. It is for this very reason that, before we start, God assures us of our eternal security in the love of God (see Rom 5:1–11). He loves us. He loved us while we were yet sinners. You know, God will never be disappointed in you. You know that, don't you? God will never be disappointed in you, for he always did know everything about you. He may oftentimes be sorrowful about you, as he is about me, but he will never be disappointed. He is under no illusions. He knows us better than we know ourselves. He knows how deceitful our hearts are, and how desperately wicked. The amazing thing is that he loved us while we were yet sinners! Being under no illusions, knowing the worst about us, he loves us just the same.

Therefore he wants us to know we are secure, so that when his Spirit begins exposing us to ourselves, and we find out that we're not necessarily the charming people we thought we were, and we discover that we are not the important people we thought we were, and we discover that God has no intention of letting us remain spoilt boys and girls, in those moments we may realize that God isn't rejecting us; he loves us still.

David Gooding, Wreckage and Recovery: God's Way of Making Believers Holy: Romans 5–8, pp. 18–19

23rd May

GOD'S TACTICS IN MAKING US HOLY

Reading: Joshua 8:20–35

But the king of Ai they took alive, and
brought him near to Joshua. (v. 23)

The tactics for overcoming Ai were altogether different from the tactics for overcoming Jericho. With Jericho God took the walls down and they went in and destroyed the people inside. With Ai it was the very opposite thing; they put an ambush behind the city, Joshua came up with the troops as they did the first time, and when the king of Ai came out they ran away as though they were defeated again. The king of Ai came out to give them the coup de grâce, then the ambush came up behind and Joshua got them in between and slaughtered every one of them. He hung the king of Ai upon a tree. That's how they did it—there were the people in the ambush behind the city, then there was that part of the army that had to go up to those walls from which they had earlier run away in defeat. They had to re-enact their defeat and run away again, as though defeated once more.

You've never done that, have you? Have you said, 'I'm never going to make that mistake again?' I've said it thousands of times. I don't know about you, but I am as liable to defeat as ever I was. But this time there was a difference—this time Joshua went with them. He wasn't with the ambush behind the city, he was with the crowd that ran away in defeat. What marvellous grace of Joshua that he should station himself with the people that re-enacted the defeat.

I'm not encouraging you to live in sin, but I want to tell you that God has a scheme to make you at last like his Son—the righteous requirement of the law shall be fulfilled in you! Is it because we have become strong? No, indeed not, we are as liable to defeat as ever. But we have with us the greater-than-Joshua, the Captain of our salvation. In those days when once more you suffer defeat and you could cry your heart out for shame, remember that the blessed Lord Jesus stands with you. What he's doing is luring out your old self—like that king of Ai, bringing him out and exposing him—so that you may repent and find that at last you get the victory.

David Gooding, *What Moses Could Not Do: Nine Studies in the Book of Joshua*, pp. 46–7

24th May

HOLINESS IN THE REAL WORLD

Reading: Matthew 10:11–25

Rise, let us go from here. (John 14:31)

We cannot be completely sure whether at that very moment they rose up, left the Upper Room, clambered down the stone staircase and out into the streets of the city; or whether, after the command to 'rise and go from here', they lingered still in the Upper Room until the remaining lessons had been completed, and then left; though the overwhelming probability is that upon the command they left immediately. But this, at least, we can say for certain: the command to arise and go hence would have taken their attention out from the cosiness of the Upper Room to the realities of the world outside where the chilly night air was laced with the murderous intentions of the priests, and somewhere in the shadow there lurked the traitor, driven by the satanic powers of hell. Now they must learn that true holiness involves not only devotion to the divine persons, but witness to and for the Father and the Son. And they must grasp the all-important fact that this witness is to be conducted not simply in the warm, safe, seclusion of the Upper Room, where all hearts in unison beat out their loyalty to the Saviour, but in the world outside, whose very streets breathed hostility to the Son of God.

Here, then, at the outset of the second half of the course, stands this simple, but searching, lesson for us too: there are two sides to holiness, and both are indispensable. One without the other is weak and inadequate. Public witness for the Lord that is not founded on private, personal devotion to him would lack its necessary foundation. Private and personal devotion to the Lord that did not go on to express itself in public witness to the Lord would be maimed and unbalanced. Still today, in the course of our private devotions and in the fellowship of the church, we shall hear from time to time the challenging call of our Lord, 'Arise, let us go from here.'

David Gooding, *In the School of Christ: Lessons on Holiness in John 13–17*, p. 124

25th May

WHAT HAPPENS WHEN WE SIN?

Reading: Leviticus 4:1–13; 1 John 2:1–2

*So Jesus also suffered outside the gate in order to sanctify
the people through his own blood. (Hebrews 13:12)*

What happens if I sin? Well, I am to realize that my sin is a murderer. It killed Christ, but because it killed him and he died willingly for me, I have access to God, and Christ in his life was *for* me. Ah, but now Christ is risen; he is at the right hand of God interceding for me, failing sinner though I am. Yes, at present our Lord in heaven is interceding for me.

We read in Leviticus 4 that when the priest had done what was required he came out with the rest of the blood, and poured out the whole of it at the base of the altar. Even if the sacrifice were for just one sin, all of the blood was poured out. The only way for my sin to be dealt with was for Christ to give his blood for me.

That wasn't the end of the priest's journey, for in sacrifices where the blood was brought into the holy place, the animals had not to be burnt on the altar; they had to be taken away outside the camp, and there burned to ashes. I am now on very safe ground, yet I stand here afraid that you will accuse me of wild symbolism. Well, this bit isn't wild. The Epistle to the Hebrews says 'the bodies of the sacrifices, whose blood was brought into the holy place, were taken outside of the camp' (13:11). You will remember it, won't you? When he died, Christ didn't die as a great hero, surrounded by the massed bands of Israel, singing his triumph as a noble hero. He was found by the highest court in the land to be guilty of heinous sin, and was bustled out of the gate of the city to Golgotha. He suffered outside the gate.

My dear brother and sister, what effect does this drama have upon you? Think now of the reality, not simply of the Old Testament picture. Do you see Christ carrying the cross they put on him, bustled outside the gate, taken to Golgotha, crucified with that wild, gruesome crew? And you say, 'Christ, did that for me?' How moving it is. I fancy if I've read your heart aright, when the Holy Spirit has brought that home to you, you will say, 'Well, God help me. I never want to sin again. I will go forth in this world unto Christ outside the gate and stand with him, because he did this all for me.'

This is, in God's word of Leviticus, the initial stages in what the book has to say about our becoming holy, as God is holy.

David Gooding, *Understanding the Old Testament: An Overview of Genesis to Joshua*, p. 28–9

THE DISCIPLE'S JOURNEY

Part 3—Faith for the Journey

26th May

ABRAHAM'S FAITH AND OURS

Reading: Genesis 15:6–21

*And he believed the LORD, and he counted
it to him as righteousness. (v. 6)*

Many people lack complete peace with God because they misunderstand what is meant by 'faith' when Scripture says: 'being justified by faith, we have peace with God' (Rom 5:1 KJV). They have read of faith in other connections in the New Testament where people are rebuked for their little faith; and they fall to thinking that the reason they have no peace with God is that their faith is not strong enough. They then imagine that faith is a kind of work that must be performed up to a certain standard before it qualifies for justification and peace.

But that is not what 'faith' means when used in the context of justification, as the analogy between Abraham's faith and ours clearly shows. It was not Abraham's faith that produced the miracle: long years of believing and hoping left his body as good as dead. It was God who accomplished the miracle. Similarly, we are justified when we put our faith in God who raised the Lord Jesus from the dead. It was not our faith, strong or weak, that raised the Lord Jesus from the dead: it was God who did it.

Imagine we were standing with the apostles round the grave of Christ before his body was raised from the dead. And imagine further that we realized the fact that Christ's body was in the grave because he died for our sins; and unless he was raised from the dead, there would be no justification for us: we would simply remain as we were, unforgiven and liable to God's wrath (1 Cor 15:17). Aware of the gravity of the situation, we say to one another: 'Look, let's stand round the grave, join hands and start believing as strongly as we can. For if only we can manage to believe with strong enough faith, our faith will cause the Lord's body to rise from the grave, and we can then be sure that we are justified and have peace with God.' Would the strength of our faith bring Jesus out of the grave? Of course not. The very idea is grotesque.

The resurrection of Christ was something that lay beyond any human power to effect. God alone could do it. In fact, if God had not done it, there would never have been any gospel for us to believe (1 Cor 15:14–17). Faith, for us, then means believing that God has done what we could never do, in raising Christ from the dead, and then resting entirely on that and on its significance.

David Gooding, *The Riches of Divine Wisdom: The New Testament's Use of the Old Testament*, pp. 135–6

27th May

ACTIVE, LIVING FAITH

Reading: Numbers 14:1–24

And without faith it is impossible to please him, for whoever would draw near to God must believe that he exists and that he rewards those who seek him. (Hebrews 11:6)

What does it mean to *live* by faith? The faith spoken of throughout the letter to the Hebrews is the faith without which no one can please God, without which we are not believers at all. The ancient Israelites in the desert failed to believe the gospel. They were not believers in any true sense of the word. They may have believed 'for a while', as the Lord phrased it (Luke 8:13); but they certainly had no root in themselves. That kind of faith is no good. When the test came, they were found never to have truly believed the gospel. Now once more at Hebrews 11:6 the writer explicitly says that by 'faith' he means that true and genuine faith by which we truly come to God and truly please him; without which it is in fact impossible to please him; without which we are not true believers at all.

On the other hand, we are about to be shown in this chapter that you cannot divide faith into nice, tidy, separate compartments and categories. We start our life with God by faith. It is not a different kind of faith that thereafter carries us on, but that same faith still. And the faith by which we start, though small at the beginning, has within it all the potential for growth, action and endurance that is about to be illustrated for us in chapter 11 of Hebrews. The faith we exercise when first we receive salvation is such that it will inevitably show itself in life. It cannot be completely hidden. It cannot completely fail to mould our lives. True faith is a living thing. It will result in an altered life, it will be courageous for God, it will act, it will persist and endure.

Sometimes I feel a little uneasy when I hear people say that to be saved you do not have to do anything at all. I know what some preachers mean when they say that. In the sense they mean, it is true. Of course, you cannot earn salvation by good works; of course, faith is rest, a resting on the work of Christ; of course, faith is a receiving and not a giving. But true faith is always active right from the very beginning.

David Gooding, An Unshakeable Kingdom: The Letter to the Hebrews for Today, pp. 200–1

28th May

FAITH'S PILGRIMAGE

Reading: Genesis 12:1–9

By faith Abraham obeyed when he was called to go out to
a place that he was to receive as an inheritance. And he went
out, not knowing where he was going. (Hebrews 11:8)

So the first step in Abraham's pilgrimage of faith was one of blind obedience. He had God's promise and that was enough. When the call came, he obeyed it. He did not demand to have everything explained to him first so that he could then make up his mind whether he would follow God's call or not. Knowing it was God's call, he obeyed it simply because it was God's call. That's what it means to follow God. If it had been the call of a mere human being, he would have been wise to demand to know and understand all the details before he decided whether to follow it. But he couldn't treat God that way. If he was the God of glory, the one, true and only God, and if Abraham really believed it, then he must be prepared to do what God said, just because it was God who said it.

And so it is with us and the Lord Jesus. He will not ask us blindly to believe that he is the Son of God. He will give us plenty of evidence on which to base our faith (John 20:30–31). But suppose we come to believe that he is the Son of God. That will do us no good whatsoever unless we then become his genuine disciples. And the very first step he will demand of us as his disciples is that we accept his lordship over everything and everybody, ourselves, our thoughts, decisions and possessions, before we go any further. And we must accept it unreservedly (Luke 14:25–27, 33). We cannot be his disciples on the understanding that he will first explain to us in detail what he would like us to do, and why; and then leave us free to decide on each occasion whether we like his demands or not and whether or not we consent to them. That would be to treat Christ not as Lord but merely as a professional adviser or as one business person treats another. If we really believe that he is the supreme Lord, we shall do what he says, just because he says it, whether we understand it or not, and whether we like it or not. What does our profession of faith amount to, if we call him 'Lord, Lord', and then do not do what he says? (Luke 6:46).

David Gooding, An Unshakeable Kingdom: The Letter to the Hebrews for Today, pp. 209–10

29th May

GROWING IN THE FAITH

Reading: Hebrews 5:11–6:12

*And we desire each one of you to show the same earnestness
to have the full assurance of hope until the end, so that you
may not be sluggish, but imitators of those who through
faith and patience inherit the promises. (6:11–12)*

Now the writer of the letter meets a difficulty. His readers had been professing Christians for a considerable time, so long indeed that they might reasonably have been expected to be able by this time to teach others. Unfortunately, they had remained spiritual babies. Far from being able to teach others, they needed someone to teach them the elementary truths of God's word all over again. Like infants they needed to be fed with milk not solid food. And being infants they had no experience of the word of righteousness and no practice in training their spiritual perception to distinguish between what was spiritually good and what was spiritually bad.

Now, however, they were in a critical situation of testing and trial and they desperately needed to know as much as ever they could about the high priest in the order of Melchizedek. But the writer fears that it will be too much for them to take in. If so, it would be cruelly sad; for these were the very things they needed to know to bring them safely through their crisis. It is always so. If we remain infants and are careless about our spiritual growth and education, all may go fair for a while; but let the storm rise and the crisis come, and we shall find that the very things that we need to know and to grasp hold of to keep us and bring us through the storm, we shall not know, and therefore shall not be able to grasp hold of.

We remember that Peter found himself in a similar situation. How it must have buoyed up his spirit, even when he went out and wept bitterly at his dismal failure, as he thought again and again of the Lord's gracious promise, 'I have prayed for you, Simon, that your faith may not fail' (Luke 22:32). And Peter came round, with all that that meant, to face his fellow disciples again, to face the Lord again, to face the public again, after such a dismal defeat. Peter came round, and he owed it to the fact that he had a high priest, and knew it. Let us be sure, when the sun shines and things go easily and we feel like singing all the day long, that we take care to store our minds and hearts with the riches of God's holy word that in the evil day we may be able to stand, and, having done all, to stand.

David Gooding, *An Unshakeable Kingdom: The Letter to the Hebrews for Today*, pp. 124–5

30th May

FAITH'S FRUITFULNESS

Reading: 2 Peter 1:3–11

*Know therefore that the LORD your God is God, the
faithful God who keeps covenant and steadfast love with
those who love him and keep his commandments, to
a thousand generations. (Deuteronomy 7:9)*

Certainly Abraham's persistence in living as a foreigner and pilgrim on earth
was no negative, barren, unproductive running away from life. Quite the
opposite. Perhaps no one else recorded in Scripture, except of course our
Lord, and perhaps also Paul (the great expounder of Abraham's life), has
had such an immense influence on his fellows. His life and Sarah's have been
astonishingly—in sober fact, miraculously—fruitful.

We think of the great and distinguished nation, influential out of all proportion to its size, which has sprung physically from him. Its birth was a miracle
directly attributable to his faith and Sarah's. More impressive still are the
multi-millions of his spiritual progeny from every nation (see Rom 4:16–17).
How many myriads of those who shall inhabit the eternal city, will, under
God, owe their initial justification by faith and their persistence in a life of
faith to the guidance and encouragement of Abraham's example.

If we would live fruitful and not barren lives (2 Pet 1:8) and influence
others for God, we must discover his secret. How did his faith manage to
be so strong that it could bring life out of veritable death? 'He counted him
faithful who had promised' (Heb 11:11 own trans.). His faith was the result of
his considered moral assessment of the character of God. God, so Abraham
decided, was faithful. He could never be anything less. Therefore, if he made
a promise, he would keep it. So Abraham believed the promise, and kept on
believing it in spite of the all-too-real difficulties and the long delay in the
fulfilment. Abraham could not give up believing the promise. To have done
so would have been to imply unfaithfulness and moral defect in God.

That is faith, then. It is not some high feeling, mood or emotion, worked
up by psychological or religious techniques. It is the result of calm, deliberate
moral assessment of the character of God. The Apostle John remarks that if
you don't believe God's word, you make him out to be a liar (1 John 5:10). In
that case true faith is not long in deciding what to do.

David Gooding, *An Unshakeable Kingdom: The Letter to the Hebrews for Today*, pp. 211–2

31st May

FAITH AND WORKS

Reading: Genesis 22:9–19

Do not lay your hand on the boy or do anything to him,
for now I know that you fear God, seeing you have not
withheld your son, your only son, from me. (v. 12)

Abraham's faith was genuine. But at first his genuine faith was mixed up with a certain amount of dross. He thought, for instance, that faith in God's promise to give him a son meant really that it depended on his and Sarah's efforts and scheming whether that promise would be fulfilled or not. But he had to learn that that was wrong. His efforts would not fulfil God's promise. What God had promised was a gift that would be given by God's grace and miraculous power

At length the promised seed, Isaac, was born; and in a very real sense all God's promises to Abraham and all Abraham's future were centred in Isaac. But now there was a danger that Abraham's faith for the future would come to rest partly in Isaac instead of resting solely in God. And that would never do. For his own sake, if for no other reason, Abraham must learn that no one can enjoy total security for the future unless his faith is solely and utterly in God and God alone.

And so, if I may reverently paraphrase the situation, God came to Abraham and said, 'Abraham, when I first promised to give you a son and offspring as numerous as the stars, you said you believed me. Did you really mean it?' 'Oh, yes,' said Abraham, 'of course I did.' 'Well, what does your faith for the future rest in now?' 'In you, of course,' said Abraham. 'Are you sure it rests only and altogether in me, and not partly in me and partly in Isaac?' 'Oh, not in Isaac,' said Abraham, 'in you and only in you.' 'Then, Abraham,' said God, 'I ask you to demonstrate that your faith is in fact in me and in nothing and no one else. Please give me Isaac.'

And Abraham gave up Isaac to God and demonstrated by this act that his faith was totally and altogether and solely in God. He justified his profession of faith and showed it was genuine; he was justified by his works. And God's reply was 'Now I know that you fear God, because you have not withheld from me your son, your only son' (vv. 11–12). With that God gathered up all his previous promises, renewed them and confirmed them with a mighty oath, so that Abraham and all others whose faith is in God alone might enjoy the 'strong encouragement' of absolute, unchangeable and eternal security.

David Gooding, *An Unshakeable Kingdom: The Letter to the Hebrews for Today*, pp. 141–2

1st June

THE TESTING OF FAITH

Reading: Genesis 22:1–8

*Abraham reasoned that God could even raise the
dead, and so in a manner of speaking he did receive
Isaac back from death. (Hebrews 11:19 NIV)*

True faith must and will be tested. It is not enough to say, 'I believe.' Sooner
or later we shall be called upon to justify our profession of faith by our works.
Abraham was; and we have already considered what the issues at stake were,
and what it was that had to be demonstrated, and to whom it had to be
demonstrated, when Abraham was asked to offer up Isaac to God.

What interests us here is to discover how his faith found the strength to go
through this extreme test so triumphantly. It found it in logic. I don't suppose
for one moment that Abraham ran up the mountain singing and shouting
'Hallelujah!' It was not exuberant spirits or waves of emotion that sustained
him in his grim task. It was logic. Abraham reasoned the matter out. God
had not only promised that he would have many descendants; God had
specified that it was through Isaac that these descendants would come. Isaac
as yet had no children. He was not even married. If God was now asking that
Isaac be slain, that could not mean that God was going back on his promise.
There was only one way out. God would have to raise him from the dead.
He could; and he would. So presently Abraham told his servants to stay put:
he and Isaac were going to the mountain top to worship and both of them
would come back again (Gen 22:5).

The logic was simple but breathtaking. It was also sound; and God was
delighted to honour it, and to make the giving back of Isaac from virtual
death a prototype of our Lord's death and resurrection (Heb 11:19).

Faith's logic does not reason that if God loves us he must save us from
difficulty, disease, sacrifice and death. It argues rather, 'I am persuaded that
neither life nor death can separate us from the love of God, or from the
fulfilment of his promises' (see Rom 8:38–39).

David Gooding, An Unshakeable Kingdom: The Letter to the Hebrews for Today, pp. 214–15

2nd June

FAITH UNDER PRESSURE

Reading: Genesis 20

*I did it because I thought, There is no fear of God at all in
this place, and they will kill me because of my wife. (v. 11)*

Think how serious it was for Abraham and Sarah at this stage of the proceedings. God had appeared to Abraham in his tent and told him that his
wife would have a son, and now some weeks, perhaps months, after this,
Abraham is taking that same wife and allowing her to be taken off by the
Philistines. Was he not taking a very big risk about the eventual paternity
of the child and putting the whole purpose of God at risk? God's purpose
was not ultimately to save Abraham's skin; it was to conform Abraham to
the character of God. If I cannot fulfil the purpose of God and still keep on
living, I would be better dead. I say that advisedly. To keep hold of physical
life by compromising the purposes of God is a sad and sorry thing, for that
is to confuse the end with the means and the means with the end.

I picture another great saint of God, standing on the deck of a ship that is
nearly going under the Mediterranean in the middle of a storm. He stands
in front of the frightened crew and passengers and he says,

> This very night there stood before me an angel of the God to whom
> I belong and whom I worship, and he said, 'Do not be afraid, Paul;
> you must stand before Caesar. (Acts 27:23–24)

'I do not care what seas there are around me, I shall not be drowned here.
God has said that I am going to preach the gospel in Rome!'

Abraham might have argued like that. God said that he was going to have
a son. Therefore, it was impossible that the Philistines should slit his throat, at
least before the son was born. But these were early days and Abraham's knees
were a bit wobbly. It's all right meeting the Lord at his table; what giants of faith
we are then. And it's wonderful what faith we can rise to in the secret place when
we are interceding with God for the salvation of our relatives, as Abraham did
over the salvation of Lot. It is another story in an ungodly, unprincipled, sinful
world. It's not so easy then to stand for true morality and not dodge the issue
by all sorts of shady things, half-truths and lies. Let me be the first to confess
that I have fallen right there. Afraid, for security reasons.

David Gooding, The God of New Beginnings: Eighteen Seminars on the Book of Genesis, p. 128

3rd June

THE EVIDENCE AND COST OF FAITH

Reading: Matthew 13:1–23; Acts 14:8–28

When they had preached the gospel to that city and had made
many disciples, they returned to Lystra and to Iconium and to
Antioch, strengthening the souls of the disciples, encouraging
them to continue in the faith, and saying that through many
tribulations we must enter the kingdom of God. (Acts 14:21–22)

The happenings at Lystra show us this: the Christian doctrine of salvation by grace through faith was as insistent on maintaining the moral law of God as the Jews—more insistent than some of them, in fact. And now in this brief final part of this first movement we shall meet another side to the Christian doctrine. Forgiveness, justification, acceptance with God, eternal life, these all are perfectly free gifts; but those who receive them may well find that there is a heavy cost involved in receiving them.

Recovering from the near fatal assault he had suffered at Lystra, Paul went on—amazing man—to Derbe, preached the gospel there, and made many disciples (14:20–21). That for the moment was his farthermost point. From there he and Barnabas began the return journey. They visited again, in reverse order, Lystra, Iconium, and Pisidian Antioch. On the way from there back to (Syrian) Antioch, their home church, they preached in Perga. But what they said, and what the results were, Luke does not tell us.

What he does concentrate on is what they said and did in the infant churches that they had recently founded in Lystra, Iconium, and Pisidian Antioch. They strengthened the souls of the disciples, encouraging them to continue in the faith (14:22). We observe once more the term 'the faith'—that is, the body of Christian doctrine—which has so marked this section of Acts. But now let us notice the term 'continue in' ('remain true to', NIV). Salvation is by grace, the gift of God to every believer. But the evidence that someone is a true believer is that he or she continues in the faith. This is what our Lord said to those who professed to believe on him: 'If you continue in my word, you are truly my disciples' (John 8:31 RSV). Those who did not 'continue in his word', he pointed out, were not, and never had been, children of God. This is the message of all the Epistles likewise. 'Continuing in the faith' is not a condition of being justified. But it is the natural outcome and the necessary evidence of being a genuine believer.

David Gooding, *True to the Faith: The Acts of the Apostles–Defining and Defending the Gospel*, pp. 263-4

4th June

FAITH AND RISK

Reading: Acts 27:9–20

Sirs, I perceive that the voyage will be with injury and much loss,
not only of the cargo and the ship, but also of our lives. (v. 10)

Faith thrives on taking risks for God's sake; but there comes a point where the risk is unjustified, and taking it is not faith but presumption. Paul was prepared to die for the sake of the gospel, but not needlessly. He was no expert sailor, but it was accepted wisdom based on years of experience in the nautical world that the season for sailing was already past for that year. To put to sea from Fair Havens so late in the year was to take an enormous and foolish risk (vv. 9–11). The purpose of putting to sea again was to reach a more commodious harbour in which it would be more comfortable and convenient to spend the winter. But to risk shipwreck, with loss of the cargo and above all of the two hundred and seventy-six lives on board, simply in order to gain a slightly better harbour than the one they already had, was to Paul's way of thinking foolish; and he spoke his mind.

But the captain and the owner of the vessel wanted to take the risk. Expertise and professional pride can often breed over-confidence; and the centurion in charge took their advice rather than Paul's. All the same, it is instructive to notice Paul's attitude. His faith was not of the kind that would argue: 'Yes, take what risks you like. I'm God's special ambassador. God would not allow me to suffer any disaster. If necessary, he will do a miracle and keep the seas calm until we get to the next harbour.' It wasn't that he did not believe in miracles, or in God's willingness to do them where absolutely necessary. But they had no compelling need to go on to the next harbour; and to take unnecessary risks and then count on God to do miracles in nature to obviate disaster is not faith but presumption. At this point, therefore, Paul appears in Luke's record not as some super-spiritual hero, but as a man whose humble but real faith knew its proper limits.

David Gooding, *True to the Faith: The Acts of the Apostles–Defining and Defending the Gospel*, pp. 486-7

5th June

THE POWER OF FAITH OVER DESPAIR

Reading: Acts 27:21–42

Therefore I urge you to take some food. For it will give you strength,
for not a hair is to perish from the head of any of you. (v. 34)

For two weeks passengers and crew had scarcely eaten anything. Which is no wonder: below deck everything was probably in chaos if not awash. And anyway, in their fear and misery people would have had no stomach for food, even those who were not hopelessly seasick. But once more Paul's faith took a grip of the practical situation. He got up and addressed all two hundred and seventy-five of his fellow passengers. Reminding them of God's promise that they would all get safely to land, he urged them to eat something. No angelic chairlift would miraculously waft them to the shore. They would need every calorie of energy for their last battle with the crashing waves and undertow. So he set them an example. Openly demonstrating the secret of his calm and confidence, he took bread, gave thanks to God before them all while the gale still raged, ate, and encouraged them all to do the same (vv. 35–36).

Observe, then, the role of faith in this whole affair. It was not that Paul simply believed that because God had a work for him to do in Rome, God would bring him and all the others safely through, in spite of the storm. It was Paul's faith in response to God's promise that he would survive to see his task of witnessing completed that enabled him to take control of the psychological situation, and to see to it that all the necessary practical steps were taken to keep the ship afloat and bring her, as best as might be, to the shore.

Ultimately it takes a faith and a purpose that are anchored beyond nature, to give one the strength and courage to persist with life and life's endeavours in the face of nature's storms, when it appears on other grounds that all hope is gone. Indeed, why would God himself continue with nature any longer if he had not magnificent and eternal purposes beyond all her ragings? For this reason it is that even when (and if) we lose our last struggle with nature, and she overwhelms us in death, we shall be more than conquerors through him who loved us (Rom 8:37).

David Gooding, *True to the Faith: The Acts of the Apostles–Defining and Defending the Gospel*, pp. 489-90

6th June

FAITH IN GOD'S PROGRAMME

Reading: Genesis 50:15–26

Then Joseph made the sons of Israel swear, saying, 'God will surely visit you, and you shall carry up my bones from here'. (v. 25)

Perhaps the greatest test of faith is not sacrifice but success, worldly success. If so, Joseph's faith was supremely triumphant. The remarkable thing about Joseph is that, being in the position he was in, he still retained his boyhood faith that God had a prophetic programme for this world and that that programme was centred in, and would be carried by, Israel and not Egypt.

Egypt in those days was the dominant world power. Israel was a tiny tribe, scarcely more than an extended family. For a member of that family to emigrate to Egypt and eventually to become the vice-president of the country was not all that remarkable. Such things have often happened in the history of superpowers. But for such a vice-president, while still in office, to believe and announce that hope for the world's future lies not with superpowers, but with tiny Israel and with her God-given prophetic role in history—that is quite another thing. It takes a lot of faith to believe that nowadays. It must have taken a lot more in Joseph's day.

Yet that is what he had learnt from Abraham, Isaac and Jacob, and he continued to believe it. He lived in a day when there was an interlude in God's programme for Israel, and Israel was out of the promised land and living among the Gentiles. During that interlude Joseph was happy to serve in Egypt's administration. But he believed the promise given to Abraham (Gen 15:13–16). The interlude would one day end, Israel would return to the land. God's prophetic programme would be on the march again. When that happened, Joseph wanted to be identified with it. His bones were not to be left in Egypt to await the general resurrection at the last day. Even in death he wanted to be remembered not as a famous prime minister of Egypt, but as one link in the long chain of the fulfilment of God's purpose through Israel. In this, Scripture says, he acted in faith. That is, his action was based on the explicit word of God recorded in Genesis, interpreted literally, and believed wholeheartedly.

God give us the faith of Joseph to believe that before this planet comes to its end, there will be a time of unparalleled blessing for our world. The present interlude in Israel's history, marked by her unbelief in the Messiah and her scattering among the Gentile nations, will one day end. Her Messiah shall return. Israel shall be reconciled and restored.

David Gooding, *An Unshakeable Kingdom: The Letter to the Hebrews for Today*, pp. 218–19

7th June

FAITH'S VICTORIES AND APPARENT DEFEATS

Reading: Hebrews 11:32–12:2

*Let us run with endurance the race that is set before us, looking
to Jesus, the founder and perfecter of our faith, who for the joy
that was set before him endured the cross, despising the shame,
and is seated at the right hand of the throne of God. (12:1–2)*

And now the author summarizes in a very impressive and moving list the
exploits of numerous men and women of faith. Some were obviously victorious by faith even in their lifetimes. Others, equally men and women of faith,
suffered apparent defeat. They died without being vindicated. Faith is not
always seen to be triumphant in this life. And it takes greater faith to suffer
apparent disaster, unvindicated, and to go on believing still.

Now all in the list of those who faced disaster through faith are nameless,
except one. Of him we read in chapter 12. For when all the vast army of
witnesses has gone past, there comes one at last who takes our attention
away from all else and fastens it on himself. We look off to the author and
perfecter of our faith. And what do we observe? A great success in this life,
with people thronging round to praise him that his way has worked and
has been vindicated and proved right? No. We follow the man of faith to
Golgotha's hill and see him trust God's leading and guidance till it brings
him to the cross. We watch the nails driven in, and we say, 'Surely God will
vindicate his faith now and work a miracle to bring him down'. The crowds
pass by and say, 'He saved others, but he can't save himself. Let this Christ,
this King of Israel, come down' (Mark 15:31-32).

But he doesn't. The hours pass, and he dies. The world says, 'There you
are. He was an impostor'.

What is there to prove otherwise? Why, the one who went to the cross is
risen now, seated on the right hand of the throne of God. And he who once
seemed such a victim of circumstances, sits on the right hand of the very
throne that controls the universe. Courage! If you dare to believe this Christ
and follow him, come what may, you too shall sit down on his throne, as he
also overcame and sat down on his Father's throne. This is Christ's explicit
promise (Rev 3:21; 2 Tim 2:12). Let us dare to believe it.

David Gooding, An Unshakeable Kingdom: The Letter to the Hebrews for Today, pp. 224–5

8th June

THAT CHRIST MAY DWELL IN YOUR HEARTS THROUGH FAITH

Reading: Ephesians 3:7–21

. . . so that Christ may dwell in your hearts through faith. (v. 17)

Paul tells us here that he is praying—and he makes it explicit—for people who are already believers. They already have the Holy Spirit, but he prays that God would give them the workings of the Holy Spirit in their hearts, so that they may be strengthened in their inner being by that Holy Spirit. What for? 'So that Christ may dwell in your hearts through faith' (vv. 16–17).

You say, 'But Christ is dwelling in my heart'.

Well, of course he is. If you are a believer, Christ is dwelling in your heart. God's desire is to dwell in us; but do you think God is satisfied with what he has got yet? You would be disappointed, and you might have your doubts about heaven, if he were! No; the final product will be that I shall be 'filled with all the fullness of God' (v. 19). All the glory of God and all the character of God will find its expression in me until there is not a part of me that he does not fill.

When they built the tabernacle and presented it to Moses, Moses erected it and presented it to God, then God came down and filled it. There was no room for anybody else and the priests had to get out. God is not going to be content with us either, until his dwelling in us means that he has filled us in every part of our being and all the fullness of God is in us. It has not happened yet.

You say: 'It will happen when the Lord comes.'

So it will, my brothers and sisters, but it had better start happening now. Why do you suppose the Lord has left us here and not taken us at once to heaven? We should not just be sitting around, wasting our time. The Lord has left us down here to do something. History is more real than that. The purpose of time is that we make progress. The years of our converted life are not to be frittered away by standing still. They are the time when, by God's Spirit, our hearts might be strengthened; that Christ might come and take his abode ever more fully in our hearts. That is a process, and a process that takes a necessary preparation. It involves the strengthening of my inner being by God's Spirit, and it involves that I become more and more rooted in the love of God (v. 17).

David Gooding, *Ephesians: A Bird's Eye View of the Major Movements of Thought*, p. 77

9th June

POOR BUT RICH IN FAITH

Reading: James 2:1–11

*Listen, my beloved brothers, has not God chosen those who
are poor in the world to be rich in faith and heirs of the
kingdom, which he has promised to those who love him? (v. 5)*

'God has chosen the poor,' and James brings home his exhortation to us by saying, 'but you have from time to time been known to despise the poor.' Be very careful!

It sometimes happens that a young gentleman falls in love with a young lady, proposes marriage and marries her. But some of his friends mutter to themselves, 'I can't think what he saw in the woman! What on earth did he see in her to marry a woman like that?' If you must say it, be careful not to let your friend who married the girl hear it! You won't say in his presence, 'I can't think what you saw in that woman.' You won't say that, when he has chosen her, will you? Not unless you want to insult his choice.

You had better watch what you say about me, for if God has chosen me, be careful lest you criticize God for his choice. He has chosen the poor to be rich in faith. That doesn't mean that all poor people are believers, but, on the whole, a believer who is poor is generally likely to have stronger faith than people who are not poor. Why is that? Well, because they are obliged to trust God.

The miners in north east England amongst whom I once lived used to tell me what it was like in the days of the terrible Depression. They had no unemployment benefit and husbands could be out of work for ten years at a stretch. The women told me how they used to get down on their knees and pray to God for the next meal.

If you are in difficult circumstances—poor economically, physically, poor in any sense—it will take much more faith to believe that God loves you than when you are surrounded by riches galore. And yet faith is the most valuable thing in all God's universe. Faith is the thing that holds the universe together; it holds God and his people together. If we are thinking about values, then let us get Peter's perspective on it. Our faith is much more valuable than gold (see 1 Pet 1:7). Next to the blood of Christ, it is the most valuable thing in all the universe. That poor brother could be remarkably rich in faith, and faith will outshine all other riches.

David Gooding, James's Vision of the Perfect Man and Woman: The Epistle of James, p. 30

THE DISCIPLE'S JOURNEY

Part 4—Our Walk with the Lord

10th June

WALKING IN THE LIGHT

Reading: John 8:1–12

*Again Jesus spoke to them, saying, 'I am the light
of the world. Whoever follows me will not walk in
darkness, but will have the light of life.' (v. 12)*

When the scribes and Pharisees brought the woman who had been taken
in adultery before him, Christ bent down and wrote with his finger on the
ground. This was writing the first time. And when he lifted himself up the
second time they were all gone, beginning from the oldest to the youngest.
I feel like calling after them: 'Don't be daft! If you go now you are admitting
that you are sinners, aren't you? Come back! Face up to it with him!' But they
dared not. They were standing in front of him who is the light of the world.
They were standing in front of him who is the lawgiver incarnate. 'Let him
who is without sin among you be the first to throw a stone at her' (v. 7). They
slunk out. They daren't face him, for he would have exposed them.

So after the first time he wrote on the ground, he stood up and said, 'Let
him who is without sin among you be the first to throw a stone at her.' Then
he stooped down and wrote again. And they went out. When he had written
the second time he stood up and said to her:

> 'Woman, where are they? Has no one condemned you?' [that is, con-
> demned you to death] She said, 'No one, Lord.' And Jesus said, 'Nei-
> ther do I condemn you; go, and from now on sin no more.' (vv. 10–11)

He is not saying that adultery is right. He is saying, 'I don't condemn you to
suffer the penalty of death.' How could he say it when he was the lawgiver
incarnate? Well, how did he forgive Israel and write the tablets of the law
again? He could say it because in a year or two's time, he was to be 'lifted up', as
this very chapter says (v. 28), and pay the penalty of that woman's sin himself.

That is where we begin: when we begin to follow the light, and stand long
enough to let the light expose us, and in repentance and faith we cast ourselves
on the mercies of Christ. He is God incarnate, the lawgiver incarnate, a God
of all mercy who died that we might be forgiven. Then we begin the journey,
following the light of this world. He casts light on our journey. We are sure there
is a heaven to go to because he tells us where he comes from and where he is
going; and we find the transition from this life to the next because he is the I AM.

David Gooding, *Four Journeys to Jerusalem: A Series of Seminars on the Gospel of John*, p. 122

11th June

THE ATONEMENT AND WALKING IN THE LIGHT

Reading: Leviticus 16:11–19

For with you is the fountain of life; in your
light do we see light. (Psalm 36:9)

You say, 'If I come and walk in the light it will expose my sin and I'll feel so unworthy.' But John says,

> 'I am writing these things to you so that you may not sin. But if anyone does sin, we have an advocate with the Father, Jesus Christ the righteous. He is the propitiation for our sins (1 John 2:1-2).

He is the propitiation for our sins. Back in Old Testament days, when God dwelt in a tabernacle amongst his people, we're told that on the Day of Atonement there was atonement made for the tabernacle itself, because the very presence of the Israelites and their sinfulness defiled God's presence. How then could God righteously continue fellowship with them? How was it that the first time they sinned, he didn't depart from them immediately? How could he carry on with them in all their weakness and their sinning? The answer is that there was atonement made, 'to make atonement for the tent of meeting that dwells with them in the midst of their uncleanness' (see Lev 16:16).

Oh, what a mercy it is. See that poor adulteress standing exposed in the presence of the very light of the world (John 8). She can't run away; there's nowhere to run to. Exposed, confessed as a sinner. And God has to abandon her? Oh, thank God, no. The dear woman can be forgiven. And so with us: when his light exposes us and we confess our sins, our eternal life isn't broken off. It's maintained through the great atonement of Jesus Christ, our Lord. If we walk in the light, we have fellowship, and the blood of Jesus Christ cleanses us from all sin.

You may remember that in the tabernacle, as the priest came and walked to the table in the light of the great lampstand, there was a third vessel, the vessel of intercession, at which the high priest prayed. What a lovely trilogy of fellowship they make, reminding us of what John says, 'If we walk in the light, as he is in the light, we have fellowship with one another, and the blood of Jesus his Son cleanses us from all sin. . . . If we confess our sins, he is faithful and just to forgive us our sins . . . . But if anyone does sin, we have an advocate with the Father' (1 John 1:7, 9; 2:1)

David Gooding, *Life in the Family of God: Twelve Seminars on the First Epistle of John*, p. 20

12th June

FOLLOWING CHRIST ON THE
PATH OF DISCIPLESHIP

Reading: Matthew 9:18–26

*And he said to them, 'Follow me, and I will
make you fishers of men.' (Matthew 4:19)*

There is no such thing as being saved and not being a disciple. In Matthew 9, Jairus invites the Lord Jesus to come to his house and lay his hand upon his daughter because she is even now close to death. And 'Jesus arose and followed him' (v. 19). Do you know that's sometimes a dangerous thing to do? You have a need, some particular need, some particular worry, and you come to the Lord Jesus and you say, 'Now, Lord, come and deal with my need', and the Lord begins to follow you. But you'll want to watch it, because he doesn't follow you for very long. Yes, he'll let you take him to your need, whatever your need is, but presently you'll find he isn't following anymore. He's going on in front and bidding you follow him, and he'll take you right beyond your need, because he's not just interested in helping us with the need that we see. He has plans ahead for us and ideas that we haven't yet grasped, and he won't be content until he has conformed us to his own image. So our Lord began to follow Jairus.

But now notice what Matthew tells us later on: 'And as Jesus passed by from there, two blind men followed him' (v. 27). How difficult it was as these poor chaps went feeling their way all down the road. 'Where's he got to now?' So they listened for his voice, and for a while that guided them. When that went quiet they didn't know where he'd got to, and then they found he'd gone into a house.

Have you ever been trying to follow the Lord, and then everything went silent and you didn't know where the Lord had got to? You felt blind, and you were groping your way along, and you missed all your landmarks. The Lord seemed to be playing games with you. Yes, but there are lessons to be learnt on the path of discipleship, not merely at conversion but all the way along the road home to glory.

So Matthew is talking to us about discipleship and the twin ideas that lie behind it: the authority of the Lord Jesus on the one hand, and the following of the disciple on the other.

David Gooding, The Gospel of Authority and the Path of Discipleship: Studies in Matthew, pp. 6–7

13th June

THE GOSPEL OF AUTHORITY AND
THE PATH OF DISCIPLESHIP

Reading: Matthew 8:1–17

Come to me, all who labour and are heavy laden,
and I will give you rest. (Matthew 11:28)

Sometimes when we talk about discipleship we are inclined to talk as though it were something very severe and thus contrast it with the gospel. We represent the gospel as being something lovely, delightful, comforting, rich and free, and that's the bait with which we attract the unconverted. And then, after you've had the nice bit, here comes the nasty bit.

It's like it used to be at school. I went to school, and they tricked you. Oh, it was terrible. They started off with beautiful stories and toys and things. That was marvellous. They gave you the idea that this was what school was going to be like. Then when they'd got you hooked on that, they said to you: 'Arithmetic' and other such abominations. Now you found out that, along with the nice, you had to take the nasty. Horrible it was.

Sometimes we talk about discipleship like that, don't we? 'The gospel is all free, and it's glorious and it's wonderful, but then there comes this painful business of discipleship.' Matthew doesn't make that mistake, as we'll see in chapter 8. The first part deals with what you might describe, quite fairly, as the gospel of authority. What do we mean by 'the gospel of authority'? Matthew says that, as our Lord Jesus came down from the mountain, the multitudes followed him. He taught them as one having authority, not as the scribes (see 7:28–8:1). What is the nature of the Lord's authority?

This is gospel that says there has come a Saviour with authority to deliver. And so Matthew quotes to us those lovely words from Isaiah as he sums up this passage that deals with the gospel of our Lord's authority, telling us it's just like Isaiah said, 'He himself took our infirmities and bore our diseases' (see 8:17; Isa 53:4). That is, he carried them. The nature of his authority is this: that the king himself, with all his authority, lowered his shoulder and put it under our weaknesses and under our burdens, and he carried them. What a lovely thing that is, for all of us are broken in some way or another. All of us are weak in some way and defiled. We need somebody with authority against sin, with authority against weakness, with authority against fevered distress, who can come with his strong shoulder and put it underneath our weakness and underneath our disability and carry it.

David Gooding, *The Gospel of Authority and the Path of Discipleship: Studies in Matthew*, p. 7–9

14th June

THE FIRST LESSON OF DISCIPLESHIP

Reading: Matthew 8:18–22; Luke 9:57–62

But Jesus answered them, 'My Father is working
until now, and I am working.' (John 5:17)

I wonder what the Lord Jesus meant. Was this a word simply to that scribe who lived all those many years ago and to him only? Did he say, 'the Son of Man has nowhere to lay his head' to warn him that, if he followed him in the boat, it wouldn't necessarily be very comfortable; he might have to rough it, like missionaries going to various difficult places? Did he mean that, 'in this particular journey that we're taking across the lake here, you'll have to rough it'?

When the old fox gets tired after all its daily activity, nature has provided it a place to lay its head, and it is here on the earth. The bird of heaven, when it has finished its flying around the place, has a nest. But for the Lord Jesus, where was the place to lay his head when he had finished his work? Well, there was nowhere in this world, because his work wasn't ever finished.

The word is only used of our Lord Jesus once more in the New Testament, as far as I know. There was one place where he laid his head. According to the Gospel of John, he bowed his head, saying, 'It is finished: and he bowed his head, and gave up the ghost' (19:30 KJV). On Calvary alone was his work finished in this world and, in that sense, not until then did he lay down his head and rest. What a mission it was, when he came down to our world. It was never finished until the great work was accomplished.

We are called to follow him on the path of discipleship. It may be that sometimes we shall have very comfortable homes, or perhaps we shall not. Perhaps we shall have to rough it sometimes and, on the other hand, sometimes things will be comfortable. But as far as the work of our discipleship is concerned, as far as the lessons that we may learn and must learn on the path of discipleship, so far as the training goes that our Lord intends to give us on the path of discipleship, we shall *never* finish on this side of glory. We shall never be able to lay down our head and say, 'Now I've finished.'

David Gooding, *The Gospel of Authority and the Path of Discipleship: Studies in Matthew*, pp. 13–14

15th June

FEEDING ON GOD'S WORD

Reading: Psalm 119:97–104

*For even when we were with you, we would give
you this command: If anyone is not willing to
work, let him not eat. (2 Thessalonians 3:10)*

We are all good Christian men and women and so we give thanks for our daily bread, even though we've worked hard for it. We recognize that it is God who has given us our bread and butter; but that doesn't mean it falls down out of heaven on to our plates, already processed, cellophane wrapped, and all we have to do is to take the wrapper off and eat it. God gives it, but we have to work for it; and so it is with our spiritual bread. God gives it, of course, but then we have to work for it.

There are, as you know, all kinds of meals. There are those quick snacks: you go into the pantry and lift a tin of sardines, open the lid and there in half a second you have the meal already prepared; another half minute and it's eaten, and what a lot of time it saves you so that you can do other, more important things.

Then there are those other gorgeous meals, home-made plum puddings and things, and you would be mistaken to suppose that you can have a 'quick snack' plum pudding. Of course you can't. You have to start months before, with orange peel and sugar and who knows what, and you've got to stir it and mix it and let it stand and coax it and persuade it and talk nicely to it, and get out the Kenwood mixer and things. You can spend hours on this heap of stuff, and it still isn't ready to eat. If anybody was so silly as to try and eat it, he would suffer indigestion forthwith and conclude that Christmas puddings were horrible things. No, you've got to work hard for days on end, and only at the end will you get something to satisfy your hunger and your taste.

Thus it is with Scripture. We can come for quick snacks, but there are other kinds of meals, and if we would appreciate the deeper things of God we must be prepared to work hard and not demand instant results; working in faith, that if we honestly work hard at his word, God will in the end honour our faith and show us the great treasures of his word. If we don't work at this level, then we will not eat.

David Gooding, *Family Life with Abraham and Jacob: Studies in Genesis 12–50*, p. 43

16th June

DEALING WITH DOUBT

Reading: Matthew 11:1–19

Are you the one who is to come, or shall we look for another? (v. 3)

Many believers have felt a little bit nervous at the idea that John the Baptist ever came to doubt whether Jesus was really the Messiah. But then of course, there are many believers who feel that doubt is a very bad thing and something, which if it ever happens to you, you should do your best to keep in the dark. I don't know what you have found; I have found over the years there are many believers who, if you can really get close enough to them, have very serious doubts in their hearts and often about matters of their own personal salvation. They are scared stiff to let anybody know it, lest they would be thought to be terrible people and forthwith cast out of the synagogue, so to speak. Or, if they have doubts about their salvation, they wonder if that would disqualify them from being saved, and therefore they keep their doubts suppressed, with a great deal of consequent misery.

So let us, at this level, get this matter straight. If we have doubts, then let us be open and honest about them with the Lord. It has been my good fortune, having been saved I wouldn't like to tell you how many years, by God's good grace to have never doubted my salvation. It's none of my cleverness either. I have doubted many times whether there is anything true in Christianity at all. Yes, if Christianity is true, I'm saved, but is Christianity true? And is it objectively true, or have I managed simply to play a psychological trick upon myself? How do I know it's true?

And you will observe on every occasion where people have doubts that our blessed Lord, instead of rejecting them, encourages them. He might chide them for having unnecessary doubts, but he always solves those doubts for them by giving them that kind of evidence that is necessary to resolve the doubt.

Permit a grey head to turn aside to a little exhortation. If we have doubts, let's do with them what John the Baptist did: let's tell the Lord honestly about them.

David Gooding, *The Gospel of Authority and the Path of Discipleship: Studies in Matthew*, p. 43

17th June

DEALING WITH FAILURE

Reading: Psalm 51

*For sin will have no dominion over you, since you are
not under law but under grace. (Romans 6:14)*

You know there are many folks walking the streets of Belfast, who would like to be saved, only they say to themselves, 'Ah well, it's no good. I did make a profession once, but then I fell and, well, I've broken it all, and that's finished it.

So, now what?

'Well,' they say, 'might as well be killed for sheep as a lamb, mightn't you? I mean, my resistance is no good. I don't try these days at all; I just go on sinning.'

If I speak to a believer who is thinking this way, won't you listen to God's word? Won't you learn his facts? Sin need not have dominion over you! It is possible for you to get up and start again as a believer. Why? Because the penalty of sin has been paid. I'm not telling you sin doesn't matter; sin matters a lot, and if we've got away from the Lord and gone into sin as Christians, there is no penalty, but coming back can be difficult, can't it? And the lessons we shall have to face can be bitter. But courage brother and sister, you can do it! And you are free to do it! You are not chained by the penalty of the law. You are free, thank God, because of Christ's sacrifice! You are free to get up and begin again in the path of holiness and in the school of Christ. Don't let sin have dominion! Don't let it keep you down, for it needn't. Poorly as you may have done, however full of mistakes your Christian life has been, at this very moment you can say, 'Sorry, Lord. I'm coming back. Now let me start again.' And you are free to get up.

Some of us, if we'd be honest, would admit we've had to do it one thousand and one times. We've had to start again. Poor old Abraham: he wandered at times, didn't he? He went off wandering around Egypt. What circles he did make. But mercifully we read he came back to where he started; he began again. All Christian life is the story of ten thousand and one times of beginning again. I don't know about you, but there are some days I have to start again, I don't know how many times, and I am free to do it because I am not under law.

David Gooding, *Wreckage and Recovery: God's Way of Making Believers Holy: Romans 5–8*, p. 38

18th June

PRINCIPLES OF LIVING IN A NEW WORLD

Reading: Genesis 8:20–9:17

. . . for whoever has entered God's rest has also rested from his works as God did from his. (Hebrews 4:10)

When God smelled the pleasing aroma (Gen 18:21), did he say, 'Well now, Noah, you have been in the ark and you have been through the waters; I am very content with you and I now feel that I can rest'? Indeed, not! God wouldn't feel contented with Noah until he got him home to glory. Nor will he feel contented with us till he gets us home to glory either. I'm being factual. God loves us, but that is a different thing from being contented with us. Indeed, it is because he loves us that he'll be constantly trying to bring us to repentance. And we must not think he doesn't love us because he keeps pointing out things that are wrong. He won't be content until we have lost all our wrinkles, spots and blemishes and we're like Christ. We can find rest where God already finds rest, in the great sacrifice of Christ. Our peace with God and the resting place of our hearts is not based on our attainments, it is based always and only on acceptance with God through the sacrifice of Christ.

If Satan can't get at you through your being worldly, he will trip you up by your very godliness and spirituality. He doesn't mind which way he does it. You set yourself tremendously high standards (of course, you shouldn't have low standards) and he will fill you with glory on a Monday morning. You have never felt such a good Christian. You are making the grade and now you feel you can call yourself a Christian. You were always a bit uncertain before; you weren't absolutely sure you were saved, but now you feel you are. Tuesday afternoon you come a cropper and you don't think you're a Christian at all now. All the puff has gone out of it. You feel you're no good and nobody's any good and Satan has got you because your feeling of contentment was based on your attainment. It will sap every bit of strength you've got, or else turn you into a hardened Pharisee.

Learn that you are accepted through Christ's sacrifice and be content with him and permanently discontent with yourself. Come and celebrate it every Lord's Day morning. Have the courage to face all those things about yourself of which you have every right to be discontent.

David Gooding, *The God of New Beginnings: Eighteen Seminars on the Book of Genesis*, pp. 79–80

19th June

CHRISTIAN ATTITUDES

Reading: Luke 6:27–36

*You therefore must be perfect, as your heavenly
Father is perfect. (Matthew 5:48)*

Running through these exhortations are two basic principles. The first is
that followers of Christ are called upon to behave in ways far superior to
those of sinners (Luke 6:32–34). It is the fact that many of the kind and
generous attitudes and acts on which we all congratulate ourselves, are the
attitudes and acts which all members of all groups show towards members
of their own groups. We all love our fellow-socialists, or fellow-capitalists,
or fellow-nationals, or fellow-religionists. But there is nothing very special
about that. Even sinners do the same. Christ calls his followers to love their
enemies, their oppressors, their robbers and those that show them violence,
and to do them good (vv. 27–29).

The second is that followers of Christ must show the same character as
their Father (vv. 35–36). He is just, but he is more than just: he is merciful.
So must his sons be. It is not so much a question of following rules, or even
of clamouring for justice. It is a question of inheriting by the new birth the
Father's nature and exhibiting that nature by behaving as his mature sons.
Sonship, one might almost say, is the key to Christ's moral teaching. We
recall how at Luke 5:34–35 he explained that the behaviour of 'sons of the
bridechamber' (which is what the Greek calls the bridegroom's guests) will
be regulated by the presence or absence of the bridegroom. And the analogy
turned into a metaphor: he is the bridegroom and his disciples are his 'sons
of the bride-chamber'. Now here his disciples are sons of the Father. And
once more we conclude that for them true moral behaviour is not so much
a matter of keeping rules but a matter of developing a God-like character as
a result of enjoying the life of God in fellowship with Christ.

David Gooding, *According to Luke: The Third Gospel's Ordered Historical Narrative*, p. 122

20th June

DEPENDENCE ON GOD

Reading: James 4:13–17

. . . yet you do not know what tomorrow will bring.
What is your life? For you are a mist that appears
for a little time and then vanishes. (v. 14)

From verse 13 to the end of the chapter James wants us not to allow ourselves, even in our business lives, to become independent of the Lord. We so easily get enthused and rightly so; God has given us ambitions and we should be ambitious to please the Lord. If God has put the stewardship of money or capital or factory or firm into our hands, along with that stewardship come the heavy responsibilities of running the firm well. Upon its smooth and proper running depends the welfare of many a workman, his wife and family. Let us give thanks for men who know how to manage. Very often the workman goes home to bed and hasn't another care in his head until tomorrow, whereas the manager, who has got to find the funds for the salaries at the end of the week, can spend many a sleepless night.

Let's be thankful for the various gifts that God has given. If he has put us in business, it's easy for the joy, the thrill and excitement of it to carry us away. We have plans here and plans there; this is what we are going to do next year. What's wrong with that? First of all, you don't know what is going to happen tomorrow (v. 14).

'Are you proposing to be alive tomorrow?'

You say, 'I hope so!'

'Don't you know?'

Why has God left it uncertain? One effect it has is that we have to take every single day as a gift from God to which we have no right. We can't take it for granted and we are dependent each day on the Lord. Therefore, that habit of mine whereby I constantly remind myself to say, 'If the Lord wills, we will live and do this or that' (v. 15), brings us to a more realistic confrontation with life. It is not mere pharisaic religion. At the same time, it stops that incipient worldliness, which is the creeping tendency to become independent of the Lord in our lives. That, after all, is what worldliness is—getting away from the Lord and the sense of dependence upon him.

David Gooding, *James's Vision of the Perfect Man and Woman: The Epistle of James*, p. 69

21st June

DON'T BE ASHAMED OF YOUR WISDOM

Reading: Deuteronomy 4:1–14

For I am not ashamed of the gospel, for it is the power
of God for salvation to everyone who believes, to the
Jew first and also to the Greek. (Romans 1:16)

As they are about to enter the land, Moses appeals to them not to be ashamed. He says, 'Keep them (these statutes) and do them, for that will be your wisdom and your understanding in the sight of the peoples, who, when they hear all these statues, will say, "Surely this great nation is a wise and understanding people"' (Deut 4:6). *Don't be ashamed of your wisdom!*

When I first joined Queen's University there were two bodies of students that sought to witness for Christ. One of them was the Student Christian Movement and the other the Christian Union. In its early days the Student Christian Movement had set out with good and great intentions. By the time I reached Queen's they had lost their grip on the doctrines of the gospel, the deity of Christ, his virgin birth and his resurrection. The last president of the Student Christian Movement was an atheist! That movement folded up. A sociologist came to the university who was an atheist. He chose to write a PhD thesis on the Student Christian Movement and the Christian Union in Queen's University Belfast. His aim was to discover why the one institution had folded up and the other had continued vigorously. Being an atheist he was not biased, for he didn't believe any of it. He pointed out to the world that the one institution had folded up because they had lost grip of their beliefs—they had nothing to believe any more.

There are people who claim to have a religious faith, but they are prepared to compromise it all the way along the line. You can't continue if you've lost your faith in the very foundations of your beliefs. The world won't respect you for it. They won't necessarily agree that you are wise, if you do maintain your beliefs. But as far as the world is concerned, a Christianity that denies the virgin birth of Christ, his atoning death, his resurrection and his second coming might as well fold up. My good brothers and sisters, and especially you younger folks who must face this new age that we are entering, take heed to the historic facts, both of Israel's faith and of ours, and determine by God's grace not to be ashamed of them.

David Gooding, *With Moses on the Plains of Moab: Studies in Deuteronomy*, p. 13

22nd June

LOYALTY TO CHRIST AS LORD

Reading: Daniel 3

*So therefore, any one of you who does not renounce all
that he has cannot be my disciple. (Luke 14:33)*

With what right does Christ face us with such an alternative? He is God!
How little our concepts of God are these days. Christ is not a 'resource
person'. We treat him like we treat our garage man. We don't spend much
time with him, but when the car goes wrong and things have broken down
we go to him, believing he can put things right. Of course he puts it right,
but we don't ask him to get in the car and come home with us and guide
us in our lives. As soon as he has put it right, we say good-bye—until we
need him again.

In our anxiety to get converts we are tempted to preach that sort of gospel
to the people. 'Jesus Christ is a resource person. Are you feeling the blues?
Well, Christ could help you with that!' You are not feeling the blues? Well
then, you won't feel any need of Christ. The very terms of salvation are these.
If you want salvation as a free gift, it is through faith in Christ; you become
his disciple and he will demand that you renounce everything else you have
and take him as sovereign Lord.

You say, 'Why do you try to apply this ancient lesson to us in this far-off
day? Our circumstances are easy. We are not likely to come into the kind
of crisis situation that the three young Hebrew men came into in Daniel 3.'

Perhaps you may manage not to, and get home to glory before you meet
any dictator. That is not the point! This is a decision that each one must
make. Unless our hearts are surrendered absolutely to Christ—given the
choice between him and everything else we will choose Christ—we wouldn't
be safe in heaven. What do I mean? If the devil can take the little things of
this passing world and so hold them out in front of our noses that, in fear of
losing them, we grasp them and leave the Saviour, what would happen if we
were in heaven with ten thousand million delights and our hearts were not
first and foremost rooted in the Saviour and he is supreme above them all?
I fancy we would maybe turn up to a heavenly prayer meeting once in two
years and the very delights of heaven would take us away from the Saviour.

David Gooding, *Daniel: Civil Servant and Saint*, pp. 106–7

23rd June

WALKING WORTHY OF THE LORD

Reading: Colossians 1:1–12

Walk as children of light (for the fruit of light is found in all that is good and right and true), and try to discern what is pleasing to the Lord. (Ephesians 5:8–10)

I remember hearing Dr Laubach at a missionary breakfast. He was the great missionary pioneer who developed a means of teaching one-time savage tribespeople to be able to read. He told us a touching story. He'd given the chief of a tribe some lessons, and now the chief could read. So grateful was he to Dr Laubach that he came and sat by his side, and put his arm around his neck. He said, 'Dr Laubach, I am so grateful to you for teaching me to read, I'd like to do you a favour. Is there anybody around here I could kill for your sake?' He wanted to please the good doctor, but he hadn't learned what would please him!

So Paul prays that they may be filled with the knowledge of his will in all spiritual wisdom and understanding, so as to walk in a manner worthy of the Lord, fully pleasing to him.

'This will involve two things,' says Paul. It will involve good works; and in addition to good works it will always involve an increasing—with a snow-ball-like effect—knowledge of God. It is difficult for the Almighty to make himself known to us personally if we just carry on living in a way that displeases him. It is to those who please him that he can reveal himself more deeply. If we are to bear fruit in every good work, we shall need this *endurance*. But now the great question arises: from where shall we get the strength, the moral and spiritual power, to carry on enduring? Paul gives us the delightful answer: '[being] strengthened with all power, according to his glorious might' (Col 1:11). That's where we shall get the strength from to endure.

Sit back for a moment and put these things together. The great future lies ahead when we shall be presented before the throne of God's glory without charge, 'if indeed you continue in the faith' (v. 23). From where shall we get the power to continue? What if our own little strength isn't sufficient and adequate, and exhausts itself before life's race is won? Where shall we look to for strength? And the answer comes back, 'being strengthened with all power, according to his glorious might.'

David Gooding, *A Cosmic-sized Salvation: Three Studies in Colossians*, pp. 19–20

THE DISCIPLE'S JOURNEY

Part 5—Our Daily Lives

24th June

SEEKING GOD'S KINGDOM IN OUR DAILY WORK

Reading: Matthew 6:25–34

But seek first the kingdom of God and his righteousness,
and all these things will be added to you. (v. 33)

It is valuable experience as we try to carry out the Lord's rules and principles of living in our daily work. Work is not only the means of providing food and clothes. The Lord knows you need those things, of course he does. That is the normal way of providing them, but daily work is about more than that; it is about developing a Christian character. We need it, good Christian friend, for we are being trained to rule with Christ and, along with him, to put into practice the rules of the kingdom of God. How shall we be in a position to impose them if we have not learnt to keep them ourselves?

I was at dinner in a home far from here with a good Christian man who is now retired. He told me his story. In his professional life he was a company secretary (a mix between an accountant and a solicitor) and therefore had to be present at the board meetings with the directors. And on this occasion, the income tax people had become worried about certain practices that the board of directors had been following in order to cheat the income tax inspectors. The inspector demanded a meeting with the directors and my good friend, the company secretary, had to attend. The question was eventually put by the income tax inspectors, and the chairman of the board asked my friend to give the answer. My friend said, 'I knew in that moment that if I told the truth it would be the end of my job.'

What would you do? He had a wife and children and a house and a mortgage. If his prime motivation in being in business was to get food and clothes, he would have told a lie along with the directors, and kept his job. By God's grace, this noble man saw that the reason God sent him into business was that he might have practice in keeping the rules of the kingdom of God, and thus building into his life a sound character. He answered with the truth, and he lost his job. If he had told a lie he'd have kept the goods and the job, but he would have lost the prime thing for which God sent him to work.

David Gooding, *Three Creation Stories and Three Patriarchs: The Book of Genesis*, pp. 73–4

25th June

THE COST OF OUR REDEMPTION
INSPIRES US TO WORK HARD

Reading: 2 Thessalonians 3:6–15

*. . . knowing that you were ransomed from the futile ways
inherited from your forefathers, not with perishable things such
as silver or gold, but with the precious blood of Christ, like
that of a lamb without blemish or spot. (1 Peter 1:18–19)*

We too look backwards to a historic event; to that central event in all human history when Christ, the Lamb of God, died for our sins to redeem us and set us free. Indeed, we have an inalienable freedom purchased by the blood of Christ. It is God's will that we constantly remember it as the very basis of everything. Spiritual experience begins here, and to it all spiritual experience must constantly recur. So as we recall the redemption purchased for us by Christ, we too shall find the secret of living a life in full spiritual freedom.

Nevertheless, the New Testament tells us we are under obligation to lead a life of service for God. Have we ever come through a patch in life where the commandments of the Lord seemed grievous and irksome to us, and appeared as a kind of slavery? Has the recurrence of the Lord's Supper ever seemed to bind us? Has the responsibility to witness ever made us wish that preachers would move on in their sermons? If we have never had such feelings, we are unusual indeed! What is it that will take the sense of slavery out of our Christian life and work? It is the realistic remembrance of what it cost our Lord Jesus Christ to redeem us. If we forget the cost of that precious blood, then presently our hearts will start to protest that God is expecting too much from us.

If we become like the servant in the parables (Matt 25:14–30; Luke 19:11–27), who protested that his lord was a hard man, reaping where he did not sow, gathering where he did not winnow and always expecting something for nothing, then our Christian duty will appear to be a slavery imposed by a hard master. However, our protests will stop if our hearts are constantly impressed by what it cost Christ to shed for us that infinitely valuable blood. We will come to agree with Paul, that offering our bodies as living sacrifices is our reasonable service (Rom 12:1).

David Gooding, *The Feasts of the Lord: Studies on the Feasts Appointed by the Lord for Israel*, p. 15

26th June

SPIRITUAL AND SECULAR WORK

Reading: Luke 5:1–11

*But when Simon Peter saw it, he fell down at Jesus' knees, saying,
'Depart from me, for I am a sinful man, O Lord.' (Luke 5:8)*

Peter's confession of sinfulness, however, was not answered by some such
word as 'Do not be afraid, your many sins have all been forgiven'. Peter
was not thinking of specific and particular sins which he had committed,
but of his general sinfulness and unworthiness as a person: 'I am a sinful
man'. Christ's reply was, in effect, 'Don't worry; in spite of that I can make
something of you and use you: from now on you will catch men.' The phrase
'catch men' is instructive. At his daily work he caught fish and a skilful job
it was. Now those skills were not to be abandoned, but applied at a higher
level. Peter's daily work was to be elevated to the higher spiritual level for
which the lower material level is but the necessary, practical foundation.
To live we must eat, and fish will do for that as well as anything. But there
is more to life than eating: and therefore even catching fish, done for the
right motives, has ultimate purposes far beyond merely keeping people alive.
Therefore the Lord of daily work, having taught Peter to go about that work
with the right motive ('Nevertheless at your word I will'), now calls Peter
to serve at the level of the ultimate purpose of life's work. 'From now on',
he says, 'you will catch men', catch them, of course, for God and for his
kingdom. With that Peter left his secular employment to devote himself
to spiritual work (see 5:11). But it is to be remembered that the experience
which launched him on his great spiritual labours was an experience which
he had of Christ in his secular work. For the believer secular and spiritual
work are simply different ends of an undivided spectrum, and the secular
work can and must have the same ultimate objectives in view as the spiritual.
Since Messiah has come, we, in our daily work, may no longer be content to
aim at less than serving him and his cause.

David Gooding, *According to Luke: The Third Gospel's Ordered Historical Narrative*, p. 103

27th June

OUR WORK FOR THE LORD

Reading: Acts 9:36–43

. . . each one's work will become manifest, for the
Day will disclose it. (1 Corinthians 3:13)

The story is that Dorcas died, but that Peter came and raised her from the dead. Her resurrection was, presumably, only a resuscitation, like the cases reported in the Gospels. Even so, it must have been for her an amazing, unforgettable experience that remained with her for the rest of her days. Only picture her situation. She had been busy at her social relief when death intervened and brought all her work to an end. But soon she opened her eyes again, and there stood none other than the Apostle Peter himself, who raised her up and took her to the next room. And there were the people for whom she had worked so hard before she died, and they were greeting her with unbounded joy and gratitude. And there, too, was the work she had done, the garments she had made, and the widows had been showing them to the great apostle himself (9:39). Such gratitude, such honour, such recognition of her labours! If ever a woman caught sight of the lasting effect and value of her work, that woman was Dorcas when she was raised from the dead. It surely gave her an added impetus to go on working with all her might for the rest of her life.

Our work for God and man is valuable in and of itself for the good it does in this life. But its significance and value do not end in the grave. The certain fact of Christ's resurrection, the glorious prospect of our own resurrection or transformation at his coming, assure us that our labour is not in vain in the Lord (1 Cor 15:50–58). We too shall see our work again. Here then is encouragement to persist in toil, and a warning not to indulge in shoddy workmanship. When the Lord comes and the dead are raised and the living caught up together with them to meet the Lord, all must appear before the judgment seat of Christ, so that each one may receive what is due to him or her for the things done while in the body, whether good or bad (see 2 Cor 5:10). If our works survive Christ's inspection, then ours will be a fourfold joy. First, the sheer joy of knowing we have pleased the Lord. Secondly, the joy of experiencing the eternal gratitude and friendship of those we helped on earth (Luke 16:9). Thirdly, the joy of seeing the work we did in our lifetime last eternally. And on top of that, a reward from the Saviour himself (1 Cor 3:12–14).

David Gooding, *True to the Faith: The Acts of the Apostles–Defining and Defending the Gospel*, pp. 200-1

28th June

THE GOAL OF OUR EFFORTS

Reading: Daniel 4:19–37

Do nothing from rivalry or conceit, but in humility count others more significant than yourselves. (Philippians 2:3)

Nebuchadnezzar made a mistake, not only about the source of the gifts but also about the goal of them. He said, 'I have built by my mighty power as a royal residence—*and for the glory of my majesty.*' Instead of letting all his artistic gifts flow back in a paean of praise to the glory of God, he shut himself up in a dead end and posed as the goal of all his gifts, for his own glory.

Humankind is too small for that. We are not big enough to be the goal of life. The man or woman who exercises his or her gifts simply for their own glory and satisfaction soon finds that the goal they have set themselves is not big enough. All we do, from the smallest to the greatest, should be done to the glory of God.

I remember once I had a student. I had to mark his Latin prose. He was not altogether the brightest student I had ever met, but he was diligent. His name was Mullan. When he handed it in I noticed on the top of his paper were the four letters AMDG. I thought these were perhaps his initials, and that he was adding my initials on for some reason: A. Mullan, D. Gooding. It was only later I stumbled on to what he was writing. Those four letters are the initials of four Latin words, *ad majorem Dei gloriam*—to the greater glory of God. Here was the student, writing his Latin prose in school for the greater glory of God. I wish I could say I had always marked them for the greater glory of God, and not lost my temper with some of the students sometimes. Do you work your computer to the greater glory of God, and lay the bricks and repair the car and do the sewing and the cooking *ad majorem Dei gloriam*—to the greater glory of God? We are missing our vocation if we do not.

David Gooding, *Daniel: Civil Servant and Saint*, p. 52–3

29th June

PRIORITIES IN SERVICE

Reading: Luke 10:38–42

Mary has chosen the good portion, which will
not be taken away from her. (v. 42)

To Martha's way of thinking, Mary was being selfish, unprincipled and unfair. The trouble was that Christ seemed to Martha to be encouraging Mary in her wrong behaviour by letting her sit there and talking to her. That very fact, one might have thought, ought to have made Martha begin to suspect that her own ideas must be wrong somewhere; but instead of questioning her own priorities, she went up to Christ and suggested that he was being irresponsible in encouraging Mary to act so unfairly. Gently but firmly Christ had to correct her. It was not that he underestimated the importance of service in general or of her service in particular. But when he visited Martha's house, he was on a journey. The time he had to spend with the sisters was limited, and when he left, it would be a long while before he was back again. The question therefore was whether they would cut down work to a minimum and so give the Lord the maximum amount of time to talk to them and enjoy their fellowship, or whether Martha would insist on putting on elaborate meals the preparation of which left her with very little time to sit and listen to the Lord. In those circumstances there is no doubt what Christ would have preferred—he would have preferred Martha's fellowship to her service—nor what he in fact regarded as more necessary for Martha. But Martha's idea of what had to be done was different from Christ's, and as we can now see, it was false. She meant well, she loved the Lord, she thought she was serving him; but her sense of proportion with regard to what was necessary was in fact depriving the Lord of what he most wished for and depriving her of what was most necessary; and it had come about precisely because she had not first sat at his feet and listened to him long enough to find out what he regarded as the paramount necessity.

We too are on a journey. Life at the best is short. We cannot do everything: there is not enough time. Like Mary, therefore, we shall have to choose and choose very deliberately. Life's affairs will not automatically sort themselves into a true order of priorities. If we do not consciously insist on making 'sitting at the Lord's feet and listening to his word' our number one necessity, a thousand and one other things and duties, all claiming to be prior necessities, will tyrannize our time and energies and rob us of the 'good part' in life.

David Gooding, *According to Luke: The Third Gospel's Ordered Historical Narrative*, pp. 224–5

30th June

GREATER WORKS THAN THESE

Reading: Acts 10:23–48

*Truly, truly, I say to you, whoever believes in me will also
do the works that I do; and greater works than these will
he do, because I am going to the Father. (John 14:12)*

To understand how this can be, we must pay close attention to the reason which Christ gives: 'greater . . . *because* I am going to the Father'. When Christ was here on earth, he could only be in one place at a time. Even though he could exercise power and heal people at a distance (see John 4:46–53; Luke 7:2–10), there is no record of his ever being and speaking in two places at once. But when he went to the Father at the ascension, there was no longer any such limitation. For now thousands of believers all round the earth can simultaneously pray to the Father in the name of Christ, and Christ can put all the answers to their prayers into effect by working simultaneously through all those believers. The works will be greater than those Christ did on earth, greater numerically.

But they will be greater in quality as well. It is a great thing to be raised from the dead like Lazarus was (John 11) and to receive for a while (Lazarus eventually died again) the temporary gift of physical life. It is a far greater thing to receive the imperishable gift of the Holy Spirit, and by the Spirit to be incorporated into the Body of Christ (1 Cor 12:13).

Now no man, no Christian preacher, not even an apostle, can impart the Holy Spirit to anyone. But from Pentecost onwards the risen Lord has spoken through his servants, and as a result people have believed and thereupon received the gift of the Holy Spirit. Here, for instance, is Peter relating what happened when he was sent to preach to a Roman centurion and his friends 'words by which they might be saved'. 'As I began to speak, the Holy Spirit fell on them just as on us at the beginning. And I remembered the word of the Lord, how he said, "John baptized with water, but you will be baptized with the Holy Spirit"' (Acts 11:15–16). Nothing like this is ever recorded as having happened when Jesus preached here on earth. These are the 'greater works' which the risen and ascended Lord has been doing through his people since Pentecost.

David Gooding, *In the School of Christ: Lessons on Holiness in John 13–17*, pp. 89–90

1st July

THE LORD IS IN THIS PLACE

Reading: Genesis 28:10–22

*Then Jacob awoke from his sleep and said, 'Surely the
Lord is in this place, and I did not know it.' (v. 16)*

Notice that it was not let down from heaven with the bottom nearly reaching
earth, it was set up on earth and the top reached towards heaven. The angels
of God were first ascending and then descending when their task was finished. Where did God stand? Some translations say that God stood 'above'
the ladder (v. 13), and if you chose it no one can say that you are wrong. But
the Hebrew preposition is vague and can also mean 'beside'. It is the same
preposition that is used in 18:2, when Abraham was sitting at his tent door in
the heat of the day. 'He lifted up his eyes and looked, and behold, three men
were standing in front of him.' They came and stood by his side.

It is the same preposition here; God stood beside the ladder. When Jacob
woke up, he remarked, 'Surely the LORD is in this place, and I did not know
it' (28:16). The wonder of the revelation! It would have been no news to
Jacob to have a vision that told him that God was in his heaven. Jacob had
believed that for a long while. That was very convenient sometimes, if you
had rather a hard bargain to push with the man next door. But it would have
been more difficult if God had been at his elbow when he was all dressed up
to deceive Isaac. It would have been uncomfortable to feel that God was by
his side then. 'And he was afraid and said, "How awesome is this place! This
is none other than the house of God, and this is the gate of heaven"' (v. 17).

'The Lord is in this place.' I do not know whether this text raises me up
to heaven with delight, or casts me down on my knees in repentance. If
I could write 'God is in this place' on the wall of my study, my games room,
my business room, how many times should I have to add, 'and I did not
know it'? Our Lord Jesus later taught us that one greater than the temple is
here (Matt 12:6). What a magnificent blessing it would be to go through life
knowing that wherever I am, 'God is in this place'—and I didn't forget it.

David Gooding, *The God of New Beginnings: Eighteen Seminars on the Book of Genesis*, p. 172

2nd July

GODLINESS IN THE FAMILY

Reading: 1 Timothy 5:1–16

But if a widow has children or grandchildren, let them first learn
to show godliness to their own household and to make some return
to their parents, for this is pleasing in the sight of God. (v. 4)

My translation says 'show piety' (RV). The interesting thing is that this is our word for godliness that Paul has been using all the way through Timothy. The Greek word is *efséveia* which means 'to reverence well', and the noun coming from it is 'good reverence'. Normally it's understood to be reverence for God. But now Paul tells them to learn to show reverence first towards their own family. Godliness begins at home, you know! You don't have to go to some rainforest and face poisoned arrows and cannibals in order to develop godliness, you could develop it in that more dangerous situation of home life. And godliness that is not godliness at home is a questionable godliness.

Christ will call upon us as his disciples to put him first beyond the dearest and nearest of our relatives, and many of our fellow believers in other countries are daily called upon to do it. How easy it has been for many of us to believe the Saviour, and how difficult for many others. Christ demands that we put him first, but when we do, one of the first things he will do is to tell us to look after our own family.

'If anyone does not provide for his relatives, and especially for members of his household, he has denied the faith and is worse than an unbeliever' (v. 8), for unbelievers will often show responsibility to their parents, particularly in their old age.

I am not unaware what a burden this could be. There are many dear women who would have loved to be a nurse on a foreign field, serving the Lord as a missionary, and found themselves stuck with an elderly parent with incipient Alzheimer's and kept for many years frustrated. What a burden that is. Let not the brothers forget it's not always good to be so busy preaching to other people, telling them that they should obey Scripture, that you have no time to look after your elderly parents and bear some of the burden of doing it.

David Gooding, Take Hold of Eternal Life: Major Themes in Paul's First Letter to Timothy, pp. 30–1

3rd July

JACOB IS DECEIVED

Reading: Genesis 29:14–30

*And in the morning, behold, it was Leah! And Jacob said to
Laban, 'What is this you have done to me? Did I not serve with
you for Rachel? Why then have you deceived me?'(v. 25)*

Things were going well for Jacob—'God does help those who help themselves!' He had got the birthright and the blessing (maybe a little bit unpleas-
antly, but he had got it anyway). The Lord had promised to be with him and
now he had met the prettiest girl in all the countryside and her father was
willing that he should marry her. Things were going absolutely swimmingly.
Of course, they always do when the Lord is in it—don't they? But things
looked different the next day when he woke up. He had the shock of his life.
It was not Rachel at all, it was Leah. I will not pretend to know the words that
Jacob said then, but I don't think they were very gracious. It was not Leah's
fault, there's no point getting angry with her. But what would you say about
her father? How could your own uncle do a thing like that; he would need
to tell the uncle what he thought.

> 'What is this you have done to me? Did I not serve with you for Rachel?
> Why then have you deceived me?' Laban said, 'It is not so done in
> our country, to give the younger before the firstborn.' (Gen 29:25–26)

'In this country there is a little thing about the firstborn—we never cheat the
firstborn of their rights. I could not keep my face up before the community
if the younger got married before the firstborn. We do not cheat firstborn
of their rights here!'

'But you deceived me!' said Jacob.

Look who is talking! Isn't it marvellous how it looks wrong when somebody
else cheats you? The Lord could not be in that, not if somebody else cheated
you. 'The mills of God grind slowly,' but they do grind and God will have to
show Jacob that he will never condone in a believer what he condemns in a man
of the world. It is lovely that we should take God at his word and believe that
he is with us, guiding our ways. He is, of course, but that does not mean we
are God's favourites and if we do a shady thing or two, well never mind, it's in
the family. 'We are on God's side so he won't find fault with us.' Are you sure?

David Gooding, *The God of New Beginnings: Eighteen Seminars on the Book of Genesis*, p. 174

4th July

TAMING THE TONGUE

Reading: James 3:1–12

For every kind of beast and bird, of reptile and sea creature, can be tamed and has been tamed by mankind, but no human being can tame the tongue. It is a restless evil, full of deadly poison. (vv. 7–8)

Every animal has been tamed except the tongue, the human tongue. You say, 'I didn't know that was an animal.' But you will find that it is and you have got to watch it. No human being can tame it, only the Holy Spirit can tame the animal of the tongue. When it gets loose it will tear you to shreds. People can sometimes be proud of that; many a Christian church is spoiled because of the old animal, the tongue. Under the guise of being very spiritual, the gossip of the neighbourhood is carried and everybody knows about it.

I don't want to know about Mrs Smith's shortcomings unless you think that I could help. I have enough trouble keeping my own animal in place. I want you to come and tell me about Christ and his Holy Spirit. 'But if you bite and devour one another, watch out that you are not consumed by one another' (Gal 5:15).

We are in danger of confusing two things. Through the death of Christ, we have been saved from the penalty of sin, but we are not saved from its consequences. It is with my tongue that I repeat cheap gossip and minister to people's pride. If then I repent of it, there is forgiveness and there's no penalty, but there are consequences. If you sow barley when God has told you not to sow barley, what happens? If you say, 'I am very sorry, but I have grown barley and I know you said that I shouldn't sow barley. I was a fool; I don't know what made me do it. Now there are whole fields of barley, and all from that little seed! I didn't think it would come to much. O God, I am so sorry, forgive me for sowing barley.'

God will forgive you, but he won't say, 'I'll change it into wheat!' There is no penalty; we're saved from penalty, but we're not saved from consequences. 'Watch out,' says Paul. What will happen if you 'bite and devour one another'? Will it turn out all right in the end? No, 'You will be consumed by one another.' This business is real and you will reap what you sow.

David Gooding, *The God of New Beginnings: Eighteen Seminars on the Book of Genesis*, pp. 82–3

5th July

LOVING OUR ENEMIES

Reading: 2 Samuel 1

Saul and Jonathan, beloved and lovely! (v. 23)

What would you have done next, had you been David? Here you are in Ziklag, which isn't exactly in the centre of the world. You have your eyes on the throne, hoping that God has got one for you somewhere one of these days. What you want is a propaganda campaign to bring you to the nation's attention. David thought so too. He composed a poem and taught it to the people, so that everybody sang it. It was David's signature tune, and they learned a lot about David and got the political message.

Had you been writing David's propaganda poem, what would you have put in it? 'Look at how the previous government has led us to disaster'? 'Look at how the Philistines have overrun our land through the incompetence of that silly chap Saul and his policies'? 'Come over to my side'? If you had written that kind of poem, it would have been no good for David in the publicity department. His poem was altogether different and it went like this: 'Saul and Jonathan, beloved and lovely!' (1:23). 'Saul and Jonathan? David, they were your enemies, man. Saul's son Ish-bosheth is still alive and breathing, and ten, if not eleven, of the tribes are still in allegiance to him. If you go praising Saul and Jonathan like that everybody will say, "Why not keep them in the government?" You have to pick holes in them, David. You have to run them down. Look at the terrible things they've done. You get power by running down the people who have opposed you.'

Not David. Enemies they had been; terrible dark deeds they had imagined and tried to put into action against David, but Jonathan was lovely, and Saul was the Lord's anointed.

'There was another side to their characters, you know,' said David. 'They did the nation a tremendous lot of good', and he taught the people to love his enemies. My brothers and sisters, is that how you do it in your church? Or do you sometimes yield to the temptation that, when somebody has done you a dirty trick, you can't imagine that anything he could do would be right and you run him down? Be careful, for the man who sits on God's throne at this moment, and one day shall sit on his own throne governing the universe, is the man who not only taught people to love his enemies, but he loved them himself and he died for them.

David Gooding, *Governing for God: Studies in 2 Samuel*, pp. 17–18

6th July

THE VALUE OF LOYALTY

Reading: 2 Samuel 2:1–7

David sent messengers to the men of Jabesh-gilead and said
to them, 'May you be blessed by the LORD, because you
showed this loyalty to Saul your lord and buried him.' (v. 5)

The men of Judah told David that it was the men of Jabesh-gilead who had buried Saul (vv. 4–7). What would you have said to them? They had been Saul's servants, and when Saul had fallen on the battlefield the men of Jabesh-gilead risked their lives out of loyalty to him and went and collected his body and gave Saul a decent burial. What did David say to them?

'You'd better come and have a word with me and explain your actions. Don't you know that Saul was my great enemy? He tried to kill me. Now I am king in Hebron, and you tell me that you've gone and honoured Saul, and given him a decent public burial? This is nothing less than high treason against me, and must be construed as deliberate enmity, and a slap in a face that you've gone and honoured my enemy with a decent burial.'

He didn't say anything of the sort. David was a wise man. He knew loyalty when he saw it, and loyalty in itself is a quality whose value you could scarcely exaggerate. Loyalty is the thing that makes the universe hold together and stops it flying into ten million pieces. The loyalty of God to us his creatures: even when we've sinned against him, rather than we should perish, he gave his own Son for us. David wasn't going to smash the sense of loyalty in those men's hearts. What if they are loyal to his one-time enemy? If he smashed their sense of loyalty, even if they came over to him, it wouldn't make them perfectly loyal to him either, would it?

Sometimes we do misconstrue people. They're friends with the people who've just offended us, and, because they're their friends, they stick up for them. What would you expect them to do? Would you count them as enemies because they show loyalty?

'Now look,' said David, 'I am king; I'd like you to know that. Judah has now selected me as king. You have shown loyalty to your sovereign. Well done. You'll have nothing but praise from me.' There's more than a hint there that one of these days he would be delighted to see them loyal to himself. David appreciated the men's sense of loyalty.

David Gooding, *Governing for God: Studies in 2 Samuel*, pp. 18–19

7th July

RELATIVE VALUES

Reading: Luke 12:22–34

*Consider the ravens: they neither sow nor reap, they have
neither storehouse nor barn, and yet God feeds them. Of
how much more value are you than the birds! (v. 24)*

Christ is not saying that birds do not have to work to get their food. Birds
have to work very hard at it. Secondly, Christ is not saying that because
ravens do not sow or reap or store up food for the winter, we should not
either. God feeds them in spite of the fact that he has not given them the
ability to do these things. To the squirrel God has given the instinct to store
food; it is God's way of feeding the squirrel, and if the squirrel does not use
this ability, it will not be fed miraculously. We have incomparably greater
God-given abilities than either ravens or squirrels. That is God's normal way
of feeding us. Thirdly, Christ is not so unrealistic as not to have noticed that
birds fall prey to old age, disease, enemies, famine. Nor does he imply that
no believer will ever die of hunger or cold.

What Christ is saying is that as long as it is necessary for God to leave us in
this world to learn and practise the principles of the kingdom, and to work
for its extension and to pray for its coming, so long does God undertake that
we shall have the food and clothes necessary for the course. When in God's
wisdom, the time for the course runs out, we cannot by worrying add the
smallest amount to our lifespan anyway: and with that gone, we shall not need
food and clothes any more. Why, therefore, worry about them, the smaller
things, when worrying about the largest thing of all is no use? (see 12:25).

Let us take one practical example to show the bearing of all this on daily life.
To engage in bribery and corruption is obviously against the principles of the
kingdom. A Christian business man, threatened with dismissal from his firm
if he does not consent to practise bribery, will have to accept dismissal and
face many sacrifices in order to be true to the kingdom. But God guarantees
him enough goods and clothes to make obeying the rule of God in this world
practical. Suppose, on the other hand, he is afraid to trust God, and engages
in bribery in order to keep his job and get food and clothes for himself and
his family. He will, by Christ's standards, have lost the very purpose of life
which made the food and clothes necessary in the first place.

David Gooding, *According to Luke: The Third Gospel's Ordered Historical Narrative*, pp. 254–5

8th July

THE FEAR THAT STIFLES GENEROSITY

Reading: Luke 18:18–30

*Sell your possessions, and give to the needy. Provide
yourselves with money bags that do not grow old, with
a treasure in the heavens that does not fail, where no
thief approaches and no moth destroys. (Luke 12:33)*

Luke 12:22–31 has dealt with the question of getting food and clothes;
now 12:32–34 deals with the question of what we should do with life's goods
once we have got them: 'Sell your possessions and give to the needy'. To
see the command in its true proportion we must pay attention to its context. Christ is not insisting that no Christian should own anything. Martha
was not sinning in having a house in which Christ himself was glad to stay
(see also Acts 5:3–4). Nor is Christ saying that it is wrong for a Christian to
have treasure. Quite the reverse. He should aim to have as much endurable
treasure as he can. That means, however, transferring as much as he can to
the heavens, where it is safe from loss, devaluation, robbery or decay. And
that in turn means giving as much as he can now to the poor (of whatever
kind).

Here the great obstacle to obeying Christ is fear (see Luke 12:32). Our
little possessions seem to us so important and valuable that we are afraid
of the loss involved in giving them away. To counteract this Christ puts our
possessions in their right perspective: 'Fear not, little flock, your Father has
been pleased to give you the kingdom'. Notice the past tense. He has been
pleased to, he has decided to. Indeed, the inheritance has now been confirmed
and guaranteed by irrevocable covenant (see Gal 3:15–29). Heirs to an eternal
kingdom, why should we be afraid to give away a few temporary possessions?
Indeed how are we not afraid to keep hold of too many of them and so fail
to turn them into eternal treasure (see Luke 12:33)? Pray God we do not fall
into the mistake of the Pharisee of 11:39–41: externally and ritually religious,
but in practice mean and grasping.

David Gooding, *According to Luke: The Third Gospel's Ordered Historical Narrative*, p. 256

9th July

THE ETERNAL SIGNIFICANCE
OF OUR FAMILY LIVES

Reading: Genesis 29:31–30:24

When the LORD saw that Leah was hated, he opened
her womb, but Rachel was barren. (29:31)

When Laban deceived Jacob into marrying Leah instead of Rachel, it led to
Jacob having four wives instead of one, which was a complication certainly!
The experiences of his wives are recorded at some great length: the inner
feelings of those women's hearts in the years when they had to compete for
Jacob's affection (29:31–35:18). Do you think it is a nice thing to have to compete for love? Competition in business seems to be all right, but something
seems to suggest to me that competing for love is not a very happy kind of
thing in the family. Out of those experiences (and many of them were happy,
of course) children were born. More often than not the names given to the
children by their mothers expressed their feelings. They had taken the whole
matter to God in prayer and felt that he had heard them, so the boys' names
enshrined their experiences. When we come to the last book of the Bible
and the holy city is coming down from heaven, the lovely thing is that the
names of those lads are inscribed on the very gates. The experiences of those
women are eternally recorded.

Isn't that marvellous! If I may say something to you mothers in the home,
with a husband to please (difficult enough), children to bring up and trying
to keep the family together. There are some that push strongly and others
that are more sensitive, so you have all the little family upsets. Quietly you
take it to God in prayer. Sometimes you feel that it is humdrum, but that
experience of God that you are having in the home is built in to the eternal
city. That's what the eternal city is; it is made up of men and women with
their experience of God in the good things and the bad things, in the successes and the failings. Through the fire of earth's testing their characters are
purified, their personalities refined and turned into jewels that shall adorn
the eternal city forever. As men come to God in that coming day they shall
not see God whom we call the Father; they shall see God reflected through
you and through your particular personality.

David Gooding, *The God of New Beginnings: Eighteen Seminars on the Book of Genesis*, p. 175

10th July

MATERIAL POSSESSIONS AND THE LORD'S RETURN

Reading: Luke 12:35–48

*Stay dressed for action and keep your lamps burning, and
be like men who are waiting for their master to come home
from the wedding feast, so that they may open the door to
him at once when he comes and knocks. (vv. 35–36)*

And now Christ turns to another consideration that will put material possessions into their proper perspective for a disciple: the second coming of the
Lord. The lesson is twofold. First, we must not allow our attitude to material
goods to render us unprepared for the Lord's coming (vv. 35–40). Second,
when he comes, all his servants will be accountable to him for what they
have done with their material possessions and with all other gifts and trusts
committed to them (vv. 41–48).

First, then, we do not know the time of Christ's second coming; but whenever it may be, he expects to find us ready to serve him. His expectation is
reasonable. To borrow the language of his parables and similes, if we expect
God to be ready to answer us when we knock on his door (see 11:9), it is only
right that we should be ready and prepared for whatever Christ wants us
to do when he comes and knocks on our door (see 12:36). One danger with
material goods is that we get so preoccupied with them that we forget the
Lord, have little time for spiritual fellowship with him now or for his service.
In that case, if he were suddenly to come, how do we suppose that we should
instantaneously be found prepared to be granted that degree of intimate
and personal fellowship which he promises to his faithful servants (v. 37)?
Moreover daily life with its practical business of work, food and clothes, is
meant, as we have just seen, as a training ground where we learn to put into
practice the rules of God's kingdom. If like worldly men (v. 30) we have used
life simply to lay up treasures for ourselves on earth; if like the Pharisees
of 11:48 we have made little attempt to put the love and justice of God into
practice in daily living; how could we suppose that when the Lord comes we
shall suddenly find ourselves ready actively to reign with him (see 2 Tim 2:12)
and to practise and enforce love and justice as responsible executives in his
kingdom?

David Gooding, *According to Luke: The Third Gospel's Ordered Historical Narrative*, pp. 256–7

11th July

Reading: Luke 16:1–15

And I tell you, make friends for yourselves by means
of unrighteous wealth, so that when it fails they may
receive you into the eternal dwellings. (v. 9)

Nothing we have in this life belongs to us. We brought nothing into this world and we shall take nothing out of it (see 1 Tim 6:7). We are simply stewards. One day we must go and leave it all. While we have in our control, therefore, what our Lord here calls 'the mammon of unrighteousness' (so called because, in this disordered world, it is unfairly distributed), we are to use it, not indeed in order to gain salvation, for nothing can buy that: it is a gift; but given in order to make friends. Not fickle friends of the sort that the prodigal son is said to have made; but friends who will welcome us in the eternal world and remain our friends eternally. 'Make to yourselves friends by means of the mammon of unrighteousness; that, when it shall fail, they may receive you into the eternal tabernacles' (16:9 RV).

We need to bring a little practical realism into our anticipation of what heaven will be like. In some respects it may not necessarily be all that different from what life is like now. We should consider that while all believers will be equally welcome in heaven and all be loved equally, not all will have equally as many friends. If when accounts are rendered and it becomes known in heaven that it was your sacrificial giving that provided the copies of the Gospel of John which led a whole tribe out of paganism to faith in Christ, will not that whole tribe show towards you an eternal gratitude which they will not show towards me, who spent my spare cash on some luxury for my own enjoyment? Moreover when it is a question of our relationship with Christ as Saviour, then of course it is a one-way process in which he does all the saving. But when it comes to our relationship with him as Friend, the relationship is a two-way process: 'you are my friends', he says, 'if you do the things which I command you' (John 15:14). If our side of this friendship has been lacking here, will it make no difference at all there?

David Gooding, *According to Luke: The Third Gospel's Ordered Historical Narrative*, p. 287

12th July

JOSEPH—A FAITHFUL STEWARD

Reading: Genesis 39

*And the keeper of the prison put Joseph in charge of all
the prisoners who were in the prison. Whatever was
done there, he was the one who did it. (v. 22)*

We shall be tested in our stewardship, and if personal profit has been our motive it's going to lead us into all sorts of temptations and perhaps spoil our chances of being actively engaged in reigning with Christ in the age to come.

Joseph was not only faithful in his stewardship in Potiphar's house, but also when he was put into the prison. He didn't complain, 'I've given them all I've got and now they're blaming me for what I didn't do, and they've put me down in this wretched old dungeon with a lot of crooks. I shall just sit here and twiddle my thumbs. What career prospects are open to me down here; why should I bother?' If you were falsely imprisoned, with no prospect, no career, no promotion and no acknowledgement, what would you do? Joseph served down there just as he did in Potiphar's house and when he became second in command of Egypt.

That has practical implications for us, doesn't it? Stewards, wanting one day to reign with Christ—are we trying to compete with one another?

'I should try and run a bit harder than Mrs Zebedee. She's got some big ideas about her sons, you know. She's got notions of her sons being chief, but I shall see that she doesn't get her request in first. I'll get mine in first' (see Matt 20).

I would serve if you can give me a big congregation, thousands of people and much publicity, and it seems a worthwhile job. But in obscurity, under false criticism, would I be a steward when there seems no future in it, serving people who are much less intelligent, and a lot of old crooks? The way to exaltation and glory lay through that prison for Joseph, didn't it? In God's providence this was the training course for Joseph, whether you think he started off as a spoilt boy or not. Here he was in training for his position of glory, and so are we. It's how we're behaving now—how we're using our talents now in obscure and small things, how we react under criticism—that is determining what position we can be given in the coming kingdom of our Lord.

David Gooding, *Family Life with Abraham and Jacob: Studies in Genesis 12–50*, p. 68

13th July

Reading: Genesis 32:22–32

Jacob said, 'I will not let you go unless you bless me.' (v. 26)

Before crossing over and meeting Esau that night a man wrestled with Jacob there. It was the Lord himself, and Jacob tried to wrestle with God and manoeuvre God into a position.

'Let me go,' said the angel.

'I won't let you go until you have blessed me,' Jacob says. He was trying to manoeuvre God into blessing him.

Do you know my brothers, my sisters, you don't have to manoeuvre God to bless you. You don't have to twist God's arm to get him to bless you. It is his determination to bless you anyhow. The angel touched Jacob's thigh and withered the muscle so that the very leg muscle necessary to wrestle was now gone, and all Jacob could do was to hang on in dependence upon the angel of the Lord.

'Bless me,' he said.

The angel said, 'What is your name?'

It was no good now dressing up in goatskins and bringing imitation venison and pretending to be Esau. He was held in the arms of God and dependent on God. And with the angel asking the question, 'Who are you?' he replied, 'I am Jacob.'

What a blessing that is when God takes us into his arms and we can't move, and God makes us face ourselves and own our shortcomings and our way-wardness and learn the lesson of faith, which is to depend on God. And that night God blessed him, not with great herds of cattle but with the supreme blessing of changing the man's character. 'You have been called Jacob so far; from now on you shall be called Israel' (vv. 22–32). Now a prince with God, he was on the way to producing the nation that will bring in the Messiah; on the way to producing the son through whom all the nations of the earth would be blessed: through Joseph in Egypt, and eventually the Messiah. Jacob is now beginning to be a ruler for God. That is blessing.

David Gooding, *Three Creation Stories and Three Patriarchs: The Book of Genesis*, p. 77

14th July

PRESENT SATISFACTION OR FUTURE GLORY?

Reading: Genesis 25:19–34

For this light momentary affliction is preparing for us an eternal weight of glory beyond all comparison. (2 Corinthians 4:17)

With any son of Abraham or Isaac, the position of firstborn carried an immeasurable privilege. God had promised that, in Abraham and his offspring, not only would all the nations of the earth be blessed, but he had said to Abraham, 'Kings shall come from you' (35:11). It was the patriarchal belief that the great promises of God—sovereignty, reigning, being kings—reached out into the future and not only to a little patch of corn or a little well down the road that the Philistines would quarrel over. There lay a tremendous future of glory. If that was true, the firstborn would then carry the chief honour, position and glory. It was always the firstborn. You say, 'What an incalculable blessing.'

I'll tell you what Esau thought about it. For a bowl of stew, and for present immediate satisfaction, he sold the glory and the future. Even though it's ordinary material things, to enter the blessings of God will require faith. It will force choices upon us and it will test our comparative sense of values. Esau decided to go for immediate satisfaction, and satisfaction at a very lowly level. Many people have done it since.

Sooner or later the choice will come to us all, will it not? 'Beware!' says the writer to the Hebrews to those who had professed salvation.

> See to it that no one fails to obtain the grace of God; that no 'root of bitterness' springs up and causes trouble, and by it many become defiled; that no one is sexually immoral or unholy like Esau, who sold his birthright for a single meal. (Heb 12:15–16)

We cannot lose our salvation; every believer will be with Christ when Christ comes to reign. What position will I have, and how big the blessing then? It is possible to sell what could have been mine in that glory—an exalted position in the government of Christ—because I'm not prepared to go occasionally with an empty stomach and to make a sacrifice for Christ's sake, believing his word and his promise. I demand to have my blessing now. But we can't always have everything; we have to choose.

David Gooding, Family Life with Abraham and Jacob: Studies in Genesis 12–50, pp. 27–8

15th July

THE PRINCIPLE OF MERCY

Reading: James 2:12–13; 5:7–12

Mercy triumphs over judgment. (2:13)

My brothers and sisters, I tell you I am glad it is so. When I stand before the judgment seat of Christ if I get simply what strict justice would give me, how little should I get! Because the Holy Spirit is available to the youngest convert, would you say that he or she must overcome all sinful tendencies overnight? No, the Lord is merciful in his assessment of what is possible to that young convert and the Lord will be merciful. The trouble is that I am not a young convert, I have been a believer some fifty-five years and I have got less excuse. I pray that the Lord will be merciful when he assesses my reward and place in his kingdom.

But that lays on me an urgent consideration. If I want him to be merciful to me then I had better start being merciful now. Keep it in the context—James is talking about the way we treat each other. Here's this poor brother, a good man. It isn't merely that his suit is a cheap old suit and badly cut, and he hasn't had a change of shirt for a long while so it smells a bit. He hasn't had the advantage of culture and his conversation is a bit tiring; his outlook is a bit restricted and his manners are difficult. Shall I put him in a corner, or will it not move me to compassion so that, if possible, I love him all the more? Will I not have mercy and if I don't show him mercy now, when I stand before the Lord and he begins to examine the way I have behaved, my 'suit of clothes and the cut of my shirt,' as he comes to estimate my reward, then he won't have mercy on me. 'So speak, so behave, as men and women who are going to be judged' (see v. 12).

The Lord loves to be merciful in his judgment. When it comes to our judging the behaviour of our fellow-believers, God save us from an overly censorious and critical spirit. Remember how indignantly the Lord rebuked the Pharisees as they criticized his disciples for rubbing the corn in their hands on the Sabbath and would have condemned them as sinners.

David Gooding, *James's Vision of the Perfect Man and Woman: The Epistle of James*, p. 42

16th July

BEING A TRUE PRIEST

Reading: 1 Samuel 1

For this child I prayed, and the Lord has granted me my petition that I made to him. Therefore I have lent him to the Lord. As long as he lives, he is lent to the Lord. (vv. 27–28)

The first secret of the revival lay with a woman called Hannah. She was a wonderful soul. Her husband Elkanah was quite religious and went up to the festivals in the tabernacle every time he should. He had two wives, Peninnah and Hannah. I am not recommending that state of affairs! In fact it was quite unpleasant, particularly for Hannah, because Peninnah had children and Hannah had no children. Can you imagine the competition? It's a very hard thing when we have longings that nature itself has put within us, and then fulfilling them becomes impossible. That's a very big burden to bear. And as for Elkanah, he was a foolish husband! When Hannah was depressed he said to her, 'Why are you bothered about that—am I not better to you than ten sons?'

It made Hannah think of the purpose in having children. Was it just to satisfy the urges of nature, or was there more to it? She decided there was more to it. Of course she still wanted a child, but she took it to the Lord. She said, 'Lord, if you could give me a child I could devote him to your service in the tabernacle, and begin to counter the disreputable behaviour of Eli's sons.'

May I ask you a big question? Why would you want to be married (if you are not already)? Just for the sake of being married? It's a marvellous gift, but would you tell the Lord that if it could serve his purposes, that would give it infinite significance? Why would you want to be an architect or an accountant or a mechanic? Just to make money, or is that part of your priesthood? Although it is the way you get your food and clothes, is it also how you could serve the Lord and make your occupation serve his interests? In practical life, what does it mean to be a priest?

Hannah decided that she still wanted a child, but now she saw the possibility that if the Lord gave her a child it could become significant for God and his kingdom. She eventually had the child, Samuel. She waited until he was weaned, which in those days would have been about four years old, then she took him up to the tabernacle and left him. What a sacrifice that was. How it tugged at her heart—she was acting like a true priest.

David Gooding, *Priesthood and Holiness, Sin and its Consequences, Atonement and Acceptance*, pp. 6–7

THE DISCIPLE'S JOURNEY

Part 6—Prayer

17th July

THE NEW WAY OF ENTERING INTO GOD'S PRESENCE

Reading: Hebrews 10:15–25

*Let us then with confidence draw near to the throne of grace, that
we may receive mercy and find grace to help in time of need. (4:16)*

The verse is not simply saying that we can pray to God with confidence.
God's people all down the centuries have always felt free to pray to him.
Nor is it saying that Christ has opened the gates of heaven and so made it
possible for us to enter God's presence when we die. It is saying that Christ
has made a way for us to enter here and now into the immediate presence
of God. We can now do every day of the week what Israel's high priest could
only do once a year: enter the Most Holy Place. We can now do what Israel's
high priest could never do. He could enter only the Most Holy Place in
the tabernacle on earth; every day of our lives we can enter the immediate
presence of God in heaven.

To the average Jew, the idea would at first seem strange and incredible. It
might even do so to some of us. For some of us the difficulty might be to
understand what it means to enter the Most Holy Place in heaven while we
are still on earth. We say to ourselves, 'God is in heaven and we are on earth,'
and that's that. He can hear us when we pray because he is God. But how can
we enter heaven to talk to him? What we should remember is that we are now
thinking in spiritual terms, not physical. At this level, distance is not to be
measured in miles, nor in light years. Two people can be sitting in the same
room on the same sofa and yet in heart be very distant from each other. The
tax-collector in our Lord's parable (Luke 18:10–14) went up into the temple
to pray. But 'he stood at a distance. He would not even look up to heaven.'
God, of course, heard his cry for mercy and he went to his home justified
before God, whereas the Pharisee who trusted in his own good works was
not justified. But the point is that now we are justified, we need no longer
'stand at a distance'. In spirit we can come right into God's presence and stand
before his very throne, because we know that we are completely accepted by
him already and he will never cast us out. 'But now in Christ Jesus you who
were once far away have been brought near through the blood of Jesus. . . For
through him we both have access to the Father by one Spirit' (Eph 2:13, 18).

David Gooding, An Unshakeable Kingdom: The Letter to the Hebrews for Today, pp. 185–6

18th July

WHATEVER YOU ASK

Reading: John 15:1–8

*If you abide in me, and my words abide in you, ask
whatever you wish, and it will be done for you. (v. 7)*

The invitation to ask whatever we will, and the promise that it shall be done to us, is clearly not an open-ended invitation to ask for just any and everything we might happen to desire—a new car, a larger house, and so forth. The invitation is limited by two conditions: first, 'If you abide in me', that is, remain in close and intimate fellowship and communion with the Lord. Secondly, 'If my words abide in you'. Both conditions must be met. If in our private devotions we enjoy intimate communion with the Lord, we shall become increasingly aware of his love for us; and his love will certainly give us confidence to bring him our requests. But what shall we ask for? Here we shall need guidance.

In order to ask aright we must let his words abide in us, correcting our misconceived desires, opening up to us what God's purposes and objectives are for us and for others, so that we can shape our requests accordingly. But granted that, the wonderful thing is that we are invited to cooperate with the vinedresser in accomplishing his desires. After all, while we are, metaphorically speaking, vine branches, we are not literal, passive pieces of vine wood. We are redeemed personalities. As we abide in Christ and his words, abiding in us, begin to renew our minds, we shall in the first place become aware of faults in our personalities, hard knots in the vine branch, so to speak, that limit our fruitfulness and impede our growth. And when that happens we are invited to cooperate with the vinedresser, and ask for these things to be removed, so that more fruit shall result for his glory. We are not allowed to dictate to him how he shall do it: we may well find that he chooses unexpected and sometimes painful methods. Nor are we allowed to dictate how long he shall take over it. We are not to suppose that habits and complexes ingrained over many years will necessarily be removed instantaneously. But we may ask, and go on asking, in the God-given assurance that our asking is not in vain. He will do for us what we ask; and when the resultant fruit brings him the credit, we shall have the joy of knowing that we cooperated with him in achieving his glory; and the added joy of realizing that our fruit-bearing demonstrates that we are genuine disciples of Christ.

David Gooding, *In the School of Christ: Lessons on Holiness in John 13–17*, pp. 149–50

19th July

PRAYER AND THE COMING OF THE LORD

Reading: Psalm 102:1–17

*He regards the prayer of the destitute and
does not despise their prayer. (v. 17)*

Now the psalmist tells us a wonderful thing: when the Lord appears and rebuilds Zion, it will be in answer to the prayers of his destitute people. 'Let it be written down here and now', he says in effect (vv. 18–22) 'for the benefit of the future generation (that will be alive when the Lord comes) so that the people who are not yet created may (then) praise the Lord.' For they will learn from what is written that the coming of the Lord is not some arbitrary, unexpected, unannounced intervention by God. Generations of God's afflicted and persecuted people have believed it to be promised in Scripture, and have longed and prayed for it.

This then is what the psalmist wishes to be recorded. In answer to the pleas of his people: 'The Lord looked down from his sanctuary on high, from heaven he viewed the earth, to hear the groans of the prisoners and release those condemned to death' (vv. 19–20).

How graphic and moving these expressions are! He is not thinking of the distance between heaven and earth in spatial terms, as though it could be measured in light-years. He is thinking how infinitely above earth's affairs is the transcendent God; how infinitely beneath his undisturbed glory is the wretched misery of earth's prisons where people groan as they await execution. Yet the transcendent God has 'looked down', viewed earth's misery, heard the groanings of prisoners, and in response will one day appear and rebuild Zion. It is not—obviously not—that five minutes before the second coming God will suddenly turn his attention to earth, become aware of the groanings of prisoners, and decide to act. God has always looked down, always heard the prayers of his distressed people throughout all the centuries. Their prayers have not been lost (see Rev 6:9–11; 8:3–5). God will yet 'respond to the prayer of the destitute; he will not despise their plea'. The blood of the martyrs, the groans of innocent prisoners, the plea of the author of Psalm 102 and of millions of believers like him, the as yet unanswered intercessions of Daniel (see chapter 9 of his prophecy), the cries from Auschwitz and Dachau silenced by the gas chambers—all make it a moral certainty that the Lord will one day appear and rebuild Zion.

David Gooding, An Unshakeable Kingdom: The Letter to the Hebrews for Today, pp. 61–2

20th July

THE LORD'S PRAYER

Reading: Luke 11:1–4

And he said to them, 'When you pray, say: "Father, hallowed be your name. Your kingdom come."' (v. 2)

In Luke's record of the prayer which Christ taught them there are five requests. First come two requests relating to God's own interests: his name and kingdom; then three requests relating to our own: daily bread, forgiveness, and shielding from temptation. God's interests first, ours next. That obviously is the true priority for creatures at prayer. What God is, his character, his glory, these things stand first. We are to pray that his name be hallowed, that is, set apart, regarded with awe as the most holy, valuable, glorious thing in all the universe. Life's values will never be measured properly or seen in their true light unless we see that God's name is not only the chiefest value of them all but the source of all true value which any person or thing possesses. Let God's name be devalued and God himself dishonoured, then all that derives from him—which is everything—is correspondingly reduced in value and honour. Deny God altogether, and nothing ultimately will prove to have any value at all. And yet in this sorry world God's name is not hallowed as it should be, not by the greatest saints, still less by us ordinary saints, not to speak of the profane and godless. We have lost the sense of God's holiness, and we live in a world where sacred things are progressively profaned and life becomes ever more cheap.

But it will not always be so. God has his purposes and plans to bring in his kingdom universally so that his will shall be done here on earth as it is in heaven, and his name be hallowed as it should, and all life's values shine with the lustre and brightness of the jewels of the new Jerusalem. That is God's purpose and it shall be accomplished. But we are not to regard its accomplishment fatalistically. We are actively to pray for it, to align our will with God's will, and to make the coming of his kingdom our chief desire, aim and ambition.

David Gooding, *According to Luke: The Third Gospel's Ordered Historical Narrative*, pp. 226–7

21st July

Reading: Luke 11:5–13

*If you then, who are evil, know how to give good gifts to
your children, how much more will the heavenly Father
give the Holy Spirit to those who ask him! (v. 13)*

At first sight shamelessness might seem to indicate a bad quality; and on some
occasions, of course, it does. But its meaning is not always or necessarily bad.
It simply describes a person who has no sense of shame, no compunction,
in doing something or asking for something. If there are reasons why the
person ought to feel compunction or shame, then, of course, shamelessness
is a bad thing; but if a man's case is good, then shamelessness in insisting
on it, is not blameworthy, but commendable. To illustrate the point Christ
pictures a man who has an unexpected guest arrive in the middle of the
night, and finds he has no food to offer his guest (see vv. 5–8). Being an
oriental with an oriental's sense of the importance of hospitality he has no
compunction whatever in going to a friend's house, midnight though it is,
and getting him out of bed to lend him the necessary food to put before his
guest. His friend would not find fault with the man's shamelessness. Sharing
the man's oriental ideas on the duty of hospitality, he would recognize his
shamelessness as perfectly justifiable.

An equivalent in our culture would be the question whether or not you
should call a doctor out in the middle of the night to visit a sick person. We
would feel embarrassed if we called the doctor out for something that proved
to be only a minor upset. But if someone in the family suffered a massive
heart attack, we would have no compunction at all in summoning the doctor
whatever the hour of the night.

This, then, is the analogy. It tells us that while all who ask for the illumination and strengthening of their hearts by the Holy Spirit, will most certainly
receive the gifts they ask for, yet whether we ask and go on asking or not will
depend on how necessary we regard the gift. If, for instance, today we ask for
illumination by God's Spirit through his word so that we may know God and
his grace and his purposes more fully, and then tomorrow forget to ask, or to
seek in his word, or to knock on the door of heaven, and carry on forgetting
for the next six months, it is obvious that we do not regard the gift we ask
for as very important or necessary; and it is unlikely that we shall receive it.

David Gooding, *According to Luke: The Third Gospel's Ordered Historical Narrative*, pp. 229–30

22nd July

GOD LISTENED TO A MAN

Reading: Joshua 10:1–15

*And the sun stood still, and the moon stopped, until the
nation took vengeance on their enemies. . . . There has been
no day like it before or since, when the LORD heeded the
voice of a man, for the LORD fought for Israel. (vv. 13–14)*

Marvellous miracle wasn't it? And all put on to save the Gibeonites, if you
please, for God was determined to destroy the very last enemy that had ever
come against them, or ever would.

But you've missed the biggest miracle, haven't you? As the historian himself
says, 'There was no day like that before it or after it, that the Lord . . .'—That
the Lord what?—'. . . heeded the voice of a man' (v. 14).

In the process of protecting them, Joshua, who has two feet on earth, dares
address the Almighty and ask for the sun and moon to be stayed until the
last enemy is destroyed. And the Lord listens. Do you know there was never
a day like that before or after? Yes, it's inspired Scripture that says so; but
that was written centuries ago.

That record has been overtaken since then, hasn't it? For there came another
day, when another man stood on earth and he saw the people that had trusted
him, and he saw their enemies, and he prayed that they might be kept from
the evil one. And he said, as he lifted his eyes to heaven, 'Father, glorify me
with the glory I had with you before the world was' (John 17:5). Oh, what a day,
when God listened to the voice of a man, and glorified the blessed Saviour
to shine as the sun in the firmament of heaven forever, and all to protect us.
Coming to the end of that prayer he prayed again. 'Father,' he said, 'I desire
that they, whom you have given me, be with me where I am that they may
behold my glory' (17:24). And at that moment the moon appeared in the
sky in full face of the sun. You are seated already with Christ in heavenly
places, far above all principalities, powers, mights and dominions; and one
day you shall be bodily where you already are spiritually. It will be as now
it is with that old moon, looking at the sun, and the sun flooding it with its
glory. And to think that you were once afar off, under the threat of God's
judgment, alienated from God and with no hope in the world, and today
you are eternally secure and seated with Christ in heavenly places. It's fit to
make your lungs burst with joy!

David Gooding, *Entering the Inheritance: Studies in Joshua 1–12*, pp. 45–6

23rd July

ASKING FOR MORE

Reading: Joshua 14:6–15; Judges 1:11–15

*Give me a blessing. Since you have set me in the land of
the Negeb, give me also springs of water. (Judges 1:15)*

Caleb wholly followed the Lord and showed himself a genuine Old Testament believer. There were many more who followed him and at last when the Lord Jesus came he showed them the full revelation of God. Then there were Achsah and Othniel (Josh 15:17). They didn't claim what was promised, they asked for more. Can you imagine it! Said Achsah: 'Daddy, you know that I'm grateful for this bit of ground you've given us for my inheritance, but it's a bit of dry ground in the southern Negev—you couldn't grow anything on it! You must give us some water.' Caleb was moved and said, 'You're right, my dear. I tell you what; I'll give you the upper and the lower springs as well' (see v. 15). Now Othniel and Achsah could make something of it, they grew the fruits of Zion with these upper and lower springs.

They asked for more. Should not we? We've been brought into our inheritance and we have the Holy Spirit, so why should we ever ask for more? Well precisely because we have the Holy Spirit! Paul prayed for the Christians in Ephesus:

> That the God of our Lord Jesus Christ, the Father of glory, may give
> you a spirit of wisdom and of revelation in the knowledge of him,
> having the eyes of your hearts enlightened, that you may know what
> is the hope to which he has called you, what are the riches of his
> glorious inheritance in the saints, and what is the immeasurable
> greatness of his power towards us who believe. (Eph 1:17–19)

My heart is so small and my imagination so poverty stricken. I am saved, but I haven't the beginnings of a notion of what the great hope is that is set before me. I need more. Shall I not come, like Othniel's wife, to the blessed Lord and pray for the ever-increasing illumination of his Spirit, that I may grasp what is the hope of his calling? What will it be to be with Christ, to dwell with the Lord, to be part of his bride? Queen when he is king. What shall it be, with him to rule and reign and to administer the great universe that yet shall be? Who can tell the wonder of it, that little bits of clay should not only be forgiven, but united with a divine person, the Son of God himself—who can explain the mystery?

David Gooding, *What Moses Could Not Do: Nine Studies in the Book of Joshua*, pp. 68–9

THE DISCIPLE'S JOURNEY

Part 7—Hindrances, Challenges and Trials

24th July

ABRAHAM'S IDOLATRY AND OURS

Reading: Genesis 14:18—15:5

After these things the word of the Lord came to Abram in a vision: 'Fear not, Abram, I am your shield; your reward shall be very great.' (15:1)

For Abraham in those early days, life was simply his goods. He lived down in Ur of the Chaldeans in beautiful houses with all kinds of magnificent art and conveniences. It was a very civilized existence. For some years that was the sum total of his life. He had no sense of the living reality of faith in the living God. None whatsoever!

What broke his idolatry? As ever, God took the initiative. Sooner or later in every person's life God approaches and makes him or her conscious that there is something bigger than food and clothes. Behind this vast world there is a personal God, who has given us richly all things to enjoy in order that they may lead us to him, and to put our faith in him. It breaks his heart that men will take the glorious gifts he gives them, and instead of letting those gifts lead them to God they lead them away from him.

This is not something confined to those far off days. It happens again and again. It happened to the nation of Israel centuries later. Through the prophets, God laments over what they had done. He brought them out of one of their bondages, put them in the land of Canaan and blessed them with solid houses, beautiful fields and abundant crops. Instead of that leading them to him, it led them away.

'She said, "I will go after my lovers, who give me my bread and my water, my wool and my flax, my oil and my drink"' (Hos 2:5). Israel took the gifts that God had given them and went after other gods. There burns in the God of this universe a passionate but exceedingly grieved heart.

Does your heart burn with love for God? You say, 'I've got my business and my home!' Could it be that your business and the lovely home that God has given you have so swamped you that it leaves you with no time for God or any faith in him? You're not vicious, you're not wildly immoral, but sheer goods have robbed God of your faith and you have made an idol of this passing world. You say, 'I've got a future; I cannot always be thinking of God.' But there is no future without God! If you would have a future, you must learn with Abraham this basic lesson—forsake your idols and put your faith in the living God.

David Gooding, *The God of New Beginnings: Eighteen Seminars on the Book of Genesis*, p. 87

25th July

LIVING IN THE POWER OF THE FLESH

Reading: Genesis 16

Now Sarai, Abram's wife, had borne him no children. She had a female Egyptian servant whose name was Hagar. (v. 1)

Sarah came to Abraham, and said to him, 'God has promised us that we shall have a child, and in our seed shall the nations of the world be blessed. Wouldn't it be a good thing, if somehow we contrived to have child?' Then she said a very strange thing, 'The Lord has prevented me from bearing children.' If that was what the Lord had done, she should have said, 'We shall have to wait for God's time for him to fulfil his promise!' But she added, 'Go in to my servant; it may be that I shall obtain children by her.' I don't think Sarah realized that what she was proposing was independence of God. With the very best will in the world, they decided to proceed to fulfil the glorious promise of God in their own way.

I wonder if we feel much more of an arrow of conviction here than when we were thinking about Lot. We have been justified by faith, are at peace with God and determined now to live godly lives and see that all God's purposes for us are fulfilled. How many of us have gone past the stage of simply cooperating with the power of God and have attempted to do it in our own religious flesh? We forget that a believer's flesh is no more acceptable to God than it was in his unregenerate days. It can no more accomplish things for God than it could before conversion. A great deal of the frustration and disillusionment that we experience in our Christian lives is because we act simply in the power of the flesh. We have not yet come to a radical enough assessment of the evil, wickedness, rebellion and weakness of the flesh.

> For I know that nothing good dwells in me, that is, in my flesh. For I have the desire to do what is right, but not the ability to carry it out. (Rom 7:18)

How many churches have been disturbed by men who thought they were standing for God's truth, but stood for it by the ugly, fleshly energies of their own powers? The resulting squabbles and Pharisaism are open evidence for all to see that it is not the work of God's Holy Spirit.

David Gooding, *The God of New Beginnings: Eighteen Seminars on the Book of Genesis*, p. 109

26th July

Reading: James 4:4–12

*Do you suppose it is to no purpose that the
Scripture says, 'He yearns jealously over the spirit
that he has made to dwell in us'? (v. 5)*

Once we have eaten of that living bread and drunk of that living water, it doesn't mean that all our desires and pleasures are at once put into orbit. We notice how possible it is for believers still to find their desires and their pleasures out of gear with the Lord and his word. It is possible for a believer to allow the enemy to dangle before him, not some vicious way of behaving, but lovely and delightful things and, by that means, draw a believer away from the Lord.

When that happens it is exceedingly serious; James says that it is spiritual adultery and disloyalty of heart to the Lord Jesus. He calls believers who give way to this kind of thing 'adulterous people' (4:4). It is not a very pleasant word—it is an ugly word that describes an ugly thing. Paul naturally agrees with James in everything and he says, 'I betrothed you to one husband, to present you as a pure virgin to Christ. But I am afraid that as the serpent deceived Eve by his cunning, your thoughts will be led astray from a sincere and pure devotion to Christ' (2 Cor 11:2–3). That is precisely what Satan tries to do to get us divided in our hearts and in our loyalties to the Lord Jesus.

Young folks, if I may talk to you. Satan will do his best to get you to be intellectually dishonest and disloyal to the Lord Jesus, using that lovely thing God has given you, your intellect, the longing and desire to know. Then craftily he says, 'Look here, you are an intelligent person. If you are going to satisfy your thirst for knowledge and your enquiring mind, you are not going to be satisfied with just any old explanation. You like to go into the deep things.'

Little by little he will siphon off that intellectual desire and get it involved in all sorts of things that are lovely in themselves. It could be science, physics or chemistry. It is a lovely thing to study God's handiwork, but it is a tragic thing to let your science so absorb you that, little by little, prayer, Bible reading and communion with the Lord Jesus are abandoned and presently nothing remains of church fellowship but a formal attendance and a man who at fifty-five is a brilliant physicist and a dwarf Christian.

David Gooding, *James's Vision of the Perfect Man and Woman: The Epistle of James*, pp. 65–6

27th July

ATTITUDES TO INEVITABLE OCCASIONS OF STUMBLING

Reading: Luke 17:1–10

And he said to his disciples, 'Temptations to sin are sure to come, but woe to the one through whom they come'! (v. 1)

If true, genuine and active faith is as eternally important as we have just seen it is, no sin against a fellow-man can possibly be more serious than to do something by act or word to stumble him in his faith, or to break that faith in God, in the deity of Christ, in the authority of his word, in the value of his redemption or the reality of his salvation. In this imperfect world, Christ says, it is impossible but that such stumbling-blocks will occur; but the consequences for the people responsible for their occurrence will be so grave, that it would have been better for them, before they injured someone's faith, to have been flung into the sea with a millstone round the neck where they would be safely out of the way and unable to influence anybody.

A true disciple, therefore, has two special duties in this connection. First, he must rebuke his brother when he sins (v. 3). Some people seem to enjoy doing it; and if they do, they are obviously not doing it in the manner in which it should be done. Most of us find it unpleasant and in cowardly fashion err by not doing it at all. But if our silence encourages a man to think that his sin does not matter, where might he not end up? In this as in all things Christ is our example. He rebuked 'that fox Herod', for example, even though in doing so he was, humanly speaking, endangering his own life (see 13:31–33). Secondly, the true disciple must forgive his repentant brother, even if he sins and then repents seven times a day (17:4). God himself never refuses forgiveness to genuine repentants. But what a tragedy it would be, if a man who professed to know Christ were to refuse to forgive his fellow man when he repented, and his fellow man got the impression that repentance is useless, and therefore ceased to repent thereafter of his sins towards men or towards God either. So if seven times a day seems an impossible number of times to have to forgive a sinning brother, let the disciple remember Christ. He called on Jerusalem to accept his protection. How many times they rebuffed him. And how many times, in spite of it, he renewed his offer of mercy (see 13:34).

David Gooding, *According to Luke: The Third Gospel's Ordered Historical Narrative*, pp. 293–4

28th July

PROBLEMS OF MIDDLE AGE

Reading: 2 Samuel 11

In the spring of the year, the time when kings go out to
battle, David sent Joab, and his servants with him, and
all Israel. And they ravaged the Ammonites and besieged
Rabbah. But David remained at Jerusalem. (v. 1)

This is the middle period of his reign and David has become middle aged.
He's victor, he's arrived. He's head, not only of the two tribes, but of the ten
tribes as well, monarch of the whole lot. His kingdom extended until it was
bigger than anything he'd ever dreamed of. His treasuries were rich, his
harem very thickly populated.

But as he begins to feel the weight of middle age spread, and when Moab
and Ammon and others rebelled, David sent Joab and the army to fight and
he stayed at home. This is the period when the difficulties began, the real
difficulties, and David's sorry mistakes were made. You know, even if we
went no further, that passage seems to preach an exceedingly practical lesson.

We do well to hold meetings for young folks. We must encourage them
when they're young. Of course we must; you can't work too hard for the
young folks. You must come to their level and help them all you can. These
are the men and women of the future, and what big battles they have to face.
But they don't have to face half as big battles as the middle aged do. Who
are the folks that cause all the disturbance in assemblies, by and large—is it
the seventeen-year-olds? Who is it that, when they quarrel, split assemblies
wide open? Is it the eighteen-year-old young ladies? Not normally, is it? It's
the middle aged who do that.

I sometimes think it's about time we had some meetings for the middle
aged and somebody talked to us straight about the perils of middle life.
When people who once were full of ideas, and would have given up anything
for the Lord to work for him, somehow get caught up in the humdrum of
daily living. Things are not so difficult as they were in youth, they've arrived
a bit and circumstances are easier. But they've got podgy spiritually as well
as physically and aren't really doing anything much for the Lord now. They
stay at home while others do it.

David Gooding, *Governing for God: Studies in 2 Samuel*, pp. 9–10

29th July

KEEPING GOING IN OLD AGE

Reading: 2 Samuel 24

David's heart struck him after he had numbered the people.
And David said to the Lord, 'I have sinned greatly in what
I have done. But now, O LORD, please take away the iniquity
of your servant, for I have done very foolishly.' (v. 10)

There is of course another part to 2 Samuel that fills the rest of the book. These are David's declining days, and when the book comes to its end you will find David getting out his harp and singing his poetry in praise to God as he reflects on the goodness of God all through the years of his long life. As he sums up the difficulties he has known and the problems of actually trying to govern for God, they are creating within him a sense that, whatever you do, in the end you cannot be perfect here on earth. It has increased in his heart the longing for the day when the Sun of righteousness shall arise; a morning without clouds (Mal 4:2; 2 Sam 23:4); when the perfect King shall come, undo earth's tangles, and rule perfectly for God.

In his last years, white haired (if he'd got any left), far too old to go out to battle, they persuaded him to stay at home. The wise old man, advising the elders, the captains, and the commanders who were still in middle life and carrying the burden of the day, David was loved and respected by all.

You say, 'Well, he'll be safe now.'

Really? Do you think old age is a safe haven? Then let's learn from David. The most terrible sin wasn't with Bathsheba. The most terrible sin, that nearly ruined the whole purpose of God in David's life as king of Israel, he committed in his old age when he insisted on numbering the people (24:10).

I said a moment ago, I thought we ought to have some meetings for the middle aged. Do you know, verging there myself, I think we ought to have some special meetings for the old aged. You organize them and I shall be there. It's a mistake to think that if we patiently get past thirty we've seen all the spiritual battles we're ever going to have. Some of the biggest battles lie at the end; they don't get easier, they get harder. David stands before us, the great sweet psalmist of Israel singing his poetry, as a reminder that it is possible to grievously sin in our old age.

David Gooding, Governing for God: Studies in 2 Samuel, p. 10

30th July

ENDURING OPPOSITION

Reading: 1 Peter 2:18–25

*Consider him who endured from sinners such
hostility against himself, so that you may not grow
weary or faint-hearted. (Hebrews 12:3)*

Arguments, painful disputes, accusations, contradictions, bitter words, hurt feelings, broken friendships—all are very wearisome and wearing. No wonder if the readers of the letter to the Hebrews were discouraged, and sometimes felt like giving up altogether. Since they had been converted there had doubtless been many such arguments. Friends of years had become virtual enemies, relatives had been alienated. The rabbis had been ferocious in their opposition, and on top of all that there had been the physical persecution, damage and loss. It is not surprising if they felt spiritually and mentally drained.

But there is relief for mind and heart. 'Consider him', says the writer, 'who endured such opposition from sinful men, so that you will not grow weary and lose heart'. The mind finds healing and encouragement in its distress, sometimes, by forgetting itself and thinking of the greater distress of someone else. And there was never distress like that which the Lord suffered.

Israel were running true to type when they disputed the claims of their Messiah, mocked and crucified him. But he endured it without retaliation and without giving up. 'When they hurled their insults at him, he did not retaliate . . . Instead . . . he bore our sins in his body on the tree, so that we might die to sins and live for righteousness' (1 Pet 2:23–24). If he had refused to endure it, all sinners everywhere would have perished along with their sins. Shall we not show similar endurance? We too are involved in a fight against sin; in our own lives as we endeavour to progress in holiness; and in other people's lives as we preach the gospel, teach God's word and pastor people in difficulties. The fight is real and costly. We must expect opposition. We must expect to get hurt. But cheer up, says the writer, you're not dead yet! (Heb 12:4). It's not that bad—yet. You have not resisted to the point of shedding your blood in your struggle against sin. But one day we might have to, who knows? The battle is as serious as that. Anyone who thinks that the struggle against sin is a pastime or hobby probably hasn't joined in the war yet.

David Gooding, *An Unshakeable Kingdom: The Letter to the Hebrews for Today*, pp. 226–7

31st July

THE PURPOSE OF TRIALS

Reading: Hebrews 12:1–13

For the moment all discipline seems painful rather than pleasant, but later it yields the peaceful fruit of righteousness to those who have been trained by it. (v. 11)

Let us see what it is that God is doing in our trials. Things went so smoothly for us at first, perhaps, and we were enjoying spiritual life so much—and then days of difficulty came. We look back with a sigh to the earlier days and wish we were there still. We enjoyed spiritual life then, but not now; it is all so difficult. Why can't we go back? To reason like this is to reason like a child in the nursery. She has been enjoying life so far. There have been gifts from the parents, and endless play, and the child has enjoyed it. But now comes the day when the parents take the child off to school, and the child does not care for it. Why can't she go back and play as she used to instead of having to be made to face lessons in school that are tedious and uninteresting? But see that child in ten years' time, and she will not want to go back to the nursery. She has now been trained so that she sees greater possibilities in life.

And though God gives us times of great enjoyment in spiritual life, yet sooner or later he allows things to become difficult, so that he might develop us, and so that we get more out of spiritual life. And that is not only here; God thinks not only about the few years of our preparation in this life, but has in mind a whole eternity. We have to learn to share in his holiness, to behave as he behaves. It is the way the divine persons behave that makes heaven heaven. How short life is to prepare us for eternity! Shall we not rather, then, submit to him? Shall we not trust his wisdom? Shall we not agree that he sees and foresees far better than we do? And shall we not cooperate with him and live? Why, of course! By his grace we will. Now at the time discipline seems painful and not at all pleasant. Afterwards, however, it produces a harvest of righteousness and peace for those who have been trained by it.

David Gooding, *An Unshakeable Kingdom: The Letter to the Hebrews for Today*, pp. 229–30

1st August

TRIALS PRODUCE ENDURANCE

Reading: James 1:1–12

You know that the testing of your faith produces steadfastness. (v. 3)

Listen to James, 'Count it all joy . . . for you *know* . . .'. Mark the verb. He doesn't say, 'you hope'; he says, 'you know.' This is the secret of facing such a trial with joy; we can face it knowing, on God's authority, that the trying, the proving of our faith produces endurance, perseverance. It doesn't simply mean that it turns us into persevering men and women. This is the word that the Lord Jesus used in that famous parable in Luke 8, 'But the seed in the good soil, these are the ones who have heard the word in an honest and good heart, and hold it fast, and bear fruit with *perseverance*' (v. 15 NASB). With *endurance*—not with *patience*, at least if you understand the word 'patience' in the modern English sense—patience, as distinct from *impatience*. Some of God's good saints are horribly impatient! But we are talking here about perseverance, endurance; the good seed that grows and brings forth fruit with endurance.

There is only one way known in this life to bring forth fruit in a plant. That is, if the plant persists in growing through the rainy days and through the sunny days, through the wind and through the calm. By nature using these forces (the sun and the wind, the calm and the storm, the cold and the heat) in the end it brings forth fruit. The same forces that would destroy a plant that had no root contribute to the maturing and the fruitfulness of a plant that has a root.

As we face trials that will test whether we are believers or not we are to count it all joy, for we have it on the authority of God himself that trials produce endurance and in that confidence we can go through the storm. Paul says the same thing in Romans 5: we glory—not only in hope—we boast, we exult in confidence in the face of tribulation, *knowing that* tribulation works persistence, that is, endurance, perseverance (see vv. 3–5).

This is what makes life and trial faceable by a believer. And if I speak to some fellow-believer whose heart is besieged by difficulty, whose life is almost overwhelmed by trial and you feel it is almost impossible to carry on, courage up! The blessed Lord himself says that you may count it all joy. Grim kind of joy, maybe, but count it joy, knowing that where there is true faith to begin with, tribulation produces endurance.

David Gooding, James's Vision of the Perfect Man and Woman: The Epistle of James, pp. 7–8

2nd August

FAITH AND HEALING

Reading: Job 2:1–10

*But stretch out your hand and touch his bone and his
flesh, and he will curse you to your face. (v. 5)*

If someone becomes ill, what should we do? You say, 'Ask God immediately
to heal him.' James tells us that if someone gets ill we are allowed to pray and,
as it suits his wisdom and good plan, God is prepared to listen to us and heal
a brother or sister (5:14–15). That is still true, but you could have prayed a long
while for Job and nothing would have got better, for Job's story tells us why
God allows some illnesses to last for so long.

There came a day when the sons of God came to present themselves before
God, and God said to Satan, 'Have you considered my servant Job?'

'Yes, I have', said Satan.

'What do you think of him?'

Said Satan, 'You think he is one of your trusted people, full of faith and he
loves you. That's just because you have made life easy for him; he has the best
of health, beautiful daughters, lovely sons. It pays him because you feather his
nest. Let me take away his prosperity and touch his health, and you will find out
whether he has faith in you or not. He will curse you to your face!' Does God
take notice when Satan talks like that? Yes, he does. God has to justify himself
before the intelligentsia of heaven. If he is going to save you on the grounds of
faith that you are a genuine believer, then God is concerned about his character.
If Satan accuses God and says, 'This is not genuine faith at all', God is prepared
to go to tremendous lengths to demonstrate before principalities and powers
that his people's faith is genuine faith.

In the early days Job didn't know what was going on and it led to much
anguish of heart. 'Why does the Lord let me suffer?' He was serving a greater
cause than he knew; his very suffering was clearing God of the charge of favour-
itism and demonstrating God to be just, because Job's faith was genuine. It is
a marvellous thing when God saves his people from sickness. He is prepared
to do it. But it can be a bigger marvel and a bigger triumph when God allows
his people to suffer and in their anguish they come through and bless God and
refuse to allow any accusation against God or his love. God is vindicated by
their unbroken faith and that is a victory that eternity itself will never forget.

David Gooding, James's Vision of the Perfect Man and Woman: The Epistle of James, p. 73

3rd August

FILLING UP WHAT IS LACKING
IN CHRIST'S AFFLICTIONS

Reading: Colossians 1:24–29

*Now I rejoice in my sufferings for your sake, and in my
flesh I am filling up what is lacking in Christ's afflictions
for the sake of his body, that is, the church. (v. 24)*

They are the afflictions of Christ—not, of course, his atoning sufferings;
they are finished and have been since Calvary. The afflictions of the Lord
are for his body's sake: sufferings and afflictions involved in care for his
church. Ephesians chapter 5 has a delightful phrase. In the course of exhorting husbands how to behave, Paul says that your wife is part of you—you
are 'one flesh' (v. 31). 'For no one ever hated his own flesh, but nourishes
and cherishes it, just as Christ does the church' (v. 29). This is not about
Christ's sufferings at Calvary but of his present ministry in nourishing and
cherishing the church, 'so that he might present the church to himself in
splendour, without spot or wrinkle or any such thing, that she might be holy
and without blemish' (v. 27). Of course it involves suffering.

This process of being perfected will involve suffering for the church, as Paul
well knew. In his unconverted days God allowed him to persecute that church
and attack them ferociously. He drove them to prison and stood over them
and tortured them in order to try and get them to blaspheme the holy and
lovely name of the Lord Jesus. Why did the Lord Jesus allow Saul of Tarsus
to persecute his church like that? Had he no concept of the suffering they
were going through? Yes, indeed he had. Listen to what he said as he shone
forth on Saul of Tarsus and brought that persecutor to his knees: 'Saul, Saul,
why are you persecuting *me*?' (Acts 9:4).

You say, 'Surely the Lord is in heaven, and up in heaven they don't feel any
sufferings.' What would you make out of what is said of God in Isaiah 63:9,
talking of the afflictions through which his people Israel went through—'In
all their affliction he was afflicted'? What, God up in heaven? I've no right
to dispute it; it is in Scripture! Do you think that God sits in his heaven and,
even when his people go astray, he doesn't feel any sorrow? Perhaps we should
revise our notions of what heavenly joy is like. Certainly the Lord himself feels
for his people, 'For we do not have a high priest who is unable to sympathize
with our weaknesses' (Heb 4:15). He shares in the afflictions of his people.

David Gooding, *Christ Is All: Twelve Seminars on the Letter to the Colossians*, p. 39

4th August

GOD CAN USE MY DISABILITY

Reading: Exodus 4:1–17

Now therefore go, and I will be with your mouth
and teach you what you shall speak. (v. 12)

Finally, as Moses thought about it and prepared himself to go to Pharaoh and preach the message, once more he felt he was too weak to go. Said Moses to God, 'This is all very nice, but I am a poor speaker. I wouldn't know what to say, my words would stumble because I can't speak very well. You know I have a disability' (see Exod 6:12, 30).

Said God to Moses, 'I'm the God of your disability as well. Who made man's mouth? Who made the blind and the mute?'

We are not to suppose that God directly makes people deaf or mute or blind—for a multitude of thousands of causes lie in between the original creation and what happens to each individual born. But you know, in the last analysis, nothing happens but what God permits. Have you got some disability that nags you and chains you and frustrates you, and you feel there can't be a God who allowed such a major disability in your life? You feel it frustrates the lifework that you could have done and it is all so unfair. Daren't you believe that behind that disability is God himself? You say, 'But how can I believe that God would allow such a thing to happen to me?' Well, friend, I know it's hard, but it's harder not to. For if it isn't God behind it, then it's a freak of chance and it's meaningless.

But if there is a God who has permitted your disability, as he permitted Moses' disability, he is a God big enough to take you—disability and all—and use you significantly now in this life. He can use even that disability to be a means in his hand of preparing you for greater glory.

'It's hard to believe that!' you say. My friend, it's desperately hard. It depends what you think of God, doesn't it? If it's true that he loved you enough to give Christ to die for you, then he loved you like that when he allowed that disability to overtake you. Though you cannot understand it, if you know his love and you dare to trust his wisdom, rest assured that the God of your past, the God of your future, the God of your present—God your Creator and Redeemer—is the God ultimately behind that disability and he can turn it to your blessing now and to your greater glory and enjoyment hereafter.

David Gooding, *No Longer Bondmen: Thirteen Studies in the Book of Exodus*, p. 36

5th August

OUR RESPONSE TO DISCIPLINE

Reading: Hebrews 10:32–39

*Therefore, since we are surrounded by so great a cloud
of witnesses, let us also lay aside every weight, and sin
which clings so closely, and let us run with endurance
the race that is set before us. (Hebrews 12:1)*

I suppose trial trains us all to some extent; but just as it is possible to waste money on some people's education, it is possible for us to despise God's discipline and not value it; and thus much of his care goes unrewarded. We need to let ourselves be trained by the discipline. Look on to the afterward and lift up those hands that hang down, strengthen those paralysed knees, and though you feel fit to drop, your knees sag in the middle and your hands hang down, press on! For there is an afterward.

Our Father knows. While we think at times that things are well, our Father can see a hidden weakness within us, and allows a trial to come that exposes that very weakness in a way that is unpleasant. We ask God for the trial to be taken away so that the weakness will not be exposed so much. But God probes it all the more. Just as a physician will come to an ailing body and put his finger right on the mark, and of course it hurts—you would rather he put his finger anywhere else than there—so God, with unerring skill, very often allows a trial to come that exposes the very weakness that up till now we have sheltered and tried to forget. He is not fault finding, delighting to criticize and to humiliate us. He is out to heal our weaknesses. Let us only understand this, and then in time of trial we shall find grace to pray not so much that the trial be stopped, but that the weakness be dealt with and we come through refined.

Yet what do we know of trial? As once more we remember the plight of those to whom this letter was written, we must admit that we scarcely know anything. Many of them stood with broken homes, with everything lost, family connections severed. Their knees were sagging, their hands were hanging down. In spite of it, many of them, with their eyes on the mark, valiantly ran to the end and gained the winning-post somehow. The Lord help us in our easier circumstances to run with perseverance, putting off everything that hinders and the sin that so easily entangles us, running with endurance till we sit down beside the Lord at the winning-post above.

David Gooding, *An Unshakeable Kingdom: The Letter to the Hebrews for Today*, pp. 230–31

6th August

THE SOURCE OF TEMPTATION

Reading: James 1:12–18

*Let no one say when he is tempted, 'I am being
tempted by God', for God cannot be tempted with
evil, and he himself tempts no one. (v. 13)*

There are some areas in particular where we could be deceived by bogus spirituality. James 1:13 is set in the context of temptation. We are not to be deceived; 'Let no one say when he is tempted, "I am being tempted by God", for God cannot be tempted with evil and he himself tempts no one.' *It is exceedingly important when we are tempted to recognize what the source of temptation is.*

What would you say to a man who let it slip that he was thinking of joining the Freemasons, with all their old idolatry? He says, 'I was out of work and desperately needing a job and I believe the Lord opened the way for me to enter this firm. It was of the Lord; he opened the way. The principals of the firm said I would have to join the Freemasons. I knew it wasn't for the best, but if the Lord opened the way it must be right.' What would you say to him? We should need to say, firmly and lovingly, 'Don't be deceived, my brother; God never leads anybody, or lures somebody, into sin.'

Joseph believed with all his heart that it was God who had overruled that he should be put down into the pit and then find himself in Potiphar's house as his chief steward. That was the Lord's leading; but when Potiphar's wife made her advances Joseph did not say, 'Well it was the Lord who put me into this situation. He must know about it and perhaps it's OK because the Lord led me.' *Be not deceived, God does not tempt us.*

We mustn't blame the devil too much either; he is a common scapegoat. He certainly does enough damage, but sometimes we are inclined to blame him when we should be blaming ourselves. 'That wasn't me,' says somebody, 'it was the devil.' Somebody else says, 'It wasn't me, it was my ugly temper.' Well, who is your ugly temper if it isn't part of you?

Part of our growing up into maturity is to *face the reality of ourselves*; not to keep blaming our faults on other things and other forces, but to face the fact that it is me. I am the one who is guilty of the pride and the jealousy and I must repent and seek deliverance. I must learn to stand against it and put to death the things of the flesh.

David Gooding, *James's Vision of the Perfect Man and Woman: The Epistle of James*, pp. 15–16

7th August

THE EXTENT OF GOD'S DISCIPLINE

Reading: Exodus 34:1–14

Then the angel of the LORD said, 'O LORD of hosts, how long will you have no mercy on Jerusalem and the cities of Judah, against which you have been angry these seventy years?' (Zechariah 1:12)

Our Lord is interceding for his people and for the cessation of discipline. You must not think that there is any conflict within the Godhead. You must not fall into the pagan superstition that God the Father is stern and severe, and God the Son is kindly; for the second person of the Trinity tells out what is in the Father's heart. But here lies the problem for God, who loves his people and will spare them pain, but loves them too much to permit their unchecked sinning. Here is the problem for God who has set his hand to our salvation—not merely our salvation in the sense of forgiveness of sins, but our salvation from our failings here in life; our salvation in the sense of our ultimate glorification, our conformity to the image of God's Son. Because we are never-dying spirits, God's love determines that he will not give us up until he has fulfilled his purpose and we are finally like Christ. Therefore God's love cannot always afford to be kind, with that type of superficial kindness with which an indulgent parent will excuse the child its school lessons because the child finds them difficult. Yielding to indulge the child now risks his whole future. Not so God. Be the pains of spiritual education ever so severe, God will educate us, his people, correcting us when we go astray; disciplining us by positive training, severe as it may seem, so that our faith may grow and our likeness to Christ increase.

You will think I'm a terrible man and in need of restoration, and you would be correct. Watching the way of God with his people, I have long since decided myself that God is very tough. You will forgive me, and I'm sure God does, when I say that I wouldn't treat my dog, nor allow it to suffer, as God sometimes allows his people to suffer. But then, you see, my dog has a very limited future, and if he should get some illness it would be a kindness to put him down. But you are eternal spirits, begotten of God, children of God with an eternity of glory before you, so God will not give you up until he has brought you through. Be the suffering ever so great, yet here as the angel of the Lord he pleads before God and asks now for a cessation of the discipline and for happier days ahead. God comes out of the shadow, so to speak, and orders that his reply to the intercessor be published abroad so that all may know it.

David Gooding, *The God of Restoration: Four Studies in the Prophecy of Zechariah*, p. 9

8th August

LOVING THE WORLD

Reading: 1 John 2:12–17

*. . . but of the tree of the knowledge of good and
evil you shall not eat, for in the day that you eat
of it you shall surely die. (Genesis 2:17)*

The devil came along and said, 'Well, that's God all over. He puts a beautiful tree in front of you, all attractive and lovely, and then he says you can't have it. He is always tantalizing people with all the lovely things in life that you must not enjoy.'

The world has swallowed the lie and they have no time for God. Time for music, but not for the God who made music. Time for food, but not for the God whose hand provided it. Time for art, but not for the God who gave them the ability and the eye to see with. They are like the girl who takes an engagement ring, but is not interested in the fellow who gave it to her.

The Apostle John has to warn us: 'Do not love the world or the things in the world. If anyone loves the world, the love of the Father is not in him. For all that is in the world—the desires of the flesh and the desires of the eyes and pride in possessions—is not from the Father but is from the world' (1 John 2:15–16).

What's wrong with loving the world? If the world is understood as those lovely things—not wrong in themselves but things that would draw your heart away from God the Father—then those very things become perniciously dangerous. Instead of the love of them leading me nearer the Lord, if they lead me away from him that is an unqualified disaster.

Imagine a wealthy father who took his son, on becoming twenty-one, outside on to the lawn in front of his stately home. He said, 'You are my son, and I would love to mark your coming of age by a beautiful present. Here is your own private jet aeroplane.' There's nothing wrong with jet aeroplanes. But suppose the boy got into the cockpit, started the engines, waved good-bye to his father and never came back again. He had no time for his father. Don't you suppose his father would curse the very day he gave the boy the aeroplane?

Our hearts are such deceitful things. We enjoy what God gives, but we must love the Father and let all his gracious gifts draw us nearer to him.

David Gooding, *Daniel: Civil Servant and Saint*, pp. 53–4

THE DISCIPLE'S JOURNEY

Part 8—The World and Our Warfare

9th August

ATHEISTIC MATERIALISM AND GOD'S ANSWER

Reading: Acts 2:22–36

I have not come of my own accord. He who sent me
is true, and him you do not know. I know him, for
I come from him, and he sent me. (John 7:28–29)

Atheistic materialism denies that there was ever any purpose, divine or otherwise, behind the appearance of the human race itself upon earth, let alone behind the birth of any individual person. It likewise denies that there is any future for the individual beyond his or her life on this planet, or any divinely planned future for the planet itself. Thirdly, it denies that there is any genuine non-materialistic, spiritual dimension to human life even during the short time each individual lives on the planet.

In holding this view atheistic materialism turns our planet into a prison; and the more truly intellectual a person is, the more intellectually cruel the prison will appear. For materialism insists that human rationality is the unplanned, unpurposed, product of mindless forces, which eventually proceed systematically to annihilate every individual's intelligence, love, hope and very existence. In the end these same mindless forces will destroy planet earth and every vestige of intelligence upon it, and—ultimate irony—when they have done it, they won't even know they have done it. Human intelligence, therefore, is the ultimately helpless prisoner of mindless matter.

The fact that this philosophical materialism is often urged upon us and taught to our children as the acme of intellectual thought, shows what its ultimate anti-intellectual source is. It comes from the 'prince of this world' of whom Christ says in the Gospel of John: 'He was a murderer from the beginning, and stood not in the truth, because there is no truth in him. When he speaks a lie, he speaks of his own; for he is a liar, and the father thereof' (John 8:44).

The incarnation of the Son of God, his death, resurrection and ascension are God's answer to Satan's attempt to banish God from the world, and to persuade mankind that this world is all there is. Summing up his mission, Christ said to his disciples: 'I came out from the Father, and have come into the world; again I leave the world, and go unto the Father' (John 16:28). There is another world; this world is not all there is.

David Gooding, *The Riches of Divine Wisdom: The New Testament's Use of the Old Testament*, pp. 219–20

10th August

THE WORLD AS A DEAD WEIGHT TO BE OVERCOME

Reading: John 15:18–25

For this is the love of God, that we keep his commandments.
And his commandments are not burdensome. For everyone
who has been born of God overcomes the world. And this is the
victory that has overcome the world—our faith. (1 John 5:3–4)

True love for God, says John, means keeping his commandments. But the plain fact is that the world often makes it difficult for a believer to keep God's commandments. It is not necessarily because the world is hostile to believers. It is simply the way that the world is organized and the principles on which it conducts its affairs. The director of a factory, trying to evade his creditors, may well instruct his secretary to tell any callers that the director is away travelling—when all the while he is in fact in his office on the premises. If the secretary is a believer, and for conscience sake refuses to tell this lie, she may well lose her job.

A friend of mine, in a country that shall be nameless, complained to his local income tax inspector about the excessive amount of tax which the government demanded of him. The inspector explained that most people he knew cheated the government by not declaring large parts of their income. The government, therefore, tried to compensate for this loss of taxes by raising the rate of tax on the amount that people did declare. Said the inspector to my friend: 'If for the sake of your Christian principles you refuse to cheat, and honestly declare all your income, there is nothing we can do about it: we shall have to charge you this enormous amount of tax.'

Obviously, one could cite many other, different kinds of situations where the way the world runs makes it difficult for a believer to keep God's commandments. But then, says John, for a believer God's commandments are not burdensome, 'for everyone who has been born of God overcomes the world' (v. 4).

David Gooding, *The Riches of Divine Wisdom: The New Testament's Use of the Old Testament*, p. 215

11th August

BREAKING THE POWER OF WORLDLINESS

Reading: Isaiah 44:6–11

*Come, you who are blessed by my Father, inherit
the kingdom prepared for you from the foundation
of the world'. (Matthew 25:34)*

One of the things guaranteed to break the grip of worldliness upon our hearts, is to awake to the notion that God is the God of our past. Long before you came into this world as an infant and were laid in a cradle, God had been thinking of you, talking of you, planning for you; it wasn't an accident that you came. It wasn't that you arrived in this planet by some accident and God scratched his divine head (if I may so speak, reverently) and said, 'Now what shall I do? I wasn't expecting him to come here and now I'm landed with him!' No! The divine Creator, who foresees and foreknows, had anticipated your coming and in Christ had chosen you before the foundation of the world. This temporary little world wasn't the beginning and neither shall it be the end. We are passengers through this temporary planet—*every mark of it is temporary*. But we come with plans of eternity behind us. It begins already to add dimension to life, as we discover the name of our God—the God of our past. He is the God who in that past made sundry covenants and declared that he will be faithful to them.

'I am the God of Abraham,' he said to Moses (see Exod 3:6).

'Abraham—who is Abraham, and what about him?'

'Well, Moses, I made a covenant with him. Don't you know I covenanted with Abraham that in him and in his seed all the world should be blessed? I covenanted with Abraham and his offspring that I would give him these vast territories for his possession.'

Doesn't that excite you? I hear some staid Christian say, 'Well yes, I would get excited if I were a Jew, but what on earth has Abraham got to do with me?' O my brothers and sisters, let me spell out the riches. If you are Christ's, then you are Abraham's seed and heirs according to that promise (Gal 3:29). All those glorious promises made to Abraham and his seed in those far off days, God will keep them and honour and fulfil them to you. The God who came down to this planet and dined with Abraham outside his tent door on those rude and plain benches such as Abraham would have had—that God hasn't forgotten Abraham and he hasn't forgotten me. I'm not to be regarded as some flotsam and jetsam on the river of time; I've come into this planet with God and his eternal plans behind me, 'even as he chose us in [Christ] before the foundation of the world' (Eph 1:4).

David Gooding, *No Longer Bondmen: Thirteen Studies in the Book of Exodus*, p. 30

12th August

OVERCOMING THE FLESH

Reading: 2 Kings 2:1–15

And behold, I am sending the promise of my Father upon you. But stay in the city until you are clothed with power from on high. (Luke 24:49)

As the two went together, Elijah was taken up by whirlwind in a chariot into heaven, and Elisha saw him go into heaven. As he stood watching that ascending figure, there fell down from the rising and ascending Elijah his cloak, and Elisha took it. Therein lay his secret: actually seeing a man going into heaven. He was from then on clothed with the very cloak of a man who was now in heaven.

What then is the secret for overcoming the flesh? The New Testament records the words of our blessed Lord in those last hours before he left his disciples to go to Calvary. 'Yet a little while and the world will see me no more, but you will see me. Because I live, you also will live' (John 14:19). Then, before he left them at the end of the forty days he said, 'But stay in the city until you are clothed with power from on high' (Luke 24:49). Down from the ascended Christ there came God's Holy Spirit, to clothe the believer in the power of the risen Lord. What a wonderful day that was for the apostles as they stood on Mount Olivet, facing the task that the risen Lord had given them, of being his witnesses in Jerusalem, in Judea, in Samaria and to the outermost parts of the earth. Where should mere mortal men, subject to the same passions as we are, get the power to be witnesses for Christ? As they stood and he was commissioning them, he was parted from them and carried up into heaven, and they stood looking with literal eyes, seeing him go.

We haven't seen him with our physical eyes ascend from Mount Olivet to heaven. Yet there is a sense in which we can see him. The Lord explained it to Judas (not Iscariot) when he asked, 'Lord, how is it that you will manifest yourself to us, and not to the world?' And Jesus replied, 'If anyone loves me, he will keep my word, and my Father will love him, and we will come to him and make our home with him' (John 14:22–23). That is precisely what happens as the Holy Spirit reveals to our inner spiritual sight, not spooky visions, but the glorious reality that there is this man in heaven, Jesus Christ our Lord, and we are imbued with his power. Have you seen him lately?

David Gooding, *Studies in the Life of the Prophet Elisha*, p. 24

13th August

THE BATTLE FOR THE MIND

Reading: 1 John 4:1–6

*Now this I say and testify in the Lord, that you
must no longer walk as the Gentiles do, in the
futility of their minds. (Ephesians 4:17)*

First of all we shall think in our own Christian terms of the Gentile attitude
to God's salvation and to his purposes. The New Testament warns us of
the workings of Satan through unregenerate and carnal men. Ephesians 4
is dealing with the topic of the risen Christ, who has given gifts to men—
apostles, prophets, pastors and teachers and evangelists, 'until we all attain
to the unity of the faith and of the knowledge of the Son of God, to mature
manhood, to the measure of the stature of the fullness of Christ' (v. 13). That
is, the revealed doctrine, until we all come to believe exactly the same thing.

The enemies are vigorous. 'They lie in wait to deceive,' says Paul, with 'the
sleight of men, and cunning craftiness' (v. 14 KJV). John warns us about the same
thing, 'So now many antichrists have come' (1 John 2:18). How will you know an
antichrist when you see one? By his doctrine! How will you distinguish a genuine
gift from a false gift? By its doctrinal content and whether the spirit involved
will confess that Jesus Christ has come in the flesh—that 'Jesus Christ is Lord.'

We face now an enemy that is not merely concerned with people's bellies,
but with people's brains. Not merely with the indulgence of the flesh, but
with what they believe. This is a spiritual universe and what people actually
believe about God is the most important stronghold of all. Satan may have
his red light areas in our modern cities to attract some, but perhaps he is far
more active in circles where men use their brains and think. He can pervert
their minds from the truth and sidetrack believers by his cunning craftiness.
'In the very bosom of the church at that time,' says John, 'there were these
false teachers. They were anti-Christ. They were not of us,' he says, 'for if
they had been of us they would have continued with us. They went out to
manifest that they never were of us—they are antichrists.'

Colossians similarly warns us, 'See to it that no one takes you captive by
philosophy and empty deceit, according to human tradition, according to
the elemental spirits of the world, and not according to Christ' (Col 2:8). The
battle is for people's minds. Paul therefore pleads with us not to think like
Gentiles do, in the darkness of their minds, alienated from the life of God
that is in them (Eph 4:18).

David Gooding, *The Lord Saves His People: Fourteen Seminars on the Book of Judges*, p. 52

14th August

OVERCOMING WORLDLINESS

Reading: Judges 3:7–11

*All that the Father has is mine; therefore I said that he will
take what is mine and declare it to you. (John 16:15)*

It is no good just being negative, hoping thus to escape worldliness. The
only victory against worldliness is a heart filled into all the fullness of God.
Motivated by such things Othniel went out to war and fought, and his hand
prevailed, which reminds us that this matter will involve us in a war to the
end of our days.

Our foe is dastardly cunning. Says John, 'I write to you, young men,
because . . . you have overcome the evil one' (1 John 2:14). If only God's word
had been deeper in Eve's heart when that sophisticated tempter confronted
her! But he made out that if you listen too much to God's word it will make
you a bit cranky, cramp your style and stop your enjoyment. So the minimum
of the word of God, please, and then we can get on with enjoying ourselves!
Rather, see our Lord in the desert, who, having the powers to make the stones
bread, declined, saying to Satan, 'Man shall not live by bread alone, but by
every word that comes from the mouth of God' (Matt 4:4). Thank God for
his victory. 'The ruler of this world is coming', he said. 'He has no claim on
me' (John 14:30).

Who shall measure the fight and the heat of the battle, when the Son of
God and heir of all creation came down and, in obedience to his Father's
will, hung naked on a cross? They laughed at him for his faith in God as
he hung abandoned at Calvary. Do you know what sustained him in those
terrible moments in his battle against worldliness, when the prince of this
world came and mocked him?

'You fool,' said Satan, 'I offered you all the kingdoms of the world if you
would fall down and worship me, and you refused. Now you hang naked,
ruined, your career at an end, going down to death vilified and traduced as
an impostor.'

In that holy heart there surged again and again, 'All that the Father has
is mine.' As he stood on the verge of Gethsemane he repeated it over to his
apostles—'All that the Father has is mine' (John 16:15). After they had sung
a hymn they went out into the darkness and to Calvary. 'But take heart; I have
overcome the world,' said he (v. 33).

David Gooding, The Lord Saves His People: Fourteen Seminars on the Book of Judges, p. 34

15th August

Reading: Daniel 10:7–11:1

. . . and especially those who indulge in the lust of defiling passion and despise authority. Bold and wilful, they do not tremble as they blaspheme the glorious ones. (2 Peter 2:10)

As he outlines history, the man who spoke with Daniel is to be heard talking of powers greater than human: of the prince of Persia that has power enough to withstand the pre-incarnate Son of God; of battles in the heavenly places, of demonic forces, of satanic attack. In previous visions in the book of Daniel we have seen human empires under the guise of wild animals fighting it out between them, but the distinctive thing of this vision is not wild animals but mighty spirit forces waging their warfare, going about their deadly and devilish designs.

If you would account for the endless disasters, the miseries and warfare that have come upon the human race, then according to this vision you must not put it down, altogether and unqualified, to the responsibility of mere human beings. This vision says there is more to human warfare and disasters than mere humans. There is a spirit realm; there are demonic forces, and they fight battles.

It is easy to laugh at that kind of thing, and it is not merely modern men who laugh at it. Peter had occasion to warn his fellow-believers that certain false teachers had crept into the church. Among the wares of their trade they taught that it was perfectly acceptable for Christian people to live a permissive lifestyle of pre-marital and post-marital unchastity and unfaithfulness, but another element in their false teaching was that they laughed at the whole idea of spirits and angels and a devil. 'But these, as natural brute beasts, made to be taken and destroyed, speak evil of the things that they understand not; and shall utterly perish in their own corruption' (2 Pet 2:12 KJV).

If we are to be balanced men and women we must realize that we stand in the middle, in tension between two realms. Beneath us there is the animal realm. We have certain things in common with the animals; we have bodies, we have stomachs and we have lungs and things. But at the other side we stand in contact with the spirit realm. Man is not just body and not just physical. Man has a spiritual dimension and therefore has contact with a world of spirits. If we refuse to face the fact that there is a spiritual dimension to humankind and to world affairs, as Peter tells us, we will sink to the level of mere animal behaviour.

David Gooding, *Daniel: Civil Servant and Saint*, pp. 93–4

16th August

COMING TO HELP THE LORD IN THE BATTLE

Reading: Judges 5:1–23

Gilead stayed beyond the Jordan; and Dan, why did he stay with the ships? Asher sat still at the coast of the sea, staying by his landings. (v. 17)

We are talking about this in the context of this great battle that raged in olden times, when the Canaanites in all their massive technology, brains, industry and commerce oppressed the people of God. Great things are at stake. Now listen to Deborah as she summons the tribes of Israel up to Mount Tabor. Not now the matter of getting the clothes or other possessions we need; the whole battle for truth is at stake. Is Israel the vehicle of God's revelation to the Gentiles, or is the whole thing going to be obliterated and shattered? With prophetic voice she calls Israel to the battle of the Lord and some came—glorious men, hazarding their lives in the thick of the battle. But when the battle was at its thickest the inhabitants of Meroz did not come to the help of the Lord. 'Curse you Meroz,' said the angel of the Lord (Judg 5:23).

Around this big world there is a battle on for the minds of men. Whether we know it or not the Lord is involved, striving against the mighty, and you and I have a chance to join in the battle. God forbid that we get so lost in the occupations of life, so oppressed and obsessed by our material needs and business that the angel of the Lord has to say, 'Where are the men?' (There are women pioneering in Africa, lonely and alone, but where are the men?) 'Curse you Meroz,' said the angel of the Lord, 'that you didn't come to the help of the Lord in the day of battle.' It would be a tragedy if we were trying to get too many coats and didn't have enough time to join in this battle.

'Why did Dan remain in ships?' (v. 17). I don't know whether this can be answered. Remaining in the ships, messing about in boats when such a tremendous battle was at stake. Young men were facing the enemy on the battlefield and some of them getting wounded, why did Dan stay with the ships? I don't know, but he remained in the ships and forever lost his chance to have the honour of coming to the aid of the Lord in the battle against the mighty.

David Gooding, *The Lord Saves His People: Fourteen Seminars on the Book of Judges*, p. 62

17th August

THE 'TENT PEG' THAT GIVES US SECURITY

Reading: Judges 4:8–24

And he said to her, 'Stand at the opening of the tent, and if any man comes and asks you, "Is anyone here?" say, "No."' (v. 20)

That was more than she dared to do. What if an Israelite was to come up the path and say, 'Is there any man here,' and Jael said 'No'? That would have been the end of Jael. Not to speak of what would have happened when her husband came home and found a curious lump in the back of the tent in the women's quarters! The only thing she could have done was to tell the truth. Sisera knew what it might mean for her to tell a lie and that made up her mind for her.

In the ancient east it was the woman's job to put up the tent and to take it down. Women may not have had much to do with armies and fighting, but they did have their own battles to fight. It was the women who drove the stakes into the ground, put the tents up and made a secure home for their husbands and children. A tent peg may be a very simple thing, but it means a lot if you are living in tents. For the ancient easterner how easily it became a figure, 'The peg that was fastened in a secure place' (Isa 22:25). To the prophet it represented life's security.

In this great world in which the battles run to and fro, how nervous mothers feel when their teenagers go up to university, out into the world not yet saved. What is the security you want for them? It's not primarily a pension, is it? What security is there in earth or heaven, except in a faith that is tied to that great peg in a secure place, our blessed Lord? What is your own life built around for its security?

There was Sisera, coaxed to sleep with the milk, and Jael got the tent peg and she hammered it through his brain.

God be praised for the intellect he has given us and we must love him with all our minds, hearts, souls and strength. But in this fallen world we shall not find security and the ultimate solution by our unaided Gentile intellect, we shall only find security, certainty and truth in God and his self-revelation in Christ. If my Gentile unregenerate intellect comes into conflict with Jesus Christ and God's revelation, I shall have to decide what I am going to stake my life round. As my ultimate security for time and eternity, what is the truth? God help us in the home, in business and in all our preaching, for the thing is more than simple theory. If Jesus Christ is truth, if the Bible is God's revelation, then we shall have to stake our very life and all that we have on it.

David Gooding, *The Lord Saves His People: Fourteen Seminars on the Book of Judges*, p. 63

18th August

FIGHTING THE RIGHT BATTLES

Reading: Judges 7:22–8:3

*Then the men of Ephraim said to him, 'What is this that
you have done to us, not to call us when you went to fight
against Midian?' And they accused him fiercely. (8:1)*

So Midian was subdued, and if we had been able to leave the story there it
would be a happy story indeed. But the record goes on in all realism to tell
us that the wonderful fruits of the victory were followed by a success that
was in part flawed. In the first place, now that they had deliverance from the
Midianite raiders you might have thought that, without exception, all the
people of God would come crowding round, praising the Lord and patting
old Gideon on the back. Not so the Ephraimites. 'Why didn't you call us? We
have a right to be called,' they said (8:1). And here they are, getting angry and
stirring up more strife. You say, 'Why can't those petty-minded Ephraimites
rejoice in the victory, never mind who won it?' They didn't have a part, and
weren't asked.

I have known churches ruined from end to end because Mrs. So-and-So
wasn't asked to arrange the flowers—you must have a nice pot of flowers
under the preacher's desk! Somebody went and asked Mrs. Jones and didn't
ask Mrs. Smith. Woe betide the gospel meeting now; it becomes irrelevant
and the battles of the Lord irrelevant. The peace of a church can be smashed
over such stupid trifles.

My brothers and sisters, we know our own hearts. We would love to be the
preacher who preached and thousands came to Christ. When I am not the
preacher, but somebody else is, my narrow heart knows a pang of jealousy.
God give us some sense of proportion, with the world outside perishing and
the battles of the Lord in progress. God save us from being people who are
prepared to make trouble in the church and disarray in the armies of the
Lord because of personal grievance that we were not invited to do something.

Gideon managed to find grace enough to calm these people before their
indignation broke out into serious trouble.

David Gooding, *The Lord Saves His People: Fourteen Seminars on the Book of Judges*, pp. 74–5

19th August

PASSIONS OF THE FLESH WAGE
WAR AGAINST OUR SOULS

Reading: Numbers 11:1–25

*Beloved, I urge you as sojourners and exiles to
abstain from the passions of the flesh, which
wage war against your soul. (1 Peter 2:11)*

When God delivered the Israelites out of Canaan and they began to march towards their inheritance flowing with milk and honey, Amalek came with all his forces and fought against them. He would stop them making any progress and he came to war against them. 'The passions of the flesh,' says Paul, 'wage war against the soul. As you pilgrims and exiles are on your way to glory, these fleshly desires will wage a campaign against you to stop your progress. 'Watch your soul.'

Who exactly were these Israelites? They had come out of Egypt and there they were, foot slogging along the desert because there was a great inheritance out there, flowing with milk and honey. But after a while the going got a bit tough. The sand got hot during the daytime; there wasn't too much water about, and they felt a bit thirsty and began to think of all the onions and cucumbers and garlic that they ate in Egypt. Then their appetites got involved and they began to crave those onions and garlic and cucumbers and things, so they came to Moses and they nearly stoned him. They started weeping over cucumbers. 'We remember what we had in Egypt and we ate it for nothing.' What a lot of nonsense that was. Nothing? They got it by being slaves! 'We remember the cucumbers and things. Now there's nothing but this dry old manna stuff,' and they all wept. What a sorry sight. I try to imagine it sometimes—600,000 grown men weeping their eyes out over cucumbers. They can't work it out in their heads that they have a glorious inheritance ahead, and for the time being the road may be a bit tough. They haven't the sense to judge the one thing by the other and be prepared to endure the toughness now because they're going to the glory beyond.

And how about us? Says Peter, 'You're travelling to an inheritance that is imperishable, undefiled, and unfading, kept in heaven for you . . . In this you rejoice, though now for a little while, if necessary, you have been grieved by various trials' (see 1 Pet 1:4, 6). Can't we see the proportion of things? It's worth enduring a little discomfort that's unavoidable on a journey that is taking us to the imperishable inheritance above.

David Gooding, The Saving and Losing of a Soul, pp. 9–10

20th August

NOT ALONE IN THE BATTLE

Reading: Exodus 17:7–16

*For it is God who works in you, both to will and to
work for his good pleasure. (Philippians 2:13)*

First of all there was Moses, sitting upon the mountain. Can you see him
there, a noble figure with his beard and white hair? Thank God for Moses.
When Amalek came down the road Moses raised up his hands; and when
Moses stands in front of you and puts his hands up and says, 'O no you
don't!' he is a force to be reckoned with. I hope you haven't dismissed him,
for you'll need him. We are not under Law as a system of earning salvation,
thank God, but we still need Moses. When the enemy comes along to my
unsuspecting soul and puts distractions in front of me, in those moments
when I would give in I need Moses to say, 'O no you don't!'

Secondly, Moses' hands were weak; both Moses and his law combined would
be weak because of the weakness of the flesh. I shall need something more than
Moses; so there came those two priestly men, Aaron and Hur, and they held
up Moses' hands. Thank God for a high priest. On those days when the battle
is hard and it's difficult to go against my feelings—difficult not to side with
my own rebellious heart—thank God for that ever-vigilant High Priest who
intercedes and sends me the succour that I need to avail in the fight.

And then, thirdly, not only the priests up above on the mountain; there
was Joshua down on the ground, bearing his lovely name of Saviour because
God designed him to be a picture of that greater saviour who is in heaven
interceding for us. When the battle is hard he is down here fighting our battles
with us and in us, so that we might get the victory.

May the Lord so encourage us by his word. God is going to win the battle—'For it is God who works in you, both to will and to work for his good
pleasure'—may he give us the grace to cooperate with him in his war and
work out our own salvation.

David Gooding, No Longer Bondmen: Thirteen Studies in the Book of Exodus, pp. 107–8

THE DISCIPLE'S JOURNEY

Part 9—Looking to the End

21st August

THE FINAL VICTORY OF TRUE FAITH

Reading: John 21:15–23

. . . so that the tested genuineness of your faith—more precious than gold that perishes though it is tested by fire—may be found to result in praise and glory and honour at the revelation of Jesus Christ. (1 Peter 1:7)

And so Peter came back. Christ's prayer had prevailed. It was not for nothing that Christ had made a covenant in his own blood to write his laws on Peter's heart and turn Peter into a true and loyal man of God. Nor had the interlude of his failure been without its part to play in the process of making him, and through him untold numbers of other people, holy. 'And when you have turned again, strengthen your brothers,' said Christ (Luke 22:32).

Peter remembered the charge; and in his first letter he set out to do just that. Your faith, he points out to his fellow Christians, is like gold, incalculably precious. But like gold, it is all mixed up at the beginning with dross of one kind and another: excitement, it may be, or self-confidence and pride, or second-hand experience or even childish father-fixations. And so it has to be purified, and like a goldsmith purifies his gold by putting it into the crucible and subjecting it to intense heat, so God must allow you from time to time to pass through suffering of various kinds.

But don't be surprised when it happens, as though some strange thing happened to you. Your faith shall eventually be found unto praise and glory and honour at the revelation of Jesus Christ (1 Pet 1:6–9; 4:12). Whence Peter's confidence? Why first the word and intercession of Christ, and then his own experience. Of course, anyone knows that though a goldsmith may put his gold through the fire until it reaches melting point and beyond, he never allows any of the real gold to be destroyed; all he's getting rid of is the dross.

David Gooding, *Windows on Paradise: Scenes of Hope and Salvation in the Gospel of Luke*, pp. 110–1

22nd August

FAITH'S ULTIMATE GOAL

Reading: Hebrews 11:8–10, 13–16

We look not to the things that are seen but to the things that are unseen. For the things that are seen are transient, but the things that are unseen are eternal. (2 Corinthians 4:18)

If it is important that we start our pilgrimage on the right foot, so to speak, it is also important that we get our ultimate goal clearly in our sights from the very beginning. Abraham did, and so did the other patriarchs. They arrived in the promised land and were informed by God that this was the land which was to be theirs and their descendants. But they made no attempt to build a city there and to settle down. They continued to live in tents like strangers in a foreign country. It was not that they were ungrateful or that they despised the great earthly possessions that God was giving them or the brilliant career that God had in mind for their descendants in that land. All that was good. They would enjoy it in its day. But nothing on this temporary earth could be their main goal. In their hearts they had already left it all. Only the eternal city could be their goal. So Abraham continued to live as a pilgrim and foreigner. It doubtless took a lot of faith to do so. His secret was that he kept his sights on the eternal city. That nourished his faith in its reality; and faith in its reality kept him from treating anything in this world as though it were his main objective.

His secret may be ours. We are meant to enjoy our God-given present and future earthly blessings and careers; but we must not let them loom so large in our thinking that they virtually become life's chief goal. If we do, the danger is that we shall settle down in this world as if it were our home, cease to live like pilgrims and foreigners, and belie our professed faith that we are looking for the eternal city. Our goals and way of life will then be no different from those of people of the world.

David Gooding, An Unshakeable Kingdom: The Letter to the Hebrews for Today, p. 210

23rd August

FAITH IS NECESSARY EVEN IN HEAVEN

Reading: Luke 19:11–26

No longer will there be anything accursed, but the throne of God and of the Lamb will be in it, and his servants will worship him. They will see his face, and his name will be on their foreheads. (Revelation 22:3–4)

It is a common thing to be heard many times repeated—in fact it has the backing of holy Scripture—that 'now we walk by faith.' And then the hymn says that faith will give way to sight—'And Lord, haste the day when my faith shall be sight.' Of course it will! We can't see heaven now; we have not yet seen its glories and its joys and its wonders, many of them we can't even visualize, but one day we shall see them. And, wonder of wonders, we shall see the blessed Lord himself; not having seen him, and still not seeing him, we love him. One day we shall see him and, in that sense, faith will give way to sight.

But tell me, when we get home to heaven will that mean we won't have to trust the Lord? We'll be at liberty then—we won't need faith any more! Will you have permission not to trust the Lord up there? When he says to you, 'My redeemed child, I've appointed to you galaxy 2304 in the nebula of Orion—I want you to go out there, taking all the helpers that I shall give you to develop it for me and I want you to do it this way.' When you get out there you say, 'This is a tremendous job—I don't know if I can do it! Is this the right way of going about it?' Will you not have to trust the Lord still—or are you going to be as infinite and omniscient as God when you get home? If he asks you to do something and tells you the way to do it, will you say, 'I'm as good as he is, I don't have to trust him—I could have told him how to do it!' Or will God not always be bigger than you are and his thoughts immensely and infinitely greater than your thoughts, so that there will always be occasion for you to trust him, because you won't understand everything about God? Are you going to be omniscient when you get home? No, indeed not! We shall still have to trust the Lord. If there came a moment in that glorious place when our faith in God wavered but a centimetre, then the lights of heaven would begin to dim.

David Gooding, *No Longer Bondmen: Thirteen Studies in the Book of Exodus*, p. 86

24th August

THE GOAL OF OUR REDEMPTION

Reading: Deuteronomy 4:32–40

God himself will be with them as their God. (Revelation 21:3)

What is the chief point of redemption? What is its goal, its chief enjoyment? Let this ancient text tell us what in God's mind was the chief benefit he would confer upon the children of Israel when they came into the land of Canaan. There would be grass and cows and bees and honey and flowers, wine and olive presses and a bungalow or two. But what were they compared with this supreme benefit, that even there in Canaan the transcendent Lord of all creation, time and space, condescended to come down and dwell among them? What joy could you compare with that? How would you rate the grass and the honey compared with having the living God dwell in your midst? You could go to his tent of meeting and know that your prayers reached the very heart of God. He was not a long, long way off in his heaven; he had come down to dwell in your very midst.

Oh my brother, my sister, the real point of going home to heaven is not a few golden streets and pearly gates and one or two angels around you as servants. The real goal that you're longing for is to see the great tabernacle of God descend from heaven. When time was no more and the present earth and heaven had fled away, John waited to see where all history had led and the goal of all God's redemptive ways. He tells us:

> I saw a new heaven and a new earth, for the first heaven and the first earth had passed away, and the sea was no more. And I saw the holy city, new Jerusalem, coming down out of heaven from God, prepared as a bride adorned for her husband. And I heard a loud voice from the throne saying, 'Behold, the dwelling place of God is with man. He will dwell with them.' (Rev 21:1–3)

A moment's thought tells us that must surely be so. The virgin birth, the manger, all the sorrows of Gethsemane and Calvary, the cross and the resurrection, were not done simply so that we should tread golden streets. They come from the very heart of God who proposes to confer on us the biggest joy and wonder that little creatures could know—to have the living God dwelling in our midst. Isn't that why you want to go?

David Gooding, *What Moses Could Not Do: Nine Studies in the Book of Joshua*, p. 63

THE FATHER'S PLAN OF REDEMPTION

Part 1—God's Character and Government

25th August

GOD IS LIGHT

Reading: 2 Corinthians 4:1–6

This is the message we have heard from him and proclaim to you,
that God is light, and in him is no darkness at all. (1 John 1:5)

It is this fundamental characteristic of God that is going to control the condition upon which we may come and have fellowship with God. God is light and in him is no darkness at all. What shall we understand by the phrase 'God is light'? I suggest that there are at least two realms in which we can think of God as light.

God is light intellectually. God is self-revealing energy. It's his very nature to make himself known. Self-revealing energy. That means he's the source of all reality and truth. The truth about a daisy ultimately is God. The truth about a sunset is God. Trace all this vast creation to its source—what's the truth about it? The truth is that it comes from God, part of his self-revelation. Therefore it's the source of meaning and purpose. He's the giver of understanding and knowledge. And if you'll allow me a little fancifulness, he's the revealer of beauty and colour. As we nowadays know, colour resides in the light. If a certain source of light doesn't include a certain element, then you'll not see the colour in the lady's dress. What you thought was red will look a very funny, pale colour because there isn't the stuff in the light sufficient to bring out that colour in the dress. It's the light that brings out the colour, and God is the source of all beauty. And God is light morally. As light, he exposes all that's not true, exposes what's false and unreal and perverse. He's pure and holy and righteous.

Not only is God light, but we read that God is *in* the light (1:7). That is to say, that in the person of our blessed Lord, God now stands completely revealed. When King Solomon was praying at the inauguration of the temple, he reminded God that God had said that he would dwell in the thick darkness. But nowadays, since our blessed Lord has come, God doesn't dwell in the thick darkness: God is in the light. He has been manifested. He can be seen in the person of Jesus Christ our Lord. God is light, and in him there's no darkness at all—no cover-up, no compromise, no place where I can come in order to shield my weakness and have it compromised with. God is light, and in him is no darkness at all.

David Gooding, *Life in the Family of God: Twelve Seminars on the First Epistle of John*, p. 17

26th August

THE THRONE OF GOD

Reading: Revelation 4:1–6

From the throne came flashes of lightning, and rumblings and peals of thunder, and before the throne were burning seven torches of fire, which are the seven spirits of God. (v. 5)

So these torches are burning and they're giving light. Do you know what the power is on this throne? Well, you know at once that it certainly isn't 'the power of darkness.' It is the very opposite: the power of light. That's very important. When God says that he's delivered us from 'the power of darkness' through Christ, he's describing the devil's domain (see Col 1:13 KJV).

When our Lord was brought before Pilate, 'they began to accuse him, saying, "We found this man misleading our nation and forbidding us to give tribute to Caesar, and saying that he himself is Christ, a king"' (Luke 23:2). And poor old Peter came near to putting his foot in it, didn't he? The devil nearly succeeded in his plot when Peter drew his sword to cut off a man's head. If Peter had succeeded the devil would have laughed. He wanted Christ to be caught in a situation where there was political strife, and one of his followers could be accused of starting a war. Lies and falsehood: that's the power of darkness. God's power is light. He never rules by keeping you in the dark.

I've known some people to be afraid of science. I was afraid of it because I hadn't the brains for it, but that's another story. Some people say, 'Do you think you ought to investigate as far as that?' Well, as far as I know, you can look down your powerful microscope and keep on looking, and you'll never come across a notice that says, 'Trespassers will be prosecuted beyond here.' God isn't afraid of light. He doesn't rule you by keeping you in the dark; he rules you by flooding you with light and telling you the truth.

Christendom hasn't always understood the principle, and for centuries unreformed Christendom forbade people to have the Bible. They ruled by keeping them in the dark. Our Lord's techniques are the opposite, 'I am the light of the world . . . If you abide in my word . . . you will know the truth, and the truth will set you free' (John 8:12, 31–32). This is the power of light, but it's a burning light and you have to be very careful how you handle it. The light of God's truth will burn up perversity.

Daniel and Revelation: A Comparative Study, pp. 91–2

27th August

GOD COMMENDS HIS LOVE TO US

Reading: 1 John 5:6–15

God commends his love toward us, in that, while we were
yet sinners, Christ died for us. (Romans 5:8 KJV)

The point of the Holy Spirit's argument is this. First of all, consider what is the greatest thing that God will ever do for you. I don't want to disappoint you, but whatever you expect God to give you when you get home to glory—a few galaxies to look after or to play with—I don't know what you're expecting, but the fact is, the biggest thing that God will ever do for any one of us, he has already done. He has given his Son for us. The question, therefore, is: when did he do that? Did he do it after we were somewhat improved, and only on the condition that we had improved? 'No,' says the Holy Spirit. Pray, do observe that it was 'while we were yet weak', while we were yet 'ungodly', while we were 'sinners', while we were 'enemies', that Christ died for us, and thus we were reconciled to God through the death of his Son.

If that is so, then the logic of the situation is this. God gave his Son to die for you when you were still a sinner. Do you think, now that you have been justified by his grace, he will give you up? If he did, it would suggest an inconsistency in the character of God, would it not? He loved you while you were a sinner, loved you so much that he gave his Son for you; but now that you have become justified, might he let you go? That wouldn't make logical sense, would it? While we were enemies we were reconciled to God through the death of his Son. That is an extraordinary statement.

It is a powerful argument. It is the Holy Spirit's argument. Notice it depends on logic, and on the character of God, and that God is not inconsistent. 'God commends his love towards us.' That is a vivid phrase.

Oh, what a concept it is for God Almighty, maker of heaven and earth, to have to come down and recommend his love to us and put his foot in the door, so to speak, to gain a hearing and argue the case for his love and character!

David Gooding, *God's Power for Salvation: Paul's Letter to the Romans*, p. 86

28th August

RIGHTLY REPRESENTING GOD TO PEOPLE

Reading: Numbers 20:1–13

And the LORD *said to Moses and Aaron, 'Because you did not believe in me, to uphold me as holy in the eyes of the people of Israel, therefore you shall not bring this assembly into the land that I have given them.' (v. 12)*

Moses had just about had enough, but here were the people, and they'd run out of water. This time, had Moses eyes to see it, they were not rebelling against God. They were faced with the reality: their little children had no water, their stock had no water. And Moses took the matter to the Lord, and this time the Lord, in his great compassion, understood their suffering and why they pleaded for water, and was going to give it to them.

He told Moses and Aaron to take the rod: be careful that you get the rod right, which rod it was. It was not the rod of God's judgment, that Moses lifted up over the Nile and turned it to blood. It was the rod that was set up before the Lord, and that blossomed and brought forth almonds, and confirmed the priesthood of Aaron (see Num 17). What an exhibition of the mercies of God it was going to be. In answer to the people's cry, there was Moses, there was Aaron, and there was the rod of his priesthood. It was going to be a magnificent example of the mercies of God that had provided a priest to intercede for them. Instead of that, between the two of them, they called the people rebels, instead of just speaking to the rock; and it would have listened to them, so to speak, and God would have given them water. But they belaboured the rock. God gave the people water, for he was merciful to the people, but Aaron and Moses had grievously misrepresented God.

As I speak as a teacher, I'm not unaware of the problem of rightly representing God to his people. What if I were over-harsh, and to people in trouble who were having difficulty carrying on believing that God cares for them, what if I simply diagnosed their trouble as sheer rebellion and rebuked them and called them rebels? Oh no, it is a serious thing to represent God, and very serious if we misrepresent him. Moses didn't lose his salvation; we shall meet him in heaven. But it put a limit on his usefulness. What a thing this journey was.

David Gooding, *Understanding the Old Testament: An Overview of Genesis to Joshua*, pp. 40–1

29th August

OUR SECURITY AS BELIEVERS

Reading: Romans 8:12–17

See what kind of love the Father has given to us, that we should be called children of God; and so we are. The reason why the world does not know us is that it did not know him. (1 John 3:1)

There was a friend of mine once who told me the following little homely story. He went upstairs one night to find his little girl in bed and deeply distressed. It turned out that she was worried at the prospect of her exams and what he would say if she did not pass. Would he be terribly angry and offended? The father was concerned that she had those thoughts in her mind. Who had put them there? She imagined that her father's acceptance of her depended on whether she passed the exams or not.

What would you have said to her? 'That's right, my dear! Get down to your studies! Do that algebra one hundred per cent and the essays ten out of ten. I am not going to tell you that I accept you in my family; I'm going to leave it uncertain. If you get through your exams, I shall accept you and if you don't there is a very real possibility that I shall throw you out!'

No father would talk like that. Nor did my friend; he did the obvious thing that a father would do. He said, 'My dear good girl, I shall love it if you get through the exams, but I shall love you still if you don't.' She was a child of the father first, with a right in his home because she was his child. She would never cease to be his child and knew the strength and security of a father's love. Then she found the courage to go out and face the exams.

It is curious how there are parents who would never treat their children like that, but imagine it is how God is proposing to treat them. We need to pass all our spiritual examinations. At length finals come and the great final judgment. They imagine God is saying to them, 'It will all depend on whether you pass your final exams whether I accept you into my presence or not!'

But it is not that way round. God is not like that; he is not cruel. God's way is to give us salvation for Christ's sake. He loves us and will receive us and accept us. He will assure our timid hearts that we have been accepted. We are members of his family; we are born again children of God and heirs of his kingdom. It is because we are secure and loved for Christ's sake that we have the strength to face our spiritual training within the family and school of God.

David Gooding, *The God of New Beginnings: Eighteen Seminars on the Book of Genesis*, p. 115

30th August

THE VIBRANT LIFE OF GOD

Reading: 1 Kings 6:19–38

And round the throne, on each side of the throne, are four living creatures, full of eyes in front and behind. (Revelation 4:6)

It was marvellous to be inside because of the décor. In the house of the Lord, you didn't have to walk two inches in before you saw that the leading motif was all living things—trees and open flowers, and then there were these cherubim everywhere. And if you had been allowed to go into the holiest of all, there were not only a couple of cherubim on the ark, but in Solomon's house there were two mighty olive wood cherubim that stood facing you when you went in, with their wings outstretched from one wall to the middle, and from the middle to the other wall.

Cherubim everywhere, and it wasn't just to make the house look pretty. As other parts of Scripture tell us, the cherubim were the *living* creatures. In Revelation 4, where God's throne is seen and pictured to us, it is said to be resting on the backs of the living creatures, and they are the cherubim. For this you must know about God and his government—and here we're using the picture and metaphorical language of Scripture—his throne rests on living things. This is not a set of doctrines, this is the living God. What would you suppose the decorative motif of his house to be? Everywhere around the walls in the Holy Place and the Most Holy Place is the expression of life. That's how he governs, ultimately. That's how God gets apples to grow on a tree: he gives the apple tree life and the life he gives it brings the apples.

And that's how he governs his people, he gives them his own life—he begets them again by his Holy Spirit; and by that very life of God within them, he governs them. The living God is known in the life of his people. And you can't visualize that tremendous decorative motif in the house of God without thinking once more of Paul's words to Timothy: 'I hope to come to you soon, but I am writing these things to you so that, if I delay, you may know how one ought to behave in the house of God, which is the church of the living God' (1 Tim 3:14–15). What a wonderful thing it would be if, by God's grace, we could recapture the reality. A church is not just a place where we come as an evening club. It's a place where we can know the presence of the living God and sense the vibrancy of his life.

David Gooding, God's Programme and Provision: Lessons from History in Chronicles and Kings, pp. 20–1

31st August

THE THRONE OF GOD

Reading: 2 Timothy 2:8–13; Matthew 19:28–30

*Round the throne were twenty-four thrones, and seated on the
thrones were twenty-four elders, clothed in white garments,
with golden crowns on their heads. (Revelation 4:4)*

This is the throne of almighty God, the sole ruler of the universe. Why are
there other thrones around his throne, and what are they there for? Is it for
decoration, or are they real thrones? 'They're occupied,' says John, 'with elders.'
Well, this much is certain, those elders must be creatures, mustn't they? Can
you believe this: creatures sharing the government of God? Tell me, are they
real? Have they got real power, or are they merely puppets? They've got golden
crowns on. Does it represent any reality? What do you think?

I reckon, if we'd been painting a scene of the throne, we'd never have
dared to say there were other thrones sharing the government of God, but
it's the fact. Almighty as he is, the Sovereign of the universe has chosen to
delegate power at various levels throughout his creation. Listen to Scripture
describing the great beings that inhabited the heavens in God's original
creation: angels, principalities, powers, mights, dominions—each term
indicating rule and authority.

I can go one better than that in my exposition. If I examined your heart
deeply enough, I fancy I should find you are hoping that one of these days
you are going to share the government of the universe with God. We are
reliably told, 'If we endure, we shall also reign with him' (2 Tim 2:12). But
don't think merely of your glory, think of the character of God who designed
it. If you'd been the sovereign ruler of the universe, would you have delegated
your authority to any of us?

You say, 'Who are these elders?' I'm not going to tell you. But I know that,
without exception, all of those who shall reign with Christ started off by being
rebels against the throne of God. If we had the time to shut our books, this
magnificent thing alone would lead us to start worshipping the God of the
universe. Satan has done his worst to represent God's rule as that of an almighty
tyrant. But that is not so—round about the throne, there were other thrones.

Daniel and Revelation: A Comparative Study, pp. 88–9

1st September

THE LOYAL LOVE OF THE ONE WHO IS WORTHY

Reading: Revelation 5

Worthy are you to take the scroll and to open its seals, for you were slain, and by your blood you ransomed people for God. (v. 9)

Why do the judgments of the Revelation come? They start with the throne, of course, and its creatorial rights. The only way the universe will be made to work sensibly is if it is brought back to serve the will and purpose of the one who made it. If men will not repent, the only way the world can be brought back is by God's intervening judgment. But that raises a very big moral problem: who is worthy to execute the judgment?

That's why the cry goes out in Revelation 5. There was a book in the hand of him who sat upon the throne, written inside and out, and sealed with many seals. Once those seals are opened, the judgments will begin, but who's worthy to take it and open it?

You say, 'God is. Why doesn't he get at it?'

And there you meet the magnificence of God. He has all power to do the judgment, and every right. Then why doesn't he? Because the ultimate question in the universe is not, who has the biggest power?—the ultimate moral judgment is, who has the biggest love and loyalty? A God who, without asking permission, made a creature and brought it into the world, and was not loyal to that creature, would be an immoral God.

If as parents you bring a child into the world, you don't ask the child's permission, do you? You bring it into the world. Does that not create in you a moral responsibility for that child, and will you not be loyal to that child to the last? A God who could create human beings, bring them into the world and not be loyal to them, would be seriously defective morally. The God and Father of our Lord Jesus Christ is not just power; the God and Father of our Lord Jesus Christ is love. Before he brings his judgments, even upon an aberrant world, he will be loyal to them.

The judgment is committed to a human being. How is he worthy to do this? Well, precisely because he is 'the Lamb who was slain' (5:12), and this world would not be able to complain that it's unfair. The one who will deluge the world in judgment to bring it back to God first died, so that no one needs to perish and a rebel world might be brought back to God.

Daniel and Revelation: A Comparative Study, pp. 94–5

2nd September

THE WAY GOD ESTABLISHES HIS GOVERNMENT

Reading: 1 Samuel 15:34—16:13

It was necessary that the word of God be spoken first to you.
Since you thrust it aside and judge yourselves unworthy of
eternal life, behold, we are turning to the Gentiles. (Acts 13:46)

Ask any church elder who is trying to govern for God about the one thousand and one problems that arise in the course of trying to shepherd the people of God. It's not easy to come to a right decision here, a fair decision there, knowing what to do next, how to reconcile differences and mend things that are broken that perhaps will never be fully put together on earth again. Any elder will tell you that governing for God is not, and cannot be, a simple matter.

It is with the question of *governing for God* that the books of 1 and 2 Samuel deal. As we read the story of 2 Samuel, we can see the great similarity between God's methods in appointing David to be king, and the methods he has employed in appointing Jesus Christ our Lord to the throne of the universe. First Samuel is particularly interested in how God went about that. He could have destroyed the wicked and rebellious Saul and put David in his place. That would have been simple, but God didn't do it. God could have let King Saul carry on right to the bitter end, until eventually he was destroyed by his enemies, and only then anoint David as king over Israel in his place, but God didn't do that either. God did a very curious thing. He let King Saul continue for years as king, but had David anointed king while the false king was still reigning. So David was anointed king, and for years after he was anointed he was persecuted and driven out into the wilderness and rejected by Israel. So persistent was the official rejection of her anointed king that Israel lost him to the Gentiles for a long time.

You can't read it but your mind goes to the method God has used for appointing Jesus Christ our Lord as king. Certainly God has anointed him with the Holy Spirit and with power. He was anointed by the Holy Spirit at his baptism and raised to the Father's throne at the right hand of God. But God has not yet intervened in our world to remove rebellious human government; he has let it go on. God has not moved in our world to destroy the rebellious in Israel who have rejected their Messiah. So we have the situation now, where Israel has officially rejected her anointed Messiah so persistently that he has been lost to the Gentiles these last two thousand years. The parallel between the two arrangements is striking, and easy to perceive.

David Gooding, Governing for God: Studies in 2 Samuel, pp. 4–5

3rd September

GOD LETS US TASTE THE BITTERNESS OF OUR CHOICES

Reading: Exodus 32:1–30

Your evil will chastise you, and your apostasy will reprove you. Know and see that it is evil and bitter for you to forsake the LORD your God. (Jeremiah 2:19)

When Israel turned to worshipping idols in the wilderness, Moses made them drink the ground up idol mixed into their water, until its bitterness nauseated them. When, under the kings, they turned to idolatry and proved incorrigible, at length the divine wisdom threw them out of the land and took them down to Babylon. Once more God was saying, 'If you want idolatry, have idolatry! You don't want to be my people and worship me, you want the ways of the nations—then go and learn the ways of the nations! Go down to Babylon where every street corner is full of temples with idols. Go there and have it!'

At the end of this age, men and women who have abandoned faith in the living God and put their ultimate faith in their own intellects, brains and brawn, will find that God will do the same thing. 'If you won't have me, the living God, have your idols!' And this age shall end with people turning from the living God and bowing down at the feet of an image. It will be an image set up by that last ruler of this present age, the man of sin himself, who exalts himself above all that is called God and in the place of the living God puts man. People shall worship and trust in a man. The modern world has gone a long way down the road that shall lead them there. One fears there is no turning back now for the multitudes. The little kiddies from their earliest age are taught that this whole universe needs no further explanation than mindless materialistic evolution. Man is the one you must trust; man's brain is what ultimately you must trust to solve all your problems. In the end God will let man have his idol and find out the fearful bitterness of tyranny that shall come upon humankind when, forsaking the living God, man goes the whole road of idolatry and bows down at the feet of his fellow man.

David Gooding, *No Longer Bondmen: Thirteen Studies in the Book of Exodus*, p. 144

4th September

THE BEAUTY OF GOD'S WRATH

Reading: Revelation 15

*And out of the sanctuary came the seven angels with
the seven plagues, clothed in pure, bright linen, with
golden sashes round their chests. (v. 6)*

It is no wonder that, at this stage, the holiest of all is filled with smoke—an expression of the feelings of God, of the character of God. And when the angels who have the vials full of these plagues come out, do notice how they are clothed.

Did you notice that? This section has a lot to say about clothing. How would you expect angels to be clothed, who come out with these dire judgments, to inflict pain and dishonour and eventual destruction upon men and women?

You say, 'I'd expect them to come out there dressed in funereal black, solemn looking, almost hideous hags dripping and oozing blood.'

No, that's a pagan conception. The angels that come out to execute the wrath of God at this stage, oh do look at their clothing! It is fantastically beautiful. It is white, of course, but not a dull old white that you put on the walls of your sitting room. This is brilliant white and marvellously attractive. Oh, the purity of it! Yes, they are beautiful. I tell you, my brothers and sisters, the wrath of God is something exceedingly beautiful.

Check yourself if ever you find yourself apologizing for the wrath of God, as though it were something to be ashamed of. As if we had to say, 'Well, you know, God does get wroth sometimes. That's like him, but it doesn't last, and he's altogether nice and good really, on the whole. It's just sometimes he loses his temper...'

No, he doesn't; he doesn't lose his temper.

The wrath of God is like God himself: it is a beautiful thing, for it is the expression of the character of God. It isn't a question of losing his temper. He stands for all that is true, and therefore his whole being vibrates against what is false and unreal and insincere. He is the sum total of all holiness, and when he meets unholiness the whole of his character is moved against it. In him are located all true values, and it is a part of the beauty of his character that he reacts against perversion of beauty, and demands its destruction.

David Gooding, *The Book of the Revelation: Major Themes of Revelation's Six Sections*, pp. 98–9

5th September

MERCY EVEN IN JUDGMENT

Reading: Joshua 6:22–27

*For we have heard how the LORD dried up the water of the Red
Sea before you when you came out of Egypt. (Joshua 2:10)*

If perchance you have ever been troubled by the seeming severity of the
judgment of which you read in the book of Joshua, pause again to consider its historical context. There were four hundred years of the mercy and
long-suffering of God to this ancient, sinful nation before he executed his
judgment. Now the time of his long-suffering had come to its end. Only
days from now Jericho must be destroyed. But even so, God is rich in mercy.

Forty years before the judgment fell he preached the gospel to them. With
every tramp of every foot of the thousands of Israel as they marched across
that wilderness, God had preached the gospel to Canaan. Some, thank God,
heard the message. As we listen to Rahab the harlot speaking to the spies she
had received, she tells how she had heard of the wonders of the living God.
'We have heard what your God did in Egypt, how he brought you out with
a high hand, cleared the Red Sea and brought you through. We see clearly
that your God is the true God. He is Lord in heaven above and on the earth
beneath.' Those judgments upon Pharaoh, that 'vessel of wrath', had not
simply been the penalty of his obstinacy. God had made him a vessel of wrath
so that Pharaoh might speak to other Gentiles and lead them to repentance.
God will save men and women, even if he has to use the punishment of the
ungodly to induce them to repent.

What a God we serve: he's determined to save people. He'll save them
every way he knows how. In that poor, darkened, benighted mind of a harlot
woman in Jericho, the light of God's gospel has begun to dawn, and she sees
the difference between the idols of Canaan and the true and living God.
What a spectacle you are about to witness again in this passage, though
you've often rejoiced in seeing it. On the eve of judgment, a pagan heart is
touched by the gospel and turns from idols to serve the living and the true
God. If in those days she didn't know how to wait for his Son from heaven,
she knows now, for she is at home with the Lord. There were forty years of
gospel, and some heard it and repented and were saved; for in his judgment,
God remembers mercy.

David Gooding, *Entering the Inheritance: Studies in Joshua 1–12*, pp. 15–16

6th September

THE LONGSUFFERING AND JUDGMENT OF GOD

Reading: Joshua 11:1–9

They refused to love the truth and so be saved. Therefore
God sends them a strong delusion, so that they may
believe what is false. (2 Thessalonians 2:10–11)

A second confederacy came and positively attacked Joshua. Now, you will notice that Jericho didn't do that, and Ai didn't do that; Joshua had attacked them. But this northern confederacy came and attacked Israel, and met disaster. How did it happen? Well, it was of the Lord, for he hardened their hearts. They'd heard the gospel just like Rahab had heard the gospel, and they could have been saved like Rahab. They had heard what Moses said about coming judgment, and they could have been saved like the Gibeonites. But they rejected the gospel, and determined to attack and destroy Joshua and Israel. There came a point where God hardened their hearts, and coming finally against Joshua they were destroyed. It can happen to anybody, can't it?

It will happen historically in a very big way. The Acts of the Apostles tells us there was a tremendous confederacy against our Joshua, Jesus, when he came first (Joshua is the Hebrew form of that hero's name, and in the Greek translation his name becomes Jesus). The heathen raged and the people imagined a vain thing, and they rose up against God and against his anointed (Ps 2:1-2). They put the blessed Lord Jesus on the cross, but God answered it by raising him to the very heaven (see Acts 5:30).

The gospel has gone out, but at the end of this age, when men have deliberately with eyes open rejected the gospel and refused the love of the truth so that they might be saved, God shall send them a strong delusion. They shall believe the lie. The beast shall lead his armies against the coming blessed Saviour, Jesus. What fatuous folly, thinking with his space age equipment to be able to resist the glorious coming of Jesus Christ our Lord. It will spell for him instantaneous destruction. 'Behold the goodness and the severity of God' (Rom 11:22).

David Gooding, *Entering the Inheritance: Studies in Joshua 1–12*, pp. 46–7

7th September

THE WRATH OF GOD IS PART OF HIS GLORY

Reading: Exodus 1:8–22

Then the Lord said, 'I have surely seen the affliction of my
people who are in Egypt and have heard their cry because of
their taskmasters. I know their sufferings'. (Exodus 3:7)

The wrath of God is an essential part of his activity. It demonstrates his
holy character to us and we are to worship him for it. It shows us what
God himself is like. A God who could look upon sin with equanimity and
tolerance, a God who could face sin and say that sin did not matter, would
be a God convicted of sin himself and a God who would immediately lose
the reverence and respect of any moral being. Sin matters, and God will
never say that it does not matter. In God's wrath we see God's values; we
see God's love.

Pharaoh had his sense of values. He had treasure cities and filled them with
wealth. His values were of the sort that if the building of those cities meant
the hard lash of the taskmaster on the backs of his unfortunate slaves, what
did it matter if they were crippled in the course of their work, or if a stone
block fell off its rollers and crushed half a dozen Israelites to death? What
were they but slaves. Yes, Pharaoh had his values.

And would you have God stand by and say it didn't matter? Am I to
presume that God doesn't care for human beings; that the odd half dozen
perishing under those blocks of stone don't really matter? No indeed! In
getting angry with Pharaoh the God of heaven that created them shows us
beyond all manner of doubt the value he places upon his people, upon the
individual human being. Let all systems of economics hold it in mind, God
values one human beyond all the material wealth of the world.

While I speak in general of the wrath of God, I am provoked to say—if
I may say it with reverence—that, far from God's wrath being something
to be apologized for, the fact that God gets angry with human beings is
the biggest compliment that was ever paid to them. I think of God and his
infinity, his greatness and his might and his splendour; I think of how tiny
human beings are and I say to myself, why should God bother with them?
For God to count them significant enough to take seriously what they do is
an indescribable compliment paid by the almighty Creator to his creatures.

David Gooding, *No Longer Bondmen: Thirteen Studies in the Book of Exodus*, pp. 38–9

THE FATHER'S PLAN
OF REDEMPTION

Part 2—The Purpose of Our Redemption

8th September

THE PURPOSE OF OUR REDEMPTION
IS TO BE BEFORE HIM

Reading: Leviticus 23:15–21

*. . . in order to present you holy and blameless and
above reproach before him. (Colossians 1:22)*

In the coming age God has the one who shall head up the whole of his
administration, Jesus Christ our Lord. Under him will be his redeemed
people, trained and ready to engage with Christ in all the tasks that God
has in mind. Before that active side of God's purposes there is a passive one,
which comes first. It is that we should be before him. What does that mean?
Is there much of a purpose in being 'before him'?

Ask a married man why he married his wife. Did he just want someone
to cook his meals, or dig his garden, or clean his house? Even if he did, they
were not the primary reasons. There is a higher reason: so that she might
be 'before him.' In early days nothing would have delighted him more than
her sitting before him so that he could just look at her! Men are not content
just to have their wives in the kitchen twenty-four hours a day, they want
them to sit down beside them and talk. Almighty God, who is in need of
nothing because he is perfect, deliberately chose to need us. Wonder of
wonders, he created us so that he might have us before him, to gratify his
heart and fill it with joy! It is the most tremendous compliment he has paid
us, in making us and redeeming us so that we should be before him. We
do not need to wait until the fulfilment of that great purpose, we can be
in his company now. Of course, our conversation may be rather limited.
'God, help my arthritis; give me a good job; help my little boy to pass his
exam.' One day we shall be better company for him, but we do not have
to wait. The coming of the Holy Spirit on the day of Pentecost has already
begun that great work in us. Even in this imperfect world, still beset with
sin, we can be before him and gratify his heart.

The loaves spoken of in Leviticus 23 had leaven in them, but with what
pride the farmer in Israel would reap his corn, mill it fine and offer it to God.
And with what pride and joy does God's Holy Spirit take men and women
and bring them to Christ for cleansing from sin; thus cleansed, forgiven and
made holy, he presents them to God to be before him.

David Gooding, *The Feasts of the Lord: Studies on the Feasts Appointed by the Lord for Israel*, p. 33

9th September

SHINING BEFORE THE LORD

Reading: Leviticus 24:1–3

*Command the Israelites to bring you clear oil
of pressed olives for the light so that the lamps
may be kept burning. (Exodus 27:20 NIV)*

Let us look briefly at another object that was before the Lord: the lampstand, the lights of which burned continually. The Israelites had a problem with them too. They found it odd that the lamps had to burn even when no one was there. Why would God need lamps in the Holy Place? We need light, so that we can see; but God doesn't need us to give him light, because he is the author of light. Why would he need human beings to give him light? The lamps were burning before the Lord.

And now we know the features of it, don't we? It was an emblem, a prototype of what has become the great reality. He who is the light of God has shone into this world. When you come to Christ, he shines upon you, exposes your sin and shows you the way of forgiveness and eternal life. But there is more. The very Light of the World by his Spirit is now in you. Why and for what reason? *So that you might shine.*

You say, 'So that I might take the gospel to the next door neighbour.' Yes, that is so, and I hope you do. But it's more than that.

'So that I can be a missionary?' I hope you will, but it's more than that. The very Light of the World is in you by his Spirit, so that you might shine before the Lord.

'I don't get that,' says someone. 'How could I shine before the Lord?'

Let me use an illustration. An artist tries to express the ideas that have been burning in his head for the past twenty years and he paints an enormous great oil painting. When it's all done, it's hung and the crowd comes in. Some think it's wonderful, some think it's hopeless, and some want to slash it with a knife. But there are nights, when the museum is closed and nobody else is about except one person. It is the artist, and he sits and looks at it. He hopes that the crowd enjoys it; but he doesn't care all that much, because he does. It was his idea and he expressed himself, but now he sits there looking at it.

God decided to have the likes of you and me to feed him and to shine before him, so that he might eternally look at, listen to and enjoy us.

David Gooding, *Ephesians: A Bird's Eye View of the Major Movements of Thought*, p. 22

10th September

HE WILL BRING US TO GLORY HIMSELF

Reading: John 14:1–3; Philippians 1:20–26

You yourselves have seen what I did to Egypt, and how I carried you on eagles' wings and brought you to myself. (Exodus 19:4)

I wonder will they have to adapt heaven to receive human beings. Was heaven made for humans, or when God designed the human race did he design them in such a way that they could eventually be changed? Could beings made for the murky atmosphere of this little temporary planet be changed in such fashion as to still remain human and yet be able to inhabit the very dwelling place of God? I don't know, for it lies in the future and he's gone to prepare a place for us. He says, 'I will come again and will take you to myself, that where I am you may be also' (John 14:3). That will be glorious—but we're still in the wilderness! Listen, as the departing Lord goes on to speak, 'If a man really loves me, my Father will love him. And if you love me you will keep my commandments [of course you will], and we [the divine persons] will come and make our abiding place with you' (see v. 23).

And you see it, don't you? The love of God's heart is impatient, as love always is. He can't wait until he gets us home to heaven; he must have a tabernacle with us now. He cannot stand at heaven's door and greet us when at last we arrive; he must come down to the desert and dwell amongst us as we travel, walking each patient footstep with us the journey through. But he must have a tabernacle to do it in, and he proposes that that tabernacle shall be the hearts of those who love him. 'It's like heaven begun,' you say. 'Is this what redemption is? Not merely heaven some way off out there, but heaven begun now. The divine persons coming out on the road to meet us, to live with us from Monday through to Sunday and travel with us the road home to glory.'

David Gooding, *No Longer Bondmen: Thirteen Studies in the Book of Exodus*, p. 115

11th September

TO WIN A BRIDE

Reading: Genesis 24:1–50

Go to my country and to my kindred, and
take a wife for my son Isaac. (v. 4)

So Abraham sent his servant, and he preached it in glowing colours—it's an extraordinary story. 'God has blessed my master with everything that his hands could hold and his heart could long for. He has one son, and has given to him all that he has. The proposition is, Rebekah, would you care to be the wife of my master's son?' (see vv. 34–49).

She heard the story and decided to leave the Gentiles to go to be the bride of a man she had never seen, yet having not seen she loved. Though she still didn't see him, as every foot of the camels went that little bit further, she rejoiced with joy already tinged with the glory that should be. She had got an earring or two already, and they were tremendous, and a coat or two, and they were glorious. If this was *the earnest*, the guarantee of the inheritance, what would the inheritance itself be? If these were the gifts, what would the giver be?

You know how to make the application of the story, don't you? It's the fact that there once we were, a lot of old Gentiles. The God of glory appeared to Abraham our father, and called him out. He lived as a patriarch in the land of promise until the seed was born, and the seed was offered. His descendants eventually again came into the land; they were put under the law until the seed was born and the son was offered.

Then what happened? Why, there broke out another great movement of the Gentiles, and it hasn't stopped yet. Vast multi-millions of Gentiles doing what Abraham once did, for the God of glory has appeared to them too. It started at Pentecost, and God has brought them out from the Gentiles to be a bride for Abraham's seed, God's Son (see Gal 3:14).

We've now gone back in history; whether you accept this as a prototype or not, this is history. Abraham came out from the Gentiles those thousands of years ago and the Jewish nation was born. Since Pentecost, and since the death and resurrection of Jesus, multi-millions of Gentiles have repeated what Abraham did. They've learned to love a man they've never seen, and believing in him have come out of the Gentiles and are on their way to glory to meet the loved one of their hearts.

David Gooding, *Family Life with Abraham and Jacob: Studies in Genesis 12–50*, p. 21

12th September

THE REALISM OF GOD'S PURPOSES FOR US

Reading: Zechariah 1:7–13

But one thing I do: forgetting what lies behind and straining forward to what lies ahead, I press on towards the goal for the prize of the upward call of God in Christ Jesus. (Philippians 3:13–14)

In the first vision, as the man stood in the myrtle trees, there was a fearful and frightful complacency—the whole earth was at rest, and even the Israelites themselves had settled down into a desperate complacency. No movement for God. No progress. No real concern about the poverty of spirit and the brokenness of Israel. By the intercessions of the angel of the Lord that complacency was broken and spiritual energy set loose that got Israel moving again, to restore the priesthood and restore the temple, and begin the long drawn out work of delivering God's people from evil.

The God who is against complacency is a God of realism and he sets realistic objectives for his people. Here in Zechariah's day, it was not the final triumph. That would in fact take centuries to come, but there had been movement and there had been progress. Many long miles are yet to be covered, but God can announce that in some sense his spirit is quieted and at rest. That may not mean much to you, but it means volumes to me. You don't need to tell me that I'm a long way off heaven, and I don't mean geographically. I mean in my spiritual experience, building the temple of the Lord, in the execution of my priesthood and in the pursuit of holiness. You don't need to tell me I'm not in heaven yet. I stand with the apostle, though miles behind him, and say that I have not already attained (Phil 3:12).

How far off the goal seems to be some days, and the question arises, 'Shall I ever get there?' And then I consider all the mercies of what God has already done, all the graciousness of God. As a wise teacher and father, he takes us by realistic stages and says, 'Yes, there is some progress and I can make known my satisfaction.' Courage, my brother and sister, granted that there is within you a heart to go on with God and not rest in complacency. Don't vex your souls too much that you have not yet attained what for the moment are impossible goals. But as you press on, learn to draw strength and comfort and courage from this, that if you're walking with God and doing the best you know how to walk with him, pursuing and gaining your short-term victories, the heart of God can find satisfaction and rest for the moment in you as you are.

David Gooding, *The God of Restoration: Four Studies in the Prophecy of Zechariah*, p. 31

13th September

MATURE IN CHRIST

Reading: 1 Corinthians 3:1–15

Him we proclaim, warning everyone and teaching
everyone with all wisdom, that we may present
everyone mature in Christ. (Colossians 1:28)

We shall all be presented holy and blameless and above reproach, and none shall be able to lay any charge against God's elect—but shall we all be presented mature, fully grown, perfect? What do you say? I'm tempted in my simplicity to say, 'Of course, we shan't.' Take the dying thief: converted one minute, and within a few hours in paradise. Shall he be as mature and fully developed as the Apostle Paul? Without turning to God's word for a moment, my natural answer to that would be, 'How could it possibly be, unless life is a mockery?'

Do we really think that he will be equally as mature and spiritually developed as the godly sister? If that were so, it would begin to suggest that there's no pressing need of 'bringing holiness to completion in the fear of God' (2 Cor 7:1). So long as we're believers, the careless and the careful, the worldly and the godly will all end up the same.

'Before you go any further,' says somebody, 'I'd have you know that holy Scripture tells us that, when we see the Lord Jesus, all of us shall be like him. "We shall be like him, because we shall see him as he is"' (1 John 3:2).

Thank God it's true, we shall be like him. But I want to add, what there is of us. A baby is like his father, and still is when he's a fully grown man of fifty. There is, to be sure, a difference between the two: the man has grown, and there's more of him than there was of the baby.

I don't need to rely upon my own conjecture for an answer to my question. In his second Epistle, Peter deals precisely with this particular question, and in more detail than Paul applies here. 'His divine power has granted to us all things that pertain to life and godliness' (2 Pet 1:3). But alongside that, we ourselves are to 'make every effort to supplement [our] faith with virtue, and virtue with knowledge, and knowledge with self-control, and self-control with steadfastness, and steadfastness with godliness, and godliness with brotherly affection, and brotherly affection with love' (vv. 5–7). We are diligently and by considered effort to add these qualities to our life, to our character, to our personalities.

David Gooding, A Cosmic-sized Salvation: Three Studies in Colossians, pp. 22–3

14th September

TRANSFORMED BY SEEING THE GLORY OF CHRIST

Reading: Exodus 34:29–35

*And we all, with unveiled face, beholding the glory of
the Lord, are being transformed into the same image
from one degree of glory to another. For this comes
from the Lord who is the Spirit. (2 Corinthians 3:18)*

Show me your way; show me your glory! How shall I be kept on course,
to arrive home at last and be like the Saviour? How shall I be saved from
being turned aside to the little baubles that Satan throws in my way? How
shall I ever be saved from the glitter of the golden calf and all idolatry, if
from time to time he doesn't come near me and show me his glory? So that
the very glory of God overpowers all else, demolishes all other attractions
and wins my heart so overwhelmingly that before I know what I am doing
I am up and moving ever more readily and steadily to where I see the glory
shining—the glory of God in the face of Jesus Christ.

I think you have seen him, my brother, my sister! How do I know? When
you have made every allowance for all the failures and weaknesses of God's
people, a glory is being written upon your heart that is beginning to dawn
already on your personality. 'Beloved, we are God's children now, and what
we will be has not yet appeared' (1 John 3:2). Already the family likeness is
being formed; I thought I saw it just now in the way you forgave that other
sister. I thought I saw it in the way your heart went out for the preaching of
God's gospel. I thought I saw it when you didn't grasp for place, but knelt and
scrubbed the floor of that lonely widow because she was Christ's. I thought
I saw the glory of God in the face of Jesus Christ beginning to dawn in your
face—you must have been looking at him!

There's a lot of road yet to go, but keep on looking at him, and as you look
at that glorified Lord Jesus Christ the glory of God fills your soul. It will keep
you like nothing else on earth; keep you journeying on and bring you at last
to where you shall sit down with him, fully transformed and conformed to
the image of God's Son.

David Gooding, *No Longer Bondmen: Thirteen Studies in the Book of Exodus*, pp. 151–2

THE FATHER'S PLAN OF REDEMPTION

Part 3—Implementing the Plan: Creation and the Fall

15th September

GOD'S PLAN REQUIRED A UNIVERSE

Reading: Isaiah 45:18–25

Even as he chose us in him before the foundation
of the world, that we should be holy and without
blemish before him in love. (Ephesians 1:4 RV)

One of the first things that we are told about the good purposes of God as we find them in Ephesians 1:1–14 is that these purposes were made before the foundation of the world. We were 'chosen in him before the foundation of the world', and we must stop to enquire why it is that God tells us that his choice was made before the foundation of the world.

If we weren't to think very carefully, but merely read these things superficially, we might suppose that God chose in this remark simply to communicate the fact that he chose us rather a long time ago. Not yesterday, nor last century, nor in times BC, but a long, long time ago—why, even before the foundation of the world! And then, having chosen us, for some reason or other he went on to do other interesting things, like making a few galaxies, or making our planet.

We might fall into the mistake of thinking that these two things were unrelated. Of course, they are not unrelated. We are told that he chose us before the foundation of the world because that very fact and plan will explain to us why the world was ever founded; why the galaxies were made; why the moon, the stars and our planet were made. Before he made them he had a plan: the plan and purpose was such that inevitably it involved God in making our world and our universe as a stepping stone towards the achievement of that entire intention and purpose.

As to why it's there at all, you'll have to go back before the foundation of the world and allow God to let you into the secret of his plans and purposes. Why did he have the whole thing? He had it because of his prior intention: 'He was pleased to determine that he wanted us before him in love, as sons of God.' That was the plan. Because God set his sights on such an elevated plan it then demanded that God create a vast universe, such as we see around us, in order to be the means for the staging by which he would see the fulfilment of his plan. That was the order of events.

David Gooding, *Ephesians: A Bird's Eye View of the Major Movements of Thought*, pp. 14–15, 17

16th September

THE PURPOSE OF CREATION

Reading: Hebrews 1:1–4

*For by him all things were created, in heaven and
on earth, visible and invisible, whether thrones or
dominions or rulers or authorities—all things were
created through him and for him. (Colossians 1:16)*

Imagine visiting a brand new vast factory with all its complicated machines
and technology and the five or six thousand people that run it. I say to the
managing director, 'Where did this all begin?' Would you expect him to
answer, 'When they laid the first bricks,' or 'When the sand and cement were
created'? I'm not thinking in those terms at all, and he knows I'm not. He'll
say, 'This great factory that you see is the result of an idea that happened in
my brain. That's where it all started!'

If you want to know where this universe started, it's no good analysing the
chemistry or the physics of it. That will tell you one or two things, but it can't
tell you where it all started. 'In him', says verse 16. He is the beginning: 'In the
beginning God created . . .' (Gen 1:1). That is to say, he was the great beginning
in which the whole thing was conceived. What a mind this great agent of
deity has. You are Christ's idea, you know! That's where you started as well.

It was not only made *in him*, it was made *through him*: 'All things were made
through him' (John 1:3). Whatever processes have gone on in the formation
and development of the universe it was because he engineered and sustained
them, and sustains them still.

What's it all for? I wonder have you ever stood watching the stars at night,
burdened maybe with the cares of your business, with family problems, finding life exceedingly complicated and perplexing. You say to yourself, 'What
is it all about, where is it all going?' We're corkscrewing in space, following
the sun. Where is it all going, where are you going? Were you designed to go
anywhere in particular? The answer comes back from the measureless past.
When it was made, it was made *for him*. If there has been any genuine progress
in the history of our planet, in the end he shall be the heir of all things and
inherit it. Was I made for him? It's obvious that I haven't always lived for him,
and that's part of the great disorder. Men and women were made for him, but
'all we like sheep have gone astray; we have turned—every one—to his own
way' (Isa 53:6). That's cardinal sin No. 1 in the logic of creation.

David Gooding, *Christ Is All: Twelve Seminars on the Letter to the Colossians*, p. 30

17th September

GOD'S PURPOSE IN CREATING MAN

Reading: Genesis 2:4–17

*And raised us up with him and seated us with him in
the heavenly places in Christ Jesus. (Ephesians 2:6)*

In this third creation story it is important to follow the language throughout
the succeeding chapters. It is the story of 'man', this strange new creature, the
like of whom there had never been before. There were endless teeming forms
of life, and the angels clapped their hands with sheer joy at the ingenuity and
imagination of the Creator. Lastly there came this thing. 'What on earth is that?'
And God informed them that this was *man*. 'Is he an animal?'

'Well, partly so. He's got a lot in common with animals.'

'He's not only an animal?'

'No, he is spirit too.'

I wonder if Michael said, 'We are spirits. You're not putting him above
us, are you?'

'No. I made him a little lower than you,' God says.

'Well, that's all right,' says Michael, breathing a sigh of relief.

How exciting to be alive in those days and to see this new creature, man!
What a story man's story has been, for we who are Christians cannot forget the
day when the serried ranks of angels saw the Son of the Father stooping, and for
a little while he was made lower than the angels and became human. I wonder
what Michael said to Gabriel then. 'What, the Son of the Father, lower than us?'

And what did he say when he saw that the Son of God, the Son of Man, was
nailed to a cross and God didn't obliterate the planet right then? That the Son
of God should die for simple man: the angels have not got over it yet. And what
did Michael or the others say when they saw the man Jesus summoned, rising
into glory and invited to sit at the right hand of God, far above principalities,
mights, powers and dominions (see Eph 1:21)? That the Son of God sits there
is only reasonable, but for the *man* Jesus to be raised above angels?

There is a rumour going around (and I for one believe it is true) that you
who were sinners, humans, are seated with Christ in heavenly places far above
principalities, powers, mights and dominions; and one day where you are
already seated spiritually, you shall be literally and physically seated with Christ.
This is God's purpose for humanity redeemed through the man Jesus Christ,
the Son of God, our Lord. What a fantastic story this is.

David Gooding, *Three Creation Stories and Three Patriarchs: The Book of Genesis*, pp. 34–5

18th September

Reading: Genesis 1:11–27

*Why are you anxious about clothing? Consider the
lilies of the field, how they grow: they neither toil nor
spin, yet I tell you, even Solomon in all his glory was
not arrayed like one of these. (Matthew 6:28–29)*

First of all, God made trees that are good to look at, and then trees that are
good for food. Man's physical life will need to be provided for. It is interesting that God made trees that are good to look at first, and then trees that are
good for food. That's God's order of priorities. Isn't it a curious thing how
sometimes Puritanism has reversed the order and exalted the importance
of the stomach far beyond the importance of the brain? Good Christian
folks think that eating your food is a very good thing, but they're not quite
so sure about art. But God's very sure about art; he invented it. He made
trees in that garden that were good to look at. I love God for that! God is no
utility God; he could have made us a colourless world full of concrete, like
men do nowadays. That's not God. I suppose we could live without colour
and without beautiful things to look at, but I should imagine that more often
than not we should be very difficult to get on with.

So God wants us to live. He has ministered to our aesthetic life and to our
sound mental health by giving us tulips and daffodils and forget-me-nots.
When we come in all steamed up from work we can go and sit in the garden
and have a look at the tulips and all those beautiful things and let them calm
us down. And when a husband wants to please his wife he can give her a nice
bunch of flowers. Many an invalid has found a renewed desire to live (not by
the injections, important as they are) but by the lovely colours of a bunch of
flowers somebody has put next to his bed.

Isn't he a lovely God! He made trees that are good to look at, to cope with
our aesthetic sense. But I shall have to add to this. We need to be careful as
Christians what we spend on these things. God has given us richly all things
to enjoy and he wants us to enjoy them with a very good conscience, but we
must remember that we are living in a fallen world and get our priorities
right. There are men wanting to be redeemed and that means that we shall
not always have the time to enjoy the nice things as much as we would like.

David Gooding, The God of New Beginnings: Eighteen Seminars on the Book of Genesis, pp. 33–4

19th September

THE WORLD GOD HAS MADE

Reading: Genesis 1:27–31

*Then God said, 'Let us make man in our image, after our likeness.
And let them have dominion over the fish of the sea and over the
birds of the heavens and over the livestock and over all the earth
and over every creeping thing that creeps on the earth.' (v. 26)*

The pinnacle and goal is man, and he was made to have dominion, so let us
consider that term just for a moment. The Hebrew word means not so much,
'to have *dominion*,' as being a king, politically. It means to have dominion in
the sense of being the one to organize, administer, run the place and develop
it. I do admire the genius of God's inventions. All the glorious fun that he
proposed when he invented a universe and then made a man in his image,
to whom he could talk; a man who could respond to God and feel how God
feels, think how God thinks and take part with God in developing the thing.

Thus the heavens and the earth were finished, and all the host of them. And
on the seventh day God finished his work that he had done, and he rested
on the seventh day from all his work that he had done. (2:1–2)

God didn't make it in its final form, there was still a lot to be done; the
world still had to be developed. God subsequently planted a garden, 'The
LORD God took the man and put him in the garden of Eden to work it and
keep it' (v. 15). I think that is lovely! God didn't put man in a world that was
finished to the last crossing of the 't' and dotting of the 'i', he left something
for man to do and to develop.

I don't know what your father was like when he gave you presents, a bicycle
maybe or a toy train. I can distinctly remember that it was usually some
older person who would give you a train. The adult wanted to show how it
should be done, so he hitched the engine up; he even wanted to show you
how the signals went. As the evening went by you hadn't been allowed to do
anything, the adult had done it all!

I'm glad God isn't like that. He invented a big world for man, put him on
it and said, 'Adam, you develop it!' God has packed his world with all sorts
of surprises to keep man interested and entertained. On that physical level,
in doing things with God, man might then grow up and get to know God,
just as a child grows up and gets to know his father, and advance into those
deeper spiritual lessons and get to know God on that highest of all levels.

David Gooding, *The God of New Beginnings: Eighteen Seminars on the Book of Genesis*, pp. 17–18

20th September

MAN'S PLACE IN CREATION

Reading: Psalm 8

When I look at your heavens, the work of your fingers,
the moon and the stars, which you have set in place,
what is man that you are mindful of him? (vv. 3–4)

Genesis 1 tells us of an ongoing process that was designed from the very start to lead to a glorious climax and goal, the very pinnacle of the works of God. It is an exciting thing when we find Genesis 1 telling us what that pinnacle is, and what goal God had in mind when he began these creative acts and as they continued, becoming ever more complicated and colourful. The goal he had in mind was *man*. We who believe God's holy word should lift up our heads as we observe what a dignified and glorious concept the Bible has of human beings. *We were made in the image of God, to have dominion over the creation.*

For centuries men and women have lived in indescribable slavery and fear, for letting go of this glorious truth and not believing that man owes his position in the world to an almighty Creator. Man was the pinnacle of his creation; God made him to be viceroy of it, to control it, to be lord of it. Generations have slipped into idolatry and superstition: by banning the knowledge of God from their minds they thought they would strike a blow for freedom, but they have descended into being slaves.

If you look around the world it will not take you five minutes to observe that there are colossal, almost immeasurable, elemental and physical powers—powers that we have not even a hope of controlling in our own strength. Sooner or later we must ask ourselves what is our relation to those great powers. If there is no God, and our world is merely the result of chance—working on blind matter without forethought or plan, then we are slaves indeed. We are beings with intelligence who can think and reflect and we find ourselves in the universe surrounded by colossal powers that we cannot control.

Sin has done its deadly work. Mankind has rebelled against God and sought a false independence, and God is in the process of teaching us where independence of God will lead. But God has not given up his intention and glorious adventure of having a thing called man. This creature in the image of God can have fellowship with God, and on a smaller scale do the kind of things that God does and rule God's universe for him. God still adheres to the programme, and the glorious adventure will go on until one day it is finally realized in full.

David Gooding, *The God of New Beginnings: Eighteen Seminars on the Book of Genesis*, pp. 16–17

21st September

LIFE, LANGUAGE AND HUMAN RELATIONSHIPS

Reading: Genesis 2:18–25

*The man gave names to all livestock and to the birds of
the heavens and to every beast of the field. But for Adam
there was not found a helper fit for him. (v. 20)*

God brought all the animals and Adam named them. But among them there
was not found a 'a helper fit' for Adam. Isn't that interesting! The first man
was not a somewhat improved animal. An animal that was just a little bit
improved might have been delighted to have a lion for his wife, or an ape
for all I know, but Genesis roundly declares that in the entire animal world
there was not an affinity in any of them with the first man. Mark that carefully; we are required to believe it.

Adam gave names to the animals. I can't tell you what language he used.
Unless God gave him a language already invented and complete, we have here
evidence of a tremendous mental capacity. Inventing language was one of the
most brilliant things that man ever did. Animals communicate with nods
and grunts, and as far as we know none of them has a developed language
system like humans. It was somebody's genius that hit upon the system of
using an arbitrary sound to represent a thing or person.

This matter of language is first introduced when Adam is presented with his
wife, Eve. If ever there was a place for them to use words, beautiful words, and
to really act like human beings it was in human relationships. When the lion
thinks his lioness is pretty he has ways of expressing it—he nibbles her ear and
pats her on the back. But there is not much he can say to make her heart glad.
What marvellous things words are! Christians should never be found saying, 'This
holy book; it's only words.' What do you mean it's *only* words? It is the highest
expression of fellowship and life. Adam found his language and a wife to talk to.
The second man came to win a bride—he is called 'the Word' (John 1:1).

Are you alive at every level? Are you alive and enjoying the beauty and
aesthetics of creation? Alive and enjoying its fascination and exploration, its
challenge and its interests? Are you alive in your relationships with your fellow
men and women? Alive to the Scriptures, those inspired words? Are you alive
supremely to God as he has expressed himself not only in creation but also in
the Word, Jesus Christ our Lord? In all the experiences of life are you really
enjoying God? May the Lord help us to have that as our supreme aim in life.

David Gooding, The God of New Beginnings: Eighteen Seminars on the Book of Genesis, pp. 37–8

22nd September

MAN'S MORAL RELATIONSHIP WITH GOD

Reading: Joshua 24:1–21

*God said, 'You shall not eat of the fruit of the tree
that is in the midst of the garden, neither shall
you touch it, lest you die.' (Genesis 3:3)*

Man is in a moral relationship with God. What does that mean? It means a relationship where God declares himself Creator and Lord by laying down a command, which man is expected to reply to through loving obedience and trust. It is a relationship at the level of one's morality and behaviour, choice and moral judgment. God says, 'You shall not eat of it.' And if man asks 'why?' God says, 'Because I say so.' Man has to decide what he's going to do with this prohibition and consequently his relationship with God.

Now see a wonderful thing! It's a little bit difficult to explain, so if you think I'm saying heresy, I'm not. In order that mankind might have this relationship with God, God had to give them the ability to sin. And I repeat that last phrase, God gave them the *ability* to sin. I hasten to add God didn't give them *permission* to sin. In fact, God very strictly forbade it.

When Adam was faced with that prohibition he was able to disobey it, and he did. God didn't make him like a caterpillar. He could have made us, like he made many of his creatures, simply to go by instinct. They have no choice what they do, they just do it by the mechanism inside that keeps them going. They don't even know they are doing it; they have no choice in the matter. A bumblebee that gets on your arm doesn't sit there pondering if it would be a Christian thing to do if it were to sting you. It doesn't ask itself if its Creator would want it to sting you, it just reacts blindly. God could have made us like bumble bees with no choice. We should all have been the best behaved, but there wouldn't have been much significance in it.

It would have cut out love in its highest and truest sense; what the Bible means by loving God. It would have made a high relationship with God at a moral level impossible. You can't have love in that sense unless people have a choice.

David Gooding, *The God of New Beginnings: Eighteen Seminars on the Book of Genesis*, pp. 35–6

23rd September

FREEDOM AND LOVE

Reading: Ruth 3:1–10

Go and proclaim in the hearing of Jerusalem, Thus
says the LORD, *'I remember the devotion of your*
youth, your love as a bride, how you followed me in
the wilderness, in a land not sown'. (Jeremiah 2:2)

God gave his creature the ability to say No to him. I don't know whether it is an appropriate remark, but I feel I want to say what tremendous courage it showed in God. It was so that he might give us the opportunity of the very highest fellowship and love. He did strictly forbid Adam and Eve to eat of that tree and warned them of the consequences of disobeying him.

Do I think that it was a real tree? I don't see why not; it didn't need to be any particular or special tree. In order to set up this relationship, there just had to be one prohibition. You say, 'That's God, he spoils it all. When you think he's given you some lovely gift, then he adds some kind of snide prohibition and makes life difficult.' No! God put the prohibition there so that man might learn freedom and exercise it. You never know what freedom is until you meet a prohibition.

I come into your house, and you say, 'You're very welcome here. You may do as you like; make yourself at home.' You don't know what I do at home and yet you say, 'make yourself at home!'

I say, 'Really?'

'Yes, there isn't anything you mustn't do!'

What a pity, for now I have no choice. I can't do anything wrong, even if I want to. I can't express my personality; there is nothing that I mustn't do. God was bigger than that. He said there's one thing you mustn't do and he therefore let man sense his freedom of choice. We know too well the sad results. But before we get to the end of Genesis we shall be told what glorious things have developed from this marvellous concept of life that God has designed for human beings. In chapter 24 we shall read the story of a servant who came to a girl and said, 'My master is exceedingly rich, has one son, and has given him all that he has. Would you like to be his bride?' It was a free choice; she didn't have to go. The marriage supper of the Lamb will go on for all eternity. And this is the thing that shall fill heaven with consummate delight: men and women freely saying Yes to God's Son, not because they have to, but because they want to.

David Gooding, *The God of New Beginnings: Eighteen Seminars on the Book of Genesis*, pp. 36–7

24th September

WE ARE MADE FOR CHRIST—NOT THE OTHER WAY ROUND

Reading: Romans 11:33–12:2

Worthy are you, our Lord and God, to receive glory and honour and power, for you created all things, and by your will they existed and were created. (Revelation 4:11)

Sometimes, even after we get saved, it doesn't dawn on us how immensely sinful our sin is. If we are not careful we could misapprehend salvation in the same way and imagine that salvation is geared to have us at the centre of it, and Jesus Christ is there to minister to us in our times of need.

Last year my doctor sent me to see a surgeon because he was worried about one of my big toes. The surgeon was explaining to me how good a surgeon he was and what a marvellous operation he could do, and to encourage me he told me about one of his colleagues. He said, 'One of my colleagues let me do the operation the other month because his left toe had become very rigid, like yours. It was interfering with his golf swing. I did the operation for him and now he's rejoicing because he can swing his golf club again!' I pondered the idea that the National Health Service was geared through the surgeon to putting right his colleague's rigid toe to facilitate his golf swing.

Sometimes we have that concept of Christ, don't we? When our marriages break down, Christ is there to fix them. When we get depressed, he's there to encourage us. If we fall into sin, he's there to forgive us. He's there and his salvation is there for us. If we're not careful we will continue in that same old egocentric attitude to life—hedonistic and pleasure-seeking—and feel that, when we get into trouble, Christ exists to put us right.

We could be in danger of preaching a gospel to men and women today, which suggests that that's what Christ is. He's the universal 'fixer-up' of human beings when they get into difficulty. He exists for them, and that's the sum of the matter. To misrepresent the gospel like that would be what Chuck Colson calls a 'hedonistic blasphemy'. Christ doesn't exist in that sense for us, we were made for him; but the terrible fact is that we took our free will, rebelled against him and went our own way. We must not interpret salvation as merely a fixing up job that Christ does for us to put us on our 'feet' again.

David Gooding, *A Cosmic-sized Salvation: Three Studies in Colossians*, pp. 12–13

25th September

AN ANCIENT SIN

Reading: Genesis 3:1–7

*For although they knew God, they did not honour him as God
or give thanks to him, but they became futile in their thinking,
and their foolish hearts were darkened. (Romans 1:21)*

This false, unholy attitude of heart is the sin into which Satan originally lured Adam and Eve. Genesis 3 describes how he pointed to the tree of the knowledge of good and evil and made Eve aware that it was good for food: that is, for physical satisfaction; that it was good to look at, that is, for aesthetic satisfaction; and desirable to make one wise, that is, intellectual satisfaction. He put to Eve the lie that it is possible to enjoy these lovely things—in a word, to enjoy life to the full—independently of God and without regard either for him or for his word.

Adam and Eve believed the lie and inevitably it reorientated mankind's attitude to life, to its resources and relationships. Life's benefits ceased to be regarded as gifts from the gracious hand of God to be enjoyed in fellowship with God, drawing their hearts into ever closer friendship with God, so that, when life on earth ceased and life's temporary gifts were gone, the friendship with God would continue eternally in God's heaven. Now life's benefits became an end in themselves, drawing their hearts away from God instead of to him. Moreover, their alienation from God made them afraid of God. He was someone to hide from; no longer a source of their enjoyment of life but a threat to that enjoyment. The poison of this false attitude to God has infiltrated the veins of every human being.

It is the world's typical sin, so much so that the Bible often uses the word 'world' in a bad sense to refer to human society, organized and living on the basis of this false heart attitude to God.

David Gooding, *In the School of Christ: Lessons on Holiness in John 13–17*, p. 53

26th September

HOPE EVEN IN THE FALL

Reading: Genesis 3:8–15

I will put enmity between thee and the woman, and between thy seed and her seed; it shall bruise thy head, and thou shalt bruise his heel. (v. 15 KJV)

The sorry story of the fall is nevertheless a story that brims over with wonderful hope. It tells not merely of a creature of God who wilfully disobeyed him, and therefore fell. It tells also of a Creator whose heart was full of love for that very creature, and who was moved with compassion at the sorry state that his sinfulness has brought upon him. When God came down into the garden that he had made, almost the first word that he spoke to Adam was a word of hope. He told him that one day the whole thing would be put right again. I am proud of this story and of the God who tells it. As Adam and Eve stood there, shivering in their fig leaves and tortured in their consciences, they were beginning to be dimly aware of the terrible thing that they had done. But God told them that he would go on with the adventure, and what they had spoiled he would put right. It is a wonderful story.

It is even more wonderful! God did not merely say they were foolish creatures who had spoiled it all and he would come and put it right; God said that it would be one who should come from the human race who would put it right. A man shall be born, the seed of the woman, and he shall put it right. A man put it wrong and a man shall put it right! This wonderful new kind of man, bigger and infinitely better than Adam was even before he fell, shall 'bruise the serpent's head.' God will not have to write off humankind as an experiment that went wrong. Man shall yet be God's great and wonderful masterpiece through that second man, Jesus Christ our Lord.

So, the story of the fall is brim full of hope. Man put it wrong, but God is going to put it right. The story is also kind, fair and just, and we are not merely victims of chance. Listen to holy Scripture's comment upon it, 'For as by the one man's disobedience the many were made sinners, so by the one man's obedience the many will be made righteous.' (Rom 5:19)

David Gooding, *The God of New Beginnings: Eighteen Seminars on the Book of Genesis*, pp. 50–1

27th September

GOD CALLS

Reading: Revelation 22:1–6

And I, when I am lifted up from the earth, will
draw all people to myself. (John 12:32)

In the book of Genesis we read that God called to Adam in the garden of Eden, 'Where are you, Adam?' (3:9). Adam was busy trying to hide himself behind the wonders of creation from creation's Lord. The merciful Creator was urging Adam to come and stand before him and let his sin be exposed, to stop running away and find the beginnings of his way back to God.

In Exodus 3 God is calling again. This time the scene is very different. No longer the luscious trees of the beautiful garden of Eden with all their greenery and fruit and delight. Sin has had some centuries to get working, and now when God calls, he calls out of the midst of a thorn bush burning with fire. What things sin can do: it has transformed our world from a garden of Eden to a weary old desert full of thorn bushes whose end is to be cursed. Moses had fled from all the complicated politics of Egypt, where both the oppressed and the oppressor were found to be unreasonable. He fled away from it all into a desert, solitary and cursed, and there he heard God calling out of life's thorn bushes. Here is a God who had not forsaken his people, a God who had come down to stand with them. Here is God in the very thorn bush, which explains why it burned but was not consumed.

Give history some more centuries to wreak worse havoc and you will find a figure on a cross, crowned with twisted thorns. That's the kind of thing sin does. Yet from that figure crowned with thorns, God calls to men and women whose lives deserve the curse and tells of somebody who has been made a curse for them. The tangled thorns can be undone and woven into a veritable crown of glory.

David Gooding, *The Beauty of Holiness: Israel's Sacrificial System and the Christian Faith*, p. 8

28th September

BORN IN SIN

Reading: Romans 5:12–21

For as by the one man's disobedience the many
were made sinners, so by the one man's obedience
the many will be made righteous. (v. 19)

It is not our fault we were born sinners. It was by one man's disobedience that the many were constituted sinners. This is the Christian doctrine of the fall. Adam was not born in sin but he disobeyed God, and as the founder and first member of the human race from whom all others have come, the human race was in that sense perverted in Adam and all who have been born since have been born sinners. By his one act of disobedience all have been constituted sinners. It is not our fault, therefore. The doctrine of the fall is in one sense a very glad (I almost said 'happy') doctrine. People who say, 'I don't see why I should be condemned because of what Adam did,' can be answered with the assurance that nobody will ever be condemned because of what Adam did. People will be condemned for what they've done themselves, but not for what Adam did. We shall not be condemned because we were born sinners—that wasn't our fault; we shall be condemned for rejecting salvation. And salvation is on these terms: 'For as through the one man's disobedience the many were constituted [were made] sinners, even so through the obedience of the one shall the many be made righteous'. If we were born sinners by what somebody else did, we can be made righteous by what somebody else did. God's ways are fair, aren't they?

This is a very merciful doctrine. We all are guilty, and to that extent it is our fault. But do have compassion on people. They were born sinners, you know. It wasn't their fault that they were born sinners. They didn't ask to be born, or to be born of a fallen race. In that sense, then it is not their fault they were born sinners. Since God's ways are just, and more than just, if they were born sinners by what somebody else did, namely Adam, they can be saved by what somebody else did: 'By the obedience of the one, the many shall be constituted righteous.'

We have to be careful in applying these things. In the diagnosis of sin that we find in this Epistle's explanation of the gospel, the first point to notice is that we are responsible before God (1:1–5:11). We deserve his wrath. We are guilty sinners.

David Gooding, *God's Power for Salvation: Paul's Letter to the Romans*, p. 91

THE FATHER'S PLAN OF REDEMPTION

Part 4—Implementing the Plan:
God's Strategy in Redemption

29th September

GOD'S PLAN WAS NOT A CONTINGENCY PLAN

Reading: Isaiah 46:8–13

I bring near my righteousness; it is not far off, and
my salvation will not delay; I will put salvation
in Zion, for Israel my glory. (v. 13)

Sometimes we are inclined to think and talk of our world as though it was some kind of a glorified Sunday School trip that went wrong—as very often they do. You plan to go to Bangor, and the sun will shine and all will be well. But the day comes and Bangor is doing what Bangor often does: it's pouring with rain. You stick it out as long as you can, until four thirty in the afternoon.

Having visited Woolworths and any other shops that you can find in Bangor, you then say, 'It's too bad; we shall have to think of something else. We can't go on with this. The whole scheme has broken down, what shall we do now? Shall we take the children home and give them a slide show or something?' And you try and think of another scheme to fill in the time because the first thing went wrong.

God's scheme didn't go wrong. Sometimes people speak of God's great purposes of redemption as though it was like that. First of all he created the world and man on it, and then alas the whole scheme went wrong and God Almighty had to sit down and lament the fact, and say, 'Now, what shall I do? The whole thing has gone amiss and astray. What shall I do with this world of sinners? I know: what about inventing a heaven?'

No, no! Not only was it before the fall, but before there was a world anyway, God had his purpose that we should come to be; that we should eventually be before him, and before him as sons. To that end, God made the universe and put mankind in it. In spite of the fall, God has been steadily fulfilling that purpose and it will be achieved.

David Gooding, *Ephesians: A Bird's Eye View of the Major Movements of Thought*, pp. 17–18

30th September

THE GOSPEL ACCORDING TO GENESIS

Reading: Psalm 40

. . . but the righteous shall live by his faith. (Habakkuk 2:4)

Genesis tells us how earth came to its present chaos. Man was made dependent on God and put in a world so organized that it would emphasize his dependence. But he chose to grasp at independence of God and came to a point where he was no longer content to accept God's judgments and decisions. He insisted on knowing good and evil for himself, so that he might make his own decisions independent of God. In the very moment of grasping that independence, he quite logically lost a great deal of his dominion. Not only in the world external to him, but he lost a good deal of dominion of the world that is internal to him. Very often he is unable to govern even his own passions.

Let's anticipate it a bit further. Genesis not only tells us of man's folly at grasping independence and of the fall that followed; Genesis preaches to us the gospel. If you ask what is the gospel message particular to Genesis, then it is not so much the message of redemption by blood and sacrifice. It is hinted at in Genesis, but that message of salvation is left to books like Exodus and Leviticus to spell out in detail. The great message of salvation in the book of Genesis is *justification by faith*.

If we pondered it a moment, we would see how that method of salvation is admirably and exactly suited to man's need as disclosed in Genesis. If his ruin has come by grasping at independence, his salvation will come as he learns in true repentance to come back and be utterly dependent upon God. The New Testament quotes Genesis 15:6, 'Abraham believed God and it was counted to him as righteousness' (Rom 4:3; Gal 3:6). It explains what it means to believe God. Taking Abraham as an example, it points out how God waited until Abraham was physically quite incompetent. He and Sarah knew that their bodies were as good as dead, and if ever they were to have a son it would be God who did it all. So, from the very first chapter of Genesis, we get lines of thought that will tell us not merely what was originally intended to be, and how the fall came about, but how mankind is in the process of being redeemed and one day in Christ we shall reach the goal that God originally planned.

David Gooding, *The God of New Beginnings: Eighteen Seminars on the Book of Genesis*, pp. 29–30

1st October

HOW GOD OVERCOMES SATAN

Reading: Philippians 2:5–11

Worthy are you to take the scroll and to open its seals, for you were slain, and by your blood you ransomed people for God from every tribe and language and people and nation. (Revelation 5:9)

How shall God overcome Satan when he is persuading man to climb up and be as God? 'Watch,' says God, 'I shall answer that by becoming man.'

Oh, the divine subtlety and wisdom there is in the story of how God moves against his arch-enemy. When man in his rebellion is trying to be God, God says, 'I will become man.' Oh, what a lovely story. God was manifest in flesh, born into the human race, so that one day Satan might come across a man, the God-man, impervious to all his temptation, who would triumph. And triumph how? Did he triumph by promoting and glorifying himself, and putting himself on a pinnacle and demanding that men worship him at the pain of death? Oh no, no, no! How will he get men to bow at his feet? Oh, here is the story:

> Who, being in the form of God, thought it not a thing to be grasped at to be equal with God, but made himself of no reputation. . . and humbled himself, and became obedient unto death, even the death of the cross. Wherefore God has highly exalted him. (see Phil 2:6–9)

Why do you bow at the feet of Christ? What has overcome your rebellion as a sinner, an enemy of God? Why do you give him the loyalty of your heart? Is it because he is exalted and a heavenly tyrant, and he compelled you? You say, 'No, no. The way that God Almighty has got at me and my heart is by becoming man and dying for me at the place called Calvary. I am the rebel, and the very God whose shins I kicked, died for me.'

Oh, what a mystery! What a gospel! What divine wisdom! This is self-evidently of God. It has already worked, you know. Millions have been transferred from the kingdom of darkness into the kingdom of God's dear Son, brought by a power that Satan never knew how to wield. He gave himself to the cross, and God has highly exalted him beyond Satan's ability to capture. Satan's empire is doomed.

David Gooding, *The Book of the Revelation: Major Themes of Revelation's Six Sections*, p. 88

2nd October

GOD'S LOVE OVERCAME THE DIFFICULTIES

Reading: Leviticus 16:20–28; Hebrews 13:10–13

In this is love, not that we have loved God but that he loved us and sent his Son to be the propitiation for our sins. (1 John 4:10)

How could the holy God of heaven have any involvement with us at all? If he came and had fellowship with evil men and women, the whole universe would want to know what he was doing. Wouldn't that compromise his holiness? And doesn't it compromise his holiness still, because we are far from perfect?

Think then of the difficulties that lay in the way of God demonstrating his love to us, and the divine ingenuity and love that overcame the difficulty. There will have to be a propitiation for our sins—a sacrifice that demonstrates to the whole universe that God, in being friendly with us, is not compromising his holiness. In order to love us, and to demonstrate his love, God sent his Son to be the propitiation for our sins, and it is an incredible story.

In in the desert, living around the tabernacle of God and having fellowship with God, Israel were made aware of their sinfulness and the difficulty God had in staying with them, because the uncleanness of their sins defiled the tabernacle of his presence. They were told to bring a propitiatory sacrifice and they took two goats and confessed their sins over the head of the second goat and they took it out into a land uninhabited. First John 4:10 tells us the cost to God of loving us. That he who was the eternal Word of God, who was with the Father, whose being was enough to satisfy all the infinite desires of God, was led out into the land of abandonment and forsakenness so that God might have and enjoy our fellowship. Herein is love, and what it will do to overcome the difficulties in the way. It is an awesome thing to think of that God who has begotten us and who, as John will go on to tell us, lives in us. 'Beloved,' says John, 'if God so loved us, we ought also to love one another' (v. 11).

David Gooding, *Life in the Family of God: Twelve Seminars on the First Epistle of John*, pp. 68–9

3rd October

GOD CHOSE US

Reading: 1 Thessalonians 1

For we know, brothers loved by God, that he has chosen you,
because our gospel came to you not only in word, but also in power
and in the Holy Spirit and with full conviction. You know what
kind of men we proved to be among you for your sake. (vv. 4–5)

You are not believers by accident, you know. You didn't have to pester God to take you in, and he regretfully or reluctantly accepted you. No, God positively chose you. Ephesians 1:4 tells us he has 'chosen us in [Christ] before the foundation of the world.' Therefore his choice is not affected by the ups and downs and the changing circumstances of life. His choice doesn't depend on that. He chose us before the foundation of the world, and what is true about our salvation is true of us as servants of the Lord.

Paul says to Timothy, '[God] saved us and called us to a holy calling, not because of our works but because of his own purpose and grace, which he gave us in Christ Jesus before the ages began' (2 Tim 1:9). 'So pull up your socks, Timothy,' says Paul, 'fan into flame the gift that is in you' (see v. 6). God chose you from the very beginning, before times eternal; not only for salvation but for the work you have to do.

What a marvellous thing it is to come to the Sunday School class, or the toddlers' group, or whatever it is you come to, with the knowledge that from eternity God chose you for this task. Elders, don't lose heart when you meet to consider the welfare of the saints and whether they're doing well or badly; behind your work are the eternal counsels of God.

Other manuscripts read, 'he chose you as the firstfruits', and that is probably the original thing that Paul wrote. It means simply that when God saved the Thessalonians he didn't have them only in mind; he meant also to save other people and so they were the firstfruits of a bigger harvest that was going to be. That's a lovely thought, isn't it? When God chose Abraham he didn't choose him for himself alone; and when God chose the Israelites he didn't choose them for themselves alone. He chose them, so that in them all the nations of the earth should be blessed (see Gen 18:18). My brothers and sisters, when God decided to save you, he didn't do it just for your sakes. It was for your sakes, of course, but he chose you so that through you others might be reached in an ever extending and widening circle. He chose you as the firstfruits of a coming harvest.

David Gooding, *Eternal Encouragement and Good Hope: 2 Thessalonians 2:13-17*, p. 4

4th October

GOD'S CHOICE OF HIS SERVANTS

Reading: Romans 9:6–29

So then it depends not on human will or
exertion, but on God, who has mercy. (v. 16)

On what ground did he choose Jacob then? Well, obviously not on the grounds of merit! 'In fact,' says Paul, 'God chose Jacob even before the boy was born, so that it might be apparent to all that God's choice in this matter does not depend on a man's merit, nor upon his performance. It is not of works. It is not of him that wills, nor of him that runs, and that has always been so'.

My brother, and you too my sister, who serve the Lord in your particular sphere, might I ask you on what ground did God call you to that holy task of being a witness for Christ? Was it because of your special godliness and you were better than your next door neighbour? Perish the thought! It wasn't that God had a scheme for salvation and then left it to volunteers to come forward, and then he chose the best he could get hold of. We who sit here today may be grateful for that.

Just imagine what it would be like at the final judgment if this kind of thing could happen. Here comes a man, and in all the solemnity of that court God has to sentence him to eternal perdition. The man says, 'But why? Why, Lord?'

'Because you didn't believe the gospel.'

'What gospel? I never heard any gospel.'

'No, I know you didn't,' says God. 'I did have some servants, but they didn't make much of a go of it. They were a poor crowd and they never actually got round to coming to you with the gospel. That isn't my fault, it's their fault! They just weren't good enough.'

Must the man perish because the whole thing turned on the ability, faithfulness and godliness of the witnesses? How could it be? How would you even sustain the weight of your gospel ministry if you thought that somebody could be in hell forever because one day you slipped and fell? Oh, thank God we serve a bigger God than that! He chooses his witnesses, not according to their work: 'So then it depends not on human will or exertion, but on God, who has mercy.'

David Gooding, *The Power, the Wisdom and the Glory: Romans 9–11*, pp. 22–3

5th October

ISRAEL'S STUMBLING AND THE GENTILES' BLESSING

Reading: Romans 9:30–10:4

*Israel who pursued a law that would lead to righteousness
did not succeed in reaching that law. Why? Because they
did not pursue it by faith, but as if it were based on works.
They have stumbled over the stumbling stone. (9:31–32)*

Let it be clear in our minds what we mean when we read that Israel has 'stumbled', and thus the gospel has gone to the Gentiles. It isn't merely that when the apostles went forth (as recorded in the Acts of the Apostles) that the Jews rejected them and often stoned them so that the apostles then said, 'All right, if you won't have the gospel, we go to the Gentiles then.' That is true, but there is a deeper point at issue.

'Israel stumbled,' says Paul. Alas they did. They stumbled at the stone of stumbling, Jesus Christ our Lord (1 Cor 1:23). They thought they were going to welcome a Messiah who should make them the head of the nations; and then the Messiah came and began to talk to them about their sin, about the way they had come short. For all their Pharisaism they had come short of the standard of God and they were miserable sinners. Israel didn't like it; they objected, and they stumbled at the stone! They neither wanted his message that called them to repentance, nor would they have forgiveness at his hand. Religious though they were, they took him and nailed him to a tree. Oh, what a stumbling it was! How can you describe a nation chosen by God, so religious in its attitude and full of zeal that they should take God's own Son, their Saviour, and put him on a tree?

What a stumbling, and yet what a marvellous thing it has been for us Gentiles. From that moment there started out of Judaism an evangelization such as Judaism had never seen all down the centuries! It began in Jerusalem—a little trickle at first and then a river. It has come to be a vast ocean of evangelization. Why? Because now at last, with Messiah crucified, Judaism had a gospel message to preach. Before that day they preached the law, and it was useful, but it didn't make them very good evangelists.

That was what lay behind the great evangelization that broke out of Jerusalem from the day of Pentecost onward, so that the very murder of Jesus Christ becomes in God's hand the sacrifice of reconciliation.

David Gooding, The Power, the Wisdom and the Glory: Romans 9–11, p. 42

6th October

HOW GOD RECONCILES US

Reading: 1 Timothy 1:12–20

. . . and through [Christ] to reconcile to himself
all things, whether on earth or in heaven, making
peace by the blood of his cross. (Colossians 1:20)

One day the blessed Lord Jesus will present us before the throne of God's glory with exceeding joy, perfectly reconciled to God by the death of his Son, and God himself shall be unable to find a blemish within us. Ponder for a moment not only the wonder of that fact, but the wonder of the method that God has chosen to accomplish it. He shall 'reconcile to himself all things . . . making peace by the blood of his cross'.

The slander of the devil and all his hosts has been that, in making our world and all that is in it, God has laid down such conditions of life and stringent laws that show him to be an intolerable tyrant. The slander that God is a tyrant has gained the hearts and minds of multitudes of our fellow men and women. How will God reconcile the world to himself, if that is what is in their hearts? We've had it too, haven't we? Shall it be by some exhibition of power? No, of course not. There has never been any doubt in the universe who holds the ultimate power.

The question has always been, who has the greatest claim to man's loyalty? Who really loves? You see, when we first sinned, God could have squashed us out of existence. But what would that have proved? It would have demonstrated that, while God was almighty to create and almighty to destroy, he was not almighty in his love. A God who could not retain the loyalty and love of his creatures is a God who, in that sense, has failed.

God set out to reconcile all things to himself, so that all might come to know and acknowledge that he is not a tyrant. He is the God of almighty power and measureless love; and thus the method. To bring us rebels back to God, he ordained that in Christ should all the fullness dwell, and that Christ should die for us. We have been made for him. In our sin we had rebelled against him, and the divine decree was that he should die, not us. He, for whom we were made, should die for those who had rebelled against him.

Well, if God is like that, I can't fight him any more. If God will do that for me, then by his grace I will be his slave for ever.

David Gooding, *A Cosmic-sized Salvation: Three Studies in Colossians*, pp. 13–14

7th October

RECONCILING ONE NEW MAN

Reading: 1 Corinthians 12:7–13

. . . that he might create in himself one new man in
place of the two, so making peace. (Ephesians 2:15)

Like a good builder when he has demolished the bad things, he starts to build the good things. Having abolished the old, God started to create the new, and this was the very exciting bit. People had heard of forgiveness before, but they had never heard of this before. He took the Jew and he took the Gentile, and of the two he made 'one new man' (v. 15). That was utterly revolutionary. Notice, he did not take the Jew and then say, 'we will add a lot of Gentiles to you'. If he had, the Jews would have said, 'Yes, we are the originals. Allow them to come in, but we were here first!'

God saw to it that nothing like that ever happened, because they were not there first. I know that they were first in history, but not in the Body of Christ. The Body of Christ is not old Judaism with a few Gentiles tagged on; it is an utterly new thing. He created one new man by baptizing both Jew and Gentile in one Spirit into one Body (1 Cor 12:13).

Then he introduced them both to God and both were reconciled to God through the cross (Eph 2:16). Do you see how the thought is going? We are thinking about God's purpose: God wanted a dwelling place in time and space. He had that old dwelling place in Israel with the tabernacle, the law inside it and the wall around it that kept Gentiles out. That could never be the final answer. God in a little tabernacle in a corner of the wilderness, and a vast world lost to him. He not only wanted the old wall down and Jews and Gentiles in one new man, but here comes the purpose: they've got to be reconciled to God. On what grounds was he able to do the reconciliation? There was no privilege or superiority; they were both reconciled to God in one body. He introduced them to God on the same ground and reconciled them 'through the cross, thereby killing the hostility'.

Then, the crowning thing. Both have access in one Spirit to the Father (v. 18). If God wants to dwell amongst men, the opposite side of that coin is that men must have access to God. With the distance eventually covered the plan is now really progressing. God had set his heart upon having a dwelling place, a temple; the foundation being laid, we are being built and are growing into a holy temple in the Lord (v. 21).

David Gooding, *Ephesians: A Bird's Eye View of the Major Movements of Thought*, p. 72

8th October

PROGRESS IN HISTORY

Reading: 1 Corinthians 2:1–10

Behold, I am doing a new thing; now it springs forth,
do you not perceive it? I will make a way in the
wilderness and rivers in the desert. (Isaiah 43:19)

When Jesus came the Jews rejected him. To this present day, officially and as a nation, they reject Jesus the Messiah, who has proved to millions beyond doubt that he is the Saviour of the world. They did not invent the idea. Those centuries that God spent raising up that nation in history, giving them his laws and giving them hope, were years that have pointed conclusively to where you may find the true God within history.

But that is not the end of the story. When it seemed as if this too had all gone wrong, then God intervened in history once more and set going another move. That is the kind of a God he is. When the world nearly destroyed itself with its violence and sin God had to destroy it with the flood, but he showed that he had a new thing and invented an ark and began again. When the nations were lost in idolatry God did another new thing: he created the Hebrew race of Israel and began again. Next, when Israel had gone almost beyond repair, God intervened once more, began again and carried it one stage further.

If we are beginning to get the idea, we shall find our hearts rising with expectation and we shall say, 'I know what that new stage is and how wonderful it is compared with the previous stage. It was good, but now I can see its purpose and how much more wonderful this new stage is.'

Once you start talking like that you will find yourself presently saying, 'And if this present stage is wonderful, what will the next one be, when the Lord comes and God's great plan has been brought to fruition?'

When that begins to rise in your heart, then you will find that it has a practical implication in its tail. If God has been on the move; if the thing is even now moving forward, what progress am I making? Since I got converted, what progress have I made? Is it visible? How much shall the progress of my life contribute to the final achievement of God's purpose?

The Lord encourage our hearts and give us visions of his purposes and vistas of the future, so that we might now give ourselves seriously to the business of making progress along with his purposes.

David Gooding, *Ephesians: A Bird's Eye View of the Major Movements of Thought*, pp. 66–7

THE FATHER'S PLAN OF REDEMPTION

Part 5—Implementing the Plan:
Israel and the Purposes of God

9th October

HOW GOD WENT ABOUT THE PROCESS OF REDEMPTION

Reading: Exodus 24:9–18

[God] who went before you in the way to seek you out a place to pitch your tents, in fire by night and in the cloud by day, to show you by what way you should go. (Deuteronomy 1:33)

When God determined to save us by sending his Son, he didn't send him all of a sudden one Tuesday afternoon without any warning, did he? What use would it have been? What use would it be if God sent his Son to call upon men to be reconciled with God, if men had gone so far into idolatry that they didn't even know what God was like? What good would God sending his Son to die for us be if we hadn't been prepared, by all sorts of illustrations and pictures and experiences, to see the need of the death of Christ and to see what the significance of that death would be?

So God in his wisdom had long since started the early stages for the redemption of mankind. He summoned out from the mass of the Gentiles a man called Abraham and began from him a brand new nation that never had existed before. It wasn't that God was saying there was nobody else saved in the whole world except Abraham. But when the nations at large were beginning to sink into idolatry, God began again and took out Abraham and gave him a special status before God and gave that special status to all his seed. As Paul remarks, the first thing to get hold of about Israel is this: theirs is 'the adoption' (9:4) (Rom 9:4), that is, the placing as sons. It may not mean 'son' in the sense that we evangelicals are used to employing the term, but listen to God speaking to Pharaoh. 'Pharaoh,' he says, 'let Israel go. Israel is my firstborn' (see Exod 4:22). So God gave Abraham and his seed this special status before God, to be sons of God.

Then God did a marvellous thing, almost too marvellous to believe. The transcendent Lord came down into space and time, positioned himself on Mount Sinai and revealed himself to Israel in all the splendour of his glory! In doing so he made his mark in our world, that this world is not a closed shop; it is not just a closed system of materialism.

As that little tribe went across the wilderness, the very glory of the unseen God shone in their midst. Here was the very beginning of redemption, and God made his promise to the people that through them, through Abraham and his seed, would all the nations of the world be blessed.

David Gooding, *The Power, the Wisdom and the Glory: Romans 9–11*, p. 7

10th October

GOD'S PURPOSE IN FOUNDING
THE HEBREW NATION

Reading: Psalm 53

In days to come Jacob shall take root, Israel shall blossom and put forth shoots and fill the whole world with fruit. (Isaiah 27:6)

God did a unique thing when he called out Abraham, but he didn't leave the rest of the world lost and doomed to perish. In those days, the Gentile world—therefore, the whole world—had slithered down the slippery slope into idolatry. They were fast going down into the bondage and immorality that accompanies such an idolatrous interpretation of the universe. When God in his mercy raised up a protest and drew Abraham out of the Gentile world, he gave him a vision of the glory of the true God and set him and his descendants up as a witness. There was one place on earth at least where Gentiles might see the truth of the true God and be delivered from their bondage and superstitions.

We need that message still. People in the west do not generally bow down before idols; but our modern world is saturated with agnosticism, if not atheism, which, as any schoolboy knows, reintroduces into people's thinking an idolatrous interpretation of the universe. It doesn't really matter whether you say the sun is a bit of stuff, or it's a god. It doesn't matter whether you call the basic forces of the universe weak atomic power or strong atomic power, gravity or electromagnetism. Call them what you will. If you hold that there is no personal Creator, then you are driven to the idolatrous view of the universe that the ancient Gentile nations had. They called these forces, as far as they understood them, gods. We don't call them gods, but the atheist proclaims what the old idolatrous Gentiles believed. These are the ultimate powers that control man: his birth, his life, his death and eventual extinction; and they leave our modern world as they left the ancient world, in the darkness of ultimate hopelessness. Slaves to the great physical forces of the universe that man cannot ultimately control, but will one day destroy him.

It was a glorious gospel message that God preached to mankind, when he led Abraham out of that Gentile morass and showed him a sight of his own true glory as the living God Creator, and set up a relationship between himself and Abraham that should be a pattern for all men everywhere. He taught Abraham not only the truth of God, but how to be right with God, thus delivering him from the slaveries of religion, teaching Abraham and millions since that man is justified by faith without works (see Rom 4).

David Gooding, *A Proud Tyrant Brought Down, The Suffering Servant Exalted: A Study in Isaiah*, p. 5

11th October

ISRAEL'S ROLE IN HISTORY AND THE PURPOSES OF GOD

Reading: Deuteronomy 4:15–20; Romans 9:1–4

For what great nation is there that has a god so near to it as the LORD our God is to us, whenever we call upon him? And what great nation is there, that has statutes and rules so righteous as all this law that I set before you today? (Deuteronomy 4:7–8)

Our Christian faith is bound up with these historical things. It is not a philosophy—almost anyone can invent a philosophy. There are plenty on offer—you could invent another one if you had the mind to. However, Christianity is not a philosophy that someone thought up. Christianity is the fulfilling of a great movement in history. God called out Abraham and then his successors, Israel, to be a nation to whom God would reveal himself and through whom the Christ would come. Matthew tells us that our gospel is about the Lord Jesus who was the son of David, the son of Abraham (1:1). Paul reminds us that the gospel is about Jesus Christ, who was born of the seed of David according to the flesh (Rom 1:3). Why is that important? Because no mere man can decide where he's going to be born and by whom he shall be born. Because Jesus Christ was born of the seed of David, that in itself is an indication of God's authority behind the Christian gospel. It was announced in the Old Testament, fulfilled in the New—not only his birth and the place of his birth, but the purpose for which he came and that he should die as a sacrifice for the sins of the world.

Christianity then is rooted in history and God's self-revelation to Israel is part of our Christian testimony. Paul wrote his great exposition of the Christian gospel in the Epistle to the Romans. It is in four major parts, and the third is a discussion of the role Israel has played in God's self-manifestation to the world. 'They are Israelites, and to them belong the adoption, the glory, the covenants, the giving of the law, the worship and the promises' (9:4). All so utterly different from pagan service—there was no image of any god inside the temple. 'To them belong the patriarchs, and from their race, according to the flesh, is the Christ who is God over all, blessed for ever' (v. 5). We thank God for Israel and their testimony to the uniqueness of God, the distinction between Jehovah and all idols.

David Gooding, *With Moses on the Plains of Moab: Studies in Deuteronomy*, p. 12

12th October

ISRAEL IN GOD'S PLAN OF SALVATION

Reading: Romans 10

Know, therefore, that the LORD your God is not giving you
this good land to possess because of your righteousness,
for you are a stubborn people. (Deuteronomy 9:6)

As we read the second part of the book of Genesis we see God taking the early steps in the great programme that would eventually bring in our Lord and Messiah. God had already made his sovereign choice of the nation of Israel as the vehicle of his blessing and all these centuries later this is a striking piece of evidence.

That nation has lived down the centuries to prove that it is indeed unique among the nations of men. Unique in their history, they have given us the Old Testament and it was into that nation that Jesus Christ our Lord was born.

When the Bible talks about God's sovereign choice of the Jew as his elect, special people, many find a number of difficulties. They first think that it is very unfair that God should choose somebody and give him special blessings and privileges. But that is true of every man and woman. You are a brilliant pianist; when you sit down to play everybody stops talking and listens. How did you get that gift? Not by your merits; you were born with it. Every single man and woman born into this world has certain gifts by the sovereign providence of God.

Israel was given a special task and a high privilege to be the nation through whom God would give us the Old Testament and his Messiah, our Saviour, and through whom God will eventually govern this world. It is no exception to the general rule that God's gifts are given by his sovereign choice; it is not unfair. If God has chosen you to be a daisy and not an oak tree, then thank God for being a daisy; be a good daisy and don't try to be an oak tree!

But let us think again. God's sovereign choice does not mean that those men or women are automatically good. You may be a very good person as well as being a good pianist, but there are plenty of brilliant pianists that are morally very sorry people. We must learn to distinguish between a man's gifts and a man's moral character, and let us all remember that the possession of many distinguished gifts does not mean that you are automatically saved. It does not even mean that you are especially good morally, and of course goodness is infinitely more important than gifts.

David Gooding, *The God of New Beginnings: Eighteen Seminars on the Book of Genesis*, pp. 148–9

13th October

THE RISE OF ISRAEL AS A BASIS FOR HOPE

Reading: 2 Samuel 7:1–16

David himself, in the Holy Spirit, declared, 'The Lord
said to my Lord, Sit at my right hand, until I put
your enemies under your feet.' (Mark 12:36–37)

If you look back at the early chapters of 1 Chronicles, from chapter 1 to the end of chapter 10, you will find that it is mainly a list of names—genealogies galore. Starting with Adam, and developing the course of the human race from him, the historian very soon comes to what, for him, is the most significant thing in these chapters. And that is, the rise of Israel from among the nations; and presently the rise from among Israel of their most famous king, King David.

That is where I would put my hope, if I were surveying history and asking if there was any evidence or ground for hope that one day the human race will see an age of bliss and glory and plenty. I wouldn't put it in the United Nations. May God help them in this difficult time in history, when they grapple with the problems of a world becoming ever smaller, and therefore ever more explosive. They try to grapple with problems that now must be grappled with at world level, as our little planet becomes one great world village. But I would not put my final hopes in them, for the evidence is ambivalent; politics has been as much a curse as it has been a blessing.

I would put my hope on this extraordinary phenomenon among the nations—the rise of Israel. A tiny little nation, but raised up of God in those far distant days with a mission to the world. A mission to protest against every idolatrous interpretation of the universe; to stand for the fact of the great Creator, and that man is made by a personal Creator in the image of that Creator. And when she has not compromised herself (she has, alas, many times) that is Israel's message to the nations.

But more important still, is the rise from Israel not only of David, but David's greater Son. It is a unique nation whom God raised up to be his mouthpiece, and her prophets pointed the way to the great Saviour of the world. It was through Israel that he came, and he remains still the only credible name in the whole of history that offers himself as the Saviour of the world.

David Gooding, God's Great Salvation: Lessons from the Lives of Old Testament Characters, pp. 27–8

14th October

THE PROMISED SEED

Reading: Genesis 16:7–16

Now Hagar is Mount Sinai in Arabia; she
corresponds to the present Jerusalem, for she is in
slavery with her children. (Galatians 4:25)

God took Hagar and Ishmael, and he put them back into Abraham's dwelling place. What a difficult and trying time it was for Abraham when Ishmael was born. A wild donkey of a man he proved to be; his hand against every man and every man's hand against him (see Gen 16:12). Controlling the young outlaw was difficult enough. Oh, those long years when no promised seed appeared, and all Abraham had was this wild donkey of a boy, son of a slave woman, sharing his tent and home with him. You can imagine the sigh of relief when at long last the promised seed was born (Gen 21:2). Then the very next paragraph tells us that, when it came to the time of weaning, God gave the command through the words of Sarah, 'Cast out the bond woman and her son, for the bond woman and her son shall not inherit along with the free-born Isaac' (see v. 10). It was shortly after this that the promised seed was taken to be sacrificed upon an altar on Mount Moriah (ch. 22).

Yes, that's the original story, and I've not strayed from the serious, solemn, straightforward and pedestrian history. But, as I proceed with the analogy, listen to what Paul has to say about that very chunk of history (Gal 3–4).

The promise was given to Abraham that he should have the seed, but many centuries passed before the seed came. And who was he? The 'seed' was not Isaac, but Isaac's greater Son, our blessed Lord and Saviour, Jesus Christ (3:16). 'In those intervening centuries' says Paul, 'just like God had put Hagar and Ishmael in Abraham's tent until the promised seed Isaac came, so did he put Moses and the law in the midst of Israel until the promised seed should come.' Then he says, with a tremendous sigh of relief, 'The promised seed has come and you're no longer under the law. You are under Christ, and it is common knowledge that when the blessed seed was born the law had finished its function as a way of life, that is, as a way of justification. When the promised seed came to manhood like Isaac, only more so, he was sacrificed upon Mount Calvary.'

David Gooding, *Entering the Inheritance: Studies in Joshua 1–12*, pp. 8–9

15th October

THE BRIDEGROOM OF OUR HEARTS

Reading: Jeremiah 2:1–8

*Thus you shall say to the house of Jacob, and tell the
people of Israel: You yourselves have seen what I did
to the Egyptians, and how I bore you on eagles' wings
and brought you to myself. (Exodus 19:3–4)*

Let's look at the proposal God made to Israel when they came out of Egypt. The goal of Israel's redemption was not the promised land—that was their destination. Here God specifies exactly the goal that he had in mind when he delivered them out of Egypt: 'You've seen what I did to the Egyptians, I bore you on eagles' wings, and brought you to *myself.* This is the lover of men's souls speaking. Israel came out of Egypt under the gracious influence of God, who brought them to himself and sought their hearts' affection, so that they should receive his covenant and be his. 'Now therefore, if you will indeed obey my voice and keep my covenant, you shall be my treasured possession among all peoples, for all the earth is mine; and you shall be to me a kingdom of priests and a holy nation. These are the words that you shall speak to the people of Israel' (vv. 5–6).

God going courting and giving his proposal—'If you keep my covenant.' He's talking now of the covenant as a marriage contract. If you keep my covenant indeed, then you shall be (as the King James Version puts it) 'a peculiar treasure'. Not our modern sense of the word *peculiar* (odd though some of us are!), but in the sense of his private, personal property—his personal treasure. It's as if God is saying to them, 'Oh, my treasure! If you keep my covenant, you shall be my very own, my personal delight, my personal joy and my personal treasure. All the nations are mine, but you shall be distinct, you shall be my special love.'

Can you imagine it? The God of the universe, of all of the billions of galaxies and uncountable numbers of angels that excel in strength—he comes to a band of one-time slaves and says that, if they keep his covenant, they shall be the darling of his heart. And he says the same to us! Through the grace and redemption that is in Christ Jesus he has made us a peculiar treasure and God is now looking for what he can get from us (1 Pet 2:9–10). It would delight him to see us going out after him, like Israel went after God in the wilderness.

David Gooding, *With Moses on the Plains of Moab: Studies in Deuteronomy*, p. 20

16th October

ISRAEL'S ROLE IN HISTORY—AND OURS

Reading: Deuteronomy 11:22-28; 28:63-64

You shall therefore love the LORD your God and keep his charge,
his statutes, his rules, and his commandments always. (11:1)

Please notice that Moses is giving the people the warnings of these curses in advance, and as they hear them they say, 'Amen'—let it be so (27:15). We further notice that the issuing of these warnings didn't make the sin unavoidable. They didn't have to sin: the curses didn't need to come upon them. Moses reminded them that they had the choice. It was a stern lesson. In the mention of the curses, the description frequently reverts to phraseology like, 'I brought you up out of the land of Egypt, redeemed you and gave you this land. If you reject me, now that you are in the land, you must not suppose that you can keep the land. If you reject me, I shall turn you back to Egypt.' That is understandable, isn't it?

If one could only take the courage to say to modern Israel, 'You cannot reject your Messiah and still claim the land.' But there is coming a day when the Messiah shall come and Israel shall be saved. O thank God, 'they shall look upon him, whom they pierced,' and will say with consternation and repentance, 'We thought he was smitten by God, and afflicted—"But he was wounded for our transgressions; he was crushed for our iniquities"' (Zech 12:10; Isa 53:4-5).

In passing, we ought just to have a little word in our own ears. Christendom's reputation has been blotted with ghastly sins. When the Church thought it ought to be the reigning political power, it began to persecute Jews. We pause to think of the Inquisition and how King John of England persecuted Jews; and the Russian pogroms; and Hitler's gas chambers, though Hitler's Germany professed to be Christian. It was a serious error when the Church got into its head that there was no future for Israel, the Church had replaced Israel—when God's own word said, 'For the gifts and calling of God are irrevocable' (Rom 11:29). Israel, raised up to be the olive tree of witness for God in the world, failed. Some branches have broken off and a responsibility to witness for Christ has been given to the church. 'But beware,' says Paul to the Gentiles, 'for if you go and apostatize, you shall be cut off too' (v. 21). We live in an advanced age, when so-called Christian theologians deny the very basis of Christianity—the deity of our Lord, his incarnation, resurrection, ascension and his second coming. Let them all be warned: if they apostatize, Christendom shall be cut off.

David Gooding, With Moses on the Plains of Moab: Studies in Deuteronomy, pp. 36–7

17th October

SATAN'S WAR AGAINST ISRAEL

Reading: Daniel 8:9–26

*Then Satan stood against Israel and incited David
to number Israel. (1 Chronicles 21:1)*

It started with Abraham, and God's calling-out of Abraham to form a unique nation. Israel, that latecomer among the nations, was distinct in the fact that she did not worship idols (officially, at least). She bore witness to the one true God and to the fact that the God of heaven did have a purpose on earth. Israel was to be the favoured nation; one day it would bring in the coming Messiah and deliverer. Because of that very fact Satan has set himself all the way down history to destroy that people, if possible, and to destroy their city and their testimony to the coming of Messiah.

He did it in Egypt when he raised up a genocidal pharaoh who attempted to wipe out the nation of Israel by casting every new born baby boy into the Nile (Exodus 1). Insane, of course. He did it again in Athaliah's time when that daughter of Ahab rose up and slaughtered all the royal family of Judah (2 Kings 11). Apart from God's good providence she would have destroyed the line of Messiah, but God in his mercy saved little Joash as a baby. And again under the absurd Antiochus Epiphanes. When at last our blessed Lord came, Satan had the outrage to attack him. Trying not now to conquer him by fears, but to overcome him by corruption. 'And the devil took him up and showed him all the kingdoms of the world in a moment of time, and said to him, "To you I will give all this authority and their glory, for it has been delivered to me, and I give it to whom I will. If you, then, will worship me, it will all be yours"' (Luke 4:5–7).

Skipping the centuries, we can watch it happening again in the insanities of Hitler's gas chambers. Can you explain it to me in any rational terms? How did any human get it into his head to eliminate a whole nation? It wasn't a pagan, savage nation that did it; it was a nation that led the world in its intellectual advances. Don't blame it on mere mortals altogether. There is a devil. Whatever power lusts and war games fill men's little minds, the devil uses them for the bigger purpose that he has in his own heart, to discredit God's people and to destroy them; and to destroy the nation of Israel and make the fulfilment of God's purpose impossible.

David Gooding, *Daniel: Civil Servant and Saint*, pp. 94–5

18th October

LEADING CAPTIVITY CAPTIVE

Reading: Judges 4:4–16

Arise, Barak, and lead thy captivity captive,
thou son of Abinoam. (5:12 KJV)

After years in which the enemy had oppressed Israel and scattered them until all was fragmentation, Barak stood there upon the mountain. 'Get up,' said Deborah, 'turn the tables on your enemy and the people that have mastered you by their big brain, technology and science. Don't let them triumph over all that Israel has ever stood for. Lead your captivity captive!' And that is precisely what Barak proceeded to do.

Israel's poets never forgot it. When the psalmist makes his historical account he has interesting phrases to use, 'You ascended on high, leading a host of captives in your train and receiving gifts among men' (Ps 68:18). The phrase has a long history and appears once more in the crucial passage of Ephesians 4 from the pen of Paul. He is thinking of the warfare, the great objective of bringing the saints to the unity of the faith and the enemies that are all around, of the battle faced by the evangelist, pastor and teacher, and he comes with this glorious observation: 'But grace was given to each one of us according to the measure of Christ's gift. Therefore it says, "When he ascended on high he led a host of captives, and he gave gifts to men"' (vv. 7–8).

Who is big enough to fulfil this but the Messiah? 'In that case,' says Paul, 'if it says he ascended up on high, it must imply that before he ascended he descended into the very lower parts of our planet' (v. 9). He did indeed! Coming down in his incarnation our blessed Lord descended and in the return he 'ascended far above all the heavens, that he might fill all things' (v. 10), and from the spoil that he has taken from the conquering general he has distributed gifts.

There were some pretty hardheaded military commanders on the other side. I can think of Saul of Tarsus, whose pen wrote these words. What an opponent he would have been in any debate, what a campaigner against the truth revealed in Jesus Christ our Lord. How mercilessly he harassed the early believers. The ascended Christ met and conquered him, took him as spoil and gave him to the church as a gift, an apostle for the building up of the church. What a tremendous victory it was on the Damascus road when the ascended Christ conquered his chief enemy, Paul.

David Gooding, The Lord Saves His People: Fourteen Seminars on the Book of Judges, p. 58

19th October

THE DESTRUCTION AND REDEMPTION OF JERUSALEM

Reading: Luke 21:5–31

So also, when you see these things taking place, you
know that the kingdom of God is near. (v. 31)

The temple would of course be destroyed, its age-long testimony to God obliterated (see vv. 5–6). But when its chief priests took the Father's well beloved Son and killed him, God was not prepared to allow their temple to continue indefinitely as an alternative witness to the true God. A religion which officially denies that Jesus is the Son of God 'has not the Father', says John (see 1 John 2:23 KJV).

Here we should perhaps make the obvious, naive point that the destruction of Jerusalem was not something God gave to the Christians to do: he gave the task to pagan Gentiles, as in earlier centuries he had given it to the Assyrians (see Isa 10:5–15). The anti-Semitism of mediaeval and modern so-called Christian countries has been nothing but diabolical and satanic in its origin.

But next we should notice that divine mercy had limited the divine wrath on Jerusalem even before it began: Jerusalem, said Christ, was to be trodden down by the Gentiles but only 'until the times of the Gentiles be fulfilled' (Luke 21:24). The times of the Gentiles would be marked by centuries of opportunity for the Gentiles to hear of the Saviour and of the gospel which Judaism had officially rejected; and, as we now know, millions would respond. But in themselves the pagan nations would prove to be no better, or less sinful, than Israel; their opportunity to receive the gospel would not last for ever either, nor their ascendancy over Jerusalem. Moreover, as Paul later had to remind his Gentile fellow-Christians, apostasy would eventually rob Christendom of its role as the leading witness to God in the earth as surely as it had robbed Judaism of it; and Israel being at last converted would be restored to her place of witness for God (see Rom 11:13–32). One day, then, Jerusalem's desolations shall be over. The Son of Man shall come in power and great glory amid premonitory cosmic disturbance; redemption shall be completed; the kingdom of God shall come (see Luke 21:26–28, 31). The long waiting will be past.

David Gooding, *According to Luke: The Third Gospel's Ordered Historical Narrative*, pp. 345–6

THE FATHER'S PLAN OF REDEMPTION

Part 6—God's Object Lessons: The Tabernacle

20th October

THE HOLY GOD COMES NEAR

Reading: Psalm 27

*The life was made manifest, and we have seen it, and testify
to it and proclaim to you the eternal life, which was with
the Father and was made manifest to us. (1 John 1:2)*

All the vast universes in space are not big enough to contain the transcendent Lord, yet he volunteered to come and presence himself in the tabernacle, so that his people could come near and know him and discover at close quarters what God was like. They could see the awesomeness of his holiness; and yet they could come unafraid and see the beauty of his holiness.

What a marvel God is. He's done the same for us, you know. Not waiting until we get home at last to heaven, even though for us to be in heaven is a condescension for God, he has come down in the person of Jesus Christ our Lord, making himself such that men might come and retain their awe of him, yet be unafraid and come near enough to see his beauty. I know they had no concepts like you have. 'Blessed are your eyes, for they see what prophets and kings longed to see, and never saw' (see Matt 13:16-17). But even in those far off days something of the beauty of God got through to them. Did you recognize those lovely words from Psalm 27? They were written by a man who knew life's troubles; he had enemies galore on every side, threatening to eat his very flesh. He comforts himself with this: 'In life, through thick and thin, good and ill, this I have made this my one ambition in life, that I might dwell in the house of the Lord, to behold the beauty of the Lord' (v. 4).

Some of you would spend a whole holiday's money to go to Naples or Florence, to see the masterpieces of beauty that men have contrived in this world, and why shouldn't you? Oh, my friend, the God who made beauty, who is beauty, has not only redeemed us, but he invites us to come near to see the beauty of his holiness. If you respond to his invitation, it will while away many an otherwise dreary day, many a difficult patch in life. In business, in politics, even in the home, when difficulties come and life all seems tangled and at cross purposes, there is an escape, my brother, my sister. Not from reality, but, thank God, *into* reality. Into that reality which, in the last analysis, is the whole reason why we were made. Little bits of human clay given eternal life by God, so that we might be able to come and see the beauty of God and enjoy our Creator, who has become our Father and redeemer. That's what life is about: that is reality.

David Gooding, *The Beauty of Holiness: Israel's Sacrificial System and the Christian Faith*, pp. 9–10

21st October

A WAY FOR GOD TO DWELL WITH HIS PEOPLE

Reading: Exodus 40:17–38

And they shall know that I am the LORD their God, who brought them out of the land of Egypt that I might dwell among them. I am the LORD their God. (29:46)

Let's start at the very beginning with that literal generation in the wilderness. God was proposing to take them across it to their promised inheritance; how should he ever get them there?

More than that, God had come down to Sinai to explain to them, 'I bore you on eagles' wings, and brought you to myself' (Exod 19:4). This was no vague typology that didn't apply to them but would apply to the Christian church one day. It was spoken to those folks in the wilderness as well, and God meant it. He was to be their goal, and to be their goal right then. He offered them a personal relationship on the terms of that covenant. In the goodness of his heart he offered a tabernacle so that he might dwell with them. He wanted them and loved them. They were real people, not just pictures in an album for the benefit and instruction of Christians. Insofar as was possible God longed for an experience of them, and for them to have an experience of him. Not when they got into Canaan at last and Solomon should arise and build a temple in all its magnificence; now on the desert sands God would come down and meet with them, form this relationship with them and know them. And they would know him as best they could.

You say, 'How is it possible? How could they—poor, broken, feeble, erring people—maintain any significant and real relationship with the living God in that wilderness?' I'll tell you how. Even the first covenant had a tabernacle and vessels for divine service (see Heb 9:1). Divine ingenuity was not hard up for finding a way and a means whereby those pilgrim ex-slaves might enjoy his company as they travelled home to Canaan. As we read it, two things shall strike us: the tremendous grace of God to those ancient people; and his grace to us in the exceeding glory of the favours we have been given in Christ.

David Gooding, *No Longer Bondmen: Thirteen Studies in the Book of Exodus*, p. 125

22nd October

THE FOUNDATION OF UNITY

Reading: Exodus 26:15–29; 38:25–28

*The hundred talents of silver were for casting the bases of
the sanctuary and the bases of the veil; a hundred bases
for the hundred talents, a talent a base. (38:27)*

We could learn a lesson or two from this God-given illustration. Part of the success of the frames to perform their function of holding up the *mishkān*, the dwelling place of God, was that *they stood in sockets of silver*—every one of them. Each frame had two struts that went down, like a ladder, and there were two sockets, one under each strut. And it wasn't just any old silver; the silver for these sockets came from the *ransom money*. When the census was held in Israel everyone had to bring a ransom [an atonement] for his life in order for God to allow him or her still to live as a registered member of Israel (30:12). That ransom money, being silver, was then taken and moulded and it became, among other things, the bases for the frames—the sockets that gave them solidity. The centre of gravity was lowered and now the heavy weight at the bottom made the frames less likely to topple over. The silver came from the ransom money.

It is a foundational provision and requirement for the true church of God that every believer should stand on the ransom that Christ has provided for our souls. We are redeemed, 'not with perishable things such as silver or gold, but with the precious blood of Christ' (1 Pet 1:18–19). Here is the basis of all Christian unity; to be a true child of God we must each be 'standing' on the precious blood of Christ as our ransom, for Christ gave himself a ransom for all (1 Tim 2:6). Only those who in true repentance and faith receive Christ and take their stand upon his redeeming blood are ransomed. It is a source of serious weakness if the church forgets to proclaim that membership of the house of God depends on an individual's acceptance of the ransom and taking his and her stand on the redeeming blood of Christ.

It is a sorry state of affairs when an evangelical can write in a newspaper, 'If the theory of propitiation is right—that God laid on Christ the iniquity of us all and he suffered the indignation of God against our sin—then God ought to be had up for child abuse.' That was written and published by a professed evangelical. I cite it simply to show the importance of getting our foundation right. Every frame stood on the redemption money and every believer in the house and family of God must be redeemed by the precious blood of Christ.

David Gooding, *The Approach to God: Studies in the Tabernacle*, p. 83

23rd October

THE TABERNACLE—A MODEL OF HEAVENLY THINGS

Reading: Hebrews 8:1–6

They serve a copy and shadow of the heavenly things. For when Moses was about to erect the tent, he was instructed by God, saying, 'See that you make everything according to the pattern that was shown you on the mountain.' (v. 5)

Let's grasp the tabernacle's original, practical purpose: that God might walk with his people. But why should we study it? Well, God thought it was important. Hebrews 8:5 says that God commissioned Moses to make the tabernacle, and charged him that he was to copy exactly the model shown him on the mountain.

'Set your affection on things that are above,' says Paul to us Christians (Col 3:2). Well, how do you do that? 'Set your thoughts,' the Greek actually says. What is heaven like? You'll recall the story of Genesis, when God made man and woman, and put them in the garden, and they broke God's command and sinned and were cast out from the tree of life. When Israel were redeemed, God came down and dwelled in the tabernacle, and the priests were allowed at least into the first division of the tabernacle. I wonder what they felt like. Imagine a young priest, and he's all scrubbed up and the right clothes on, and he's going for the first time ever into the holy place. When he gets in, he sees cherubim all around the place: on the roof, on the side curtain, on the veil. If he knew his Old Testament—let's hope he did—he would have remembered that when Adam and Eve were cast out of the garden, God sent cherubim to guard the way of the tree of life, so the guilty man might not come to it. Here, when he gets into the holy place, are cherubim galore, and they're not preventing his entrance. 'Oh, that thing there looks very much like a tree.' Well, it was. It was a lampstand, actually, but made to look like a tree, with blossoms, buds, and fruit, as if it were alive; a symbol of the tree of life. There is such a tree, isn't there? We don't know really what it's like botanically, but we're told in the last book of the Bible about the tree of life, which is in the paradise of God (Rev 22:7).

I need some help to think about it. I need someone to stimulate my imagination as well as my logical thinking, so I feel eternally grateful to God, because he's condescended to my level and given me symbols of great eternal realities on which I can feast my thoughts.

David Gooding, *Understanding the Old Testament: An Overview of Genesis to Joshua*, pp. 19–20

24th October

THE ALTAR AND COMPLETE FORGIVENESS

Reading: Psalm 130

He himself bore our sins in his body on the tree, that
we might die to sin and live to righteousness. By his
wounds you have been healed. (1 Peter 2:24)

The gospel is so wonderful that it defies human language to describe it. God has promised never to rake up our sins and iniquities against us any more and punish us for them. Why not? Because the punishment was borne by Christ! And because that is so, where you've got forgiveness like that 'there is no longer any offering for sin' (Hebrews 10:18).

Let me use a little analogy. Here's a young couple—at least they were young when it all started. Mr and Mrs Smith are newly married and they've bought a house. They couldn't pay cash so they got a mortgage. They thought they could afford it, but as the days went by and the date came for paying the monthly mortgage it was a bit of a strain. When it was paid they felt marvellous relief. But as the next month came, and then another one they had to keep paying the mortgage. They were paying it like that for thirty-five years. What a strain, constantly having to pay, but the time came when they paid the last monthly mortgage and the whole thing was paid off. Marvellous! As the next month comes to its end, Mrs Smith says to her husband, 'Now, don't you think, just to make sure, we ought to go and pay another instalment?' I don't think Mrs Smith would say anything so silly, do you? It's been paid—there's nothing more to be paid.

That is the glorious fact for all who trust Christ; you don't have to offer anything to get forgiveness. If you should ever come across somebody who feels it's necessary to join in offering God something to get forgiveness, you may be sure that he or she has not 'a conscience yet made perfect,' to use the term that the Bible uses (see 9:9). Once we see that Christ's death for us paid the penalty completely and there's nothing more for us to pay, we can have God's assurance, 'I will remember their sins and their lawless deeds no more' (10:17).

Marvellous, isn't it? I trust we've all been by the cross of Christ, standing at that 'altar', and have had the experience of knowing that God has forgiven and accepted us, and our pathway to him and to his heaven is clear, open and wide.

David Gooding, *The Approach to God: Studies in the Tabernacle*, p. 11

25th October

THE NEED FOR REGULAR WASHING

Reading: Exodus 29:1–4; 30:17–21

Jesus said to him, 'The one who has bathed does not need to wash, except for his feet, but is completely clean. And you are clean, but not every one of you.' (John 13:10)

One of these days the Saviour, in all his rightful glory (and I nearly said pride), shall present the redeemed to his Father with exceeding joy. I wonder whether the Father will say to him, 'Where did you get this bunch of people from?' I can almost hear him saying, 'I got them from a place called Aughrim.' The vast multitude of the redeemed won't know where Aughrim was or is, but never mind! You will be part of the bride that Christ shall present to the Father without any spot or wrinkle, or any such thing.

Why is the constant rinsing, the washing of the feet, important? Well, as our Lord observed to Peter, 'If I do not wash you, you have no share. . . ' (John 13:8). Now notice exactly the preposition he uses. He doesn't say, 'you have no share *in* me'. He says, 'you have no share *with* me'. With him in what? In his work of evangelizing the lost; in his work of tending the redeemed.

You know what young boys are like—they will play football on the road. They stand up against my laurel hedge that I have tended with great care over the years, and if the one who's supposed to be in goal doesn't catch the ball it goes right through my hedge, breaks the whole thing down and I boil inside! In that moment, suppose I saw their parents coming and I say to them, 'Look here! I'm tired of these brats of yours destroying my hedge!' I carry on a bit more like that, and just as they're going away in disgust I say, 'O, we've got some special gospel meetings on at our church, would you like to come?' What do you suppose they would say? If as a businessman I've done a sharp deal with them, how can I sincerely invite them to hear the gospel? Would they even come?

Says Christ, 'If you don't let me begin to cope with those defects, then you will have no share with me in my work of seeking the lost and tending the redeemed (or it will be limited).' That's what is at stake.

David Gooding, The Approach to God: Studies in the Tabernacle, pp. 19–20

26th October

CHRIST—THE LIFE THAT CARRIES THE LIGHT

Reading: Exodus 25:31–40

In him was life, and the life was the light of men. (John 1:4)

We have authority for feeling that the lampstand, like the rest of the tabernacle, was 'a shadow of the good things to come,' a foreshadowing of Christ. And what in particular about Christ did it foreshadow? This was a tree; it looked as if it was alive—buds, branches, blossoms, fruit—and yet it was the thing that carried the light. Seven lamps, one on the central trunk and six on the branches. It reminds me of what John's Gospel says,

> In the beginning was the Word, and the Word was with God, and the Word was God. He was in the beginning with God. All things were made through him, and without him was not any thing made that was made. In him was life, and *the life was the light* of men. (1:1–4)

The lampstand was like a tree; symbolically saying that in it was life, all the stages of life, yet it carried the light! What a superb representation in prophecy of the coming of our Lord, for 'in him was life, and the life was the light of men.'

To understand what John is saying, we must of course read this verse in its context. What life is John talking about? 'All things were made through him, and without him was not any thing made that was made' (v. 3). It's talking about the creation of our vast universe and stating simply but emphatically that everything was made through him and by him. Nor is there anything in the vast universe that wasn't made through him. Where did he get the life from, because, as well as stars and galaxies and rocks and mountains and oceans, this planet is marked by life? It remains still the only one that, as far as we know, has life in it. Where did he get the life from to make it? He didn't get it from anywhere! 'In him was life'—*he is the source of all created life*. 'All things were made through him, and without him was not any thing made that was made. In him was life, and the life was the light of men.' The existence of life in this universe still remains a light to human beings, if they will listen.

David Gooding, The Approach to God: Studies in the Tabernacle, p. 36

27th October

Reading: Exodus 25:23–30

Every Sabbath day Aaron shall arrange it before
the LORD regularly; it is from the people of Israel
as a covenant for ever. (Leviticus 24:8)

Like the lampstand, the table, which stood opposite it on the other side of the Holy Place, was a vessel of presentation. Its function was to hold up and present twelve loaves of bread and a quantity of incense before the presence of the Lord continually (Exod 25:30; 40:23; Lev 24:6–8).

The twelve loaves, then, represented the twelve tribes of Israel; but the table that upheld them and presented them before the Lord did not represent them. Only look at its grandeur. It was made of acacia wood and then overlaid with gold. But not with just any grade of gold: it had to be pure gold, that is, gold of the highest purity obtainable. Round the top of the table ran a moulding of gold. This, apparently, was of solid gold, that is, not wood overlaid with gold. Encircling the table (whether vertically or horizontally is not clear) was a border a hand-breadth deep, and that too had a moulding of solid gold. When the tabernacle was on the move, the table had to be carried. For this purpose four rings were attached, one each on the outside of the four legs, so that two carrying poles could be inserted through them along the length of the table. Even these rings had to be of gold, and the wooden carrying poles had to be overlaid with gold. Then the table had to be equipped with various utensils to be used in the service of the table. There were plates and dishes, pitchers and bowls: and all these too had to be of pure gold, no less. No wonder the table is referred to as 'the pure table' (Lev 24:6) just as the lampstand is called 'the pure lampstand' (v. 4).

This, then, was no ordinary table of merely functional design. It was sumptuously grand in its every detail. It was in fact God's own provision for upholding and presenting his people before his presence for his own satisfaction and delight. That loaves made of common-though-fine-flour should be placed on such a majestic table is for its very contrast striking enough. But that these loaves should by God's own choice symbolically represent the twelve tribes of his redeemed, but often erring, people bespeaks a wealth of divine grace that is uncountable.

David Gooding, *The Riches of Divine Wisdom: The New Testament's Use of the Old Testament*, pp. 289–90

28th October

THE INCENSE OF OUR WORSHIP

Reading: Exodus 30:1–10, 34–38

For we are the aroma of Christ to God among those who are being
saved and among those who are perishing. (2 Corinthians 2:15)

Aaron had to burn incense twice a day: in the morning when he dressed
the lamps, and again in the evening when he lit them. Now the oil for the
lamps was extracted from olives by beating them. Then the oil had to be
refined to remove any particles of the skin or flesh of the olives that may
have fallen into the oil (Lev 24:2). Even so, the trimming of wicks when
they were burnt and greasy would have been a smelly business; and a new
wick, when it is lit can at first emit more fumes than light. This was, of
course, a natural weakness inherent in the use of oil lamps in the ceremonial
service of God. Some have suggested, therefore, that the twice daily burning
of incense was originally intended to cover the unpleasant smell from the
lamps that otherwise would be unacceptable in the presence of God, and
perhaps offensive to him.

Scripture does not explain why the burning of the incense had to coincide
with the trimming and lighting of the lamps. But of this we can be sure: God
was pleased with the fragrance of the incense; for it was he who specified
its ingredients, and commanded it to be made for his pleasure and no one
else's (Exod 30:34–38). It is not inconceivable that in the years of Israel's
spiritual childhood (see Gal 4:1–3), the fragrance of the incense could have
carried a metaphorical, if not a symbolical, meaning. We know from God's
explicit statements elsewhere that God dislikes bad smells, both moral and
ceremonial; and he is not afraid to express his disgust in metaphorical language. He warns Israel that, should their physically sweet-smelling sacrifices
be accompanied by lives of immorality and religious infidelity, 'I will make
your sanctuaries desolate, and I will not smell your pleasing aromas' (Lev 26:31
ESV). Again, when Israel adopted pagan rituals with their pseudo–recipes
for holiness, God's disgust was outspoken: 'These are a smoke in my nostrils,
a fire that burns all the day' (Isa 65:5).

This carries a voice for us even today. Not all forms of worship are acceptable
to God. On the other hand, sacrificial giving in the cause of Christ is 'an odour
of a sweet smell, a sacrifice acceptable, well-pleasing to God' (Phil 4:18 KJV).
God still likes nice smells!

David Gooding, The Riches of Divine Wisdom: The New Testament's Use of the Old Testament, pp. 293–4

THE FATHER'S PLAN OF REDEMPTION

Part 7—God's Object Lessons:
Holy Days, Feasts and Sacrifices

29th October

NOT LED BY A SPIRIT OF SLAVERY

Reading: Galatians 5:1–15

*I am the LORD your God, who brought you out of the land
of Egypt, out of the house of slavery. (Exodus 20:2)*

Israel's year was punctuated by certain holy days, which God himself had
instituted for the good of his people. It was not that God disagreed with
work, even with hard work; he is a tremendous believer in work. What
a sane and salutary thing it is to have a job of work to occupy muscles and
brain. God instituted these holidays because he was against slavery and it
is so very easy in this fallen world for work of various kinds to descend
into being slavery. God was against slavery in Israel in regard to their daily
toil; he is still against slavery when it comes to the matter of our Christian
salvation and the manner in which we lead our Christian lives.

Paul tells us, 'You did not receive the spirit of slavery to fall back into fear,
but you have received the Spirit of adoption as sons, by whom we cry, "Abba!
Father!"' (Rom 8:15). It is a very kind and loving thing of God to tell us about
the Holy Spirit's working in our lives in negative terms. We are surrounded,
both without and within, by all sorts of urgings and demands, and at times
we need to be able to know which of them are from God's Holy Spirit and
which are false urges that would lead us into slavery. If younger Christians
find urges within themselves that terrify them, or run their Christian work
into a kind of bondage that somehow they feel they dare not stop—for if
they did they would in some way be displeasing God—they should bear this
verse in mind. God's Holy Spirit will never reduce our lives to slavery; we
have not received the spirit of bondage again to fear. God wants hard work
and sacrifice from us, but certainly not slavery.

Young people sometimes start with good and admirable zeal for the Lord.
They set about serving him, praying, witnessing and striving until, before
they are aware of it, they become so involved that their nerves are frayed and
they may become victim to psychological urges that will drive them towards
breakdown. Sometimes they find that they cannot stop, for the voice that
urges them simulates the Holy Spirit and they feel that it would be a sin to
stop. It is a merciful provision of our Father, and absolutely typical of his heart,
that he reminds us that the Spirit by whom he leads us is not a spirit of slavery.

David Gooding, *The Feasts of the Lord: Studies on the Feasts Appointed by the Lord for Israel*, p. 13

30th October

THE SABBATH

Reading: Isaiah 46:1–7

*So God blessed the seventh day and made it
holy, because on it God rested from all his work
that he had done in creation. (Genesis 2:3)*

God made the heaven and earth in six days and rested on the seventh day. He made the seventh day holy, so Israelites were to work six days each week and rest on the seventh day. Why? To remind them that God made the world—they didn't make it! When we go about sad-faced, heaving and sighing, you would think we had the responsibility for keeping the whole universe going, but we do not. God made it and he made us; but not so that life should crowd out our joy and gladness and burden us with an impossible slavery. He made us to be free. Sin would make slaves of us, but he redeemed us so we may increasingly know what it is to be a freeborn child of the God who made everything.

If we are wise, we shall learn the spirit of this. We are not obliged by the requirements of the law to observe one day in seven as a Sabbath, but we allow ourselves time from our daily work—and indeed, from our spiritual responsibilities—to sit back and rest in God. We are to contemplate the fact that it is he who has made us and that he said, 'I have made, and I will bear; I will carry and will save' (Isa 46:4).

There are many who have burdens that are utterly crushing. Don't criticize them and say that they should have a smiling face, or that they are a bad testimony for Christ. That would be very hurtful. They may have personal pain, bereavement, or sorrow in their family. Those people should not reasonably be expected to laugh and smile. Life brings great burdens, but even under the burdens God invites us to pause and remember that it is he who started the whole world and us in it. He longs to carry us, and we shall find true rest of heart when we learn to let God carry the heaviness.

David Gooding, *The Feasts of the Lord: Studies on the Feasts Appointed by the Lord for Israel*, p. 7

31st October

THE SABBATH REST

Reading: Hebrews 4:1–11

Come to me, all who labour and are heavy laden,
and I will give you rest. (Matthew 11:28)

The Sabbath, a day of rest, was enjoined on Israel to remind them that once they were slaves in Egypt and God delivered them out of bondage. So now they were also to allow their servants a day of rest. We have been redeemed by God and brought into rest, so we have the responsibility if we are employers to see that we do not make life a misery for our employees. In consequence of this ordinance the nation of Israel has, even to this day, kept the Sabbath—externally at least. By the time of the New Testament, however, we find that they had made two main mistakes.

They thought they couldn't trust God, so they were tempted to work on the Sabbath. If a Jew in a competitive line of business saw someone up the road open his shop on the Sabbath, he might feel that he could not afford to keep his store shut and so he broke the Sabbath law. That failure to trust God took away his rest and turned life once more into slavery.

At the other extreme there were some religious people who turned the Sabbath into a legal enactment that had to be kept with the strictest observance. They added all sorts of rules and regulations that God never intended and turned the Sabbath of rest into a bondage of misery.

Against that background, our Lord presented himself as the Creator incarnate, the upholder of heaven and earth, the heir of all things; and he stands before us still, saying, 'Come to me, all who labour and are heavy laden, and I will give you rest. Take my yoke upon you, and learn from me, for I am gentle and lowly in heart, and you will find rest for your souls. For my yoke is easy, and my burden is light' (Matt 11:28–30).

We live in an age sadly distraught by all sorts of unrest that takes its terrible toll on our minds and nerves, and hence on our bodies. We need to know the rest of heart that Christ speaks of, and take our spiritual holidays—to come apart with God from our ordinary work and even from our spiritual work, and allow the Lord to refresh our souls and put within us a sense of his rest. Then we can go out to work again; stronger because we are the more secure and more effective since we are the more at peace.

David Gooding, *The Feasts of the Lord: Studies on the Feasts Appointed by the Lord for Israel*, p. 8

1st November

PASSOVER—THE BEGINNING OF THE YEAR

Reading: Numbers 9

For Christ, our Passover lamb, has been
sacrificed. (1 Corinthians 5:7)

There would not have been a nation to celebrate any new year had it not been for Passover. The first Passover was that tremendous occasion when God visited them in Egypt, redeemed them, and set them free to work with him and serve him. This reminds us at once that there can be no true serving of God until we know the grace and wonder of personal redemption through Christ. God's original Passover was precisely and explicitly a deliverance from the house of bondage. They were slaves before, and God visited them for the express purpose that they should be slaves no longer but be free to worship and serve him as his freeborn sons. He instituted this yearly feast of remembrance so that as the years went by they might annually be reminded of God's tremendous intervention to set them free from bondage. He purposed that the yearly remembrance of that deliverance should be the means of keeping them free and save them from lapsing again into all kinds of slavery.

There would be, among others, two prominent elements in their remembrance. Firstly, how God visited Egypt and delivered them through the blood of the Passover lamb. With solemn and humble gratitude, they remembered the cost of that deliverance from the wrath of God, and with it came a godly concern that their lives should be maintained free for the service of God. Secondly, they would recall how God had delivered them not only by the blood of the Passover lamb, but also with a stretched-out arm and mighty power demonstrated at the Red Sea. If they would start wondering from time to time how they could find strength to perform all the duties God had laid on them, they would be reminded of the source of that strength and the power that God exerted to set them free. Thus each generation would be moved to experience for themselves the power of that self-same God, and that seems to be where the lesson lies for us today.

> Knowing that you were ransomed from the futile ways inherited from your forefathers, not with perishable things such as silver or gold, but with the precious blood of Christ, like that of a lamb without blemish or spot. He was foreknown before the foundation of the world but was made manifest in the last times for the sake of you. (1 Pet 1:18–20)

David Gooding, *The Feasts of the Lord: Studies on the Feasts Appointed by the Lord for Israel*, pp. 14–15

2nd November

Reading: John 11:45–57

*Now that you have come to know God, or rather to be
known by God, how can you turn back again to the weak
and worthless elementary principles of the world, whose
slaves you want to be once more? (Galatians 4:9)*

Then there came the last Passover that our Lord attended (John 18:28). The Jews assembled and refused to go into Pilate's hall to accuse Christ and further his execution lest they be defiled, because they wanted to keep the Passover. They kept it, but it had become an utterly empty and meaningless thing. Once their forefathers had been in Egypt under the domination of a cruel Pharaoh, God had broken their chains and set them free. Now, in that moment, those responsible leaders hugged their chains to themselves.

Coming to the end of his Gospel, John records our Lord's conversation as the cross drew near. Three times he repeated the phrase, 'the ruler of this world' (12:31; 14:30; 16:11). He was the cruel master over so many of those who kept the Passover. Think of Caiaphas, so enamoured of his place in society as high priest and his comfortable occupation under the Romans that he would choose his career and position in this world rather than God's Christ. Think of Judas, whom the ruler of this world had claimed as slave for only thirty pieces of silver. They were dangled so close to his eyes that they blotted out God's divine Son and all that went with him. And what do you think of those disciples who were sitting around when Judas began complaining about the money being spent on Christ? Did the ruler of this world perhaps think of insinuating himself into their hearts a little? He is always up to his tricks. It is not always in great things like wealth or exalted position that he gets his grip on our hearts, but often by little things here and there. He will move us from 'using' this world, until we love it; whatever we say with our lips, when given the choice we will choose things rather than Christ. That is *worldliness*. We can be worldly with very respectable things. Satan can get us to adopt an attitude of heart towards things that are good, lovely, legitimate, or even God-given, until we just take them without allowing them to lead us eventually to God. Our only protection is to dwell constantly near our Lord and near in spirit to his cross. Rules and regulations will never deliver us from worldliness. What a sad mistake some have made who, with all goodwill, have tried to save themselves and their fellow Christians by inventing all sorts of rules.

David Gooding, *The Feasts of the Lord: Studies on the Feasts Appointed by the Lord for Israel*, pp. 18–19

3rd November

THE FEAST OF UNLEAVENED BREAD

Reading: Deuteronomy 16:1–8

*Let us therefore celebrate the festival, not with the old leaven,
the leaven of malice and evil, but with the unleavened
bread of sincerity and truth. (1 Corinthians 5:8)*

The Feast of Passover was immediately followed by the Feast of Unleavened Bread. In fact, so immediately that there was not a day's gap between them. So closely were they together that in subsequent Judaistic history the Feast of Unleavened Bread was, so to speak, extended backwards to include Passover. In Israel, the one could not be kept without the other; both had to be kept together. Unleavened Bread inevitably followed Passover, as night follows day.

The historical reason for this is given to us in Exodus 12:39. The Israelites left Egypt in a hurry and they did not have time to go through the process of making dough and leavened bread. As the years passed the Jewish rabbis came to see in the Feast of Unleavened Bread not only that reminder of a historical fact, which they never forgot, but an added significance. To them, leaven was a symbol of corruption and they swept their houses clear of all leaven for the time of that feast. This symbolized the cleaning out of the unclean thing that comes to roost in one's life from time to time. So they searched their houses high and low for leaven and cast it all out, feeling that it was symbolic of a yearly spring-cleaning and casting out of all that was foul, corrupt and corrupting from their lives.

It is not a bad idea to have such a yearly spring cleaning. Perhaps some of us should do it more regularly, but a yearly stocktaking would be a good thing as well. What have we been allowing, perhaps unconsciously, to infiltrate our lives during this past year? Has there been a deterioration in our standard of holiness? The Apostle Paul learned this idea as a young Jew and he uses it to illustrate a practical exhortation for Christians.

> For Christ, our Passover lamb, has been sacrificed. Let us therefore celebrate the festival, not with the old leaven, the leaven of malice and evil, but with the unleavened bread of sincerity and truth. (1 Cor 5:7–8)

Just as Passover was followed by the Feast of Unleavened Bread, so personal redemption is followed by a holy life where 'leaven' has been cast out.

David Gooding, *The Feasts of the Lord: Studies on the Feasts Appointed by the Lord for Israel*, pp. 19–20

4th November

A HOLY LIFE WITH NO LEAVEN

Reading: James 3:13–4:3

Search me, O God, and know my heart! Try me and know
my thoughts! And see if there be any grievous way in me,
and lead me in the way everlasting! (Psalm 139:23–24)

Were the disciples sincere as they sat in the Upper Room with our Lord, when three times he told them that he would not drink wine again until everything was fulfilled? Wine was something you drank two or three times a day with meals in Palestine. Could the cross be so near that he would not drink another cup of wine with them? They thought they were sincere, but the disciples could not have dreamt it was so near. They had been disputing about who should be first and chief (Matt 20:20–28); then our Lord said, 'One of you will betray me!' (Matt 26:21). They could not grasp that. Surely their hearts could not be so evil?

Evil is nearer than we think! From their experience we too must learn not to trust our own judgment. It is bad enough to tolerate malicious gossiping over dinner tables, but it is a fearful thing to sit at the Lord's Supper having spread or about to spread some malice about a fellow Christian. We are worse than we think we are; so may he make us realists and sincere. We can but tell the Lord, as best we know how, that we want to serve him. He will search us, prove our hearts, and see if there is any wicked way in us, and there is enough in his love, grace and power to help us.

Was our Lord sincere? Let us listen to him as he approached the cross to accomplish our redemption. 'And he said, "Abba, Father, all things are possible for you. Remove this cup from me. Yet not what I will, but what you will' (Mark 14:36). It was no superficial tide of excitement that carried our Lord to the cross. He prayed with all the sincerity of his heart that the cup might pass; but as emotions are not our final guide, neither were they his. Having looked at the very last degree of what it would mean, he said, 'Nevertheless, not my will, but yours, be done' (Luke 22:42).

We are saved because in him and in his life there was no leaven; nothing but absolute sincerity and complete truth. May God make us like him. May he take his word and purify our hearts, and lead us yet more to discover his grace, love and power so that, as freeborn children, we may journey resolutely towards home.

David Gooding, *The Feasts of the Lord: Studies on the Feasts Appointed by the Lord for Israel*, p. 22

5th November

THE FEAST OF FIRSTFRUITS

Reading: 1 Corinthians 15:12–34

When the perishable puts on the imperishable, and the mortal
puts on immortality, then shall come to pass the saying that
is written: 'Death is swallowed up in victory'. (v. 54)

At the Feast of Firstfruits, the farmer in Israel would be truly thankful for the corn having gone into the ground and dying, coming up again and producing his sheaf. If it hadn't come up, he would have had no business and he and his family would have died. Then he got to thinking, 'What will happen when I die? Do I come up again?' They had looked forward to coming into the promised land and reaping the harvest, but when they had eaten the grapes and they were gone once again, was that all there was to it?

God was ready with the answer for them, 'No, that is not all there is to it!' His words are marvellous, and beyond description,

> On this mountain the LORD of hosts will make for all peoples a feast of rich food, a feast of well-aged wine, of rich food full of marrow, of aged wine well refined. And he will swallow up on this mountain the covering that is cast over all peoples, the veil that is spread over all nations. He will swallow up death for ever; and the LORD GOD will wipe away tears from all faces, and the reproach of his people he will take away from all the earth, for the LORD has spoken. It will be said on that day, 'Behold, this is our God; we have waited for him, that he might save us. This is the LORD; we have waited for him; let us be glad and rejoice in his salvation.' (Isa 25:6–9)

Glorious as the harvest was, it was really only a faint glimmering in advance, at the physical level, of a vastly more glorious future that God had waiting for them. God said, 'I shall bring up my vintage wine one of these days. You have not tasted wine yet; you have not known what joy is yet. One day I shall make this a feast of wine, well prepared. I shall wipe away tears and death itself shall be swallowed up in victory. And then you shall be so full of unutterable joy!'

And they would say, 'Yes, we always thought there was more to it than this!'

When death is swallowed up in victory, how men shall laugh and cry in the very joy of their gladness, and their tears will be done away with forever.

David Gooding, The Feasts of the Lord: Studies on the Feasts Appointed by the Lord for Israel, pp. 10–11

6th November

THE FEAST OF TABERNACLES

Reading: Leviticus 23:33–44

*He will wipe away every tear from their eyes, and death shall be
no more, neither shall there be mourning, nor crying, nor pain any
more, for the former things have passed away. (Revelation 21:4)*

There was a second stage of the harvest. It gave way to the Feast of Tabernacles, when men forgot their groans and tears and difficulties, put on their holiday-best and went camping with God for the sheer delight of it. God commanded that they do this. They joined in that week of freedom and release, which they could not enjoy for the rest of the year. They lived in booths and took time to remember how their ancestors had come out of Egypt, and God had made them live in tents as they journeyed across the Sinai Peninsula to their inheritance. There had been many dangers, and some of them concluded that because the journey across the wilderness was so long, there was no inheritance to go to. Some had lost heart, but some persevered and came through.

So it is with us. As we shall look back on life's journey and pilgrimage, we shall smile over those problems and heartaches that now seem so insurmountable and we shall understand why God led us that way.

The people of Israel liked being in their booths so much that God gave them permission to have an eighth day as well. Seven days, and then an eighth! Of course it always ended, and they went back home. But the time is coming when it shall not end. There is a millennium coming, and afterwards a glorious 'eighth day' that shall never end. The programme is that the Lord shall come for us and raise the dead saints and change the living ones, and we shall be caught up together to meet him in the air. Death shall be swallowed up in victory.

That is not true now. Death is still a defeat; but when children get tired and beyond themselves, sleep is no disaster. As we lay our elderly loved ones to rest, we comfort our hearts that God will bring with him those who have fallen asleep when the Lord comes (1 Thess 4:14). But when death attacks a man or woman in his or her prime, what an ugly thing it is, what a defeat. We should cry if we have to when we sorrow over the death of a loved one. *It is not supposed to be a victory.* But although that battle is lost, the war will not be lost. When the Lord comes, he shall raise the dead and change the living.

David Gooding, The Feasts of the Lord: Studies on the Feasts Appointed by the Lord for Israel, pp. 38–9

7th November

THE PURPOSE OF THE OLD TESTAMENT SACRIFICES

Reading: Hebrews 10:1–14

But in these sacrifices there is a reminder of sins
every year. For it is impossible for the blood of
bulls and goats to take away sins. (vv. 3–4)

I had five brothers and sisters and when we were children our parents gave us a toy sweet shop. Perhaps their hope was that it would keep us quiet on a wet Saturday afternoon! Of course the girls were in charge of the shop and they dispensed the sweets. Then we were given toy money—it wasn't real money. So we had to come to the girls and order the sweets and pay the toy money. Even when I was an infant I knew the sweets weren't genuine; they tasted horrible if you tried to eat them. And I knew the money wasn't real money. But you see my parents were a little bit crafty, weren't they? They were teaching these infants, right from the earliest time onwards, that even sweets cost money, which served us in good stead when we grew up a little bit further and we had to deal with real sweets and real money.

In his mercy to the people of Israel in their spiritual infancy, God taught them the cost of sin. The shedding of the blood of animals was like the toy money; it was impossible that the blood of bulls and goats should put away sin. Animals know nothing of a bad conscience; it's we human beings who sometimes go to bed with a bad conscience. That is the glory and the burden of being human. So in the days of their spiritual infancy God was teaching his people the cost of sin, and in parable how the cost might be paid for.

It was fulfilled of course in the coming of our blessed Lord Jesus Christ, who with his assembled apostles around him chose to be remembered for all time in the form of bread and wine. And of the wine he said, 'This is my blood of the covenant, which is poured out for many' (Mark 14:24). Thus we remember our Lord primarily as the one who gave his body and his blood for the forgiveness of our sins.

David Gooding, The Approach to God: Studies in the Tabernacle, pp. 12–13

8th November

BURNING THE FAT

Reading: Leviticus 6:8–13

He shall arrange the burnt offering on it and shall
burn on it the fat of the peace offerings. (v. 12)

Why were they to burn the fat? Well, here you must forget for a moment all the spiritual interpretations of the fat. You put the fat on because it helped the fire to burn, didn't you? In my youth sometimes people tried to light the fire and it didn't go very well, and they poked it and it didn't flame. It was quite a bad thing to do, but they would go out and get a can of paraffin, and throw some on the fire. They had to be very careful that it didn't scorch their eyebrows off and explode in their face, but paraffin helped the thing get going. So it was with the fat. None of the Israelites was allowed to take the fat from any offering; it was the Lord's. But one of its uses was to keep the fire burning. Fat was regarded in ancient Israel as the best of anything. You talked about the fat of your wheat, for instance, meaning the best part of your wheat. The most luscious part, the very good wheat, was the fat of the wheat, and fat represents the health of the bullock. My brothers, my sisters, if we want to keep the fire going, how shall we do it? We shall bring and prepare to sacrifice the best we have, the best we can do. Is that too much?

'He . . . shall burn on it the fat of the peace offerings' (v. 12). The peace offerings were an elaborate system. They could be used in thanksgiving to God for all his benefits; as the basis of a meal, where you invited your friends around to celebrate with them God's goodness to you; and you could make a feast for others. The best we have, given over to Christ to keep the fire going. Our zeal for the Lord, our zeal for the lost, our persistence in Sunday school teaching or whatever it is we do for the Lord, our persistence in looking after the elderly believers; it will require the best we have. 'Fire shall be kept burning upon the altar continually; it shall not go out' (v. 13).

David Gooding, *Understanding the Old Testament: An Overview of Genesis to Joshua*, pp. 33–4

9th November

ACCEPTABLE GIFTS

Reading: Leviticus 22:17–33

Therefore let us be grateful for receiving a kingdom that cannot be shaken, and thus let us offer to God acceptable worship, with reverence and awe, for our God is a consuming fire. (Heb 12:28–29)

As the people drew near to God, they were to be allowed to bring their gifts. That was an awesome privilege, but what gifts should they bring? God in his mercy supplied them with a high priest who could tell them what the Lord would find acceptable. I guarantee that if you had it in your heart one of these days to give the Queen a gift, you might scratch your head a little bit. What could you possibly get that the Queen would find acceptable; and whether Woolworths would have it, or Marks and Spencer. She's a little bit difficult to please, for the simple reason that she, as they say, has everything.

To be allowed to bring gifts to almighty God who has everything—what do I bring? They were humble gifts that God allowed his people to bring, but even then they needed a priest to help them. Imagine old Zedekiah from Galilee, coming down with a pig under his arm! He meant it well, but a horrified priest grabs him just as he's about to come into the gate of the tabernacle.

'Wait a minute, you can't come in here with that.'

'What's wrong with it? It's a beautiful pig.'

'Well, so it might be, and your intention was very good, but I'm afraid God doesn't like pigs. Not as gifts.'

'Oh, but my Gentile neighbours—'

'I know, Athenians and everybody else bring pigs, but God doesn't like pigs.'

Have you ever felt that difficulty when you come to worship the Lord bringing your gifts? What shall you say or what shall you do? Where will you begin and where will you stop? Oh, thank God, he's given us a great high priest. If you find worship difficult and you don't know what to say, come to your high priest, my dear brother, my sister, tell him you find this too big a thing to do, and please will he help you. That's what he's for.

David Gooding, *The Beauty of Holiness: Israel's Sacrificial System and the Christian Faith*, p. 10

THE FATHER'S PLAN OF REDEMPTION

Part 8—The Promised Inheritance

10th November

WHAT THE LAW COULD NOT DO

Reading: Galatians 3:5–25

And he said to them, 'I am 120 years old today. I am no longer able to go out and come in. The LORD has said to me, "You shall not go over this Jordan."' (Deuteronomy 31:2)

Moses had delivered the Israelites from Egypt, but he could not bring them into their inheritance. That had to wait for the coming of Joshua, and what Moses couldn't do Joshua did.

We have a vested interest and as we think about it we shall see the parallel between that history and ours. In Galatians 3 Paul is arguing about how the inheritance is to be secured. Is it by the keeping of the law? 'Certainly not,' says Paul. The covenant was made with Abraham long before the law was given (see v. 17). In the covenant there was no mention of the keeping of the law; it was a covenant of God's absolute grace, given as a gift to Abraham and to his offspring, and therefore utterly irrevocable. The law that came in between cannot alter it. How then is that covenant to be realized and all its blessings secured?

Certainly not through Moses or through the keeping of the law, but through Jesus Christ our Lord. It is 'kept in heaven for you' (1 Pet 1:4). The Holy Spirit is the earnest of the inheritance and one day our very bodies shall be glorified like the body of the Lord Jesus. A vast eternity of God's ingenuity awaits us, providing delight and entertainment beyond our imagination. If we thought that all that blessing depended on our ability to keep the Law of Moses, all of us without exception would give up any hope of ever inheriting so much as one blade of grass or one pot of honey. 'For the law brings wrath' (Rom 4:15)—the law works condemnation. If the inheritance were of the law none of us would have any hope, but it is all of grace. 'That is why it depends on faith, in order that the promise may rest on grace and be guaranteed to all his offspring' (v. 16).

So, in the days when God's promise was being fulfilled at the level of the prototype, it wasn't Moses who brought them into Canaan. He was not allowed to do it. In fact, he couldn't do it. But what Moses couldn't do, Joshua did. In the extended sense it is the same with us. The law could never turn us into heirs of God and joint heirs with Christ, but our blessed Joshua, the captain of our salvation—Jesus Christ our Lord—has done it.

David Gooding, What Moses Could Not Do: Nine Studies in the Book of Joshua, pp. 11–12

11th November

CROSSING THE JORDAN

Reading: Joshua 4:10–18

According to his great mercy, he has caused us to be born again
to a living hope through the resurrection of Jesus Christ from
the dead, to an inheritance that is imperishable, undefiled,
and unfading, kept in heaven for you. (1 Peter 1:3–4)

The people of Israel didn't have to cross the Jordan by themselves. A great miracle was done, designed to glorify Joshua and set Israel's heart aflame with the wonder of their God. God himself went through the river. The priests were told to take up the ark and the people were told to follow it at a distance. All eyes were to be concentrated on the priests, and in particular upon that ark as it approached the river.

If we are going to understand the significance of it, we must start by believing what Israel believed. At this stage in our studies I have not begun typology. I'm talking now of an event that happened thirteen hundred years BC in the physical country of Palestine, at the literal river Jordan. Jordan is in flood and Israel are waiting to go through. They watch as the ark is lifted up by the priests and as it proceeds towards the river. Israel believed that that ark was the very throne of the Lord of the whole earth. They believed that Jehovah was God, the maker and owner of heaven and earth, and that, in his great mercy, the transcendent Lord had come down and presenced himself upon that ark.

Nature had put a great barrier in front of them, the river Jordan and its threat of death. How would Israel get through it? Watch the great miracle as the Lord of heaven and earth comes, seated upon his throne on the ark. The priests' feet came to the borders of the water, nature recognized her great Creator, and the Creator went through. I don't know if the king of Jericho thought that the river Jordan being in flood was his first line of defence, and that it would stop Israel getting in. But I know this: if God is determined to bring his people into their inheritance there is no force or obstacle in the whole of nature—be it on earth, in heaven, or under the earth—that can stand in his way. Jordan, with its threat of death, bowed and allowed the Creator through.

David Gooding, *What Moses Could Not Do: Nine Studies in the Book of Joshua*, p. 27

12th November

OUR INHERITANCE IS NOT ONLY HEAVEN

Reading: Psalm 105

Now therefore arise, go over this Jordan, you and all this people,
into the land that I am giving to them, to the people of Israel.
Every place that the sole of your foot will tread upon I have
given to you, just as I promised to Moses. (Joshua 1:2–3)

I'm aware, of course, that I shall inherit the heavenlies with Christ. But I'm not altogether convinced I ought not to inherit Palestine as well. Are you? Tell me, is the Lord Jesus going to inherit Palestine, or not? You say, 'Of course he'll inherit Palestine: he'll inherit the whole earth.' Perhaps you think that our Lord shouldn't be so interested in earth, but in heavenly things. But listen, 'Ask of me,' says God to the Messiah, 'and I'll give you the uttermost part of the earth as well' (see Ps 2:8). I tell you, there's not one square inch of territory in heaven nor on earth, but that our Lord shall inherit it all. And I've read in the Bible somewhere that we're heirs of God and joint heirs with our Lord Jesus Christ, are we not? (see Rom 8:17). On what ground do you suppose and presume that you're going to have this inheritance?

Oh, I thank God we're not dependent on some verses and analogies from the Old Testament to decide that matter. The Epistle to the Galatians is abundantly clear, and so is Romans 4. That promise made to Abraham and all those blessings and that inheritance and that covenant, all come to us on these terms—that Christ was made a curse for us. We had broken God's law and were under its curse, and had failed every test that Moses proposed, and therefore merited destruction as equally as any old Canaanite ever merited it. But the glorious news is this: that in our great Joshua, Jesus Christ, we may enter that inheritance.

The promise to Abraham and to his seed that he should be heir, not only of Canaan but of the world, was not given to him when he was in circumcision, but before he was circumcised. It was given to him by that same promise by which he was justified by faith in Genesis 15, and in that very same breath he was given a covenant that guaranteed him the inheritance. Oh, how lovely to think together of our great Joshua who brings us, even us sorry sinners, into the great inheritance.

David Gooding, *Entering the Inheritance: Studies in Joshua 1–12*, pp. 10–11

13th November

THE EARNEST OF OUR INHERITANCE

Reading: Ephesians 1:13–23

In him you also, when you heard the word of truth, the gospel of your salvation, and believed in him, were sealed with the promised Holy Spirit, who is the guarantee of our inheritance until we acquire possession of it, to the praise of his glory. (vv. 13–14)

If we want to know more of what our inheritance means to us as Christians, we could start by considering the *earnest* of our inheritance. The New Testament uses that term more than once. Not only do we have an 'inheritance that is imperishable, undefiled and unfading, kept in heaven for [us]' (1 Pet 1:4), but God has already given us a part payment, an earnest (Eph 1:14). Already now we have some of the joys that we shall have in full one day. The great earnest of our inheritance is the Holy Spirit of God himself (2 Cor 5:5). We have the earnest of the Spirit in our hearts. I have no need to remind you of all that that means and what the blessed Holy Spirit has done within us, regenerating us, giving us the very life of God already, introducing us into peace with God. We 'have access in one Spirit to the Father' (Eph 2:18), giving us that deep sense of assurance as he pours out the love of God in to our hearts, leading us to cry in genuine reality, 'Abba, Father.' Already sensing and knowing that God is our Father, we are children of God; and if children of God then heirs of God, and joint heirs with Jesus Christ our Lord (see Rom 8:14–17). The very terminology here is based on those ancient parts of the Old Testament and the book of Joshua in particular.

Not only is our inheritance concerned with spiritual blessings. Paul reminds us that the bodies in which we dwell are but fragile tents, blown about with the winds, dilapidated and coming down. It is but temporary accommodation. 'For we know that if the tent that is our earthly home is destroyed, we have a building from God, a house not made with hands, eternal in the heavens' (2 Cor 5:1).

We long, therefore, to 'be away from the body and at home with the Lord' (v. 8). This is not escapism. It isn't the word and attitude of somebody for whom life has been too much and he's glad to escape it. 'The thing that has made heaven real to us,' said Paul, 'and the certainty that we shall have an eternal building—our bodies suited to our glorified personalities—is that God has already given us an earnest of it, the Holy Spirit in our hearts' (1:22).

David Gooding, *What Moses Could Not Do: Nine Studies in the Book of Joshua*, pp. 6–7

14th November

OUR INDIVIDUAL INHERITANCE

Reading: Psalm 16:1–6

*The LORD is my chosen portion and my cup; you hold
my lot. The lines have fallen for me in pleasant places;
indeed, I have a beautiful inheritance. (vv. 5–6)*

When they got into the land the surveyors went round and measured out the farms. The land was divided up and given to each of the Israelites for their enjoyment.

As the centuries went by and the Israelites pondered the tremendous blessing that God had given them in their inheritance, they went beyond the literal land of Canaan—beyond the grass and the cows and the milk and the honey.

What does David mean, 'The lines have fallen for me'? He's thinking of the ancient story—when Israel went into the land, eventually they described the land and wrote it down in a book. Lots were cast and each citizen received his bit of land. Some of the citizens thought it was marvellous, because they got rich countryside. Some of them weren't so pleased, as they got bits that were difficult to farm. Some were very content and some were not so content. As the centuries went by, the great prophets and psalmists thought not only of the physical inheritance that God had given them; they began to think of the great spiritual inheritance they enjoyed, even in that far off day. The psalmist says, 'It's the Lord who has given me this three acres and a cow! The Lord himself is behind the inheritance that is the portion of my cup. I can honestly and sincerely say that in the bit that's been measured out for me, the lines have fallen for me in pleasant places; indeed, I have a beautiful inheritance.'

If we went no further than that, we've been moved to think of a wonderful thing. The infinite God has not only brought us into an inheritance and qualified us to enjoy it, but he has given to each one of us our particular share of that inheritance. You have an experience of the Lord in common with me; and then you have your own experience of the Lord that is totally peculiar to you. As you think of the glorious inheritance that God has given you in Christ, I wonder can you honestly say, 'Thank God, the lines have fallen for me in pleasant places; I have a beautiful inheritance'?

David Gooding, *What Moses Could Not Do: Nine Studies in the Book of Joshua*, pp. 5–6

15th November

USING OUR BLESSINGS FOR GOD

Reading: Joshua 20:1—21:3

Woe to me if I do not preach the gospel! (1 Corinthians 9:16)

When the seven tribes were eventually given their particular inheritances two things are specially mentioned. In the first place, they had to give up a number of cities to become cities of refuge, so that if anybody accidentally killed a fellow human being he could flee there and find security and safety from the hands of the avenger of blood. So the Israelites had to give back some of their inheritance for the salvation of men who were in mortal danger. Then they had to give up a lot more cities for the Levites to dwell in. It was marvellous to have God dwelling among them in a tabernacle; but he would need to be served, so they had to give back some of their inheritance to support the Levites who should maintain the service of God in his tabernacle on behalf of the nation.

We have a vast spiritual inheritance. It is given free, gratis, and for nothing, but am I not right in thinking that God has a claim on us and what he has given us? One of our richest blessings is the lovely bunch of grapes of forgiveness, such as David munched when he wrote his glorious psalm, 'Blessed is the one whose transgression is forgiven, whose sin is covered' (Ps 32:1). What a thing it is to sit down and enjoy those lovely grapes out of our God-given inheritance. Tell me, has God given that wonderful gift of forgiveness just for our own selfish benefit, or are there men and women around us who are in mortal danger? The avenger of blood is on their case and they need to be saved. God has a claim on us. He'll expect us to take some of the blessings that we have been given—the spiritual freedom, the spiritual joy, the knowledge of salvation—and use them to construct cities of refuge for men and women who are in mortal danger of perishing eternally. You see, there could come creeping over me at times a kind of a feeling that because I'm saved and secure and I know the wonderful forgiveness of the Lord, that's all I need. No, Christian friend, never! The Lord who has given us these great gifts requires that in return we share in the evangelization of the world.

David Gooding, What Moses Could Not Do: Nine Studies in the Book of Joshua, p. 66

16th November

BUILDING FOR THE ETERNAL CITY

Reading: 1 Chronicles 29

In addition to all that I have provided for the holy
house, I have a treasure of my own of gold and
silver, and because of my devotion to the house of
my God I give it to the house of my God. (v. 3)

When David was older he voluntarily abdicated and made Solomon his regent. Why did he do this? So that he could get on with the job that was nearer to his heart than anything else on earth. Not his great victories, nor his great palaces; not even the question of power was anything to him, such as the pursuit upon which he spent his last days to the full. And that was preparing the treasure for the building of the house of the Lord and organizing the people. So that, when the day dawned and the temple was built and the presence of God descended and filled it, the people might be ready, each in his or her place, and the glory of God might fill them and express itself through them. Their many and variegated gifts would hold forth and come back to God in a never-ceasing stream of glory.

For that, David gave his last moments. As he stood there with the pile of treasure that had been collected, and the people standing around him waiting for the day when the temple would be erected, he was moved to pray.

> And now we thank you, our God, and praise your glorious name. But who am I, and what is my people, that we should be able thus to offer willingly? For all things come from you, and of your own have we given you. For we are strangers before you and sojourners, as all our fathers were. Our days on the earth are like a shadow, and there is no abiding. (vv. 13–15)

What bearing do these words have upon us? What would we do with our life, if today it should dawn in our hearts that it is but a shadow and soon will be gone? God invites us to join King David and his hosts in preparing the material that shall adorn the eternal city of God. He gives us the grace, the energy, the time, the salvation, the knowledge of his word and the fruit of the Spirit to collect the material, quarry it, polish and shape it by our preaching, our prayers, our pastoring, our love, our kindness and our care. We are God's fellow-workers, but let us take heed how we build.

David Gooding, *God's Great Salvation: Lessons from the Lives of Old Testament Characters*, p. 30

17th November

THE FIGHT FOR OUR INHERITANCE

Reading: 2 Timothy 3

I have no greater joy than to hear that my
children are walking in the truth. (3 John 4)

We must move on now to the second phase of the Christian conquest of our inheritance. Our Lord is now risen and ascended triumphantly to glory, but the enemy still operates. The great strategic goal is that all the people of God should be brought to 'the oneness of the faith' (see Eph 4:4–6). Do you suppose that is ever possible: will there ever be a time when we shall all believe the same? Even in heaven hadn't we better agree to differ? Whatever view we take of it down here on earth, we are committed by our Sovereign Commander to that goal and objective. Realism tells us that we have not arrived there yet, but we are to push on,

> until we all attain to the unity of the faith and of the knowledge of the Son of God, to mature manhood, to the measure of the stature of the fullness of Christ, so that we may no longer be children, tossed to and fro by the waves and carried about by every wind of doctrine, by human cunning, by craftiness in deceitful schemes. (vv. 13–14)

We must not allow ourselves to become cynical. There is a battle and Paul reminds us of the craftiness of men who wait to deceive. We are well used to the idea that when the evangelist preaches the gospel he is in some sense wrestling against principalities and powers, but we sometimes forget that the same thing is true of the Christian teacher and the pastor striving to lead the Lord's people to maturity, not just in their emotions but in their beliefs, to bring them to the oneness of the faith. There is severe dishevelment of Christian belief in all directions. The reason is that there is a satanic mind behind it, far more interested in opposing your progress as a believer than in tempting you to some lurid vice. Because God is truth, Satan has his innumerable wiles and minions fighting the battle to cause disunity amongst the people of the Lord, in particular in what they believe.

David Gooding, *The Lord Saves His People: Fourteen Seminars on the Book of Judges*, p. 57

THE FATHER'S PLAN OF REDEMPTION

Part 9—God's Provision for Us on the Journey:
The Blessed Holy Spirit

18th November

CHRIST HAD TO GO AWAY

Reading: John 8:19–30

Nevertheless, I tell you the truth: it is to your advantage that
I go away, for if I do not go away, the Helper will not come
to you. But if I go, I will send him to you. (John 16:7)

Chapters 7 and 8 of John's Gospel are answers to the problem of God's strategy in sending his Son into the world to be our Saviour. And in both those chapters there is the 'going away'. It is not merely what he said and taught, important though that was, but right from the very beginning there was the announcement that he would be going away, and what that going away was about. It was to make it possible that the Holy Spirit should come; for later the Lord Jesus said, 'If I don't go away the Holy Spirit will not come'. So the 'going away' was not an accident. It was not a question of trying to make the best of it, now that the Jews had crucified him. He was always going away! His going away would make it possible for the Spirit to come. Christ is God's last *word*; he isn't God's last *testimony*. The last and final testimony is the Holy Spirit, bringing satisfaction to those who believe on the Lord Jesus.

Then there is the 'going away' in chapter 8. As we follow the light of this world on our pathway, we have the assurance, to begin with, that to those who are in Christ Jesus 'there is therefore now no condemnation' (Rom 8:1). We have met the I AM at the burning bush of Calvary and have known his forgiveness. He has written the law twice: first, on tablets of stone; and then, by writing the new covenant on the tablets of our hearts and minds (Heb 10:16). He is leading us home to glory, giving us the status of sons and daughters, and educating us as we continue in his word to behave as true, practical children of God. And he is coming one day to take us to the Father's house.

David Gooding, *Four Journeys to Jerusalem: A Series of Seminars on the Gospel of John*, pp. 122–3

19th November

THE GIFT OF THE HOLY SPIRIT

Reading: Acts 2:22–41

*And it shall come to pass afterwards, that I will
pour out my Spirit on all flesh. (Joel 2:28)*

It was this first glorious event, as Peter informed the astonished crowd, that was taking place before their very eyes in the streets of Jerusalem. They had killed God's Son and heir, but his death had not cancelled the promise of the Spirit; it had facilitated its fulfilment. The promise was meant for them and for their children, and indeed for as many the whole world over as the Lord would call (Acts 2:39). And the promise still stood. Already some had received the gracious gift; they too could receive it if they would, for the gift was utterly free. It was nothing less than the Holy Spirit. Not simply one of the Holy Spirit's gifts with which he equips God's people to serve him, but the Holy Spirit himself. 'Repent and be baptized, every one of you, in the name of Jesus Christ so that your sins may be forgiven. And you will receive the gift [note the singular] of the Holy Spirit' (v. 38). They had murdered God's Son; he was offering them his Spirit. They had crucified the second person of the Trinity; he was offering them the third. They had thrown God's Son out of the vineyard in the hope of inheriting the vineyard themselves; now he was inviting them to receive God's Spirit not just into their vineyard but into their hearts, to be their undying life, to be the earnest and guarantee of an infinite and imperishable inheritance. And the gift was offered universally: 'I will pour out my Spirit on all flesh.' In Old Testament times the Holy Spirit had come upon people and inspired them to deeds of power or skill, or to words of prophetic authority. But such people had never been more than a tiny select few. Now the Holy Spirit was offered to all indiscriminately: men and women, young and old, without distinction. Moreover, there was no need for any of them to fear the coming of the great and resplendent Day of the Lord, with all its terrifying signs and judgments. The way of salvation was still what God had said it was through Joel, and still as universally valid: 'Everyone who calls upon the name of the Lord shall be saved' (v. 21). Only now the Lord upon whom they must call was the very Jesus whom they had crucified. He was risen and exalted. God had made him both Lord and Christ (v. 36); and it was the prime purpose of the coming of the Spirit to prove to them that this was so.

David Gooding, *True to the Faith: The Acts of the Apostles–Defining and Defending the Gospel*, p. 67

20th November

BAPTISM IN THE HOLY SPIRIT

Reading: John 1:24–34

*For in one Spirit we were all baptized into one
body—Jews or Greeks, slaves or free—and all were
made to drink of one Spirit. (1 Corinthians 12:13)*

We do well to pause there to grasp the significance of what is being said. Baptism in the Holy Spirit is not some little incidental thing that, among others, happens to you when you trust the Saviour. Baptism in the Holy Spirit is the ministry of the Lord Jesus that marks him out as unique among all the prophets that ever have been, be they Moses or Elijah, or Isaiah himself, not to speak of Ezekiel, Jeremiah, Daniel and Obadiah. Great men of God, inspired as they are, but they fade into their true insignificance in the sight of Jesus Christ, God's Son. What's so different about him? Well, to begin with, he can baptize people in the Spirit. The Holy Spirit isn't just so much stuff, not merely so much power, like electricity is. The Holy Spirit is God. Think who Jesus must be if he can take you and put you in the Holy Spirit. This is one of his unique glories.

To help us see what the Lord Jesus does, we can take an analogy from what John did. John baptized in water. So you come to John and he baptizes you in water. John does the baptizing, meaning he puts you in the water and you get baptized. Then John says, 'I baptize you in water, but there stands one among you and he shall baptize you in the Holy Spirit.' Do you see the parallel? When you come to Christ, Christ does the baptizing. Christ baptizes you in the Spirit: he puts you in the Spirit. This is a magnificent part of our salvation. It is not like icing to decorate your Christian birthday cake. This is the very basis of the gospel. We are humbled at the wonder of it. Because you've met Christ and trusted him, the incarnate Son of deity has not only forgiven your sin and pardoned your transgression, he's taken you and put you in the Holy Spirit. Never let the glory of it depart, never let it be reduced to some minor ecstatic experience.

David Gooding, *The Gift and His Gifts: The Holy Spirit and the Use of Spiritual Gifts*, p. 25

21st November

CALLED ACCORDING TO GOD'S PURPOSE
AND GUIDED BY THE HOLY SPIRIT

Reading: Genesis 24:56–67; Romans 8:26–27

And [God] who searches hearts knows what is the
mind of the Spirit, because the Spirit intercedes for the
saints according to the will of God. (Romans 8:27)

God has invited us; he's called us 'according to purpose'. Having called us, he has a programme for what to do with us. It's ultimately for to be conformed to the image of his Son. Thank God, he's not left it to us to be in final control of the fulfilling of the programme, but the Holy Spirit witnesses that we are children of God (see vv. 15–17), and makes intercession for us according to the mind of God (see vv. 26–27). He knows what the necessary next step ought to be. Whether it is peace and prosperity, some tribulation, or whatever it is that would be necessary for the next step in the programme, the Holy Spirit intercedes according to the mind of God.

It's good, isn't it? The old story is true still, and the analogy is very helpful (Gen 24). When Abraham sent his servant to go down to find a wife for Isaac, and the girl eventually came to the decision, the family said, 'Well, you'd better call and ask her.' And he put the jewels on her which was a bit of diplomacy and enticement, and told her all about his master. Now the question was put by the family, 'Will you go with this man?' That is, would she go with Abraham's servant?

When she said, 'Yes,' the servant didn't say, 'Well, I'm delighted with your response, my dear, and I'm sure when you make your way across the desert to my master's son you won't be disappointed. We look forward to seeing you. Here is my visiting card, and when you come to our place you will find that everything is lovely.'

No, he didn't. When she made her decision, Abraham's servant was in charge to lead the dear woman, and conduct her step by step, and bring her at last to his master's son.

So is the Holy Spirit given, and he intercedes for us according to the mind of God, to see that God's programme is being put into action. He calls for our cooperation, of course, as we are no longer slaves but sons of God.

David Gooding, God's Power for Salvation: Paul's Letter to the Romans, pp. 139–40

22nd November

WALKING BY THE SPIRIT IN NEWNESS OF LIFE

Reading: Romans 8:1–8

. . . having been buried with him in baptism, in which you were also raised with him through faith in the powerful working of God, who raised him from the dead. (Colossians 2:12)

When Jesus of Nazareth comes to be baptized, John says 'I need to be baptized by you, and do you come to me?' (Matt 3:14). John knew the significance of his baptism; it was a confession of repentance, and this man had no sin to repent of. Why would he then be baptized? As we see him stand in the mud of Jordan along with the sinners, the poor, weak, corrupt, and the vicious, we might well ask what this holy Son of God is doing there. This is God's miracle of grace. When you face up to God's judgment and put yourself where you deserve to be—down in the mud so that you can get no lower, with the waters about to go over your head—you will feel an arm coming around you. It is God's holy, sinless Son, standing in your place. That's what he did at Calvary: no person went so low but Christ stood at his or her side.

Continuing the illustration, he came up out of Jordan. 'And when Jesus was baptized, immediately he went up from the water, and behold, the heavens were opened to him, and he saw the Spirit of God descending like a dove and coming to rest on him; and behold, a voice from heaven said, "This is my beloved Son, with whom I am well pleased"' (vv. 16–17).

And what happened next? 'Then Jesus was led up by the Spirit into the wilderness to be tempted by the devil' (4:1). There he was tempted by three great temptations. We have been saved through the judgment and have come out the other side to walk in newness of life. How do we control this unruly flesh? Godly character is built by being constantly led of the Spirit, which does not necessarily mean hearing voices from heaven.

The Holy Spirit is a person and that person is God. He's not a thing. I'm not to use him and switch him on like I switch on electricity. It is for him to use me. The glorious thing about God's Holy Spirit is that he will not repress my personality; he will develop it. He will pray within me and alongside me. He will allow me to express myself as best I can. If my expression of his desires is faltering and sometimes wrong, God will read it as the Holy Spirit intended them. But he will strive against the flesh, for I am called to live according to the Spirit.

David Gooding, *The God of New Beginnings: Eighteen Seminars on the Book of Genesis*, p. 78–9

23rd November

THE WORK OF THE SPIRIT REVEALING THE FATHER

Reading: John 14:15–24

The natural person does not accept the things of the Spirit of God,
for they are folly to him, and he is not able to understand them
because they are spiritually discerned. (1 Corinthians 2:14)

If we are to be brought increasingly closer to the Father, we shall, let us say it reverently, need more than the full revelation of God in Christ. Not of course that there is anything inadequate in that revelation. Far from it. But there is a great inadequacy in our ability to comprehend that revelation.

You can see that if you picture again the eleven men who reclined round the table with our Lord in the Upper Room. Seeing Jesus, Philip and the others were seeing the Father. But they did not properly take in and understand and enjoy all they saw. And why not? Because their minds were full of their own ideas, presuppositions, false expectations, and sheer ignorance.

If they were ever to be brought fully to the Father, they would need not only the full revelation of the Father in Christ, but something to deal with their internal intellectual and emotional blockages, to dissipate the dark clouds of their fears, doubts and misunderstandings, so as to let the light of God's revelation in Christ shine through.

They would need something more. The unaided human spirit, however intellectually sharp, cannot take in the things of God, says Scripture. Only the Spirit of God can understand the things of God. Therefore, if the disciples were ever going to know the Father, they would need the Spirit of God. This is precisely what the Lord Jesus now informs the disciples he will supply: 'I will ask the Father, and he will give you another Helper, to be with you for ever, even the Spirit of truth' (John 14:16-17).

We notice here at once the title that is given to the Spirit. It is not the Spirit of God, nor the Spirit of grace, nor the Spirit of holiness—though he is of course all these things, and is so called elsewhere in Scripture. Our Lord refers to him here as the Spirit of truth. This resonates with what our Lord said earlier: 'I am . . . the truth . . . no one comes to the Father except through me' (v. 6). So now he promises to pray the Father, who in response to his prayer will send the Spirit of truth, not only to be with his people but in them; and, by helping them to grasp the truth about the Father, to bring them ever nearer to the Father.

David Gooding, In the School of Christ: Lessons on Holiness in John 13–17, pp. 92–3

24th November

THE HOLY SPIRIT REVEALS THE
DEEP THINGS OF GOD

Reading: 1 Corinthians 2:10–16

These things God has revealed to us through the Spirit. For the
Spirit searches everything, even the depths of God. (v. 10)

What of the deep things of God? You say, 'That's too much for us, how could we understand them?' God has thought of your difficulty and he has given us his Spirit. Have you ever thought why there has to be a Holy Spirit in addition to God the Son and God the Father? God makes himself known through the Lord Jesus, so why do I need the Holy Spirit? Well, for this reason. God makes himself known perfectly in the Lord Jesus, but how would I ever grasp all that there is in the Lord Jesus? God gives me his Holy Spirit so that, coming alongside my spirit, he can help me to grasp the things of God. It's not left to me.

I have a secret little interest in physics and cosmology, and the other year I had such a lovely experience. I was at a Christian camp away out in Japan, and there I found a real live physicist! He was a good Christian man, who expounded Scripture very well. I couldn't resist the opportunity, and when the formal part of the meeting was over I went up to him with all my barrage of questions about cosmology and big bangs and black holes and all the rest of it. He looked at me benignly and smiled, and then said, 'That's not a very helpful question you've asked.'

Here was me in my ignorance, I knew so little. I didn't even know the right kind of questions to ask. I'd asked a silly question apparently! That's what comes when you're not an expert. How would I begin to know the questions to ask about the deep things of God? The physicist in Japan had done the research, so he knew what questions to ask and he could lead me to fathom some of these deep things. Oh, the wonder of it, my brother, my sister, God has given you his Holy Spirit, who fathoms the deep things of God and is able by the genius of his skill to make them real to you. What a magnificent person and what a marvellous ministry!

David Gooding, *The Gift and His Gifts: The Holy Spirit and the Use of Spiritual Gifts*, pp. 13–14

25th November

THE MINISTRY OF THE SPIRIT OF TRUTH

Reading: 2 Corinthians 3

For through him we both have access in one
Spirit to the Father. (Ephesians 2:18)

The Holy Spirit abiding in us is able to get underneath all our misconceptions and pour out the love of God in our hearts, as Paul puts it in Romans 5:5. That is, not our love for God (thus helping us to love God as we should, though doubtless the Holy Spirit does that for us as well), but God's love for us, as the context of Romans 5 shows. The Holy Spirit takes God's love for us, and pours it out into our hearts, as one might pour a glass of water out on the floor until the water trickles everywhere, into every nook and cranny. As we read the word of God, inspired by the Holy Spirit of God, and it tells us of God's love for us, the Holy Spirit dwelling within us authenticates that word, makes it credible and real, and thus, little by little, begins to disperse our misconceptions of God and undo the tangled knots of our doubts and fears; and so we come ever nearer to the Father.

Now we can begin to see what 'coming to the Father' means. It would not be enough, even if it were possible, to come to the Father in some physical sense. After all, one can come to another human being and sit so closely that our bodies touch, and yet in heart we could be light years distant from one another. It is only when heart meets heart and spirit meets spirit that we really come to a person. And so it is between us and God. And the glory of it is that coming to the Father in this sense does not require that we come to the Father physically, and therefore it does not have to wait for our being taken home to heaven at death or at the second coming of Christ. In spirit we can come to the Father now. As Paul later puts it in Ephesians 2:18, 'For through him [Christ] we both [Jew and Gentile] have access in one Spirit to the Father.' So our personalities, little by little, are transformed. In this way we become gradually more holy, more trustful, more devoted to the Lord, until, like Paul we can honestly say that, while sometimes we feel as if we were sheep daily delivered over to slaughter, yet we are fully persuaded 'that neither death nor life, nor angels nor rulers, nor things present nor things to come, nor powers, nor height nor depth, nor anything else in all creation, will be able to separate us from the love of God in Christ Jesus our Lord' (Rom 8:38–39).

David Gooding, In the School of Christ: Lessons on Holiness in John 13–17, pp. 96–7

26th November

THE HOLY SPIRIT'S WITNESS TO CHRIST

Reading: Revelation 7:9–12

But when the Helper comes, whom I will send to you from the Father, the Spirit of truth, who proceeds from the Father, he will bear witness about me. And you also will bear witness, because you have been with me from the beginning. (John 15:26–27)

He does not say, 'The world is hostile to God, but you are to go out and try to witness for me and for my Father.' He first of all announces the great provision that he has made for witnessing to himself in this world. That provision is nothing less than the coming of the Holy Spirit. 'When the Helper comes,' says Christ, '. . . he will bear witness about me.' Every believer, of course, has responsibility, according to his or her gift, to witness for the Lord, just as the apostles did: 'You also will bear witness.' But we would get things utterly out of proportion if we thought that the chief responsibility for witnessing was ours. The prime responsibility for witnessing to Christ in the world rests, not with us as individuals, nor with the church as a whole, but with the Holy Spirit. He it is who carries the heavy end of the load, who bears the chief burden. Even the apostles were but junior servants, and how much more junior are we? It is as we grasp this glorious fact that we shall be delivered from undue stress and strain in the course of service for the Lord, and shall constantly find our strength renewed as we learn to rest on the almighty Spirit of God. Indeed, it is an encouraging and invigorating thing to look back from time to time and see how effective the Holy Spirit has been in his witness to the world. In spite of mountainous seas of opposition that have continued to run all down the centuries, the gospel today is being preached around the world more than it has ever been preached in the past twenty centuries. Indeed, millions more people are currently hearing the gospel than ever was dreamed of even a century ago; walls which hostile governments built round their countries, in their attempt to stamp out the Christian faith and prevent this gospel reaching their citizens, have come tumbling down. We may then have every confidence in the power and wisdom, the tactic, the strategy and the effectiveness of the Holy Spirit's masterminding of the campaign of witness for Christ in the world. And in that confidence we may pursue our own witness for the Lord.

David Gooding, *In the School of Christ: Lessons on Holiness in John 13–17*, pp. 180

27th November

THE HOLY SPIRIT GLORIFIES CHRIST

Reading: Isaiah 40

He will glorify me, for he will take what is mine
and declare it to you. (John 16:14)

When the Holy Spirit came, that is indeed what he gave himself to do—to impress upon the apostles, and through them upon the generation of believers, the wondrous glory of the Lord Jesus. One thinks of passages like Hebrews 1 or Colossians 1, and who can take it in, for we're told that all this vast universe, which belongs to the Father, is Christ's. It was made in him, and through him, and for him. All that the Father has is his. Away with poverty—what wealth is here! To be honest, sometimes I find it difficult. I go out at night and look at the stars, as is my hobby, and see the two hundred and fifty billion suns that form the Andromeda galaxy and I say to myself, 'Is it possible, does it begin to be credible, that the maker and the owner and the goal of it all, came and died for you, Gooding? Is it true that, whereas all that the Father has is his, it is also written that we are heirs of God and joint heirs of Jesus Christ, our Lord?' The Holy Spirit has come to glorify the Lord Jesus before our very eyes!

If you would use your spiritual gifts effectively, keep before you this glorious objective which the Holy Spirit has, when he empowers you to glorify the Lord Jesus. What a marvellous thing it is to be used by the Holy Spirit to bring into the life of your fellow believer something of the unimaginable wealth of the Lord Jesus. They who know me best, feel so very often that they must use their spiritual gifts gently to chastise me, and rebuke me, and exhort me, and correct me. They're very wise, and I'm sure the Lord has given them the gifts for that purpose, and they ought to persist in that ministry. I value them, of course I do; I ought to value them more. In truth, I have a kind of a natural preference for those whose gift it is to be used of the Holy Spirit to bring a little of the wealth of God and of the risen Lord into my humdrum life. Life is full of its pains, its problems and its difficulties; and sometimes we allow our Christianity to degenerate into a mere practical how-to Bible that settles our problems.

David Gooding, *The Gift and His Gifts: The Holy Spirit and the Use of Spiritual Gifts*, p. 9

28th November

THE HOLY SPIRIT CONVICTS THE
WORLD OF RIGHTEOUSNESS

Reading: Isaiah 50:4–9

When he comes, he will convict the world concerning
sin and righteousness and judgment. (John 16:8)

The very presence of the Spirit being here is the evidence that Christ is in glory, and the fact that Christ is in glory is evidence of righteousness. The Holy Spirit will convict the world of righteousness 'because I go to the Father' (v. 10). The Lord was right then after all, and the presence of the Holy Spirit here on earth is the evidence that the world was wrong. You will remember the prophetic words spoken of Messiah in Isaiah, 'I gave my back to the smiters, and my cheeks to them that plucked off the hair: I hid not my face from shame and spitting' (Isa 50:6 KJV).

What an eloquent description of the insolence and abuse that our blessed Lord suffered. Who shall measure the strength of his endurance and his patience, when God incarnate stood before mere human creatures and they dared dispute his claim, blasphemed his person and rough handled his body? How did he stand it? Our blessed Lord was no Stoic, trying to pretend that he didn't feel the physical pain, trying to overlook the much deeper offence of their moral and spiritual hostility, their false accusations and their denunciations of his person. In the prophetic word, the Messiah tells us, 'He is near that justifies me,' (v. 8), meaning that God was at his right hand.

The Holy Spirit has now been sent down to promulgate in us the verdict that has been delivered by the supreme court of heaven—to prosecute the case here on earth in favour of Jesus Christ our Lord. And it is of God's magnificent grace that, whereas the Holy Spirit is the chief advocate pleading the case of God's risen Son before the world, he allows all of us to be junior counsel for the defence; to join in the defence of the Lord Jesus so that his name may be vindicated. To think that God would allow me that indescribable privilege, to be junior counsel to the Holy Spirit; and as the Holy Spirit vindicates the Lord Jesus, he will deign to use my little life, my stammering lips and my feeble actions as part of that great vindication of the Lord Jesus. As we contemplate things of that proportion, it begins to put the question of spiritual gifts into its true and proper context. Oh, if that be God's intention, God give me ten thousand gifts: they would be all too few to vindicate his dear Son.

David Gooding, *The Gift and His Gifts: The Holy Spirit and the Use of Spiritual Gifts*, pp. 7–8

29th November

THE HOLY SPIRIT IS OUR FIRST
RESOURCE AGAINST HERESY

Reading: 1 John 2:18–29

You have been anointed by the Holy One, and
you all have knowledge. (v. 20)

The first resource against this false doctrine and against these false teachers is the anointing of the Holy Spirit, and every believer has this anointing (v. 20). 'I've not written to you because you don't know the truth,' says John, 'but because you do know.' And subsequently he says 'have you no need that anyone should teach you?' (v. 27). Now, obviously John doesn't mean that in the absolute sense; that no believer needs anybody to teach him, for our risen Lord has put teachers in the church. He means it, however, in a slightly different fashion.

When it comes to these fundamental matters of our Christian faith, and our gospel, and our very salvation, all true believers have already within them the witness of God's Holy Spirit, and instinctively they will recognize false doctrine about the person of Christ to be what it is—and there's a very simple reason for that. If you are a believer and rejoicing in the forgiveness of your sins, and I come to you and say that the death of Christ wasn't an historical fact, you're not going to listen. If it isn't an historical fact your sins aren't forgiven, and you know it in your very heart that this is what has made your peace with God and given you living fellowship with him. The Holy Spirit's witness to that in your heart witnesses at once that this is false doctrine.

It is the Holy Spirit's prime responsibility to witness to the Lord Jesus, and he witnesses in the hearts of believers, so that instinctively they know. 'And you know that no lie is of the truth,' says John, adding a twist to his denunciation (see v. 21). There can be no compromise in it. It's no use getting up and saying in a very learned voice that somebody who has just come out with heresy that the virgin birth isn't true, and the bodily resurrection of Christ isn't true, is a very enterprising thinker, and this is a valid way of approaching Christianity, and we must be broadminded enough to include it. 'No,' says John, 'the Holy Spirit will witness in you that no lie is of the truth.' There's no alternative way of coming to the truth.

David Gooding, *Life in the Family of God: Twelve Seminars on the First Epistle of John*, p. 42

30th November

THE POWER OF SPIRITUAL GIFTS

Reading: 1 Corinthians 12:1–11

To each is given the manifestation of the
Spirit for the common good. (v. 7)

Around about Christmas time, my car, being a very venerable jalopy, broke down. It was a minor complaint, arthritis in the works somewhere. When the hours of Yuletide were gone by I called my motor mechanic. He is a bright young man, and when he arrived in all his kindness, he came up in a splendid motor car. It made my jalopy blush for shame! I cast an envious eye and said, 'That's a beautiful car,' and he said, 'Yes, I got it second-hand.' I gently enquired how much they would cost, for I had notions in my head. He told me what they cost, but then, looking at me straight in the eye, he delivered a warning, 'It's not everybody's car to drive: the thing is so powerful that, if you weren't careful, you could put your foot down and the back would come round to meet you in the front.' That would never do for me, for I wouldn't know what to do if the back came round to the front, so I said, 'Ah, yes, I understand,' and we went about our business.

You see the point. The car was very powerful, but it couldn't be entrusted to an incompetent driver like me: I wouldn't know how to drive it properly. It wouldn't be the fault of the car, it would be my fault. I could do a lot of damage to myself and other folks if I didn't learn patiently how to control this very powerful car.

I'm not denying that God's gifts, these spiritual gifts, can be exceedingly powerful. But the more powerful your spiritual gift is, the more you will need to seek the instruction of the Holy Spirit on just how to use that gift, so that you may use it to your own profit and to the profit of the church, and not do damage to yourself and others; and not damage yourself by seeking spiritual gifts that are not within your competence to use, and which the Holy Spirit has never designed to give you.

David Gooding, The Gift and His Gifts: The Holy Spirit and the Use of Spiritual Gifts, p. 18

1st December

GOD GAVE US GIFTS AS IT PLEASED HIM

Reading: 1 Corinthians 12:12–31

In fact God has placed the parts in the body, every one of them, just as he wanted them to be. (v. 18 NIV)

Have you never felt, my brother, my sister, a certain frustration—that you wish you were somebody else? You wish you had the gift of an evangelist. Fancy being a great evangelist and being able to point to fifty-six churches that you've planted, or something like that; so many souls that you've brought to the Lord. Marvellous! Have you ever felt, 'I wish I was one of them, and I wish my personality was different. I feel so inhibited, and I've not got the big gifts that the others have.' Yes, we'd like to be somebody else.

There was a programme on the BBC once, I forget what it was called, and people were asked that famous question, 'If you weren't you, who would you like to be?' Not that I have any chance of getting on the BBC, but I pondered it for a while. 'Now, Gooding,' I said to myself, 'if you weren't you, who would you like to be?' After thinking for a while, I said, 'I'd like to be me.' Yes, there have been moments when I'd like to have been you, but on sober thought I decided I'd like to be me! And I'll tell you why. First Corinthians 12:8 says 'now has God set each member in the body even as it pleased him' (RV). That's the thing: why would I want a gift at all? What do I want it for? Because it would make me feel better, if I had a big gift? But this is better: I'm set in the body 'as it pleased God.'

See that little violet blooming in the grass and scarcely noticeable? How did it come to be a violet and why wasn't it an oak tree, or an almond tree full of blossom? Why is it still a mere violet? And the answer is that it pleased almighty God. What a thing it is, my dear sister, my brother. Just now, this moment, in your heart of hearts raise your spirit to the Father himself. As to your gift, you are what pleases God you should be. You don't have to be a John Wesley to please God. Take the very first apostle, add to him the biggest deacons that you can manage to meet, put them all together in one bundle, and at the end of the day what have they done but to please God? In that you and they are equal: God gave you your gift as it pleased him.

David Gooding, The Gift and His Gifts: The Holy Spirit and the Use of Spiritual Gifts, p. 33

2nd December

GIFT OR GODLINESS?

Reading: Judges 16

Samson said, 'Let me die with the Philistines!' Then he
pushed with all his might, and down came the temple on
the rulers and all the people in it. Thus he killed many
more when he died than while he lived. (v. 30 NIV)

Samson was an extraordinarily gifted man. The power of the Holy Spirit upon him is mentioned explicitly at least four times in these chapters, and it is evident that the power he wielded was more than human power. So he had supernatural gift and power, but we mustn't let that blind our eyes, as eventually it blinded his, to the fact that the possession of spiritual gift is no guarantee of godly conduct.

All of us need to remind ourselves that gift is not necessarily the same as grace. Many a man and woman, not gifted so much as we may be, may in fact be far more godly—far more filled with God's grace; far more self-controlled and Christlike than some of the Lord's more spectacularly gifted servants. Gift is no proof against falling. The record of Samson's life will serve to remind us that just because a man is gifted we cannot afford to suppose that all he does and all his methods are necessarily right.

In 1 Corinthians 12–14 Paul discusses the gifts of the Holy Spirit. Perhaps more than in any other context he appeals to us to be critical of ourselves, 'Be infants in evil, but in your thinking be mature . . . Let two or three prophets speak, and let the others weigh what is said' (14:20, 29). Not with harsh and unbrotherly criticism of course, but with clear sighted discernment. Just because a gifted man says this or does that, we would be in danger if we automatically said that he must be right. We must learn in humility to judge.

Whilst he was tremendously gifted and called of God to be a Nazirite, failure on Samson's part to check his gift with such discernment meant that he broke almost every rule and ended in disaster. He was raised up of God as a deliverer, but when he died Israel were as much in bondage to the Philistines as they had ever been. He had done all sorts of spectacular spiritual fireworks, but if you ask what they achieved in the end you might be forgiven for thinking that it was perilously little.

David Gooding, The Lord Saves His People: Fourteen Seminars on the Book of Judges, pp. 93–4

THE FATHER'S PLAN OF REDEMPTION

Part 10—God's Provision for Us on the Journey: The Church

3rd December

THE BODY OF CHRIST IS SOMETHING NEW

Reading: Ephesians 3:1–13

This mystery is that the Gentiles are fellow heirs,
members of the same body, and partakers of the
promise in Christ Jesus through the gospel. (v. 6)

It had to wait until the Lord had come, died, risen again, gone back to the Father and sent the Spirit, that any talk of the Body of Christ would make sense.

Therefore, what Paul preaches is not just a little bit tacked on to the gospel. It is one of those next stages forward in God's progressive revelation to men. Paul says: 'I want you to get a hold of it, you Gentiles in particular, for you scarcely realize yet how important I am. I am in prison for you, and you might think (particularly if you listen to the Jews and some rather strange brethren) that I am an oddity. James is not altogether sure yet! But it is for your very glory that I am suffering; for what God has made known to me is by a dispensation that he has given me. To me, though least of all the saints, he has given this particular place in history, to make known this glorious new thing by the revelation of God' (see Eph 3:8).

It was such a new thing that even the principalities and powers in the heavens look on it aghast. It was something that the archangel Michael didn't know; and it overjoys me that there is something that the devil did not know. The Bible tells me that there are two things which none of the princes of this world knew: the hidden wisdom of God—'for if they had, they would not have crucified the Lord of glory' (1 Cor 2:8). And they did not know this great new thing that God was doing in the middle of creation, making a new kind of man, this new thing called the Body of Christ. They see it with wonder and they are agog with expectancy as they see the man Jesus raised above them, still human. And as they look at men and women on earth, they are told that these have been united with the Son of Man, and in God's purpose they too are destined to be above angels, principalities and powers. The novelty of it causes the angels themselves to bow and scrutinize and think and magnify the variegated wisdom of God (Eph 3:10).

David Gooding, Ephesians: A Bird's Eye View of the Major Movements of Thought, p. 76

4th December

THE REALITY OF THE BODY OF CHRIST

Reading: Ephesians 4:6, 26–32

There is one body and one Spirit—just as you were called to
the one hope that belongs to your call. (Ephesians 4:4)

The Body of Christ is made up of personalities that are like members of a body, kept together because the infinite power of God the Holy Spirit keeps them together. That is a reality, and we have the urgent need to open our eyes and hearts so that we live daily recognizing that it is a reality.

There have been people who have become very vexed and upset and have smitten their breasts and stamped their feet and said what fools they have been. But they do not get so angry with themselves that they get the carving knife and cut off their ears or toes or arms, or plunge it into their hearts; though there have been rare occasions when that has happened, but only by the demented. Why do people not do that? Because these are members of their bodies, and their bodies are real.

How I wish I could say the same thing about the Body of Christ. But you cannot live in this world, in Northern Ireland or England, or travel in other parts and enquire about the Lord's people, without finding that born again Christians are prepared to take the knife of their tongues and stab one another with it. It is heart breaking when the work of God in foreign places is flourishing, and then there comes a great explosion in a local church by petty jealousies brewing up until Christians are prepared to break the work of God.

Why is that? They do not believe in the Body of Christ; or, if they do, it is in the bit that is called theory. They have not got round to seeing that it is a reality, and that they might as well be cutting off their own arms (which they would never think of doing) as to behave the way they do towards their fellow believers. This behaviour is so natural, that, short of God opening our hearts by the illumination of his Spirit, we would go on acting like it, and think we were justified in doing so, unaware of the injury we inflict on the great reality which is the Body of Christ, and the grief we do to the Holy Spirit by whose life that Body lives.

David Gooding, Ephesians: A Bird's Eye View of the Major Movements of Thought, pp. 12–13

5th December

THE UNIFICATION OF GOD'S PEOPLE

Reading: 1 Chronicles 11:1–9

*Then all Israel gathered together to David at Hebron
and said, 'Behold, we are your bone and flesh'. (v. 1)*

The second great stage in Israel's history was a stroke of genius of David when he became king; he united the nation. They took an old Canaanite city called Jebus, captured it and turned it into the capital city for his people, and they called it Jerusalem. So David, by that stroke of genius, provided his nation with a capital city and a heart—a city where everybody, no matter what tribe they came from, felt they were at home. It was their city! It united the nation that had hitherto become fragmented; a nation that soon afterwards fragmented again. But for that brief period in history the nation was united in their glorious capital city, and united around David. They called it 'the City of the Great King'. However much they quarrelled amongst themselves, Israel loved David.

The two tribes and the ten gave up their quarrelling and they united under David in that lovely city. It was David who founded it. What a history it has gathered round its head in the centuries, and what a history there will yet be. That city shall yet be a troublesome stone to all the nations. One day all the nations of the world shall come against it—Antichrist's last fling to defy God and his Christ. And then the Lord shall come.

But just now, our minds go to a greater Jerusalem still, 'Jerusalem above is free, and she is our mother' (Gal 4:26). Can you believe there is going to be a heaven of bliss? You understand that the first thing that will have to happen is that everybody will have to be united. Will that be difficult? It is difficult to unite the world, but what about believers? Can we, who know the realities of life in the church of God, dare to believe there is going to be a paradise of bliss one day? Or is it all religious moonshine? No! Scratch a true believer and, however prickly the surface, underneath you will find a heart that loves the Saviour. What a genius Christ is for bringing people together. We can say to him in a far deeper sense, 'We are bone of your bone and flesh of your flesh.' We are not only forgiven by him, but eternally united with him in the very Body of Christ. That new Jerusalem is no myth; it is already being formed.

David Gooding, *God's Great Salvation: Lessons from the Lives of Old Testament Characters*, p. 28

6th December

Reading: Acts 18:1–17

I am with you, and no one will attack you to harm you, for
I have many in this city who are my people. (v. 10)

One night the Lord spoke to Paul in a vision to encourage him to persist in his preaching; and it was not simply what he said, but it was the terms he used in saying it, that proved so fruitful in Paul's understanding of the developing situation. Only, we must be careful not to miss the overtones of the biblical language as we read the words that accompanied the vision. 'Do not be afraid', said the Lord, 'keep on speaking, do not be silent. For I am with you, and no one is going to attack and harm you, because I have many people in this city' (vv. 9–10). If we are not careful we shall read the phrase 'many people' as if it meant simply 'many persons'; as though all the Lord was saying was, 'A lot of individuals in this city are going to get converted.' That would have been true, of course; but in focusing on individuals, it puts the emphasis in the wrong place. The Greek word in question, *laos*, refers to people as a group, a crowd, or a nation. Its plural does not mean 'persons', 'individuals', but 'peoples' (that is, 'nations'). The older English of the King James Version conveys the connotation rather better: 'I have much people.' Even so, to get the full flavour of the expression in this context, we must recall that *laos* is the translation of the Hebrew word that throughout the Old Testament designates the nation Israel: 'my people', God calls them. He explained through Moses (Deut 7:7–8) that he did not choose them because they were a numerous people; they were, in fact, few in number compared with other peoples. But he loved them and chose them, and they became his people. And now the Lord is telling Paul that he has 'much people' in Corinth, who are now to form 'his people' in the same sense that Israel was for many centuries his people. The difference is that in Old Testament times, while Israelites were 'the Lord's people', Gentiles were not. Now there had come a change: the Lord's people were to be made up of Gentiles as well as of Jews.

David Gooding, *True to the Faith: The Acts of the Apostles–Defining and Defending the Gospel*, p. 375

7th December

THE TRUE BODY OF CHRIST

Reading: Acts 11:1–18; 12:20–25

*And I remembered the word of the Lord, how he
said, 'John baptized with water, but you will be
baptized with the Holy Spirit.' (11:16)*

In the course of certain political negotiations Herod Agrippa arranged
a great spectacle to impress the people. Wearing his royal robes, he sat on
his throne and delivered a public address (12:21). The crowd responded by
attributing to him divine honours: 'This is the voice of a god,' they shouted,
'not of a man' (v. 22). He accepted their idolatrous and absurd adulation,
and immediately, because Herod did not give the glory to God, an angel of
the Lord struck him down, and he was eaten by worms and died'(see v. 23).

Acts 11:1–18 is talking about the baptism of both Jew and Gentile in the
Holy Spirit. This baptism brought about an immediate unity between Jewish
and Gentile believers such as had never been known before in all history.
Even so, it is unlikely that at the time they would have seen its amazing
implications. But they were later revealed to Paul, and Luke would have
learned of them from him before he wrote Acts. As Paul explained to the
Corinthians: 'we were all baptized in one Spirit into one body—whether
Jews or Greeks' (1 Cor 12:13). The body he referred to is nothing less than
'the Christ', that new and unique thing in God's universe that was brought
into being at Pentecost, the Body of Christ; that wonderful organism, created
by placing human beings in the Spirit of God, and causing them to drink of
the Spirit of God. They are thus in the Spirit of God, and the Spirit of God
is in them (Rom 8:9).

The result is that there has come into being a body of which the man Jesus
is the head, and in which every member shares the same life, and, without
losing his or her individual responsibility, is no longer a mere individual,
but is a member, along with the Lord Jesus and every other believer, in this
bigger organism, the Body of Christ. Man has been taken up into God! And
what Acts 12:20–23 presents is a sad and absurd counterfeit: man trying to
take the place of God and aping God, yielding to that ambition planted in
the human heart at the dawn of history by the great tempter himself: 'you
will be like God' (Gen 3:5).

David Gooding, *True to the Faith: The Acts of the Apostles–Defining and Defending the Gospel*, pp. 231-2

8th December

DEVELOPING OUR POTENTIAL BY GROWING UP TO MATURITY

Reading: Ephesians 4:7–16

. . . until we all attain to the unity of the faith and of the knowledge of the Son of God, to mature manhood, to the measure of the stature of the fullness of Christ. (v. 13)

If the Body of Christ has to progress and grow, then our Lord is not leaving it to chance. As the ascended head in heaven, he has ascended 'that he might fill all things' (v. 10). Magnificent warrior in the fight that he is, he has his men now—apostles, prophets, evangelists, pastors, teachers—whom he has given and whom he uses. He uses them to get all the rest of us converted to start with, and then perfect us so that we in turn might begin to do our particular job. It is all for the perfecting of the saints in their work of serving (v. 12). That is why the gifts are given.

They are not given so that the rest of us can put our feet up and say: 'Thank you, Lord. I have got servants galore waiting on me—Paul, Peter, Matthew, the elders in my church, the evangelists—I can afford to sit here, put my feet up and let them do the work.' No! They are given to us to perfect us, so that we may begin to do our job of work; and thereby the Body begins to grow 'by that which every joint supplies' (v. 16 KJV).

We must be both realistic and practical. Every joint in the Body does not have to be an apostle. We all have to grow and some of us have more potential than others. It is no good any of us getting it into our little heads that we are going to grow to be as big as Paul. Such is not within the potential of any of us, but our difficulty is in developing the potential we have got. The temptation always is to let some of it lie undeveloped.

Yet the Lord's people have far more potential than they think. Some think that because they are not preachers they do not have any potential. That is a lack of imagination, is it not? What vast potential there is of different kinds. The work of the Lord in many countries wilts because evangelists and missionaries are obliged to do not only their own work but a lot of things for which they do not have the particular potential. Other folks at home do have it, but it has not occurred to them that they could be part of the missionary team. Their professional qualifications could be part of the work for developing the Body of Christ.

David Gooding, *Ephesians: A Bird's Eye View of the Major Movements of Thought*, pp. 86–7

9th December

LIVING IN THE LIGHT OF THE REALITY OF CHRIST'S BODY

Reading: Ephesians 4:17–25

*Therefore, having put away falsehood, let each
one of you speak the truth with his neighbour, for
we are members one of another. (v. 25)*

In the final chapters of Ephesians we hear Paul asking us, not once but many times, to behave in the light of the truth. It is not merely truth in the sense of doctrine, but truth in the sense of reality. Paul tells us that we cannot behave in such and such a way. Why not? Because it is to make a mock of reality.

If we go out on a foggy, dark night and go staggering down the street without looking, we could walk into a lamp post. A lamp post is a very real thing! We had better know it is there and take a torch and look. If we want to know how to walk home in the dark without getting some great bruises, we had better investigate reality and bring a bit of light to bear on the realities of life. That is principle number one.

Why must we speak the truth with our neighbours? Because this is not just a theory—it is a reality. What unites our brothers and sisters and us together is unseen—it is the Holy Spirit himself. We are in Christ and the Holy Spirit lives in us. To hurt a Christian brother is to wound the Body of Christ and hurt the Holy Spirit. So, let us not rail at our brothers and sisters. We must be careful what we say, because the Holy Spirit is in them and we could grieve the Holy Spirit, 'by whom you were sealed for the day of redemption' (v. 30). That would be an exceedingly foolish thing to do, yet we often do it. Therefore, in order to behave in a practical way, we have got to face the truth: what do I really believe?

Certain folks nowadays say that Jesus Christ is so loving that he does not mind if young people get muddled up. The fashions of the world are changed, and if they get muddled up sexually and in other ways he will not mind. Will he not? Where do they get that idea from? They will say that even the church nowadays is more permissive. Is it really? Paul tells us to open our eyes to reality: 'But that is not the way you learned Christ!' (v. 20). See the reality in Jesus. What he actually teaches on these things is often so different from what is taught by our permissive society and permissive church leaders. May God give us the grace to let Christ so shine on us that we will reflect his light and, being light in the Lord (5:8), cast some reality around ourselves in this dark world.

David Gooding, *Ephesians: A Bird's Eye View of the Major Movements of Thought*, p. 89

10th December

LOVING ONE ANOTHER AS EVIDENCE OF LIFE

Reading: 1 John 3:15–24

*For this is the message that you have heard from the
beginning, that we should love one another. (v. 11)*

Love of the brothers is a mark of having been born again (v. 14). But here just
let me interject an observation, lest we get carried away in sentimentality.
What does it mean to love the brothers? You will notice that here the test is
not that we love men and women in general, but we love our brothers and
sisters in Christ. There is a special difficulty, ladies and gentlemen, in loving
the brothers and the more you get to know them, forgive me for saying it,
the more difficult you'll find it to love them—because God has not chosen
the wise and the powerful and the beautiful. I'm not necessarily commenting
upon you—you look very wise to me! But God says he hasn't necessarily
chosen them at all: he has chosen the broken and the humble.

Now then, just look at verses 16–18. They're not difficult to understand, are
they? They're difficult to do, maybe. The mark of true love is that [Christ]
laid down his life for us. Literally, physically, spiritually, and therefore it puts
upon us a bounden duty to lay down our lives for the brothers. We cannot,
by so doing, atone for them. In his atoning sufferings our Lord stands alone
and unique, but he calls upon us to follow him and, in our love and service
of our brothers and sisters, to be prepared to lay down our lives. He could
call us to the mission field and to who knows what diseases and early deaths,
which could be more difficult perhaps.

Our Lord laid down his life for us, but let's now take the means of life. In
verse 17 John says, 'Whoever has this world's goods. . . .'. That word in Greek
that is translated 'goods' literally means 'the means of life'. Take a situation
where a believer is faced with a brother who is in need and finds in himself
a certain desire to help him. And then he withdraws because it's going to
cost too much. How does the love of God dwell in him? If I won't give my
means of life, then with what credibility would I claim that I would freely
lay down my physical life? 'Let us not love in word or talk, but in deed and
in truth' (v. 18).

David Gooding, *Life in the Family of God: Twelve Seminars on the First Epistle of John*, p. 57

11th December

LOVE IS OF GOD

Reading: 1 John 4:7–21

Beloved, let us love one another, for love is from God, and whoever loves has been born of God and knows God. (v. 7)

Why should I love? How can I love? Considering that you are yourself beloved of God, how then is it possible that you don't begin to show that same kind of love to other people? The first secret of our loving is that we have been loved. Verses 7–8 tell us of our resources, for they show the source of our love: 'love is from God'. That is to say, God is not asking us to make bricks without straw, like Pharaoh demanded of the Israelites. When he tells us to love, he is not exhorting us to dredge up out of the bottom of our bankrupt emotions the ability to love somebody. He's pointing out that there is a vast resource. True love comes from God, and everybody who loves in this sense loves because—for this reason and by this enablement—he has been born of God.

So John says, 'You have the ability to love. You have been born of God, with the life of God and his nature, and therefore the great infinite resource of the love of God stands behind you.' It means that very often, when we are called upon in a difficult situation to love other folks, we do well to admit our own bankruptcy to the Lord. 'Lord, I can't love these people, but you can love them. You gave your Son for them, and if it is the fact that I am begotten of you and you dwell in me, then you could love those people through me.' We are not talking of some natural bonhomie. Some people are good at being charming and kind. They were probably born with an emotional silver spoon in their mouths and it's easy for them to be pleasant. Others of us were born like a lot of old frogs, awful and gnarled, with warts galore upon our emotional personalities, and we find it very difficult to love. But we're not talking about natural love; we are exhorted to love because we have been born of God and our God is love. I can lie back upon the ocean of the love of God and thus learn to allow some of that vast ocean to flow out through me.

David Gooding, *Life in the Family of God: Twelve Seminars on the First Epistle of John*, pp. 66–7

12th December

HOW SHALL WE SPEND OUR LOVE?

Reading: 1 Peter 1:13–25

You have been born again, not of perishable seed but of
imperishable, through the living and abiding word of God. (v. 23)

'What are you going to do with your love? You've got to spend it, but what will you spend your love on?', Peter asks. 'Having purified your souls by obeying the truth for a sincere brotherly love, love one another earnestly from a pure heart', he says (see v. 22). In other words, one prior claim on our love is our fellow believers: love one another, since you have purified your souls.

Am hearing straight, when I think I hear some of those early Christians saying under their breath, 'But Peter, do you happen to know my brothers and sisters? They're nice souls, but they're not quite so colourful as some of the companions I meet out in the world: they are very ingenious and forward moving and attractive. Not to be unkind, but some of my fellow Christians are not so colourful.'

What do you think Peter would say? 'You can love the world if you must, but do notice this, "All flesh is like grass and all its glory like the flower of grass. The grass withers and the flower falls"' (v. 24).

If you love this world, in that sense of the word 'world', and you spend your love on it, your love will go down the drain because the world is fading and one day it will be gone. Why should we love our brothers and sisters? 'Because,' says Peter, '"[they] have been born again, not of perishable seed but of imperishable, through the living and abiding word of God" (v. 23). Spend your love on them, whatever you do. They're going to last, and every bit of love you've given them and invested in them, by way of service or encouragement or whatever, will abide eternally.'

So you will see the profit on your investment of love in your fellow believers. That's an important lesson, isn't it?

David Gooding, *The Saving and Losing of a Soul*, p. 9

13th December

OUR CHRISTIAN COMMUNITY

Reading: Hebrews 13:1–2; 18–25

Greet all your leaders and all the saints.
Those who come from Italy send you greetings. (v. 24)

The letter to the Hebrews is finished; but as the writer adds his personal greetings, we get a brief glimpse through his eyes of the community he has been writing to. 'I want you to know that our brother Timothy has been released. If he arrives soon, I will come with him to see you' (v. 23). Our minds go to that able and sensitive young man from Lystra, who joined Paul on his missionary journeys. In the course of the years he helped to plant churches in different cities and countries, and carried the onerous task of shepherding the large, multiracial church at Ephesus. Apparently he had been imprisoned and then more recently released; and the writer wants his readers to hear the news. He had become to them, as well as to the writer, 'our brother Timothy'. Doubtless they had been interested in his work, and had prayed for him during his imprisonment. His release would be a victory for their prayers and a boost to their faith. A visit from him would be an occasion of great joy.

Pause to think of how true faith in Christ enlarges our horizons! It lifts us out of our narrow personal and selfish or even national concerns, and gives us a common international interest in Christ's work and workers throughout the world, making us feel an integral part of his great enterprise. 'Greet all your leaders and all God's people. Those from Italy send you their greetings. Grace be with you all' (v. 24). We think again. What a marvellous reality is the family of God into which faith in Christ has brought us! In spite of our family squabbles, how real is the affection, born of God's Spirit, which unites us in Christ across the world and across the ages.

Marvellous people, these ancient Hebrew Christians. We have read and thought much about them. We have been stimulated by their courage. We have profited from their mistakes. We have learned to love them in the Lord. They were real people, and even now they live with Christ. One day we shall meet them and be able to tell them how immensely we enjoyed reading the letter that was originally addressed to them.

David Gooding, *An Unshakeable Kingdom: The Letter to the Hebrews for Today*, pp. 241–2

14th December

THE PROPER PLACE OF SOCIAL ACTION

Reading: Acts 6:1–7

We will devote ourselves to prayer and to
the ministry of the word. (v. 4)

The early Christians had a very vigorous and active concern for the social needs of their members. There was a daily distribution of food to the widows. When it was discovered that some widows were being neglected, if not positively discriminated against, the apostles advised the church to appoint efficient and spiritual men to administer the common resources in a fair and systematic way. But the apostles were not prepared to administer that social relief themselves. And the reason they gave shows their urgent sense of true priorities: 'It would not be right for us to neglect the ministry of the word of God in order to wait on tables. . . Choose seven men . . . known to be full of the Spirit and wisdom. We will turn this responsibility over to them and give our attention to prayer and the ministry of the word' (see v. 4).

To press home the lesson, Luke phrases his conclusion with deliberate care: 'So the word of God spread. The number of disciples in Jerusalem increased rapidly, and a large number of priests became obedient to the faith' (v. 7). The connection between the growth of the church and the twin activities of preaching the gospel and expounding the word was not accidental, of course; and we must let this record of the beginnings of Christianity judge us and our modern practice today. As far as the front we present to the world is concerned, many churches seem to have lost their confidence in the gospel to convert sinners and turn them into disciples of the Lord Jesus. So they concentrate solely on doing social good works, and offer the world their aid. And the world, not being aware that there is any more to Christianity than that, takes the aid, but sees no need to come to Christ for salvation. No true conversions take place, and the churches dwindle. Similarly inside the churches, it can so easily happen that social activities virtually oust the preaching of the word and prayer. Some protest that nowadays one cannot expect congregations to put up with sermons that seriously and systematically expound the word of God. That may be true. But if it is, does it not suggest that they are not disciples in the apostolic sense of the term at all? If the churches find the word of God an intolerable bore, how can they expect the world to listen when they preach it? And if the word of God is not preached and does not spread, how will the number of the disciples increase at all?

David Gooding, *True to the Faith: The Acts of the Apostles–Defining and Defending the Gospel*, pp. 123–4

15th December

THE COST OF THE CHURCH

Reading: Acts 20:13–38

*Pay careful attention to yourselves and to all the flock, of which
the Holy Spirit has made you overseers, to care for the church
of God, which he obtained with his own blood. (v. 28)*

Unceasing vigilance is the essential requirement in shepherds. And first,
vigilance over themselves. A shepherd who grows careless over his own
spiritual life, moral behaviour, study of Scripture, progress in the knowledge
of God, thereby unfits himself for shepherding others.

'Shepherd the church of God, which he bought with the blood of his own'.
With this we touch the mainspring of all true defence and shepherding of
the church: the cost at which God bought it. That cost was the blood of his
own, that is, of his own dear, loved, cherished Son. The story still has power
to stagger imagination. For here is no image of a god that fell down from the
sky, but God of very God coming deliberately down. Father and Son in holy
concert paying the price that only God could measure, to obtain the repentance, faith and love of the likes of us. How cheap the silver of Demetrius's
shrines compared with this! 'For . . . it was not with perishable things such
as silver or gold that you were redeemed . . . but with the precious blood of
Christ' (1 Pet 1:18–19). This was not Artemis protecting the young of animal
and man and avenging the rape of nature with her lethal arrows. This was
not nature doing what was natural and tearing the enemy to pieces to save
her own life. Here was nature's Creator, knowingly, deliberately, of his own
free will laying down his own life for us, his sinful creatures (John 10:15–17).
This was not nature, magnificent but fallen. This was thrice holy divine grace.

The archetypal shepherd has set the pattern for the defence of the
sheep (John 10:7–13). All true defence of the gospel and of the church must
follow his example. There is nothing more destructive of the church, nor
bewildering to the sheep, than when men who profess to be shepherds teach
the sheep that the Chief Shepherd was not God incarnate, was not born of
a virgin, he was in fact mistaken in some of his teaching (particularly about
the second coming), he did not die as an atonement for sin, and did not
bodily rise from the dead. Such men are not true shepherds. They are not
even true sheep. They are wolves from the outside, of whom the shepherd
himself warned us.

David Gooding, *True to the Faith: The Acts of the Apostles–Defining and Defending the Gospel*, pp. 426-7

16th December

THE BODY OF CHRIST WILL RUN THE UNIVERSE

Reading: Revelation 2:24–29

. . . if we endure, we will also reign with him. (2 Timothy 2:12)

God has magnificent plans for running the universe, its economy; and the scheme basically is that his dear Son, our blessed Lord, will be in charge of it all.

My dear brothers and sisters, there is more than a rumour in the New Testament that if we behave ourselves properly we shall be given a practical share in the running of the whole universe for God. Isn't that marvellous? Why do you think Christ is spending so much time and patience on getting his Body formed by baptism in the Holy Spirit, and then training us in these lowly tasks that we have to do here on earth? Why spend so much time on it? Because the Body of Christ is not simply a little organizational detail just for earth. It's Christ and his Body that God in his purposes places above all principalities, mights, powers and dominions; a Body that he shall use to run the whole universe for God in those ages of unlimited bliss. Oh that I could be persuaded to take my spiritual education and practise it a bit more seriously now.

I can tell you a thing or two about her Gracious Majesty Queen Elizabeth II. She has a lot of houses; more than I have, by a long way. I contribute to their upkeep, but that's a small point! She has to run these houses. She is the boss in charge, of course, but she doesn't do all the practical things. She doesn't queue up in the supermarket to get the week's groceries for Windsor Palace, for instance. She has her stewards to do that, and very important some of them are too.

God will sum up everything in Christ, but the amazing thing is that God's way of running things in the coming eternity will be through Christ and his people. It is here and now in our churches that we are being given real practical training, learning to be God's responsible servants to run things for him as he wants them run; and there are right ways and wrong ways of doing things.

David Gooding, *Eternal Encouragement and Good Hope: 2 Thessalonians 2:13-17*, pp. 8–9

THE FATHER'S PLAN OF REDEMPTION

Part 11—God's Provision for Us on the Journey:
Sustaining Our Loyalty

17th December

SALVATION THROUGH THE JUDGMENT

Reading: Genesis 6

*We were buried therefore with him by baptism into death, in
order that, just as Christ was raised from the dead by the glory of
the Father, we too might walk in newness of life. (Romans 6:4)*

The act of baptism cannot possibly save you. Why such an elaborate symbol,
and why a symbol of a burial? Why is it necessary to go through that water?
Why not just cleansing? Cleansing wouldn't do any good. Take those fallen
men in Noah's day, carnal men who did not have the Spirit: a few bits of
water would not have been enough to cleanse them. 'No,' says God, 'I am
not prepared to go on with them.' The only answer is to destroy them, so
God drowned them and buried them. The very threshold of Christianity is
baptism, which proclaims the same thing. As a result of the fall and our own
personal sin, we are quite beyond the point of just being cleansed. Having
a little stain washed away would never make us all right. It would take nothing less than accepting God's judgment, which is death and burial.

Grace does not make nature perfect. If I would be saved I must come to
that basic, radical repentance that admits not merely that I do wrong but that
I am wrong. I am a fallen creature and I deserve God's judgment. I deserve
to be drowned, to be got rid of.

That is why Christ died. He didn't come with merely some advice; he came
to suffer the execution of God's wrath, the sentence of God upon man. Just
as the ark of Noah's time was able to go through the flood and come out the
other side, as Noah never could have done; so our blessed Lord was able to
go through the wrath of God and come out the other side. Therein is our
salvation. If I have seen the gravity of my position as a man in Adam, then the
way is open for me to enter the 'ark'—to come to Christ. And when I receive
Christ as Saviour, he shall ask me to confess my faith by being baptized—by
being buried. I say publicly that I agree with God; I deserved God's judgment
and sentence, but I have accepted his resurrection life as a sheer unmerited
gift. Noah came out of the ark to a new world and those who trust Christ
are saved from God's wrath and enter a new life.

David Gooding, *The God of New Beginnings: Eighteen Seminars on the Book of Genesis*, p. 70

18th December

A SIGN TO KEEP US FROM FORGETTING

Reading: Joshua 4:1–9; 19–24

Then you shall tell them that the waters of the Jordan were
cut off before the ark of the covenant of the LORD. (v. 7)

How easy it is for the believer, enjoying his inheritance, to live for his own
gratification, and forget the Lord and the basis of our inheritance. 'Bring
them back generation after generation,' says God to Joshua, 'and show them
those stones to remind them that when your fathers came into the land, the
ark of the covenant of the Lord of the whole earth went down into those
waters and came up again.'

Wisely, our Lord has given us a token, a sign, and bids us to meet with
bread and wine to remember him. You won't say that it isn't necessary, will
you? There was never anything more practical in a Christian's life than the
Lord's Supper. How shall my disloyal, wayward heart be kept loyal to God?
Even the very benefits of the gospel, if I'm not careful, will bring me away
from the Lord, as I get singing my hymns purely for my own enjoyment of
the tune. I'd better come back and stand by the bread and the wine, as Israel
stood by the stones on the further bank and said, 'Is it true that the ark of
the Lord of the whole earth was once down there in those swirling waters?'
How would Israel forget it? It was the basis of their being in the inheritance.

And what's our basis for enjoying our inheritance?

'Oh,' you say, 'I give thanks to the Father every day of the week. He's made
us qualified to share in the inheritance of the saints in light' (Col. 1:12).

We're redeemed, you tell me. I'm delighted to know it, my friend, but
by whose blood? Don't you know whose blood it is? It's the one who is the
beginning: 'all things were created by him, and for him. And he is before all
things, and by him all things consist' (vv. 16-17). This is the Lord of heaven
and earth, and we have redemption through his blood. The transcendent
living Lord once lay in the waters of death. We shall never forget it, not to
the remotest bounds of eternity. I think they're going to have twelve standing
stones in heaven, so that we shall remember how we got there!

David Gooding, *Entering the Inheritance: Studies in Joshua 1–12*, pp. 22–3

19th December

HOW HAVE YOU LOVED US?

Reading: Deuteronomy 6:1–12

'I have loved you,' says the LORD. But you say, 'How have you loved us?' (Malachi 1:2)

They had heard it many times. Now they were turning round and saying that they did not particularly see where God had loved them.

Is it possible for a believer today to do that? It is indeed! That is the very thing in which the first church in the book of the Revelation fell, 'But I have this against you, that you have abandoned the love you had at first' (2:4). What was their and our first love to Christ? Well, it was possibly when we realized how much Christ loved us. Why do some of us lose our love for Christ? It is because we lose the sense of Christ's love for us.

Israel did so. God had loved them, and loved them spectacularly. But they came to take it for granted and it became ordinary. Presently they could not see anything at all that told them that God loved them, and they lost their sense that he did love them. If only they could have remembered that God had poured judgment on Esau and had had mercy on Israel, though they did not deserve it. God spared them his judgment because he loved them, but they had lost sight of that.

We could all lose sight of God's love, for this or that reason. We so easily take it for granted and we forget it. That is why the Lord instituted the Lord's Supper, so that we would remember it at least once a week. It is easy to take it for granted and forget it. There have also been people so keen in the Lord's work, going out to see the whole area converted, putting their whole energy into it, praying, working—and only a few get converted. They had got so frustrated because the Lord's work did not proceed in their hands and they decided there was nothing in it. Today they are right back in the world.

How did that come about? They lost the sense of God's love for them. But if heaven does not come for another million years and the work of God in our hands goes to nothing, it will remain true that God loves us. Nothing that ever happens will be bigger than this, 'The Son of God loved me and gave himself for me' (Gal 2:20). Once the wonder of that ceases to touch our hearts, our work is on the slippery slope to disaster.

David Gooding, *Spiritual Dullness: A Study in the Prophet Malachi*, pp. 3–4

20th December

EXAMINING OURSELVES IN LIGHT OF THE NEW COVENANT

Reading: 1 Corinthians 11:23–34

*He took a cup, and when he had given thanks he gave
it to them, saying, 'Drink of it, all of you, for this is my
blood of the covenant, which is poured out for many
for the forgiveness of sins.' (Matthew 26:27–28)*

Sometimes a wicked notion comes in my head (you'll have to pardon me!). You who have many times taken the cup at the Lord's Supper—may I ask you frankly, can you recite by heart the terms of the covenant? I will suppose you can! There were days when I couldn't have done so. The terms of the covenant are repeated in the New Testament: '*I will write my laws on their hearts, and on their minds will I write them*' (Heb 8:10; 10:16). As he hands us the cup, saying, 'This is the new covenant in my blood', the gracious Lord Jesus is reminding us, 'I will write my laws on their hearts, and on their minds I will inscribe them'. As the Lord hands me that cup with his promise, my response ought to be to say, 'Lord, please write your laws more deeply on my heart, and in my mind more clearly, so that I think in terms of your will and your laws and my heart comes affectionately to long to do what you say.'

That is why, in this context, Paul gives us his apostolic advice. He says, 'As we come to the Lord's Supper, it is proper that we should examine ourselves' (v. 28). What does that mean? Well I can tell you what it means for me. I know, as I stand here—and my friends know better than I do—that I am not yet all I ought to be. I hope they find some Christian graces in me and sometimes they speak so generously as to suggest they do. But in private they say, 'You know him, his behaviour is a bit odd at times!' They mean it well, of course, and truly! But I ought to examine myself. Not to become unhealthily introspective; yet to say to the Lord, 'Lord, there are things I've done this week and they're not as I would like and not as you would require, if I were to examine myself and so come to the Lord's Supper.' It doesn't say that I have to be perfect to come, but what is required is that I discern myself. Then I may come to hear those blessed words again, 'This is my blood—the cup of the new covenant in my blood shed for the forgiveness of sins.'

David Gooding, *The Approach to God: Studies in the Tabernacle*, pp. 66–7

21st December

TEACH THE WORD

Reading: 2 Timothy 3:10–17

*Preach the word; be ready in season and out of
season; reprove, rebuke, and exhort, with complete
patience and teaching. (2 Timothy 4:2)*

When I went up to university in the post-war years there was a visible trend in England that I have to say has not led to desirable fruit. I would be invited to go to preach, perhaps one hundred miles away, on a Saturday night. You would travel all these miles and find that the thing started at, say, 7:30. There would be good singing—that's lovely; and then it would go on to all kinds of entertainment—events and question boxes and goodness knows what, and this would occupy from 7:30 round to 8:30. And then the chairman would say, 'We've got *dogsbody* here tonight. We've invited him to come and speak to you. We'll give him ten minutes, and if he should speak too long I'm sitting behind him and I can pull his coat and get him down.' He didn't quite say, 'and then we can go on with the fun,' but he might as well.

If I had been brought up in that kind of atmosphere, you would have lost me completely. If Christianity is such a bitter pill for young people to swallow that you have to offer it with liberal coatings of the sugar of second-rate entertainment, then I shouldn't have wanted it; I could get better myself elsewhere. I'd have said, 'I don't want Christianity either, if that's what God is like.' I believe in a God so stupendously marvellous and his word so wonderfully glorious that it is an insult to represent it as a bitter pill that has to be liberally sugared with the world's entertainment before it can be even contemplated by young people.

The word of God says, and all of us would agree, that 'all Scripture is breathed out by God'. All my fellow believers, of course, believe that with all their hearts. I sometimes feel that we have lost our nerve over the next bit: 'and profitable for teaching' (2 Tim 3:16).

Yes, I am aware, therefore, that we have to consider the spiritual state of those to whom we minister. But, having said that, if you can't make Chronicles, or Kings, or Samuel, or Judges and Joshua interesting, because they are the voice of the living God, let's pack up Christianity and go home. If God's word is such a bore now, what will it be to have to spend a whole eternity listening to him speaking? That would be frightful, wouldn't it? Excuse me if I speak more liberally than I should.

David Gooding, *Fundamentals of the Gospel For the Church Today*, p. 4

22nd December

DEPENDING ON FEELINGS
INSTEAD OF GOD'S WORD

Reading: Genesis 27:1–30

Great peace have those who love your law; nothing
can make them stumble. (Psalm 119:165)

Now watch Isaac and his five senses: sight, hearing, touch, taste and smell. Instead of resting on God's word he went by his sensations.

It seems to me that we should not be above learning the lesson. We may not have to learn it at this lowly, elementary level, but it applies at the spiritual level. If you want blessings, learn to seek the Lord and learn to believe his word. Thank God for every emotion and sensation he gives you as a result of believing his word and having fellowship with him. He will from time to time fill you with the most delightful emotions and their consequent sensations; but you will be most cruelly deceived if you base your idea of blessing on sensations.

If we use sensation as a judge of how well we are getting on, what is going to happen in the days when we are in the midst of bereavement, harassment, maybe partial nervous breakdown, with all sorts of curious sensations? How the devil could deceive! If we know that the blessing is in Christ, his declared word and his promise, and dare to believe it, we shall be saved. In those days when believing the promise and experiencing the Lord brings emotions of joy and sensations of blessing; and also in days when believing God's word and trusting the Saviour does not bring great emotions of joy, but perhaps solemn sensations of difficulty. And we shall be saved in the deeper sense, for it is possible to be sinful even at the spiritual level.

In our unconverted days our feelings were generally the guide and yardstick. It was what we enjoyed, what we wanted to do—these were the yardsticks of whether life was successful. It is all too easy in spiritual life to slip into the notion that satisfaction is the final yardstick. We will come to the meetings if we enjoy them, do the Lord's work if we enjoy it. If trials should come, hard work or experiences that we do not enjoy—cut it! Before we know it, we have turned spirituality back to front. Instead of seeking God and enjoying what emotions and feelings he gives us, we seek our own emotional sensations with God tacked on to the end to make it look respectable. But we then leave ourselves open to being deceived.

David Gooding, The God of New Beginnings: Eighteen Seminars on the Book of Genesis, pp. 164–5

THE FATHER'S PLAN OF REDEMPTION

Part 12—In the Fullness of Time God Sent Forth His Son

23rd December

ZECHARIAH'S UNBELIEF

Reading: Luke 1:5–25

*Zechariah said to the angel, 'How shall I know this? For I am
an old man, and my wife is advanced in years.' (v. 18)*

Had Zechariah protested to the angel that it was incredible that he and his
wife should be chosen to play even a minor part in this great event, we might
well have applauded his pious humility—though unbelief in the word of an
angel does not fit well with piety. But it was not the unlikelihood that he
should be chosen for such high office that was preoccupying Zechariah when
he replied to the angel's announcement, but simply the physical impossibility,
as he regarded it, of the angel's words coming true: 'How shall I know this?'
he protested. 'For I am an old man, and my wife is advanced in years'. For
expressing unbelief on those grounds he was rightly struck dumb.

On this day when the angel appeared to Zechariah in the temple, he was
not saying prayers for his own personal needs only. All the multitude of
the people was praying outside the temple while Zechariah was supposedly
representing them inside. In their simplicity they probably never dreamed
that at the heart of their professional priest, there nestled an unbelief that
made a mockery of prayer. If God is limited to doing only those things that
the normal course of nature could, and would, do anyway, what is the point
of asking God to do anything? To ask him to interfere in the normal working
of nature and to do something that nature left to herself would not, or could
not do, is to ask him to do a miracle. But if you do not believe he can do
miracles, why ask him to?

Appropriately the angel struck Zechariah dumb—that was the end of his
saying public prayers for the time being. Moreover, when he went outside to
bless the people who were waiting for him, he could not speak to them. But
then a priest who cannot believe in miracles has no message for the people
anyway, and certainly no gospel. If God cannot restore the body of one elderly
woman, what hope would there be that he could restore the whole universe?
If God could not give new life to a body decrepit but still living, how could
he raise from the tomb a body three days dead? And if Christ be not risen
from the dead, there is no gospel to preach, and the future holds nothing
but the dumb unbreakable silence of a universal grave.

David Gooding, *Windows on Paradise: Scenes of Hope and Salvation in the Gospel of Luke*, pp. 121–2

24th December

MARY'S FAITH

Reading: Luke 1:46–55

For he who is mighty has done great things
for me, and holy is his name. (v. 49)

By this point in the Magnificat, Mary has spoken three couplets. In all three she has said something about herself, though without either self-importance or self-centredness. There are twice as many couplets still to come, but Mary will not speak of herself personally and explicitly again. This may strike us as remarkable humility, but actually it arises naturally from the way she looks at the event itself. Utterly unique though it is in one sense, in another it appeals to Mary as nothing unusual. It is an act of God's mercy. But then, 'God's mercy comes to generations after generations for those who reverence him' (v. 50). Anyone of the millions in these innumerable generations could tell a tale of God's mercy just as she could. She does not feel the specialness of her case, because her eye is not on herself but on the constancy of God. In the infinite class of God's merciful acts, her case, however large, is but a single member.

Mary is aware of the great differences in ability, resources and power which separate the philosophers, the rich and the aristocrats from the uneducated, the poor and the weak, and she herself observes that, for the purposes of the incarnation, God has deliberately bypassed the former class and chosen someone from the latter. But to explain it she launches into a string of verbs in the aorist tense (see vv. 51–53), which have the exegetes undecided whether she is describing God's action in the past, God's action in the future viewed prophetically as though already accomplished, or God's habitual action. We need not decide the exegetes' question. Mary means all three. She sees God's choice of her as merely one example of what God always does, has done, and will do. And the reason for this is that, as she has told us in her very first couplet, what is happening to her is an activity of God as Saviour. In salvation he always scatters the proud, puts down princes, sends the rich away empty, but exalts the lowly and feeds the hungry. That is why she uses the poetic language of the centuries to describe her own experience, for this has always been the experience of any who have at any time experienced any aspect of God's salvation. Hannah (see 1 Sam 2) found it so in her domestic situation, very different though it was from Mary's. Paul was to observe that this is the principle, in the highest sense of the term, on which God's salvation works (1 Cor 1:18–31).

David Gooding, According to Luke: The Third Gospel's Ordered Historical Narrative, p. 40

25th December

ZECHARIAH'S FAITH RESTORED

Reading: Luke 1:67–79

Blessed be the Lord God of Israel, for he has
visited and redeemed his people. (v. 68)

Zechariah throughout his prophecy has been using the past tense. 'God has visited . . . has raised up a horn of salvation.' In one sense quite correctly: the Saviour had already come. But at the moment he was an unborn infant, not yet viable. As far as the world was concerned, the sun had not yet risen. It was still dark. Yet Zechariah's faith was already sensing vindication and victory. Long ago the prophets first preached the promise of God (see v. 70) and God himself swore a covenant on oath to Abraham (see v. 73). Since then faith had often been tempted to say that those old prophecies were only myths, an expression of man's belief in hope itself as a principle of life (for life without hope is unbearable). And faith had had to fight back and say that God cannot lie; that he must have meant what he said; that the prophets were not all self-deceived fools; that it was God who spoke to that long succession of unique prophets; that he must one day honour his oath, and honour the faith of generations of men.

And now it had happened. Faith had been vindicated. But faith was also sober. It could afford to be. Zechariah looks back at his own baby. 'Yes, you, my child, will have your necessary preliminary work to do. Messiah will save us from all our enemies' (see v. 74), 'the great imperialist Gentile powers included. But first, Israel must repent. There can be no salvation in other senses until Israel has learned the way to salvation in the sense of forgiveness of sins and reconciliation with God. That alone is the way out of the darkness of death's shadow and into peace. It will be Messiah's task, my son, to give his people not only forgiveness of their sins, but the knowledge that they have been forgiven. But you must go in front and prepare his road' (see vv. 76–79).

Zechariah knew the people. He was not a priest for nothing. They would be more interested in political deliverance than in repentance and forgiveness of sins and in getting right with God. It would be difficult for John building a road down which Messiah could travel to get at their hearts. But nothing could alter the fact, or spoil the triumph for Zechariah's faith. The Messiah had come. At the beginning Zechariah's faith was decidedly shaky. It is delightful here to see that before Messiah actually came physically and publicly into the world, Zechariah's faith recovered and triumphed. So may ours before Messiah comes again.

David Gooding, *According to Luke: The Third Gospel's Ordered Historical Narrative*, pp. 45–6

26th December

THE BIRTHPLACE OF JESUS AS A FULFILMENT OF PROPHECY

Reading: Luke 2:1–7

In those days a decree went out from Caesar Augustus
that all the world should be registered. (v. 1)

The gospel is not a set of timeless universal truths expressed in the language of myth. The gospel is that centuries ago God started a great movement in history with Abraham and his seed and then with David, a movement which was every bit as literal and historical as the rise of the Roman Empire; and that Jesus the Messiah and Saviour is the culmination of that historical movement, come to fulfil all the promises made to and through David. It was therefore indispensably necessary for this royal family tradition to be maintained at the birth of Jesus, and one feature of it in particular. The prophet Micah had predicted that the Messiah would be born in Bethlehem; in Bethlehem, therefore, Jesus must be born.

It was not Joseph or Mary who arranged it in order to lend credibility, when the day should come, to Jesus' claim to be David's Son. Divine providence so ordered things that it was the supreme organizing genius of the ancient world who arranged for Jesus to be born in Bethlehem. Caesar Augustus ordered a census. The organizing principle of the census was that every man must return to the city from which his family sprang in order to be registered. Joseph belonged to the house and line of David and he therefore had to go to David's city. He could not avoid maintaining the family tradition: the census compelled him. Of course Augustus knew nothing about this effect of the census, and the last thing he or his vassal Herod would have done would be to strengthen the credentials of a messianic claimant to the throne of Israel. For Augustus the taking of censuses was one of the ways he employed to get control over the various parts of his empire. But—and here is the irony of the thing—in the process, as he thought, of tightening his grip on his huge empire, he so organized things that Jesus, Son of Mary, Son of David, Son of God, destined to sit on the throne of Israel and of the world, was born in the city of David, his royal ancestor. Fulfilling, all unknowingly, the prophecy of Micah, he established this particular detail in the claim of Jesus to be the Messiah.

David Gooding, *According to Luke: The Third Gospel's Ordered Historical Narrative*, pp. 48–9

27th December

THE ARRIVAL OF THE SHEPHERDS

Reading: Luke 2:8–20

They went with haste and found Mary and Joseph,
and the baby lying in a manger. (v. 16)

At home in Nazareth Mary would have been making the best preparations she could for the birth, when the census demands had put all her plans awry. To have to take a journey, and stay in a public hotel at such a time was bad enough. Imagine her distress when she got there and found all the rooms were taken. Now she would have to give birth in some makeshift quarters, half in public. And where could she put the child when it was born? Her first baby! And God's Son! How could she put God's Son in a rough manger?

And then the shepherds arrived enquiring where the baby was. When asked how they knew where to come they replied that an angel of the Lord had told them that the Saviour had been born this very night in the city of David. With this, if not before, things must have begun to make sense to Mary. Gabriel had told her that her child should have the throne of his father David; and here was an angel sending these shepherds to David's city. She and Joseph had not intended to come to Bethlehem, but Augustus, or so it had seemed at the time, had compelled them to come to David's city. Now she saw what plan it was that lay behind Augustus and his administration, and had shepherded her and Joseph to Bethlehem. But there was another question. Perhaps, with the sudden increase in the population caused by the census, there might have been more than one baby born in David's city that night. How did the shepherds know that Mary's baby was the right one? The answer was simple: the angel had given them a sign: they would find the right baby lying in, of all places, a manger.

Ordinary women in Bethlehem did not put their firstborn infants in mangers, we may be sure. For Mary it must have been unspeakably distressing to have to do so. Yet here were these shepherds, and according to them angels knew that the Son of God was lying in a manger, and were glad of the fact: they could use it as a sign to guide humble shepherds to where they might find the Saviour. If angels were glad to use the manger as a sign for shepherds, another shepherd must have guided her and Joseph and the child to the manger in the first place. All, then, was well and would be well: the responsibility for shepherding the infant Son of God was in higher hands than hers.

David Gooding, *According to Luke: The Third Gospel's Ordered Historical Narrative*, pp. 50–2

28th December

THE CONSOLATION OF ANNA

Reading: Luke 2:36–40

She began to give thanks to God and to speak of him to all who were waiting for the redemption of Jerusalem. (v. 38)

For the incarnation Mary was first prepared by Gabriel and then her faith was further strengthened by Elizabeth; for the cross Mary will first be prepared by Simeon, and then consoled and encouraged by Anna.

Both Simeon and Anna had a vigorous and active faith in what they believed to be the divinely inspired prophetic programme for the restoration of Israel. Anna, for her part, is described as speaking of Jesus 'to all those who were looking for the redemption of Jerusalem'. That expectation, again, was not mere wishful thinking or narrow-minded jingoism. It was solidly based on the repeated promises of the prophets. Jeremiah, for instance, had spoken of the matter (see ch. 33). Daniel had been given a timetable for Jerusalem's partial restoration, its consequent renewed desolations, and its ultimate complete restoration (see ch. 9). After the return from the exile in Babylon, the prophet Zechariah had repeatedly affirmed that Jerusalem would one day be finally and permanently redeemed, and his language had made it clear that he was thinking of a restoration far more glorious than what was achieved when Nehemiah rebuilt the city's walls (see 1:12–2:13; 8:1– 23; 9:9; 12:1–13:1; 14:1–21). Since that time Jerusalem had been desecrated by Antiochus Epiphanes, and now downtrodden by the Romans. But Anna, and those like her, were undaunted in their faith: Daniel had said that after the partial restoration following the exile, desolations would supervene until the final restoration. In Anna's mind things were going according to plan. Jerusalem's 'widowhood' had lasted a long while (see Lam 1:1); but Anna, too, in the literal sense had been a widow for a very long time, and in a way her personal experience mirrored that of her city. Constant in her prayers and supplications, she was undaunted in her faith that the city's sorrows and desolations would one day be a thing of the past, and Jerusalem would be redeemed (see Luke 2:37–38). If Mary should need to be consoled and fortified to face the prospect of Messiah's 'being cut off', as Daniel had phrased it (9:26), there was none more suited to the task than Anna.

David Gooding, *According to Luke: The Third Gospel's Ordered Historical Narrative*, pp. 52–3

29th December

SIMEON AND FACING ETERNITY

Reading: Luke 2:25–35

*For my eyes have seen your salvation that you have
prepared in the presence of all peoples (v. 30–31)*

Simeon had lived a long life of consistent devotion to God and of practical righteousness, and now as a mature saint he was coming like a golden sheaf to the great harvest home. Evidently he lived in the closest intimacy with God, for God had revealed to him that he should not see death until he had seen the Lord's Christ. Coming into the temple one day, he saw Mary and Joseph with the baby Jesus. Immediately he recognized in the baby the very Saviour of whose coming God had told him; and in the same instant he realized that his own days on earth were now soon to be at an end.

There followed a wonderful scene, as the aged saint gently lifted the child from Mary, 'took him up in his arms and blessed God and said: "Lord, now you are letting your servant depart in peace, according to your word; for my eyes have seen your salvation"' (vv. 28–30). What a wonderful picture he makes as he stands there with the babe in his arms, his white hair and his noble face radiant already with the glory of eternity, like a mountain peak lit up by the rays of the rising sun!

The man is facing eternity, about to make his exodus from this world, and he is declaring how it is he can enter eternity in peace. There is therefore not a word about his own life; his eyes are resting solely on the life of another. 'My eyes have seen your salvation', he exclaims. We have no need to ask where. He is gazing intently at the Christ. True, he was not thinking selfishly of himself alone: here was a salvation big enough for all peoples and nations.

But a salvation big enough for all mankind was big enough for Simeon. He needed nothing more; he had Christ. As we turn to leave him, notice his arms. He stands there not holding Christ in one arm and grasping something else in the other. He has not only personally received Christ, but he is holding nothing else: both his arms are round Christ. Therein is the secret of his peace. And when our time to cross over comes, we too may go in profound and utter peace, if for our salvation we have personally received the Saviour and are depending on nothing but him.

David Gooding, Windows on Paradise: Scenes of Hope and Salvation in the Gospel of Luke, pp. 65–6

30th December

JESUS AS A BOY IN JERUSALEM

Reading: Luke 2:41–52

Did you not know that I must be in my Father's house? (v. 49)

Jesus is sitting among the teachers of the law, astonishing everybody by the depth of his understanding and the quality of his answers. In a situation where an unaccompanied child is found in a public building, the most natural questions for the authorities to ask are 'Hello son, are you all alone? Where's your father? Who is your father?' When therefore Jesus' parents came in and identified themselves as the child's parents by Mary's reprimand: 'Son, why have you treated us like this? Your father and I . . .', the theologians must have listened with intense interest: 'so this is his father, then; I wonder exactly who he is.'

At that moment the child spoke: 'Why were you searching for me? Did you not realize I had to be in my Father's house?' (v. 49). My Father's house? The learned doctors knew the Old Testament inside out. In all the long biblical record, no prophet, no king or commoner had ever referred to the tabernacle or temple as 'my Father's house'. The child was conscious of a relationship with God that none had conceived of, let alone expressed, before. And with that relationship, a compelling devotion: 'I had to be in my Father's house.' 'Did you not realize it?' he asked Mary and Joseph. The question was asked with all the delightful simplicity of a child.

Mary, at least, ought to have realized it, but in her defence it can be said that she was not the last one to believe Jesus to be the Son of God, and then with unfortunate inconsistency to express ideas implying that in some things Jesus was in error. Now both Mary and Joseph were flustered, and they did not understand what he said (see v. 50). Did it mean that from now on he was constantly going to assert independence of them? No, he would not be asserting premature independence. Mary and Joseph still had their task to fulfil as parents, and he would be subject to them. He was a real child. But they had been given an early warning; and Mary kept all these sayings in her heart (v. 51). The time would come when she must let him go at the level of the mere human relationship of child, that she might receive him as Saviour, Lord and God. As she thought over this incident, it would prepare her, so that when the break came it might not be so much a break as the eclipsing of one unique joy and responsibility by an infinitely greater wonder, worship and obedience.

David Gooding, According to Luke: The Third Gospel's Ordered Historical Narrative, p. 59–61

31st December

Reading: Romans 11:33–12:1

Oh, the depth of the riches and wisdom and knowledge
of God! How unsearchable are his judgments
and how inscrutable his ways! (11:33)

Father, for these wonderful things now, humbly and gratefully, we praise thee. Oh what a glorious God thou hast shown thyself to be. How majestic are thy purposes; how infinitely generous thy grace. How breathtaking are those vistas of perfection and delight and joy and living that thou hast opened up to us who know thy Son as Saviour.

We thank thee for thy divine purpose. Whom thou didst foreknow, thou didst predestinate to be conformed to the image of thy Son. Whom thou did predestinate, them also thou didst call. Those thou didst call, them thou hast justified. Those thou hast justified, thou hast glorified.

We praise thee, Lord, for the desires thou hast awakened in our hearts, not for heaven as some old people's retiring home, but for heaven as that great goal of living—that perfect sonship that we shall then enter, to be like thy Son, to be troubled no more by the battle against sin.

If Lord we have learned enough not to trust in the strength of our own desires—we have found them too often will-o'-the wisp—then in these moments, as we quieten our hearts, listen we beseech thee to the voice of thy Holy Spirit whom with incalculable grace thou hast placed in our hearts and personalities. Hear his longings and yearnings and breathings and groanings that rise from our hearts by his grace as he strives to bring us along the path thou hast marked out. Oh, God, what it is that he wills, by thy grace we would will. And though we know not what we should pray for, hear his prayers within us, and answer them according to the great tides of thy divine power and grace, so that we might walk the more firmly in thy Spirit from this moment onwards, and without faltering step, along that path until the time comes when all our prayers and wishes are turned to reality and we see Christ! Hear us we beseech thee, for thy name's sake. Amen.

David Gooding, *Wreckage and Recovery: God's Way of Making Believers Holy: Romans 5–8*, pp. 53–4

Publications by David Gooding

DOCTORAL DISSERTATION

'The Greek Deuteronomy', PhD thesis, University of Cambridge, 1954.

BOOKS

Recensions of the Septuagint Pentateuch. Cambridge: Tyndale Press, 1955.

The Account of the Tabernacle: Translation and Textual Problems of the Greek Exodus. Texts and Studies: Contributions to Biblical and Patristic Literature, ed. C. H. Dodd, no. 6. Cambridge: Cambridge University Press, 1959.

edited *The Text of the Septuagint: Its Corruptions and Their Emendation* by Peter Walters (formerly Katz). Cambridge: Cambridge University Press, 1973.

Studies in Luke's Gospel. Bible Study and Discussion Papers 1–3. Dublin: Biblical Studies Institute, 1973.

An Unshakeable Kingdom: The Letter to the Hebrews for Today. Scarborough, Ontario: Everyday Publications, 1975; [in German] *Ein unerschütterliches Reich: 10 Studien über d. Hebräerbrief.* Dillenburg: Christliche Verlagsgesellschaft, 1987; rev. ed. Leicester: Inter-Varsity Press/Grand Rapids: Eerdmans, 1989; repr. Port Colborne, Ontario: Gospel Folio Press, 1989; [in Hungarian] *Rendíthetetlen királyság*, Stuttgart: Evangéliumi Kiadó, 1991; [in Bulgarian] *Посланието към Евреите*, Sofia: Нов човек, 1995; [in Russian] *Осуществление Ожидаемого: Посланце к Евреям*, Moscow, 1996; [in Vietnamese] 2003; [in Spanish] *Según Hebreos: Un reino inconmovible*, Barcelona: Publicaciones Andamino, 2008; repr. Coleraine, N. Ireland: Myrtlefield House, 2013.

Relics of Ancient Exegesis: A Study of the Miscellanies in 3 Reigns 2. Society for Old Testament Study Monograph Series, 4. Cambridge: Cambridge University Press, 1976.

According to Luke: A new exposition of the Third Gospel. Leicester: Inter-Varsity Press, 1987; [in Polish] *Według Łukasza: nowe spojrzenie na Trzecią Ewangelię.* tr. Witold Gorecki. Wydawnictwo Ewangeliczne, 1992; [in Spanish] *Según Lucas: una nueva exposición del tercer Evangelio.* Editorial Clie/Publicaciones Andamio, 1996; [in Russian] *Новый взгяд на Евангелие от Луки.* Duncanville, USA: World Wide Printing, 1997. Duncanville, USA: World Wide Printing, 1997; repr. Port Colborne, Ontario: Gospel Folio Press, 2002; repr. Eugene, Origen: Wipf and Stock, 2005; repr. as *According to Luke: The Third Gospel's Ordered Historical Narrative.* Coleraine, N. Ireland: Myrtlefield House, 2013.

True to the Faith: A fresh approach to the Acts of the Apostles. London: Hodder & Stoughton, 1990; [in Spanish] *Según Hechos: permaneciendo fiel a la fe.* Editiorial Clie/Publicaciones Andamio, 1990, 2008; [in Russian] *Верные вере: Новый подход к Деяниям святых Апостолов.* Duncanville, USA: World Wide Printing, 1994, 1998; repr. Port Colborne, Ontario: Gospel Folio Press, 1995; [in Romanian] Cluj: Editura Logos, 1995; repr as *True to the Faith: Defining and Defending the Gospel.* Coleraine, N. Ireland: Myrtlefield House, 2013.

In the School of Christ: A Study of Christ's Teaching on Holiness. John 13–17. Port Colborne, Ontario: Gospel Folio Press, 1995, 2001; [in Spanish] *Según Juan: En la escuela de Cristo. Juan 13-17.* tr. Roger Marshall, Barcelona: Publicaciones Andamino, 1995, 2012; [in Hungarian] *Krisztus iskolájában.* Budapest: Evangéliumi Kiadó, 1996; [in Russian] *В Школе Христа (Учение Христа о святости)* Newtownards, Myrtlefield Trust, 1997; [in Bulgarian*]* *В училището на Христос.* Sofia: Veren, 2000; [in Polish] *W szkole Chrystusa: studium nauczania Chrystusa na temat świętości, Ewangelia Jana 13-17.* tr. Adam Mariuk. Areopag, 2010; [in Burmese] 2013; repr. as *In the School of Christ: Lessons on Holiness in John 13–17.* Coleraine, N. Ireland: Myrtlefield House, 2013.

Windows on Paradise. Port Colborne, Ontario: Gospel Folio Press, 1998, 2001; [in Spanish] *Ventanas al paraíso: Estudios en el evangelio de Lucas.* Talleres Gráficos de la M.C.E. 1982; [in Russian] *Окно в рай. Исследование Евангелия от Луки.* Newtownards: Myrtlefield Trust, 1993; [in Malay] *Jendela Syurga.* 2008; [in Bulgarian] *Прозорец към рая.* Sofia: Veren, 2011; [in Burmese] 2012; [in Vietnamese] 2013.

The Riches of Divine Wisdom: The New Testament's Use of the Old Testament. Coleraine, N. Ireland: Myrtlefield House, 2013.

Drawing Near to God. Belfast, Northern Ireland: Myrtlefield House, 2020.

BOOKS PUBLISHED WITH JOHN LENNOX

Christianity: Opium or Truth? Port Colborne, Ontario: Gospel Folio Press, 1997; [in Russian] Христианство: опиум или истина? Duncanville, USA: World Wide Printing, 1991; *Keresztyénség: illúziók vagy tények?* Budapest: Evangéliumi K. és Iratmisszió, 1998; [in Bulgarian] Християнството: опиум или истина? Sofia: Veren, 2004; [in German] *Opium fürs Volk?* Bielefeld: Christliche Literature-Verbreitung, 2012; [in Portuguese] *Cristianismo: Ópio do Povo?* Porto Alegre: A. Verdada, 2013.

The Definition of Christianity. Port Colborne, Ontario: Gospel Folio Press, 2001; [in Russian] Определение Христианства. 1997, 1999, 2005; [in Polish]

Definicja chrześcijaństwa. tr. Przemysław Janikowski. Areopag, 2001; [in Spanish] *Una definición del cristianismo para el siglo XXI : un estudio basado en los hechos de los Apóstoles.* Editiorial Clie; [in Bulgarian] Дефиниция на християнството. Sofia: Veren, 2004; repr. Coleraine, N. Ireland: Myrtlefield House, 2014.

Key Bible Concepts. Port Colborne, Ontario: Gospel Folio Press, 2001; [in Russian] Ключевые понятия Библии. 1997; [in Bulgarian] Ключови библейски Понятия. 1997, 2004; [in Malay] *Konsep Utama Dalam Alkitab*; [in Spanish] *Conceptos bíblicos fundamentales.* Barcelona: Editiorial Clie/Publicaciones Andamio, 2001; [in Polish] *Kluczowe koncepcje biblijne.* Areopag, 2001; [in German] *Schlüsselbegriffe der Bibel.* Bielefeld: Christliche Literatur-Verbreitung, 2013; [in Portuguese] *Conceitos-Chave da Bíblia.* Porto Alegre: A. Verdada, 2013;[in Malay] Konsep Utama Dalam Alkitab; [in Burmese]; repr. Coleraine, N. Ireland: Myrtlefield House, 2013.

Being Truly Human: The Limits of our Worth, Power, Freedom and Destiny. Belfast, Northern Ireland: Myrtlefield House, 2018.

Finding Ultimate Reality: In Search of the Best Answers to the Biggest Questions. Belfast, Northern Ireland: Myrtlefield House, 2018.

Questioning Our Knowledge: Can We Know What We Need to Know? Belfast, Northern Ireland: Myrtlefield House, 2019.

Doing What's Right: Whose System of Ethics is Good Enough? Belfast, Northern Ireland: Myrtlefield House, 2019.

Claiming to Answer: How One Person Became the Response to our Deepest Questions. Belfast, Northern Ireland: Myrtlefield House, 2019.

Suffering Life's Pain: Facing the Problems of Moral and Natural Evil. Belfast, Northern Ireland: Myrtlefield House, 2019.

PUBLISHED LECTURES AND BOOKLETS

The inspiration and authority, canon and transmission of Holy Scripture. Edinburgh: Darien Press, 1961.

How to Teach the Tabernacle. Dublin: Merrion Press, 1970; repr. Port Colborne, Ontario: Everyday Publications, 1977; [in Spanish] *Cómo enseñar el tabernáculo.* Port Colborne, Ontario: Everyday Publications, 1977.

Current Problems and Methods in the Textual Criticism of the Old Testament. Belfast: Queen's University, 1979.

How? The Search for Spiritual Satisfaction. Leicester: Inter-Varsity Press, 1980.

Freedom under God. Bath: Echoes of Service, 1985.

Unfettered Faith: The Promotion of Spiritual Freedom. Coleraine, N. Ireland: Myrtlefield Trust, 1986.

Wer glaubt muß denken. Bielefeld: Christliche Literature-Verbreitung, 1998.

Die Bibel—Mythos oder Wahrheit? Gibt es eine echte Erfüllung? Dillenburg: Christliche Verlagsgesellschaft, 1993; 2nd ed. Bielefeld: Christliche Literature-Verbreitung, 2001.

The Bible: Myth or Truth. [in Bulgarian: Библията: мит или истина] Coleraine, N. Ireland: Myrtlefield Trust, 2001.

How about God? Four broadcast talks (Belfast: Graham & Heslip, n.d.).

CHAPTERS AND MAJOR ARTICLES

'The Text of the Psalms in two Durham Bibles.' *Scriptorium* 12:1 (1958): 94–6.

'Aristeas and Septuagint Origins: A review of recent studies.' *Vetus Testamentum* 13:4 (1963): 357–379.

'Ahab According to the Septuagint.' *ZAW* 76 (1964): 269–80.

'Pedantic Timetabling in 3rd Book of Reigns.' *Vetus Testamentum* 15:2 (1965): 153–66.

'The Septuagint's Version of Solomon's Misconduct.' *Vetus Testamentum* 15:3 (1965): 325–35.

'An Impossible Shrine.' *Vetus Testamentum* 15:4 (1965): 405–20.

'Temple Specifications: A Dispute in Logical Arrangement between the MT and the LXX.' *Vetus Testamentum* 17:2 (1967): 143–72.

'The Septuagint's Rival Versions of Jeroboam's Rise to Power.' *Vetus Testamentum* 17:2 (1967): 173–89.

'The Shimei Duplicate and its Satellite Miscellanies in 3 Reigns II.' *Journal of Semitic Studies* 13:1 (1968): 76–92.

'Problems of Text and Midrash in the Third Book of Reigns.' *Textus* 7 (1969): 1–29.

'Text-Sequence and Translation-Revision in 3 Reigns IX 10 – X 33.' *Vetus Testamentum* 19:4 (1969): 448–63.

'Observations on Certain Problems Connected with the So-called Septuagint.' *TSF Bulletin* 56 (1970): 8–13.

'Jeroboam's Rise to Power: A Rejoinder.' *Journal of Biblical Literature* 91:4 (1972): 529–33.

'Two possible examples of midrashic interpretation in the Septuagint Exodus' in *Wort, Lied, und Gottesspruch: Festschrift fur Joseph Ziegler* (ed. Josef Schreiner; Echter Verlag: Katholisches Bibelwerk, 1972), 39–48.

'On the use of the LXX for dating Midrashic elements in the Targums.' *Journal of Theological Studies* ns 25:1 (1974): 1–11.

'A Recent Popularisation of Professor F. M. Cross' Theories on the Text of the Old Testament.' *Tyndale Bulletin* 26 (1975): 113–32.

'An Appeal for a Stricter Terminology in the Textual Criticism of the Old Testament.' *Journal of Semitic Studies* 21 (1976): 15–25.

'Tradition of interpretation of the circumcision at Gilgal.' Jerusalem: World Union of Jewish Studies, 1977.

'Structure littéraire de Matthieu 13:53 à 18:35.' *Revue biblique* 85:2 (1978): 227–52.

'Demythologizing, Old and New, and Luke's Description of the Ascension: A Layman's Appraisal.' *Irish Biblical Studies* 2 (1980): 95–119.

'The Literary Structure of the Book of Daniel and its Implications' (The Tyndale Old Testament Lecture, 1980). *Tyndale Bulletin* 32 (1981): 43–79.

'Demythologizing the Ascension: A Reply by D. W. Gooding.' *Irish Biblical Studies* 3 (1981): 45–54.

'A Sketch of Current Septuagint Studies.' *Proceedings of the Irish Biblical Association* 5 (1981).

'The Composition of the Book of Judges.' *Eretz-Israel*, H. M. Orlinsky Volume. Jerusalem: 1982.

'Philo's Bible in the *De Gigantibus* and *Quod Deus*.' in *Two Treatises of Philo of Alexandria: A Commentary on De Gigantibus and Quod Deus Sit Immutabilis*, with V. Nikiprowetzky (ed. D. Winston and J. Dillon; BJS 25; Chico, Calif.: Scholars Press, 1983), 89–125.

'The Problem of Pain.' *Journal of the Irish Christian Study Centre* 1 (1983):63–9.

'An Approach to the Literary and Textual Problems in the David-Goliath Story', in *The Story of David and Goliath: Papers of a Joint Research Venture* by Dominique Barthélemy et al.; Orbis Biblicus et Orientalis, no. 73 (Fribourg: Éditions Universitaires, 1986; Göttingen: Vandenhoeck & Ruprecht, 1986), 55–86.

'David-Goliath Project: Stage Four', in *The Story of David and Goliath: Papers of a Joint Research Venture* by Dominique Barthélemy et al.; Orbis Biblicus et Orientalis, no. 73 (Fribourg: Éditions Universitaires, 1986; Göttingen: Vandenhoeck & Ruprecht, 1986), 145–154.

The Bible and Moral Education for Schools, with John Lennox. Moscow: Uchitelskaya Gazeta (Newspaper for Teachers), 1993–5; repr. as *The Bible and Ethics*.

Articles in *New Bible Dictionary* on 'Bezalel, Bezaleel'; 'Capital' [in tabernacle]; 'Censer'; 'Gershom, Gershon'; 'Kaiwan'; 'Kohath, Kohathites'; 'Merari, Merarites'; 'Oholiab'; 'Rephan'; 'Snuffers'; 'Tabernacle'; 'Texts & Versions 2. The Septuagint'; 'Trays'. Leicester: Inter-Varsity Press, 1996.

'The tabernacle: no museum piece' in *The Perfect Saviour: Key themes in Hebrews* (ed. Jonathan Griffiths; Nottingham: Inter-Varsity Press, 2012), 69–88.

REVIEW ARTICLES

Review of Ilmari Soisalon-Soininen, *Der Charakter der asterisierten Zusätze in der Septuaginta. Gnomon* 33:2 (1961): 143–8.

Review of Joost Smit Sibinga, *The Old Testament Text of Justin Martyr. Journal of Theological Studies* ns 16:1 (1965): 187–92.

Review of Ilmari Soisalon-Soininen, *Die Infinitive in der Septuaginta. Journal of Theological Studies* ns 18:2 (1967): 451–5.

Review of James Donald Shenkel, *Chronology and Recensional Development in the Greek Text of Kings viii. Journal of Theological Studies* ns 21:1 (1970): 118–31.

Review of Adrian Schenker, *Hexaplarische Psalmenbruchstucke: Die hexaplarischen Psalmenfragmente der Handschriften Vaticanus graecus 752 und Canonicianus graecus 62, Journal of Theological Studies* ns 27:2 (1976): 443–5.

Review of Raija Sollamo, *Renderings of Hebrew Semiprepositions in the Septuagint. Journal of Semitic Studies* 25:2 (1980): 261–3.

Review of John W. Olley, *"Righteousness" in the Septuagint of Isaiah: A Contextual Study. Journal of Theological Studies* ns 32:1 (1981): 204–12.

Review of J. H. Charlesworth, *The Pseudographa and Modern Research. Irish Biblical Studies* 4:1 (1982): 46-49.

Review of Anneli Aejmelaeus, *Parataxis in the Septuagint. Journal of Semitic Studies* 28:2 (1983): 369–71.

Short Notice on Joseph A. Fitzmyer, *An Introductory Bibliography for the Study of Scripture. Journal of Theological Studies* ns 34:2 (1983): 693.

Review of Homer Heater, *A Septuagint Translation Technique in the Book of Job. Journal of Theological Studies* ns 35:1 (1984): 169–77.

Review of Roger Beckwith, *The Old Testament Canon of the New Testament Church. Irish Biblical Studies* 8:4 (1986): 207-211.

Review of George Alexander Kennedy, Duane Frederick Watson (eds.), *Persuasive Artistry: Studies in New Testament Rhetoric in Honour of George A Kennedy. Evangelical Quarterly* 64 (1992): 264–8.

POPULAR ARTICLES

'The True Peacemaker and Benefactor of the People.' *Precious Seed* 3:7 (1950).

'Modern Translations—Their Use and Abuse.' *Precious Seed* 7:8 (1956).

'New Testament Word Studies.' *Precious Seed* 12:1–4 & 13:1–6 (1961–62).

'How do you relate and reconcile the teaching on women in 1 Corinthians 11 and 14?' *The Word* (Belfast, 1994).

'Symbols of Headship and Glory.' *The Word* (Belfast, 1980); [in German] 'Symbole oder Zeichen von Autoritat und Herrlichkeit' tr. von G. Giesler. *Verlegerbeilage zu Die Wegweisung* 6/87 (Dillenburg, Christliche Verlagsgesellschaft, 1987).

Daily Readings and Key Verse Reference Index

WWW.MYRTLEFIELDHOUSE.COM

Our website contains hundreds of resources in a variety of formats. You can read, listen to or watch David Gooding's teaching on over 35 Bible books and 14 topics. You can also view the full catalogue of Myrtlefield House publications and download free e-book editions of all of the books and sermon transcripts found in *Bringing Us To Glory*, as well as many others. The website is optimized for both computer and mobile viewing, making it easy for you to access the resources at home or on the go.

For more information about any of our publications or resources contact us at: info@myrtlefieldhouse.com

WWW.BRINGINGUSTOGLORY.COM

MYRTLEFIELD ENCOUNTERS

Myrtlefield Encounters are complementary studies of biblical literature, Christian teaching and apologetics. The books in this series engage the minds of believers and sceptics. They show how God has spoken in the Bible to address the realities of life and its questions, problems, beauty and potential.

Key Bible Concepts
Defining the Basic Terms of the Christian Faith

Christianity: Opium or Truth?
Answering Thoughtful Objections to the Christian Faith

The Definition of Christianity
Exploring the Original Meaning of the Christian Faith

The Bible and Ethics
Finding the Moral Foundations of the Christian Faith

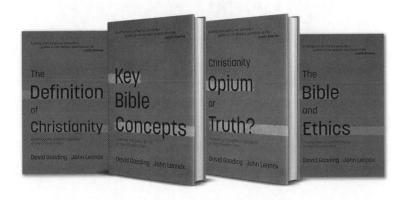

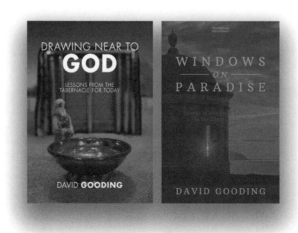

THE QUEST FOR REALITY AND SIGNIFICANCE

We need a coherent picture of our world. Life's realities won't let us ignore its fundamental questions, but with so many opposing views, how will we choose answers that are reliable? In this series of books, David Gooding and John Lennox offer a fair analysis of religious and philosophical attempts to find the truth about the world and our place in it. By listening to the Bible alongside other leading voices, they show that it is not only answering life's biggest questions—it is asking better questions than we ever thought to ask.

Book 1—Being Truly Human
The Limits of our Worth, Power, Freedom and Destiny

Book 2—Finding Ultimate Reality
In Search of the Best Answers to the Biggest Questions

Book 3—Questioning Our Knowledge
Can We Know What We Need to Know?

Book 4—Doing What's Right
Whose System of Ethics is Good Enough?

Book 5—Claiming To Answer
How One Person Became the Response to our Deepest Questions

Book 6—Suffering Life's Pain
Facing the Problems of Moral and Natural Evil

David Gooding's deep understanding of the Scriptures enables him to capture the rich truths of one passage after another in a way that encourages the weak, lifts up the lowly, and draws all closer to see Jesus. This book is filled with profound insights that again and again made me pause and marvel at the supreme kindness of our God and Saviour.

Dr Todd Bolen
Professor of Biblical Studies, The Master's University

Bringing Us To Glory combines the wisdom and warmth that characterized David Gooding's teaching with a big-picture vision of God's wonderful plan of salvation through the One who is the author's delight and the source of all wisdom. I cannot recommend this book highly enough to everyone who desires to know Christ more and to present him faithfully to others.

Dr Paul Coulter
Head of Ministry Operations with Living Leadership and Director of the Centre for Christianity in Society

David Gooding was gifted with a unique understanding of the richness of Scripture. His talks and writings are filled with gems of insight, and it is gratifying to see them being made available in the easily digestible form of short daily readings that will suffuse the reader's life with glimpses of glory.

John C. Lennox
Emeritus Professor of Mathematics, University of Oxford, Emeritus Fellow in Mathematics and Philosophy of Science, Green Templeton College, Associate Fellow of the Said Business School

Dr David Gooding was one of the finest Bible teachers that I have ever heard. Even when he said something with which I disagreed (which was rarely) he did it in such a winsome and charming way that I found him captivating. He loved the Bible, he knew the Bible, and he taught the Bible brilliantly. He knew the languages of Scripture and he was well informed of the history of interpretation of Scripture. His books are a delight to read, both for their insightful commentary and for their independence of thought. He was an original, and I am delighted that I knew him and had the opportunity to sit under his searching ministry.

David J. MacLeod
Dean for Biblical Studies and the Program Director for Biblical Studies, Bible Exposition and Theology at Emmaus Bible College, Dubuque, Iowa

In a world that lives from crisis to crisis, we need to hear this book's constant encouragement to keep our eyes on Jesus in our journey to our final goal, our Heavenly Father's house. These daily readings remind me of the way that Dr Gooding influenced my life and the lives of many in Asia, both through his writings and his willingness to make the long journey to teach us and admonish us constantly to study the Bible not just for the sake of scholarly ends but to find and strengthen our relationship with our Saviour Jesus Christ. In *Bringing Us To Glory* you will find him leading you by the hand, as it were, into the arms of our dear Lord Jesus. It has all gone as planned: this is our comfort in troubled times.

Isaac Shaw
President, Delhi Bible Institute

This is classic David Gooding with his penetrating biblical insight and extraordinary teaching—all brought together in one exceptional devotional. He not only makes the Scripture come alive, his insights reflect a lifetime of careful and detailed study of the Scriptures. He asks penetrating questions and shows how the Bible answers the longings God has placed in all humanity, something that secularism can never do. Nor is Gooding an armchair academic. It is clear we are reading a man who has fallen in love with the glory and majesty of God. It moved me to a greater love for our risen Lord who sacrificed everything for us and our salvation. *Bringing Us To Glory* tops my list of new devotionals! It is a must read!

Rebecca Manley Pippert
Author of Stay Salt

Now we have carefully selected sections from David Gooding's writings available to those who seek one of the most effective means of refreshment: the vibrant but careful exposition of Scripture that is written in a way that ministers God's healing balm to those who hunger for him.

Ajith Fernando
Teaching Director, Youth for Christ, Sri Lanka

This book is equal to a full year at any theological college. I realize more than ever why so many of my friends have been mentored by Dr Gooding.

George Verwer DD
Founder of Operation Mobilisation

Dr David Gooding's commentaries, which have been used in this new devotional, have greatly enhanced my own preaching and teaching ministry. My wife has also profited from them in her daily devotional reading. I always recommend his books to young scholars and Bible teachers, and I am very happy to do the same for this new collection.

Alexander Strauch
Author of Biblical Eldership

It was my great joy along life's journey to know and love Dr David Gooding. He was brilliant, straight as an arrow theologically and possessed the unique gift of making deep theological truths understandable to everyone. Without any reservation whatsoever I heartily recommend *Bringing Us To Glory*. You will consider it one of God's best gifts to your own devotional life. Read it—and reap!

O. S. Hawkins, PhD
Former Pastor, First Baptist Church in Dallas, Texas and
author of the best-selling Code Series of devotionals including
The Joshua Code, The Jesus Code and The Bible Code

Bringing Us To Glory is a tremendous place to begin your acquaintance with the works of Dr David Gooding. He was a legend in his own time and a household name all over the world. He was my friend and spoke for us at Westminster Chapel. We thank God that he left a legacy of his writings for the whole world to discover. I urge you to take advantage of the scholarship of a man who held to the infallibility of Scripture and whose writings will grip you no end.

R. T. Kendall
Minister, Westminster Chapel (1977–2002)

Bringing Us To Glory proves to be thoroughly biblical, genuinely God-glorifying, and eloquently thoughtful with meat for the mature Christian and milk for the new-in-Christ. I heartily commend this treasure to all who love the Lord Jesus Christ.

Richard Mayhue, Th.D.
Research Professor of Theology Emeritus, The Master's Seminary

For most of my Christian life and ministry, I have returned again and again to the beloved devotions by C H Spurgeon and Oswald Chambers, *Morning and Evening* and *My Utmost for His Highest*. Until I found *Bringing Us To Glory*, I had not found a contemporary devotional that could match the depth of theology, consistency of conviction, beauty of literacy, and sure foundation of biblical inerrancy found in those books. If you are looking for a devotion that demands a Bible, journal and pen; time to fully consider and pray; and that will demand accountability of your life according to the Scripture, then *Bringing Us To Glory* is that book.

Dr Jay Strack
President and Founder, Student Leadership University